Studies in Philosophy

R. A. HOERNLÉ

Studies in Philosophy

REINHOLD FRIEDRICH ALFRED HOERNLÉ

EDITED AND WITH A MEMOIR BY
DANIEL S. ROBINSON
Director of the School of Philosophy of the
University of South California

LONDON
GEORGE ALLEN & UNWIN LTD
RUSKIN HOUSE MUSEUM STREET

PRINTED IN GREAT BRITAIN
in 11 point Baskerville type
BY T. AND A. CONSTABLE LTD.
Printers to the University of Edinburgh

THE HERBERT WILDON CARR

PUBLICATION FUND OF

THE UNIVERSITY OF SOUTHERN CALIFORNIA

THE late Professor Herbert Wildon Carr served on the Faculty of the University of Southern California from 1925 until his death in 1931. He bequeathed to the University a sum of money to be used to subsidise the publication of meritorious works on philosophy. This fund has been designated the Herbert Wildon Carr Publication Fund.

The late Professor Reinhold Friedrich Alfred Hoernlé served as Visiting Professor on the Faculty of the School of Philosophy during the academic year 1930-31. He left a number of important essays that have never been published. Arrangements have been made with Messrs. George Allen and Unwin Ltd. to issue this material, together with some other significant essays of Professor Hoernlé.

The School of Philosophy of the University of South California has been signally honoured by having had these two distinguished British scholars as members of its faculty. We deem it especially appropriate to assist with a subvention from Dr. Carr's bequest in the publication of these original and creative philosophical essays of Professor Hoernlé.

ALBERT S. RAUBENHEIMER
Educational Vice-President

DANIEL S. ROBINSON
Director of the School of Philosophy

CONTENTS

*(These articles are reprinted by courtesy of the Editors of the Journals in which
they first appeared.)*

A MEMOIR OF
R. F. A. HOERNLÉ (1880-1943)
by DANIEL S. ROBINSON

FEW philosophers have built into their character and personality the Stoic ideal of cosmopolitanism more successfully than did Reinhold Friedrich Alfred Hoernlé. Describing this ideal in his article on the Stoics in the *Encyclopædia Britannica* (Fourteenth edition), Professor R. D. Hicks writes: "In virtue even of the freedom which belongs to the individual *qua* rational, he must recognise the society of rational beings of which he is a member, and subordinate his own ends to the ends and needs of this society. Those who own one law are citizens of one state, the city of Zeus, in which men and gods have their dwelling. In that city all is ordained by reason working intelligently, and the members exist for the sake of one another; there is an intimate connection (συμπάθεια) between them which makes all the wise and virtuous friends, even if personally unknown, and leads them to contribute to one another's good. Their intercourse should find expression in justice, in friendship, in family and political life." Add to this high stoic ideal the practice of Christian brotherly love and good-will, and anyone who had the good fortune to know Professor Hoernlé would agree that he continually sought to realise in his daily conduct this ideal of rational christian humanism. He actually succeeded in becoming a well-rounded citizen of the world.

Professor Hoernlé was richly endowed physically, mentally, and spiritually. He had a superb physique, and most of his life he enjoyed buoyant health. Personally he was always genial, affable, and sociable. In philosophical disputation he was a master. His classroom lectures were informal but always exceptionally thought-provoking and intellectually stimulating. Being a son of missionary parents and having been reared in a genuinely religious environment, his fine intellect retained always a keen sensitivity to and appreciation of religious values.

Hoernlé was born in Bonn, Germany, on November 27, 1880, but he was taken by his parents to India, where he learned

ix

to speak Hindustani as fluently as he spoke English and German. His father, Dr. A. F. Rudolph Hoernlé, was a distinguished orientalist. Hoernlé's own valuable article entitled "Solipsism" in Hastings' *Encyclopædia of Religion and Ethics* is matched by one by his father entitled: "Ājīvikas".

When the boy Hoernlé was five years old he was taken back to Germany to be educated, and he never returned to India. He lived with his grandfather in Bonn. He studied for approximately twelve years in German elementary schools and in the *Landesschule* at Pforte near Naumburg on the Saale. In 1898 he completed the course of study at this school as *primum omnium*.

Hoernlé's widow, Mrs. Winifred Hoernlé, still has the letters that he wrote to his parents while separated from them. Concerning these letters she writes: "I am a fortunate woman in that I have my husband's letters to his mother and father who were in India for twenty years. From the time they left him in Germany as a little boy of six he wrote to them; his mother preserved them and I have them all."

Continuing, Mrs. Hoernlé tells of his parents' decision to send Hoernlé to Oxford to complete his education: "Then came the wrench when his parents decided that he must go to Oxford, and that his life must be lived in the British Empire, as it then was. He was top boy of his school and a great favourite and he would dearly have loved to go to a German University and then have gone to England, but he fell in with his parents' wishes very graciously. His letters are wonderful to read. Oxford gripped him and the beauty of England, and the growth of the new Dominions beyond the seas. At this time his parents were living in Oxford, so there are no letters, and it is only one or two to his grandfather in Bonn that give an insight into the moulding that was going on. But brilliantly though he did at Oxford, Oxford never completely accepted him, for at that time, especially, he had a strong German accent, though as a child in India he had spoken perfect English, as did of course his father who was born in India and thus always a British citizen."

Mrs. Hoernlé confirms the fact that Professor Hoernlé was a genuine cosmopolite. She writes: "My husband grew to be what I call a citizen of the world understanding nationality but rising above it. He loved South Africa, but he was never

completely understood here. He learnt Afrikaans in order better
to understand the people. He wrote Afrikaans better than most
Afrikaners. But the more he knew of them the more they held
aloof from him. His breadth of vision was too great for them;
they repudiated him as they repudiated Smuts. But Smuts and
my husband were friends."[1]

Hoernlé had a brilliant academic record at Balliol College,
and at the University of Oxford. He was elected to the Jenkyns
Exhibition at Balliol College, then to the John Locke Scholarship in Mental Philosophy of the University, and a year later
he was the recipient of a Senior Demyship at Magdalen
College. He completed his work at Oxford in 1905.

Appointed Lecturer in Philosophy at St. Andrews University, Hoernlé served under Bernard Bosanquet for three years.
His keen and incisive mind fully comprehended the intricate
philosophical system which Bosanquet's genius created, but he
never became a mere disciple of the master. Although he acknowledged his indebtedness to him in his writings, Hoernlé
developed his own synoptic conception of philosophy, and
thereby enriched the British Idealism so ably represented by
Bosanquet.

In January 1908 he received an appointment to his first
professorship at what was then known as South African
College, but has since been named the University of Cape
Town. Here is Hoernlé's account of his work at that institution.
"There I spent four strenuous but happy years. Much of it was
pioneering work, but I found Schiller's saying verified in my
own experience: '*Es wächst der Mensch mit seinen gröss'ren
Zwecken*'. It was heavy work, too—rarely less than fifteen hours
of lecturing per week for thirty-six weeks of the year; and when
a Department of Education was started, I acted for a year as
Professor of Education, in addition to my work as Professor of
Philosophy, until the College funds permitted the founding of a
Chair of Education. For a year, too, I held the position of Vice-
Chairman of Senate. The Chairmanship being honorary, and
the College having no Principal, the Vice-Chairman of Senate
was the chief administrative officer, and without any relief
from his regular teaching duties, found himself engaged in

[1] From a letter to the writer dated at Johannesburg, July 19, 1950. Some
facts about Hoernlé's career in South Africa are given below.

committee-work almost every afternoon. Needless to say, the scholar in me suffered, for the time, from this burden of practical work, which left no leisure for writing and very little for keeping up with current literature. But the man and the philosopher, I think, profited by this experience of affairs and of the handling of men. I seemed to verify in myself what I take to be Plato's teaching, viz., that practical experience is a necessary element in the training, not only of a philosopher-king, but even of a philosopher. There was, moreover, one experience during these years which has proved of great value to me, especially for my understanding of political philosophy. I was fortunate enough to be a close spectator of the movement which culminated in the formation of the present Union of South Africa out of the four independent self-governing colonies. This experience of the birth of a nation, this sense of an irresistible tide of aspiration—uplifting hearts in hope, subordinating selfish and parochial interest resolutely to a large ideal of common good, undoing in generous co-operation the divisions and hatreds left behind by war—have made an abiding impression upon me and given me many a clue for the interpretation of the 'idealistic' theory of the State.''

Quoting further from his own autobiographical essay: ''In January 1912 I was recalled to England, to be the first occupant of the newly-created Chair of Philosophy at the Armstrong College (Newcastle-on-Tyne) in the University of Durham. Thence, in the summer of 1914, I moved on to join the Department of Philosophy at Harvard University, having been invited to do so after a visit to Harvard in the autumn of 1913. My six years at Harvard, during two of which I acted as Chairman of the Department, have been among the most instructive of my career. They have brought me into contact with many of the ablest and most active philosophical thinkers in the United States, among whom I must specially mention my colleagues at Harvard, Professors R. B. Perry and W. E. Hocking. They enabled me to study, from the inside, an academic system which presents a most interesting fusion of Scotch and English with German models. For the Ph.D. system has been adopted from Germany, whereas the education up to the B.A. standard has been modelled on Scotch and English traditions. I gained, too, at first hand, an insight into the various tendencies of philosophical thought in America. and especially into 'realism' in its diverse forms. And, again, I owe to America an experience which has illuminated for me the working of human nature in society. I observed there on a large scale, how, under the stress of the war-born demand for unity of action and uniformity of thought and feeling, a free people will deny liberty—even constitutionally guaranteed liberty—to unpopular views and causes; and how democracy triumphant will employ against its critics and enemies, actual or supposed, exactly the same weapons of repression and persecution as those by which auto-cracy once sought to defeat the spread of democratic ideas.

"In the summer of 1920, Armstrong College invited me back to my old Chair, but once more, as I write these lines, I am about to move on—this time, for reasons of my wife's health, back to South Africa, to the new University of the Witwaters-rand at Johannesburg."[1]

This was in 1920 and, except for an extended trip to the United States and England, during which time he served as Visiting Professor at the School of Philosophy, University of Southern California for one semester (1931), and contributed some important papers at meetings of the Aristotelian Society, Hoernlé spent the rest of his life in Johannesburg. He became deeply involved in attempts to solve the race problem in South Africa. Indeed, his strenuous activities were the cause of his death on July 21, 1943. He served as President of the South African Institute of Race Relations, and made many addresses in behalf of the Institute.[2]

In his autobiographical essay, which was quoted above, and which is entitled "On the Way to a Synoptic Philosophy", Professor Hoernlé makes some interesting comments on some of his philosophical writings, and states clearly the synoptic philosophy which he originated. During his lifetime he published three important philosophical books: *Studies in Contemporary Metaphysics* (Harcourt Brace & Co., New York, 1920); *Matter, Life, Mind and God* (1922), and *Idealism* (Doran, New York, 1926). A number of significant essays were contri-

[1] Quoted from *Contemporary British Philosophy*. Second Series. Pp. 135ff. Edited by James H. Muirhead, George Allen and Unwin, Ltd., London.
[2] The posthumously published volume entitled *Race and Reason*, edited with a Memoir by Professor I. D. MacCrone, contains a number of these addresses. Witwatersrand University Press, Johannesburg, 1945.

buted to various philosophical periodicals. He wrote: "I hope
in the near future to work up these papers and others into a
second volume of *Studies*, in which I intend also to review the
present-day issue between idealism and realism."[1] Professor
Hoernlé never completed this task. However, he left several
unpublished essays, and this volume of *Studies in Philosophy*
contains these essays, together with most of those he mentioned
in the above quoted comment.

It was the writer's privilege to study and to write his doctor's
dissertation under the direction of Professor Hoernlé. This was
during the years, 1914-17, while he was serving on the
faculty of Harvard University, and when he was at the height
of his mature philosophical development. Although he was
under the influence of Bernard Bosanquet at that time, and
throughout his life, as was mentioned above, he was keenly
aware of the need of adjusting this type of idealism to the
various tendencies of philosophical thought which he was
encountering in America. The six years he spent at Harvard
University were of the utmost importance to the maturation of
his synoptic philosophy.

Josiah Royce died two years after Professor Hoernlé came to
Harvard University. Owing to an injury received when he was
struck by a street car Royce was on the decline during these
two years. Nevertheless, Hoernlé appreciated and understood
Royce, and recognised his supremacy among American philosophers. In his essay, "The Revival of Idealism in the United
States", Professor Hoernlé wrote: "The earlier years of my
Harvard period overlapped with the closing years of Royce's
life. Illness had by then left its mark upon him, and he was but
a shadow of the brilliant self of his great days. Even so, I felt
enough of his influence to enable me to appreciate why so
many of his pupils, as is shown by the personal statements in the
two volumes of *Contemporary American Philosophy*, broke away
from his Absolutism. The very power of his dialectic, the very
masterfulness of his mind, were a challenge to them to seek
emancipation and to recover, or preserve, their own individuality as thinkers. If Idealism in the United States has suffered
a reaction, and in certain quarters even an eclipse—was not
William James himself the first of the rebels?—this is due, in

---

[1] *Loco citato*, p. 155.

part at least, to the very force and distinctiveness of Royce's thinking. Lesser men among his pupils could not effectively copy or repeat his methods, though they might regurgitate his phrases. The stronger minds were necessarily provoked into either challenging his fundamental principles or else trying to rethink them in their own ways. Men had to break Royce's spell in order to be themselves.

"Towards the end of his life, in moments of weariness, Royce would sometimes express doubts about his own effectiveness as a teacher, because so many of the doctrines which he regarded as most distinctively original—his argument that the very existence of error implies the Absolute; his distinction of the external and the internal meaning of ideas; his use of the mathematical concept of the infinite to illustrate the structure of the Absolute; his analysis of morality in terms of loyalty and of *loyalty* to *loyalty*; his concepts of interpretation and of the beloved community; his proposal to apply the principle of insurance to the prevention of war—seemed to him to have been still-born in the sense of having been received at best with barren respect, instead of being accepted, expounded, developed. He felt, I think, towards the end a growing isolation, as of one whose voice is still heard but is no longer listened to. If it is death to a philosophy to become a still backwater, whilst the main stream of thought is carving out fresh channels for itself, then that death seemed at times to be threatening Royce's own philosophy. Yet, if it is the test of a philosophical teacher to be the cause of vigorous and independent philosophising in others, then Royce was indeed a great teacher in his own generation. Nor in his own generation only: He will continue to be a fountain of philosophical life to all who are striving to learn the art of philosophising by rethinking the thoughts of a master. To any young American student of philosophy who rejects Absolute Idealism I would say that he has no right to dissent or condemn, unless he has first earned that right by a thorough study and understanding of Royce."[1]

Since it was the writer's high privilege as a graduate student to know as teachers both of these outstanding creative thinkers,

[1] *Contemporary Idealism in America*, edited by Clifford Barrett. The MacMillan Company, New York, 1932, pp. 299ff. Readers of this Memoir may be interested to learn that the writer has recently prepared for publication *Collected Logical Essays of Josiah Royce*, W. C. Brown Publishing Company, Dubuque, Iowa, 1951.

he can testify to the truth of Hoernlé's evaluation of Royce, while at the same time he can pay a well-deserved tribute to Hoernlé. Had he lived in a less turbulent period of human history than the first half of the twentieth century, had his superior gifts not been too much dissipated in struggling with the solution of acute academic and political problems generated by the extreme tension in Western Culture, and especially in the attempt to introduce reason into the solution of the race problem of South Africa, Reinhold Friedrich Alfred Hoernlé, gifted as he was, might have become a philosopher worthy to rank with the outstanding thinkers of our Western Culture. Although he did not succeed in attaining this supreme eminence, these essays that are here assembled as his literary remains will always clearly light the way of students interested in learning the living philosophical issues of our culture during the first half of the twentieth century. For Hoernlé had an intimate knowledge of what these issues are, and he wrote about them with consummate skill. No student of the philosophy of our time can afford to neglect these trenchant studies.

MY general purpose in these lectures is to defend a point of view and to sketch a programme.

On either view the question may be asked: Are these lectures original, something that no one has thought of before? I make no such claim. Certainly I am conscious that I have reached my position by the efforts of my own thinking, not by such efforts made *in vacuo*, but exercised on the problems and theories of the great classics, and of the older contemporaries who were my teachers, and of younger contemporaries. From all of them I have received much. They have made me think, and by thinking achieve the results I have here expressed in writing.

With regard to some great thinkers, I should like to say: This is what is living in their thought, this is what deserves to endure, what they wished to say but were hampered in saying. Thus, in a legitimate sense, I defend their views, and clearly I cannot claim originality for something which I seem to myself to be able to discover in doctrines of my predecessors. Mine is a contribution to that continuous debate which, retrospectively considered, is the History of Philosophy; and, as going on here and now, is Philosophy itself, as it lives in contemporary philosophising.

At the same time, I have expressed my views in the best words I could find, using historical parallels sparingly. I ask my readers to judge these lectures on their intrinsic merits, and not on the merits of any "authority" I might quote.

R. F. A. H.

PART I

UNPUBLISHED ESSAYS

Theory of Knowledge

THE theory of knowledge presents a paradox to the student of philosophy. On the one hand, it is a recognised branch of philosophy, listed in syllabuses, lectured on, made matter of examinations. The most widely studied philosophical treatise of modern times—Immanuel Kant's *Critique of Pure Reason*—is essentially a treatise on knowledge. And since Kant's time, many volumes, fat and thin, have been written on the subject by professors of philosophy in universities all over the world.[1] On the other hand, distinguished philosophers—to mention only some outstanding English names: F. H. Bradley, B. Bosanquet, J. E. MacTaggart—have denied that there is such a thing as Theory of Knowledge. Or, in other words, they have held that what goes commonly under that name is all a gigantic mistake—a tissue of ingenious theories based on false assumptions. Finally, to add to the paradox we not only find all these thinkers, commonly classed as "idealists", rejecting the theory of knowledge, but we have the anti-idealistic school which calls itself "realism", asserting that all idealists exploit a false theory of knowledge in support of an equally false metaphysics.

Let us, then, as a first step, attempt to clear up this tangle. If we can bring some order into this manifold confusion, we may hope to gain a preliminary orientation concerning the nature and locus of our problem. I take leave to assume—pending later justification of this position—that knowledge is a fact: we know, and we know that we know. The sciences are

---

[1] It is not here implied that there was no theory of knowledge before Kant. The discussion of topics belonging to its field is at least as old as Plato's *Theaetetus* and Aristotle's *Analytics*. Mediaeval philosophy, and its successor, modern scholasticism, present a definite doctrine of the nature of knowledge in the context of their total system. And Kant would not have written his *Critique of Pure Reason*, but for the epistemological problems and theories which either formed part of, or else were the main subject matter of, the writings of his rationalist and empirical predecessors. At the same time titles are here deceptive. Locke's *Essay on the Human Understanding* is a mixture of Theory of knowledge and metaphysics. Berkeley's *Principles of Human Knowledge* is pure metaphysics, being concerned with the meaning of "to exist", and with the things which "exist" in his sense of the word. Nor could a reader unfamiliar with the historical context and background expect a treatise on knowledge behind the title: *Critique of Pure Reason.*

sufficient evidence of this. Now, normally, in knowing, we are absorbed in what we know—in the object, not in the process of knowing, not in the nature of knowledge as such. But, we have it in our power to reflect, to double up—as it were—upon ourselves, to attend to attending, to think about thinking; to study not only the nature of the object known, but also the nature of the knowing of this object. In short, we not merely know that we know; but we can make the fact of our knowing—something, we can make knowing as such, an object of study and enquiry. Thus, in "theory of knowledge" we seek knowledge of knowledge: we try to understand, to know what it is to know. We try to answer the question: What is knowledge?

Now, the idealists, above mentioned, who reject theory of knowledge as a mistake, can hardly be supposed to be denying the truth of propositions such as these. What they are rejecting, as I have already suggested, is certain theories of the nature of knowledge, certain types of answers to the question: What is knowledge?

The types of answers they reject seem to me to be, mainly, these: (a) The theory which declares critical examination of the very possibility of knowledge to be fundamental, and logically prior, to the attempt to know some object, or explore some section of the universe.

In the history of modern philosophy, this sort of theory has been attempted in a variety of ways—as a classification of "ideas" into innate, adventitious, imaginary; as an enquiry into the "origin" of our "ideas"; as an examination of the "powers" or "faculties" of the human mind; as an attempt to determine the "limits" of human reason. Locke's setting himself to enquire what subjects our minds are and are not fitted to deal with here meets, verbally, at least with Kant's setting himself to enquire into the "possibility" of metaphysics by way of an analysis of the "possibility" of physical science. Here, too, belong many theories which, examining the human mind as the organ of knowledge, come to the conclusion that from the nature of this organ reality is unknowable, thus culminating in a magnified caricature of the Socratic "irony" for which wisdom lay in knowing that we know nothing.

That there is something amiss with these approaches to the problem, it is easy to realise by reflecting that, if this were the true relation of the theory of knowledge to knowledge, then our physicists, chemists, biologists, etc. would have to study, say, the psychology of cognition before turning to nature. Actually, science comes before the theory of science, just as we learn to think, and think logically, before we develop logic as a branch of philosophy. Similarly: knowledge comes before theory of knowledge, not *vice versa*. And more, a theory of knowledge which should result in denying the title of "knowledge" to most, and *a fortiori* to all, of what we value as "knowledge", thereby stands self-condemned. Somewhere or other it is mistaken. Unless we start from knowledge as, in some sense, a fact, there is nothing to examine, nothing to make a theory of.

Actually, as I shall try to show, the misleading formulations of this type of theory hide a perfectly genuine and legitimate problem, namely, the problem of the nature of the evidence available, and of the conclusions to be drawn from, or the interpretations demanded by, that evidence—be it in some special department of thought, or for some special portion or section of the universe, or be it for the universe as a whole.

As a hint for the ultimate aims of our enquiry, let me say that, for me, all debates about "faith" and "knowledge", or about what we perceive by our senses and whether physical objects are what we perceive them to be, are, in the last resort, debates about what sort of evidence is available for certain conclusions. They are debates, therefore, about truth—not about the nature of truth in the abstract, but about kinds and ranges of evidence, and the general principles of reasoning from, and interpreting, this evidence. When Descartes finds a way out of universal doubt, when Hume declares whole classes of propositions, namely, all those of the type, A is the cause of B, to be invalid, their arguments—whether in themselves sound or unsound—are contributions to *this* type of enquiry, though they may seem to talk about the "origin" of our "ideas".

(*b*) A second group of theories rejected by the idealists are all those which approach the examination of the nature of knowledge with certain antecedent metaphysical assumptions. Most common here is the metaphysical assumption that the universe consists of two heterogeneous substances, mind and matter. This theory of the nature of the universe is antecedently assumed to be *true*: it is assumed that we *know* the universe to be so. And, on this basis, in this context, the nature of knowledge is then construed. Now, knowledge is a mental possession, knowing a mental process or activity; it belongs thus to the mind side of the universe. But, in the physical sciences, at any rate, it is matter which is the object of knowledge, which is known. But, how is the gap from mind to matter bridged? How does the "inner" grasp the "outer"? What relation is there between intramental ideas and extramental objects? And how can this relation itself be known, except in its turn it become an idea and involve afresh, on this level, the problem of the "transcendence" of ideas?

The dialectics lurking in this analysis, and exhibiting it as fallacious and untenable, may be supposed to be nowadays sufficiently familiar, though it is surprising to note the extent to which verbal habits survive which, if the language used were literally interpreted, would imply this sort of discredited analysis. Idealists reject, in short, all theories of knowledge which begin with the dualism of mind and matter, or which generalise this into a dualism of idea and (non-idea) object, and then try to bring in knowledge, i.e. the truth of what we perceive and think, in the guise of the idea "representing", or "copying", or "referring to", the object, and doing so by its own implicit self-transcendence.

Once more: if there is anything living in these otherwise dead formulae, it is that, in a distorted and misoriented way, genuine problems of evidence and its interpretation are being touched on, but from a point of view which makes them in principle insoluble except by verbal hocus-pocus.

(c) Closely connected with this second type there is a third, which makes the cognitive relation of mind (idea) and (real) object rest on a causal relation—in Whitehead's words, on "what the object does to the mind". Here we are back, from another angle, at the "origin" of "ideas", as impressions produced, effected "in" the mind by the action (stimulus) of "external" objects (bodies)—an action which takes place through the body of that mind, so that this type of theory, strictly interpreted, involves not only an account of the relation of knowing mind to object known, but also of the relation of the knowing mind to its own body when that body is not itself the object known but only the intermediary through which the object "affects" the mind.

Into all the variations of this type of theory, and the criticisms by which it may be annihilated—its internal incoherencies exposed, I do not need to enter—they are, or should be, familiar ground. Their general outcome is scepticism; for they assume something to be known which, if they are true, cannot be known. But, what is, perhaps, worth stressing is that such "causal" theories of knowledge are but the highly specialised examples of a general *Einstellung* towards knowledge which may be characterised as the "naturalistic" one, and which, as such, is adopted by all those realists who are also naturalists.

In general, this point of view may be characterised as follows : Knowledge is a natural fact, a fact in "nature"; still better, perhaps, Knowing is a natural phenomenon, to be studied in its context of other phenomena. This general programme can be, and had been, worked out into a variety of special applications.

It may be given a biological interpretation according to which cognitive activities are a special kind of behaviour on the part of certain species of living beings, and cover the needs of life. To sense, to perceive, are ways of reacting, of responding, to environmental stimuli; selective responses in the service of life. For, to perceive correctly, and, on the basis of correct perception, to deal correctly with the object or situation perceived, is life-preserving, life-promoting. To misperceive, in any one of the many ways in which perceiving may fail, leads to further unadapted action and is life-burdening, life-destroying. The theory may be extended from perceiving to include remembering, thinking, reasoning, although this extension introduces awkward implications, in that direct stimuli have to be supplemented by substitute stimuli, for example, conditioned reflexes, thereby opening up the problem of imagery and language. For substitute stimuli bring in the problem of meaning, which is really present already in direct stimuli, but can be (and generally is) there ignored. At any rate, knowledge, as a biological activity, or mode of behaviour, is brought within the general framework of the physiological stimulus-response concept, though even then subject to one tacit limitation and one often unacknowledged assumption.

The tacit limitation is to the responses of animals, and especially higher animals, including man. The general concept of stimulus-response covers plant behaviour, too, but not many thinkers are prepared to say that a plant senses, perceives, let alone "knows" its environment, although they have no difficulty in saying that a plant reacts to stimuli. In this tacit limitation to animals, there lurks a hidden concession to the presence of *mind*, a concession which those naturalists and behaviourists like to keep hidden, whose preference is for the physical and the "public"—"public" in the sense of observable perception and observable by many observers. To keep "mind" "consciousness" out of the discussion as "private", "inner", not publicly observable, and thereby to keep out, too, psychology, seems to this school a merit. It wishes to rest itself securely on the standpoint of the scientific observer, who— standing over against that which he observes—has before him an animal (or, it may be, a fellow-human) in an environment. This total situation—a natural scene containing an animal in it, or the animal in that scene—is his object of observation, and in that context he observes how selected features of the scene are related as stimuli to the sense-organs of the "percipient" animal, and how these perceptual responses lead to various kinds of "practical" behaviour. Thus, the *de facto* limitation to animals—a limitation not contained in the stimulus-response concept as such, at once acknowledges that there is a difference between the responses of animals and plants, and that this is a difference of *mind*. This limitation also hinders the full recognition and discussion of mind on its merits by insisting on restricting the discussion to what is "publicly observable".

The usually unacknowledged assumption is that of the latent purposiveness of this "cognitive" behaviour. In itself, the stimulus-response concept belongs to purely *causal* thinking: it is a special form of the general cause-effect concept. And a relation of cause-effect need not logically be, although it *may* be, also a relation of means to ends. Here again there are awkward problems. Ends as aims, consciously conceived and adopted, and means consciously chosen to achieve ends consciously adopted we understand. But, can we still speak of means and ends where there is no consciousness of either? Well, we do—biologists do it, at any rate, all of them who distinguish right from wrong responses, who talk of adaptation or failure of adaptation, of conditions and actions favourable or unfavourable to the preservation of life. In short, where knowledge is treated as a mode of biological behaviour, and as an instrument useful to the living creature in the struggle for survival or in the service of a life-urge towards greater fullness of living, higher planes of fulfilment of life energies, this predication of latent, implicit purposiveness is present, and helps to make these theories plausible to their authors and the public. Here, then, belong all *instrumentalist* theories of knowledge.

Still another, more sophisticated, variety of this naturalistic point of view appears, where the thinker's *Einstellung* is not merely behaviouristic or biological, but where mind is recognised as distinct from organic life, although presupposing the latter as its basis, or, at any rate, as a higher level of evolution of organic life than the merely physical (non-mental) one. All these evolutionary theories—whether they limit themselves to three planes (matter, life, mind), or multiply these planes (e.g. Alexander)—still link knowledge with mind, consider mind to have come into being at a certain stage in the evolutionary process, and assign to it, after it is evolved, "its place among other natural phenomena". The context determining this approach is : Nature as the aggregate of all perceptible phenomena, which are, *qua* perceptible, physical; among these, some exhibit life; among living ones, some exhibit mind; some mental processes or activities are "cognitive"—there is the *locus* of knowledge. Now since it thus appears in this natural context it must be studied in it, and not apart from it.

When the idealists reject even theories of knowledge of these naturalistic types, it is not, as before, because they are self-contradictory, or self-denying, but because they are irrelevant. They are beside the point. They assume we know what knowledge is. They are not answers to the question : What is knowledge? They answer quite different questions, such as : What is the use of knowledge to a living creature? Or : Under what conditions—or at what level of evolution—does knowledge occur? Now, their answers to these questions may be either good or bad answers—let us concede for argument's sake, that they are "good", i.e. "true" answers—still they remain irrelevant to the nature, the essence of knowledge. We require a

Wesensschau. Once we have grasped the *Wesen*, the universal
nature, of knowledge, we can then also enquire, when, where,
why, how it appears in fact, i.e. when, where, why, how the
universal essence in greater or less fullness, realises itself in the
perceiving and thinking of this or that individual living being,
or historic group of beings. All these enquiries are relevant and
proper in their own place: they become irrelevant only when
they are substituted for an enquiry into the *Wesen* of knowledge;
when the theories to which they lead are offered as implying
the answer to the fundamental *Wesensfrage*, the question: What
is knowledge? What is it to know? Given the answer to this
question, the naturalistic theories may serve to round out the
Wesenstheorie, for, in the last resort, a complete theory of a *Wesen*
includes also an account of the conditions of its "ingression"
into actual events. To give only the latter, without the former,
would indeed be to present Hamlet without the Prince of
Denmark. Why, after all, is right perception biologically useful?
Because it is right, or true. But what is meant by saying that it
is right or true?

Our problem is a *Wesensbetrachtung*, or *Wesensbestimmung*—
certainly on the basis of existential examples of the realisation
of knowledge—of instances of knowing. We have no hesitation
in admitting that knowledge, or knowing, cannot occur except
where minds, or mental processes of certain sorts, occur; and
whatever existential conditions are required for the existence
of minds and, therefore, for the existence (occurrence) of knowledge, I concede in advance. But, still I want to know and still
I insist that I have not, in knowing all this, an answer to the
question: When can a mind be said to "know" something?
What must the quality of the mental processes or activities of
perceiving and thinking be, if we are to have the right to say
of them: So to perceive and think the object is to "know" it?

When the question is put in this form, does it not become
obvious that knowledge is a *value*? To claim that we know something; to attribute knowledge to another; to point to a set of
propositions as constituting scientific knowledge (or, as the
"best", the "latest", knowledge) of a given subject, is to
attribute a certain value to it. We can claim to know an object
when we are entitled to say that, as we perceive it to be, so it
really is. In short, knowledge as a value concept leads us

straight to *truth*. To know is to perceive and to think truly. Actual perceivings and thinkings—mine, yours, those of scientists or those of theologians—may succeed or fail, and both in varying degrees, to realise this value, to possess this quality of truth. But, it is only in so far as they possess it that they are "knowledge", and it is only where existing (occurring) perceivings and thinkings have this quality that knowledge and truth are realised in existent examples. Theory of knowledge thus becomes theory of truth. But a preliminary comment is in order here.

We are in the habit of distinguishing knowledge from ignorance, and truth from error. And whilst we, certainly, connect knowledge and truth, for knowledge cannot be "knowledge" if it is not "of the truth", we as certainly refuse to connect ignorance and error in the same simple way. For, although a person who is in error about something is also ignorant of it, in that he does not know the truth, a person who is ignorant of the subject is not necessarily in error about it, even though he is, by virtue of his ignorance, very liable to fall into error. A person who, in answer to the question: What is X? replies "I do not know", meaning: I can formulate no proposition whatever about it, let alone one that is true; or, who, when contemplating alternative propositions about a subject, confesses his inability to decide which one, if any, is true, and therefore accepts none— such a person is *bona fide* ignorant of the subject, but not a victim of error. On the other hand, a person who believes as true a proposition about a certain subject which is actually false, is in error. The ignorant person is unable to judge; the person in error judges falsely. (It is needless to point out that a person in error is not a liar; he speaks what he believes to be the truth. This makes it necessary to distinguish between truth and veracity.)

With ignorance, as an antithesis to knowledge, we are not, therefore, further concerned. But error, as the antithesis to truth, is part of our enquiry. A theory of knowledge need not be also a theory of ignorance; but as a theory of truth it must also be a theory of error.

Now here we enter another field full of notorious contention. And, once more, I have to try to establish my point of view, in distinction from other points of view. You are all familiar

with the fact that, usually, two types of theories of truth confront each other—the so-called Copy or Correspondence Theory
and the so-called Coherence Theory. All too often, these are
stated, examined, compared, as if they stood on the same plane
of reflection, or were rivals within a problem-situation seen from
the same point of view. This is largely an illusion begotten of
that "systematic ambiguity" of philosophical terms which I
mentioned at the outset. The difference between the points of
view to which the two theories belong goes much deeper than
is suspected. And as, from the point of view with which I am
concerned to familiarise you, the Coherence Theory is the only
possible one, I must ask you to follow me into some rather
detailed analysis.

It is usually said—and may, with proper caution, be accepted
as a common starting-point—that the predicates true and false
apply to propositions (or judgments) and to nothing else. But,
like so many happy formulae in international diplomacy, agreement on this one may express a very superficial unanimity,
while cloaking divisions of opinion which go much deeper than
all agreement. I must indicate a few of the main lines of such
disagreement.

(*a*) A "proposition" may be regarded as an entity, capable
of becoming an object of thought, towards which, equally
whether it be true or false, we can take up a variety of attitudes;
we may merely consider or entertain it, without committing
ourselves; we may commit ourselves playfully, or hypothetically
(experimentally or "supposing"), or "for argument's sake";
we may believe, accept, affirm, or, again, disbelieve, reject,
deny, and take either of these attitudes for a variety of reasons
(perhaps from a variety of causes?), among which logical
grounds, i.e. evidence for the truth or falsity of the proposition,
may, but need not, play a part, let alone be the whole and sole
motive for our attitude. Apparently, then, it is possible—and,
if possible, then for theory of knowledge also necessary?—to
distinguish between the proposition "as such", "in itself" (or,
at least, the proposition as merely contemplated, understood,
in a non-committal way, preparatory to asking oneself: now,
what attitude am I to take up to this?) and the attitude of
hypothetical supposition or categorical affirmation or denial
which can be taken up towards it. And, again, it seems possible

—and perhaps necessary?—to distinguish between the attitude taken and the motives, causes, grounds, reasons for taking just that attitude and no other. And, pondering all these distinctions which analysis thus shows to be possible, we may puzzle over the question which, if any, are relevant in considering whether the proposition is true or false. Should it be considered in itself (or as merely entertained), apart from attitude and modification of attitude, apart even from "logical" modification of attitude? Is a proposition, in short, something definite, and compact, and self-complete, as it were, which is true or false in this isolated self-containedness (so that even logical reasons for affirming it are merely *causae cognoscendi*, not *causae essendi*, of its truth)? Or is it something which is vague, fluctuating, shifting, and the truth or falsity of which cannot be assessed without taking account of—not so much the thinker's "attitude" in the abstract, as his attitude together with its motives, and especially its logical grounds? Indeed, is it not perhaps an illusion to speak of a proposition as the "same" when it figures in different minds which take up different attitudes towards it, or even the same attitude but on different grounds? When we try to think over the alternatives here suggested, we have no option but to proceed *as if* the "proposition" were the meaning conveyed by a certain form of words (a certain sentence or verbal statement). But do the same verbal formulae, in fact, have the same meaning to different minds? Let us, to give point to this question, take a proposition which may well be true (or state a "fact"), but is none the less more disputable than some other kinds of "factual" propositions. Consider this account of Hindenburg's "record": "Ludendorff won his battles for him and he betrayed Ludendorff; the Kaiser made him a Field Marshal and he betrayed the Kaiser; the Right elected him in 1925 and he betrayed the Right; the Left elected him in 1932 and he has betrayed the Left".[1] No doubt, there is here a judgment of value as well as a statement of fact, a condemnation as well as a description. And concerning both, the question of "truth" may be raised. But we can ignore the judgment of value and consider simply the truth of the description: Did Hindenburg's conduct, in fact,

[1] Uttered, in 1932, by a "German naval officer of distinction" and quoted in I. L. Wheeler-Brunck's *Hindenburg—The Wooden Titan*.

constitute betrayal? On this, different views may be taken, and are being taken, both by his fellow-actors in the German drama and by contemporary outside observers; and probably different views will be taken by later historians. In what sense "different"? Eliminating the question of moral value, whether acknowledged betrayal (or breach of faith) is sometimes, or never, justifiable, we may have differences of opinion on what constitutes betrayal; or, if there is agreement on this, then differences of opinion on whether the concept of betrayal does, in fact, apply, i.e. whether Hindenburg's actions and motives in this context possess the marks of betrayal; and behind differences on this issue will lie differences in the total view of the actions and motives in this context.

Now if different minds judge differently concerning the "true" character of an object which is, denotatively, identical for all of them we can conclude only that, connotatively, there must be a difference—that this "same" object was experienced in different ways by the several judgers. Now, you and I can treat their judgments, as based on their experiences, as "evidence" on which to found our own judgment, which may, or may not, agree with any of theirs. But, formally, our position will be analogous to theirs: they and we interpret evidence— and, if we differ, it will be because of differences in the evidence of which we, severally, take account and/or differences in our principles or methods of interpretation.

Denotative identity with connotative (qualitative) difference: a difference which need not be merely connotative and inclusive, (X sees what Y sees, but more as well), but may be truly divergent and exclusive (X sees what Y does not see, and *vice versa*)—think, for example, of the knights and the shield, and of the blind men and the elephant.

The meaning of a proposition, that is, of the form of words, will and must differ in the ways described—and in this medium truth has its being. Somewhere or another we must come to bed rock in what minds experience and what they make of their experiences. Some time or other, we must descend from abstract conceptions of truth, and try to apply our concepts to actual perceiving and thinking. And, if they prove inapplicable, the fault lies with our concepts, that is, with the abstract methods employed in determining their content and relations.

Let me try to approach this from another angle: the predicates, true and false, we have said, apply to propositions, and to propositions only. (This means that only a proposition can be either true or false; and it must be one or the other.) At once, analytically, we can distinguish between a given proposition, X, and the "being true" of that proposition X. And there will, thus, be possible a further proposition X_1, viz. the proposition that the proposition X is true. X_1 will be a proposition about the proposition X—a proposition on a higher level. And, of course, X_1, being a proposition, will in turn admit of being true, and thus of yet a further proposition, X_2, to the effect: it is true that the proposition X is true, and so on, *in infinitum*.

Is this amusing? Perhaps. Is it profitable in the sense of deepening our insight into truth? Hardly. For what evidence have we for X_2? If any, only the same evidence which we have for X_1. And what evidence do we have for X_1? Only the evidence which we have for X itself.

In other words, the evidence for X_1 and the evidence for X being true, are one and the same evidence, and this simply means that when a thinker, *bona fide*, affirms X, he affirms X-as-true. To affirm that S is P is, implicitly and *ipso facto*, also to affirm that it is true that S is P: and even that it is true that it is true that S is P. When we judge *bona fide*, we judge with conviction of truth. The "categorical" form of the proposition expresses a categorical frame of mind. And the frame of mind is categorical because of this conviction of truth realised here and now, in what I perceive and think: the object is—is truly—really *so*: It is what I perceive and think it to be. Thus "evidence" for X being the same as evidence for the truth of X, always points back to all that in the thinker's "experience" is relevant to X.

"All in the thinker's experience that is relevant to X"— once more this suggests a distinction between X and what is relevant to X (that is, relevant to the truth of X). Does the evidence for X and for X being true, lie within X itself—within its four corners so to speak—or outside X in "other" things. Are there propositions which are genuinely self-evident, as against others the evidence for which consists in their relation to "other" propositions?

c

This distinction, again—as everyone familiar with philosophical literature well knows—has given rise to an immense amount of subtle and ingenious discussion, the gross effect of which, however, might almost be characterised in Berkeley's words as raising a fog in which it is impossible to see.

Thinkers who have agreed that there are self-evident propositions have disagreed on the answer to the question: what propositions belong to the class of self-evident propositions, for example, the proposition: this is good, or this sort of thing is good. Now to say that there are self-evident propositions, but that we cannot know for certain which they are, should suggest the false method of abstraction which betrays itself by being an abstraction that lacks applicability. We want to understand the nature of that which is: the character of the real (or the real character of the real: the universal realised or realising itself). Universals abstracted from the study of which we cannot return to make our contacts with universals realised betray a false use of the method of abstraction. (I want to follow natural science in the handling of universals in relation to particulars, that is, universals abstracted and the same universals realised in instances. But this is not the "naturalism" criticised above.)

Again thinkers have said that the truth of a proposition, whether self-evident or revealed by other evidence, none the less inheres in the proposition in such a way that, even though it has been inferred from other propositions, once it is inferred as true from true premisses it can be affirmed "by itself", the nexus of evidence being discarded.

But, if we consider propositions as what a mind perceives and thinks, that context, relevant (as we have already seen) to "meaning", is equally relevant here. This means that there is no atomism of bits of meaning, standing fixed in isolation from one another. Their fixity is either that of details fixed by other details within the system, or of pervasive characters seen on reflection to run through the system as a whole. The truth of the former is inferred from other evidence: the evidence for the latter is self-evident, that is to say, they are the system holding truths themselves.

Let us make yet another approach. The word "true" must have a meaning. It must express something which we experience.

The word would be meaningless without an experience of truth. But how do we experience "truth"? Again, to give an analysis of "truth", an account and definition of the nature of truth, which is inapplicable in the sense that the attempt to apply it leads only to the conclusion that nothing we experience is true (or, at any rate, that the experience which leads to this conclusion is our only experience of truth), and the judgment that no judgment is true (other than this judgment) is the only true judgment, is an example of false abstraction.

We are easily tempted into such false abstraction by beginning, for example, with some such reflection as this: The word "true" is an adjective; adjectives name qualities, hence the word "true" names a quality (of propositions). Now, qualities constitute the essence or nature of a thing: essence is a non-relational, an absolute concept, hence if true names a quality belonging to the essence of a given proposition, then it is there, whether we happen to perceive it or not.

Note, however, that this same reasoning would hold for the quality named "false". There would, thus, be intrinsically true and intrinsically false propositions, just as there are things good and bad, regardless of desire or aversion. But the fact that we can consider whether a proposition is true or false, can ask for its verification or refutation and demand evidence, seems to conflict with this view. An absolute quality it would seem can only be perceived to be there. But, if evidence for the truth of a proposition can be demanded, its being true, or false, must consist in its relation to something else. Thus "true" will name, if a quality at all, then not an absolute but a relational quality. We shall then mean, by calling a proposition "true", that it stands in a certain relation to something else—an object or "fact". "False" similarly will name another relation, the logical opposite of the one denoted by "true": not the mere absence of the truth-relation. (Note the pitfalls involved here.)

It is not my intention to examine in detail the various theories of truth constructed on this general pattern. I want to point out only that, the evidence for the truth of a given proposition, if evidence is to be *experience* of truth, can be only an experience of a proposition standing in the required relation to the relevant fact. If, at the same time, it is held that, from the nature of the case, such an experience never does, or can, occur, once more we are in the awkward position of never being able to say what propositions are true or false. In other words, we can never use, or apply, our definition of truth.

On the other hand, if the experience of proposition-in-relation-to-object occurs, why, having the object, should we also frame the proposition? Some thinkers have strained the resources of language in order to discriminate between the fact: This-white, and the proposition: This is white—but why, at the moment of perceiving this-white, I should bother to complicate the situation by gratuitously adding "This is white" (an addition not merely of words, but of a special type of object, viz. the meaning of these words, that is to say, the proposition), is not explained. And the moment we pass beyond these simple situations, in which the theory has still a certain plausibility for innocent minds, conundrums multiply. Suppose "this is white" to be a false proposition, what is "the" object in relation to which its falsity consists? This-black? But if "this" is black, then it is presumably not the "this" in "this-is-white". Whence the assumed identity of denotation in "this"? And who, confronted with a perceived this-black would fool himself by adding "this-is-white". In fact, how can an object of perception be misjudged, let alone misperceived? And yet we know both to be possible. Again, what of the truth of negative propositions? If "this is not white" can be true, what is the object in relation to which it is true? This-black? But why add to this black perceived as such the gratuitous proposition, this is not white? Or if the object is: this-not-white is any such object ever perceived? And, then, take the objects, or facts, of general, hypothetical propositions; or propositions dealing with objects and qualities imperceptible by the senses—what sort of experience of their truth-relation to objects can be pointed out? Suppose it to be true that "every event has a cause", what experience of what relation to what fact or facts do we have which could be adduced as our experience of the truth of this proposition?

Much has been written on denoting, on knowledge by acquaintance and knowledge by description, etc. Without going into detail, I say that much of it is vitiated by a false use of abstraction. What is not so vitiated can find its place, with suitable interpretation, in the context which I am trying to establish. What is this context? It is "experience", in the widest sense, or "mind" as the context of all contexts, and, in this sense, as the absolute context.

Let me expound this more in detail. Certainly, we can distinguish mind and body, or mind and matter, or experienc*ing* and experienc*ed*, or, indeed, any one thing from any other thing—but all distinctions are within an embracing context, for which it is difficult to find a name free from ambiguity. If we distinguish "mind" from "body", it will be mind as an "empirical phenomenon" (as it is often, and aptly, expressed) from body as another sort of empirical phenomenon. That is, mind as experienced from body as experienced are two objects of experience. Thus "experience", as the aggregate of empirical phenomena or experienced objects, is the ultimate, the absolute context. Why not say that it is the Universe? All things are within the Universe, and are there distinguishable from each other. There is no reason for not using such language, provided only that the reflection is not ruled out that the "Universe" is the Universe-of-experience, the Universe-as-perceived-and-thought. Whatever language we use, the unity, or complex, of experiencing-and-experienced (of subject and object) is the ultimate prius of theory of knowledge.

Historically, this is the significance of Locke's "new" *Way Of Ideas*. According to his terminology "idea" is anything and everything that is object of thought, i.e. of apprehension in the widest sense. Among ideas, we can then distinguish ideas of this and of that, and debate which of them are real, which imaginary, etc. But the effect of projecting all things in the universe on to the common plane of "ideas" is the same as that of saying that "experience" or the Universe as experienced is the context of all contexts.

This, again, I suggest, is the real meaning of Kant's concept of "transcendental ideality" which is yet compatible with "phenomenal reality". This reminds us that everything we acclaim as "real" is an object of experience and thought—is perceived and thought just so.

Admittedly, the language one cannot help employing constantly leads one into the temptation of slipping into contexts which abandon this absolute prius. For example, if one says "perceived and thought", it may be asked, by *whom*? By *me*, by *you*, by human beings, by human minds. And at once these terms suggest the context of human versus non-human; of mind versus body; of men as an animal species in a natural environment. This is the door to the "naturalistic" plane.

However, this is not the force and meaning of these terms here. When I speak of "my" experience, I mean, not "mine" as against "yours", or human as against animal, but experience *here and now* in its immediate actuality. When I speak of "ours", the social plural invites others, each to realise the here-and-now immediacy of experience in himself. Whenever anyone perceives, thinks, feels, etc., there occurs an example of "Experience". We are to study the example, not as the particular occurrence or event, but as an illustrative instance of a universal, which universal is the real object of investigation. In experiences immediately occurring, we want to study Experience-as-such: Experience as the experiencing-of-objects no less than as objects-as-experienced, experience as the self-revelation of the Universe.

Verbs, like perceiving, thinking, etc., suffer from this same systematic ambiguity. They may be used in the context of psychology as a natural science, studying mind as a natural phenomenon: but to hold fast to this point of view in Theory of Knowledge would be *Psychologismus*.

We can think and speak of "mind" and "experience" as "natural" objects, phenomena, processes, in a context of other kinds of natural objects—and we can think and speak of them as referring to the apprehension of all objects whatsoever, or all objects whatsoever as they are and are experienced as being. There are, thus, two planes of reflection: two senses in which mind, or experience, are their own objects; the naturalistic, psychological, and the "transcendental".

Really, it is probably easiest to avoid the tangle and gain the right *Einstellung* by thinking in terms of *evidence* and the *interpretation of evidence*. They belong to the terminology of "knowledge", and they imply that we are dealing, each of us, with what he is experiencing as he is experiencing it. We could all readily agree, for example, that science as a whole, and any single science in particular, reveals to us, gives us the "truth" concerning its subject-matter. *Ipso facto*, we take for granted, in so speaking, that the subject-matter is object of perception and thought—"our" perception and thought. But the force of "our" is not to contrast ours with that of some other type of being, but simply denotes experience and thought as illustrated in *this* experience-and-thought, here and now. We are trying to speak in principle of *any* experience and thought: of the universal, and refer to "ours" simply as the example always ready at hand, the familiar instance.

There is, no doubt, a legitimate context in which it is possible and relevant to compare and distinguish different kinds of experience, in the sense of the experiences of different kinds of beings—infants, children and adults; male and female; scientific and non-scientific (or religious and irreligious); civilised and primitive; human and animal. But, even if this comparison takes the form of distinguishing between what a child *knows* of the world (that is, how the world appears to, reveals itself to a child) and what an adult knows,[1] or what a primitive people *knows* (that is, what it thinks the world to be; what the world is to it) and what civilised, i.e. scientifically trained Europeans know the world to be—the argument is not necessarily relevant to theory of knowledge? Why not? Because I can keep it on the plane of discussing and comparing merely what different kinds of beings (or different kinds of minds, human or other) believe the Universe to be, without raising the question of truth and without asking: What *is* the Universe? as distinct merely from the question: What does X believe the Universe to be?

To make an object of study of what children or primitives or scientists "know"—that is to say, of what they believe and think —is to study a certain order of facts. But knowledge in the *vital* sense is what I, the student of these things, come to think concerning these facts. It consists of the judgments with which I express the truth concerning these facts and their nature, as I apprehend it. I can study "knowledge" as a set of ideas, beliefs, and theories in certain people's minds—even in my own mind. I can note the fact that X believes so and so, and even why he does, or why he says he does, believe so and so. But this is to study knowledge in abstraction from its cognitive

---

[1] This comparison is possible on different levels of generality. For example, child and adult in the context of a given culture, and child and adult in general.

function, its "reference" to reality, and its truth-claim and truth-value.

Locke, Descartes, etc., it will be noted, started from "ideas", precisely in order to go on from there to ask the question of the nature, tests, and criteria of the cognitive function. (Think, for example, of the contrast between idea as "fact" and idea as "meaning", and that between idea as entertained and idea as judged or referred to reality.) But it is not until we come to Kant's Transcendental Logic that we find a clear and consistent discrimination between a study and description of ideas as mental facts and a study of their cognitive function, that is, their value as revealing the nature of the Universe. All too often, when the pre-Kantian thinkers did face this problem, they attempted its solution by assuming certain ideas to be true (by assuming the universe to be so and so), in order on that basis to discriminate between the truth and the falsity of ideas in general. But a general enquiry into the nature of "knowledge" or of "truth" cannot start by taking this or that particular proposition to be knowledge, or to be true, and then use that proposition as a test for all the rest. By a "particular" proposition, here, is meant one not concerned with the nature of truth in general; for, of course, reflection on the nature of truth must express itself in propositions which, once expressed, will be "particular" in the sense of being *these* propositions among a lot of others on other topics.

On the plane of mere fact, one set of beliefs actually held and another set of beliefs actually held are of equal value. There is here no ground for preferring one to the other. If primitives believe in sympathetic magic, and we do not; and if we believe in scientific determinism, and primitives do not—this is, so far, just a piece of information about them and us, relevant in an anthropological context. If, on the other hand, we start arguing that the belief in sympathetic magic is false, whereas that in scientific determinism is true; or if, among ourselves, we debate, not the relative truth of sympathetic magic and scientific determinism, but the truth of the latter relative to other beliefs of our own, which some, or all, of us also accept as true but which are incompatible with the truth, or at any rate with the absolute truth, of scientific determinism, *then* we pass into theory of knowledge. For then the real question is: is the Universe so?

where "so" means: as it is here affirmed to be—as its nature is expressed in this set of propositions affirmed by some and offered for the acceptance of all.

This is a question of evidence and interpretation of evidence. But what does "evidence" *denote*? Surely, actual or possible "experiences". And what does it *connote*? Surely, these experiences as revealing the nature of the object, in the last resort of the Universe as the object including all objects. If experiences do not reveal anything concerning the nature of the Universe, if they have no cognitive function, no truth-value —then, (*a*) What is their relevance? and (*b*) What other relevant evidence is there, if they have none?

Here we have confirmation of our starting-point. Theory of knowledge assumes that knowledge exists, that instances of knowledge occur, and that there are perceptions and thoughts to the very nature of which belongs the conviction that the object is what it is here perceived and thought to be.

So, again, with interpretation: The cognitive value, the reality-revealing function, of any bit of evidence is not restricted to what it, here and now, is; to what it reveals within its own four corners, so to speak, but extends to what it means or implies. In other words, it is what it is because other things in the Universe are what they are; and, *vice versa*, because it is what it is, other things are what they are. In this sense, each bit of evidence points beyond itself to the whole, or system, to which it belongs. This whole it reveals "so far as it goes", and this means, fragmentarily, but none the less genuinely.

So understood, the process of interpretation, however much in detail liable to error, must in principle be reality-revealing. If correctly performed, it cannot take us away from, but must take us closer to, reality. It cannot spin a web of illusions, but must cumulatively reveal Truth in a system of "truths".

Leaving aside, for the present, the here conceded fact that illusion and error do actually occur (and, therefore, are both "possible" and "necessary"), let us assume that evidence and interpretation are in fact, what they are in principle, viz. infallible—reality-revealing beyond any question, that reality is what (or as) it appears, i.e. is perceived and thought to be.

Leaving qualifications and restrictions for later consideration, this, then, is the principle. When applied to actual experiences this principle can, and must, be unfolded into a complex of more special propositions, themselves of varying degrees of generality. However these special propositions all fall within the same context of "knowledge" as revealing reality or the Universe. Such revelation takes place in and through experience, and within experience there is distinguishable evidence and interpretation.

1. In ordinary thinking "evidence" generally consists of propositions already accepted as true. But, reflection easily reveals that a large number of propositions, perhaps all, concern what is perceived or, at least, is perceptible: felt or at least feelable. Thus, we learn to distinguish modes of experience which are, or supply, evidence in an ultimate or primary sense from evidence in a secondary sense of something already elaborated by interpretation. The attempt to distinguish between datum and interpretation, where datum must mean the not-yet-interpreted, but interpretable, thus leads us to postulate, or recognise, as an ideal lower limit the existence of forms or modes of experience which function as evidence by their mere occurrence and their mere *such-ness* or *thus-ness*. "Immediate experience" this sort of evidence is technically called. Denotatively, the word refers to the experience of the senses, the "sensations", that is to say the colours, or coloured shapes, actually seen, sounds actually heard, etc. Also to the feelings of pleasantness-unpleasantness which may accompany any or all of these; and the sensations of movements. These we later learn to interpret as responses or reactions towards or away from various objects and situations, with feelings of liking and disliking, enjoyment and aversion. All of these immediate experiences come in a mass, within which they are discriminable, and they change, they come and go. If we attribute to them a sophistication which is not theirs, considering them thus as an abstract evidential starting-point, we might think of each of them as saying:

> I am I; I am what I am; and, being what I am, I am part of the Universe. In that I am part of it, the Universe is what I am. My being what I am is part of its nature; and it is such that I, being what I am, am part of it. So far as I go I reveal its nature, and its nature reveals itself in me.

These immediate experiences are "evidence" because, in occurring at all, they make this claim, and they make it absolutely. Whatever else the Universe may be, it is *this* and it is *so*. Anything and everything that in this ultimate way is, has been, will be, is a revelation of the nature of the Universe.

We may argue where to draw the line between immediate experience and other experience, what to include in the former and what to exclude. Such debates do not touch the principle just affirmed. We may argue about the transition from immediate experience to explicit judgment, or the transformation of the former into the latter, or whether this transition or that transformation can occur. But if it does, it is because this possibility is part of the nature of the evidence. The intrinsic qualitative diversity within the mass of immediate experience makes possible isolation of this from that by attention, distinction by thought of what is different in fact, and the naming of each distinct item or kind of item, may be necessary for explicit judgment, that is to say, for the affirmation as a proposition of what comes first as a bare immediate fact (or "content" of experience)—the essential thing is that the occurrence of an immediate experience is the evidential basis for the judgments: this is; this is so-and-so; this is a so-and-so; this being so-and-so is real, and part of reality; and, ultimately, whatever else reality may also be, it is this and it is such that this, being what it is, is part of it.

In these statements, I have tried to do justice to what there is of truth in the contention that in sensations, or, generally, in immediate experience, we have something infallible, indubitable, and absolute. To discredit the deliverances of immediate experience, and especially of the senses, has always been part of the case of sceptics in general and also of rationalists, as sceptics concerning the cognitive value of sense-experiences in particular. But the doubt, and denial, of truth could never touch what an immediate experience is "in itself", it could only touch the interpretations put upon it, the inferences drawn either from its occurrence (*Sein*) or its qualitative nature (*Sosein*).

At any rate, there is "truth" in immediate experience, because it commits us not only to the affirmation that *it* is so-

and-so; but also to the further affirmation that it means more than, in itself, it is—in short, that it is a clue to the wider Reality of which it is a part, and within which its being so-and-so is determined. We may misread its meaning as a clue: but even such a misinterpretation still falls, formally, under the principle of being an affirmation that Reality is such as to contain within itself this immediate experience, standing in such-and-such relations to other aspects of the Whole.

2. Now let us return to a more general consideration. The distinction between evidence and interpretation may be given a misleading distortion, which either dodges the real problem, or twists it out of shape.

The evidence, we may say, comes first and the interpretation follows after. The accumulation of evidence in successive experiences takes time; fresh evidence comes in, perhaps, during the process of interpretation and modifies its results; still further evidence may confirm or verify the results reached, or negate them. But immediate experience comes first—first in the life of the individual, as an infant; and first in the experience of the race.

Interpretations, themselves, have their history. They are built up slowly by the labour of successive generations of thinkers; they may be discarded *in toto* by large-scale revolutions in thought. Think, for example, of the history of science; the history of a theory or belief; and the history of a discovery or of an invention.

However, this temporal, historical, and genetic point of view is irrelevant. When offered as a substitute solution, it dodges the problem. When we want to know what knowledge is, it is no answer to describe to us the steps by which it has come to be realised in an individual mind or in human civilisation. When we ask: what is truth? it is beside the point to show how this or that truth came to be discovered or formulated.

Most insidious is this false twist into a genetic theory when what is meant to be a *Wesensanalyse*: an analysis of essential, constituent, factors—is turned into a general picture of genetic development: first came (or comes) this factor: on it supervenes, or out of it emerges that other factor. Kant's transcendental logic of the "possibility" of experience is meant to be an analysis of its essential constituents. However, Kant himself does not consistently escape the danger of using "genetic" language.

Most disastrously, because most insidiously, this hidden geneticism betrays itself in assessing the cognitive value of the factors distinguished in knowledge. Hence, the curious instability in Kant's theory: sensations are given to the receptive mind: thus they seem to be in some way intimations from the Beyond, from the Universe that sends these signals, that in them makes known its presence, its existence. But this "chaotic manifold of sense" with which the process of experience begins, which stimulates the mind to activity (note the genetic language), is now synthesised by the mind working with synthetic principles which constitute its nature as a logical machine, so to speak. The result of this synthetic activity exercised on the given sense-material is the affirmation of "objects"—of the empirical world in space and time, with its things—their qualities, its changes—their causes. But the synthetic principles, as contributed by the mind, seem "subjective": revealing the nature of the mind, the human mind, not that of the Beyond, the great X, which sends its intimations through the senses. Is this truth or illusion? Is reality revealed by this synthesis or disguised and distorted?

No. For if our distinction of evidence and interpretation were to be similarly read, it would be open to analogous objections. For example, it might be asked: what are your principles of interpretation? What right have you to use them? What right have you to claim that the result of their application is "the truth" concerning the matter under investigation?

The only way of avoiding this twist is to recall our starting-point. We start from knowledge as a fact, from truth realised in "truths". Knowledge is there, truths occur in human thought. If it were otherwise we could have no theory of knowledge or of truth.

Otherwise expressed, we start with the Universe, that is to say, with the Universe as it is perceived and thought to be. "But what if the Universe is utterly other than it is perceived to be by us?" "What if there be no Universe at all?" The latter question is meaningless verbiage, namely, if it means: is there anything at all? or: is there anything over and above this momentary perceiving and thinking? It is not meaningless, if its point is: is whatever may exist, a *uni*-verse or a *multi*-verse? The first question has meaning only in the sophisticated sense in which any universal may be also an ideal measured by which its realised instances are recognised as falling short. However, even then, without the clues furnished by the realised instances the ideal could not have been conceived, and this is its claim to be a "true" ideal. If a universal, when we compare instances of its realisation with each other, itself leads us to recognise degrees of perfection in its various realisations, and thus to conceive a perfection transcending any realisation with which we are actually acquainted, then this is itself a feature of that self-revelation of reality which is "knowledge".

Immediate experience, then, reveals universals and linkages of universals, which for reflection become objects of abstraction, an abstraction of which we have the simplest example when the experience of $a_1, a_2, a_3 \ldots a_x$ leads us to conceive the nature of A. Similarly, instances of identity, contradiction, etc.—are cases of the application of these principles.

In short, we come here to *Logic*. For, logic deals with universals of a high order of generality, which can be illustrated from actual instances in which they are realised, even if we regard them as holding, not only for this *actual* world, but for all other "possible" worlds. Indeed, to think of them as holding for other "possible" worlds is merely a way of emphasising their extreme generality.

If the actual world has a definite logical structure, then that structure will be realised in *what* immediate experience presents, even though this is not yet recognised as such, nor abstractly conceived. As thus realised it is part of the nature of Reality thus revealed. To recognise it there; to abstract it and study it for itself, is part of knowledge. In principle, the "truths" thus revealed are part of the Truth. Reality is such that these principles are exhibited by it: "exhibited" both in the sense that they are realised in what immediate experience gives, whether they are explicitly recognised for what they are, or not; and also in the sense that, when they are explicitly recognised, they are recognised as "true of" the given as there illustrated, as there having instances of their realisation.

Now, logic has come to mean, in modern thought, a great

many different things. One might almost speak of *logics*, each having its own concept of its subject-matter, and of the place of that subject-matter in a general theory of Reality. But I believe that it will be found true of all of them that, if they are dealing with the structure of Reality, that is, its "logical" structure, that structure will be the structure of Reality-as-object-of-experience, and will, therefore, be exemplified in the real as we perceive and think it to be.

This is obviously true of the so-called traditional logic, as is shown by the way in which all of its doctrines are illustrated from actual life, that is, from everyday experiences or from scientific thought. No doubt this logic is full of defects and limitations, considered as a theory of the most generalised universals illustrated in reality as we experience it. In making this statement I intend no illegitimate exploitation of the ego-centric predicament, but only a reminder of the self-evident truth that we can talk and think only of the real which appears, that is, the real which is object of perception and thought. That the so-called "laws of thought" of the traditional logic are "laws of reality": i.e. laws expressing the most general nature of the thinkable-as-such or whatever can be "object" of thought at all, may be taken as commonly agreed.

That the theory of judgment of traditional logic, with its doctrine of the distribution of terms, is based upon the concept of classes, and that it was born of reflection, not on the nature of classes in a realm of pure thought, but on human experience of natural classes among the objects of perception, should be equally obvious. That the individual member of a class is commonly, though not always, an object of perception, and as such a "thing", the "qualities" of which are revealed to us as perceived, or as perceptible, such as colours, shapes, odours, touch-qualities, etc., is again plain. That the entire theory of traditional logic moves in this medium, in this "empirical" atmosphere, seems to me to be undeniable. This does not mean that its principles or laws or fundamental concepts are *a posteriori*—mere empirical generalisations. They are *a priori* right enough, the empirical "particular" being only the occasion for reflection to grasp the universal which is there illustrated, for every particular is not a "mere" particular, but a this-such—a particular instance of a universal. We become acquainted with universals and universal connections between universals in instances of their empirical realisation: but we can, on the basis of such acquaintance, make them objects of reflective thought in their own right.

That there are difficulties here, in the correct definition and delimitation of universals in their relations, we know from the arguments about the principle of causality as the law of inductive inference: the principle which must be realised in the succession of natural events, if it is to be possible to infer from the actual occurrence of one kind of event that an instance of some other kind of event will follow or has preceded. But the fact that we occasionally mis-identify a relation of events as "causal"; or fail to assign an adequate cause for a given effect, is no argument against the principle as such.

Into Hume's attack on causality, I have not time here to go: and, even if recent science doubts the applicability of the principle to certain microscopic phenomena it deals with, I would still say that over the vast range of macroscopic phenomena the principle is so firmly established, that its status (subject to whatever limitations) as a law of thought which is *ipso facto* a law of reality cannot be abolished. At any rate, we reason *as if* there were causal laws, and the success of such reasoning, and our success in learning to distinguish causal from non-causal successions of events is sufficient verification. The *quaestio facti* settles the *quaestio juris*.

These terms recall Kant and his "Transcendental Deduction of the Categories". If at this point I may permit myself a digression into the History of Modern Philosophy, I would say that the point of view which I am trying to state and commend may be regarded as a "justification" of Kant. No doubt this justification is an interpretation of Kant, perhaps even an interpretation which he himself would have rejected, but none the less an interpretation which strikes through at what is *living* in Kant's thought, and has proved its aliveness by the line of thought which has been born from it. At any rate, I regard the Bradley-Bosanquet type of *Logic*, especially in its theory of judgment, as the direct heir to what is "alive" in Kant's "Transcendental Logic", however much its formulation may in detail have been influenced by the tradition of English philosophy in general ("Philosophy of the Human Mind"): by antagonism to Mill's *Logic*, in particular; by influences from Hegel, Lotze, and Sigwart. The famous, and to some critics infamous formula that judgment is "the reference of an idea to reality", is not one which I, personally, employ because the words used are loaded with "systematic ambiguity", i.e. they give no hint of the context in which they have to be interpreted, and are thus unguarded against false interpretations from critics who give them a meaning derived from other, and inapplicable, contexts.

I take the formula to mean that, in principle, Reality is what I perceive and think, or, generalised: what is perceived and thought. Reality, in short, is here identical with Kant's "empirical object", or his "world (of objects) of actual and possible (sense-) experience". That he distinguished this world as *realitas phenomenon* (appearance) from an unknown and unknowable *x*, the *Ding-an-sich*, or, again, from a *realitas noumenon*, which is object of pure thought, but not of experience, that is, of thought synthesising sense-data, is a special twist of the Kantian theory which we here discard. We keep, in short, to the central doctrine of his Transcendental Deduction, which is concerned, *at once*, with the nature of objects of perception and of the judgments in which these objects are affirmed to exist and to be so-and-so. The whole point of the Kantian analysis here turns on the "critical" reflection, which equates, for example, physical objects with objects-perceived (or "objects of experience"), and then analyses them and their nature by analysing what is perceived and thought. Deliberately, I do not say "what is perceived and thought—*of them*": for *they* ARE *what* is perceived. There is *identity* here: hence Kant's doctrine that the "object" is constituted by the synthetic activity of the judgment: it is what we perceive and think it to be. To perceive an object, to perceive it as existing and as being so-and-so is, for Kant, to judge, on the evidence of sense-data, that it exists and is so-and-so. The whole system of judgments employed in empirical science rests upon this principle, and elaborates the nature of the world perceived. The essence of the position is the rejection of the dualistic analysis which consists in contrasting the world perceived, which is regarded as being "mental", with a "real", i.e. "non-mental" world, which is existentially and qualitatively "other" than it.

The formula, "reference of an idea to reality" has a fatally

D

dualistic ring—verbally. Consequently, it belies that very identity of object of perception with the real object (object as part of the real universe) on which, taken in its genuine context, it is its purpose to insist.

At any rate, Kant's categories (to whatever criticisms his and the traditional table of categories may be open) constitute the logical structure of nature, of the Universe (or Reality), as object of perception and of natural science. That he professes to discover his categories through an analysis of judgments as acts of synthesis (*quaestio facti*); and that he attempts to justify them (*quaestio juris*) by the argument that, without them, there is no "nature", no physical thing, in general, no object having qualities and undergoing changes, does not affect the fundamental principle: They *are* the logical structure of the Universe as object of perception.

Now this line of thought, this attempt to reach through a study of judgment-forms the logical structure of Reality as object of perception and thought is characteristic also of the Bradley-Bosanquet type of theory. This theory offers no such detailed list of categories as does Kant, but it treats different judgment-forms, none the less, as expressing logical features of Reality as revealed, as it "appears", as it is perceived and thought to be.

Perhaps their analysis, even from their own point of view and on their own premises, is open to criticism and is capable of improvement. At any rate, the most recent developments in lgoical theory: Logistic, *Gegenstandstheorie*, Logical Empiricism, etc., have been inspired by other motives, have been born from another *Einstellung*. It would be interesting to examine how much of their results could be absorbed, by suitable reinterpretations, into the Bradley-Bosanquet context; how much of it, in fact, is another type of analysis of this same fundamental situation for which I know no more suitable phrase than: Reality-as-it-is-perceived-and-thought.

Truth and Error

WHAT is error? What is it in its essence and nature? I can say
only: a failure of the cognitive function, recognised as such on
the basis of a more successful functioning. *Veritas norma sui et
falsi*: as a self-revealing process cognition is self-correcting. Why
error occurs at all; or why a particular person on a particular
occasion falls into error; why doctrines which a later age ranks
as "errors", prevailed for centuries as "truths"; or why what
some of us regard as exploded errors prevail or are even
revived—all these and similar questions are not problems of
the theory of knowledge. The first of these questions belongs to
the group which includes such questions as why there is evil
in the Universe; or why human minds are finite and non-
omniscient. Whether or no it be profitable to discuss such
questions, certainly the place for such discussion is not in an
essay on theory of knowledge.

Error is recognised for what it is only by contrast with truth.
And how is truth identified? One is tempted to answer: It
shines by its own light. However, at this point such a metaphor
is unhelpful, and it is even misleading if it suggests that anyone
should be able to take any proposition and, contemplating it
thus in isolation, to decide by some intrinsic illumination that
it is true. This would be to demand for every true proposition
self-evidence.

We shall get nearer to a helpful statement by two reflections: First, when a proposition is true; then, ideally, our
conviction of its truth should be capable of being expressed
by saying: it is so, it must be so, it cannot be otherwise.

When do we approach this degree of conviction? Whenever
a proposition is exhibited, by a process of reasoning, as necessarily implied in certain others, and when these others, these
premises are true (or—and it here amounts to the same thing
—are accepted as true). The principle is this: What follows
from a true premise (or true premisses) is true. Thus, given

33

true premisses and correct reasoning the conclusion is so, must be so, cannot be otherwise.

We must remember, here, the distinction between *validity* and *truth*, for in order to reason from a proposition, we need not know whether it is true or false: a false proposition permits formally valid inferences to be drawn from it as well as a true one; but to reason from propositions which one knows to be false (except in some "indirect" proof) would be a fool's game. Hence, although we can draw conclusions from premisses the truth of which we doubt, or concerning the truth of which we are uncertain, the above principle that what follows from a true proposition is true applies here only in an hypothetical way. This means that if the premiss is true (were true or should turn out to be true) then the conclusion is (would be, or would turn out to be) true, too. Thus the logician, concerned with validity of reasoning, can abstract from the truth or falsity of the premisses and conduct his analysis on this hypothetical plane. In order to examine whether a conclusion follows validly from the given premisses, he does not need to know, or to decide first whether the premisses are true. But he would need to know this in case he had to decide, not only that the conclusion is validly drawn, but also that it is true.

Now, normally, in ordinary life and in science, we work with premisses which are true, or—what amounts to the same thing —which we *bona fide* believe to be true, either because we can prove them by valid reasoning from true premisses, or from premisses believed to be true, or because we know of no evidence to the contrary, no reason why they should not be true. And thus, we proceed from truth to truth, and knowledge "advances". The light by which truth shines and reveals itself is here, partly the light of "validity", of logical necessity or connection (this *must be* so, because that *is* so), partly the lack of any evidence (grounds) why it should not be so. Thus, logical necessity and compatibility (the relation of two propositions which can both be true, although neither can be inferred from the other) constitute that "coherence" with each other of propositions, which is the essence of truth, i.e. which entitles us to say that the Universe is as it is here judged to be.

So analysed, coherence is an *internal* characteristic of the system. To it we should add that there must be no evidence, within or without the system, which might contradict or throw doubt on any part of it, that is, which, if true and accepted as true, makes it impossible for that part also to be true. This means that the situation of "no evidence to the contrary" is an essential feature of truth.

"Without (outside) the system" may refer to *other* systems of thought *within* the range of experience and thought as a whole. "Outside" this whole, in any absolute sense of "outside", we cannot, of course, go. But, if the truth of science, as a whole, is challenged, for example, from the point of view of religion, or *vice versa*, we have such an instance of incompatibility between a system and evidence which lies, *prima facie*, "outside" it, and which, within that system is not met with, or is ruled out as "irrelevant" (for example, as "unscientific").

Truth thus appears in many places; and, ultimately, demands the total inclusion of all experience, so that the concept of "outside" drops away, and there is no quarter from which evidence to the contrary might come. And so we come to this conclusion. Theory of knowledge furnishes no definition of truth, which could be applied *ab extra* to propositions so as to determine whether they are true or false. That determination is done in the actual process of thinking and perceiving, of collecting and interpreting evidence; and what reflection on "truth" and the nature of truth, does is merely to set out, as objects of reflection, the principles already operative in truth-seeking, reality-revealing perceiving and thinking.

Thus we conceive a system of universals, interpreting the given evidence (immediate experience), and thus claiming to be "true" of it, realised in it, illustrated in it, even whilst transcending the "data" of any given moment. Yet, at the same time, the flux of data, the flow of experience, constantly "verifies", and continuously illustrates the system, while receiving from the system its meaning, so that we can, from point to point, say: "So-and-so is the (real) nature of this which is here and now perceived".

The second line of reflection, referred to above, is: Every proposition *bona fide* affirmed, is implicitly affirmed as "true". This naïve, innocent, conviction of truth can be lowered into a mere *claim* to truth, by turning in reflection, round upon the proposition and asking: But, is it really so? Is this really true?

Normally, we do not do this—we do not question or doubt—without grounds or evidence of some sort. To do so without some definite reason, would be idle. However, what can happen is that, having found definite reason for doubting, and perhaps even sufficient reason for rejecting certain propositions at first affirmed with naïve confidence, we can by generalisation move to the reflection that evidence might present itself for doubting propositions hitherto unquestioned. From the experience of actual error we might form the concept of possible error beyond the range of the actual.

Yes, but under one all-important proviso, namely that, however extensive we allow the range of possible error, even for the proposition that "such-and-such a range of affirmations is, in principle, open to challenge as potentially erroneous", we need a positive basis which stands outside the challenge and from which we can make the challenge, but which is, itself, *unchallenged*. The argument remains of the general type: this being so, such-and-such affirmations may be false. And the basis, "this being so", must be affirmed as true in order to supply evidence for the interpretation of the rest as possibly false.

No doubt, this type of challenge can operate on many planes; it can challenge an individual judgment of perception here and now; and it can challenge all judgments based on the evidence of the senses as such. But, what it cannot do is to rise to an absolute challenge. All sceptics have had to accept something as true, however little it be, from which to argue to the falsity of all the rest that claims to be "knowledge". Thus: *veritas norma sui et falsi* is once again verified.

However, to return: If we leave aside deliberate lying, imagining (for example, day-dreaming), make-believe, etc., and argue from the normal trustful and unsuspecting, but at the same time truth-seeking attitude, we can only say that every experience (evidence and *prima facie* interpretation) so to speak believes in itself, and offers itself as true. And true it is, and as true we accept it, *in the absence of reasons for thinking otherwise*. We all know that this naïve trust receives many rude shocks and jolts; we all know that often not only are "second thoughts", that is to say, interpretations, best, but even third and fourth thoughts better than firsts ("things are other than they seem").

We even may have had occasions when second and third lookings and hearings and tastings, etc., brought fresh evidence correcting the first evidence and its interpretation. Thus, even within the range of an individual thinker's perceiving and thinking, conflicts arise, and judgments have to be revised.

And, when we pass from the individual (who is, after all, an abstraction) to the individual as member of a group, perceiving the same objects as others; finding his interpretations confirmed by others, or again accepting their interpretations as authoritative; often also finding himself perceiving and interpreting differently from his associates—in this context, this intercourse of mind with mind, the coherence principle of truth has the real medium of its application. And here—I say this in passing—moral questions may enter which, as such, have nothing to do with pure theory of knowledge: such as— whether, and to what extent, the individual has the right to proclaim, or to act on (live by) the truth as he sees it when his "truth" is condemned as "error" by others perhaps better qualified to judge.

In *theory*, given equal competence, the fact that others differ from me should be ground for me to entertain some doubt concerning the absolute truth of what I believe, even if, apart from this disagreement, I have no evidence whatsoever to think otherwise than I do. "I may be mistaken, but I cannot see how or where".

In such a case, what is my moral duty? To stand by the truth as I see it, through thick and thin? To withdraw into myself, holding to my private conviction, and let others, if the majority, or if the constituted authority, have their way? Shall I take the position Martin Luther took: "*Hier stehe ich, ich kann nicht anders*", or shall I admit that I may be wrong and that I have no right to resist? What is my duty in such a situation? What does or what should conscience demand?

To be sure, even these conscience questions work out differently in different contexts. On the purely scientific plane, it may be obviously right to hold to, and to continue to argue for one's unorthodox opinion and leave the final judgment to posterity. But, on the practical plane—when it concerns truths on which common action has to be taken, or which are to supply the common foundations of belief on which communities

are to be organised for coöperative action, the vistas that open
out on freedom of thought, speech, and teaching are all-too-
often left in an obscurity which may become dangerous.

This has been a digression, interesting only as a reminder
that theory of knowledge, as theory of what Sigwart called
"the will to truth", is, after all, but one strand in the complex
web of human life, and that neither its isolation for purposes of
reflection, nor the preoccupation with the honorific name of
"truth", must betray us into thinking that we are here dealing
with a value necessarily dominant over all other values,
supreme in the realm of values.

With this remark I return to my main line of thought. Error
is discovered, propositions are judged "false" by the "light of
truth", that is, on the evidence of other propositions which are
true, in the sense that they, then and there, hold the field
according to the *implicit* working of the principle of coherence.
Whether this discovery is made by an individual thinker within
the context of his own thinking, whether one corrects oneself,
discovers one's own errors; whether a thinker's errors are
discovered by others, contemporaries or successors; whether in
the former case, the original thinker becomes himself convinced
of his error and acknowledges it, or not: what constitutes, in
each case, relevant or logical evidence for recognising a proposition as false—all of these questions, and similar ones, are
questions of detail, through all of which we must hold fast to
the self-correcting nature of knowing as the self-revelation of
the Universe. And the principle of this self-correction is the
Principle of Coherence, as above described.

I put emphasis, deliberately, on the Universe as revealing
itself, unafraid of the dialectics lurking in the question: If self-
revealing then revealing itself to—? Well to me, to us, to anyone—to all who perceive, think, and in short experience; to
"minds", if we like. In language this is dualism: here is the
Universe complete in itself, and there, over against it, are minds
to whom it displays itself. But no—the minds are in it and part
of it: with this reflection monism returns upon us. And if the
Universe reveals itself to me, it reveals itself to itself through
me: to itself *quatenus humanam mentem constituit*. But, actually,
these dialectics are not worth pursuing; certainly not worth
pursuing at the expense of the—to me—much more important

reflection that, although I write (as we all do, and cannot but, write in the grammar of languages moulded to the needs of social intercourse) of *my* knowing as my activity, of my perceiving, thinking, reasoning, as something which I *do*, yet am I conscious, on deeper reflection, that what I do is as much, and more, a something done to me; that I am in the grip of the Universe which uses me, which has made me, and is making me, what I am. There is a passivity, a receptivity, not merely in respect of the impressions of my senses, the feelings which spontaneously accompany them, the reactions or responses which "automatically", or "reflexly" they evoke. There is a passivity also in the play (or, if you prefer, the "work") of my thinking. Thoughts comes to me, especially fresh, unexpected thoughts; and even in my attitudes towards these, when my thinking seems most "mine", it is, none the less, mine only as the relatively enduring deposit, or system, of thoughts which once "came" (*einfallen*) and which, coming again and again have become an habitual apparatus for evaluating fresh thoughts; a company of associates, more or less closely organised, which a fresh thought has to join, with or without modification of itself and others, or else be rejected as "false".

Does not the judgment which becomes recognised as an "error" remain as *prima facie* evidence against the "truth" of the judgments on the basis of which it has been labelled "error"? For example, consider judgment A over against judgments B, C, D. Let B, C, and D be true and in their light let A be false. Now can we not invert the argument and say that, if we suppose the truth accent shifted to A, then A is, so far, evidence for the falsity of B, C, and D? The situation arises in our experience when the judgments are distributed over different thinkers. For example, X, believing A to be true, judges B, C, and D false, whereas Y, believing B, C, and D to be true, judges A to be false. But, in principle, the objection misses the point. The difficulty is raised in a wrong context. Admittedly, thinkers who disagree in their judgments and accuse each other of error may fail to convince each other, to extract one from the other a confession of error. But, the theory of error, as part of the theory of truth, assumes the context of acknowledged recognition of error—the experience of judging for oneself, on evidence duly considered and accepted by oneself, that a certain judgment, previously affirmed as true, is in fact false. This experienced process of self-correction, in its context of truth-seeking thinking, is the basis of the theory of error.

The aspect of passivity: of the Universe communicating itself to me is present throughout. Always I perceive, feel, think what, then and there, I do perceive, feel, think: and what, as thus *actual*, I cannot help perceiving, feeling, thinking— what I am *compelled* to perceive, feel, and think.

This is generally recognised concerning the evidence of our senses, the bare sense-data, abstracted for interpretation. What I see, I see. If I hit on the table, the bang which you hear is an ultimate datum for all who hear it. It is just so, and, as being just so, it is an indelible part of the Universe as each of you experiences it.

Now this principle, so plain and obvious here, extends to other planes in the realm of knowledge. There is more variation in interpretation, in the meanings which we judge data to bear. But, again, for each of us, in categorical interpretations the meaning is just this which we put upon the data and cannot help putting upon them. If other meanings are suggested, we may consider them, on evidence which we judge sufficient, reject them as "impossible", or at least as less probable than the meanings accepted. Always, the urge is towards the position: It is so; it must be so; it cannot be otherwise.

What is the meaning of this "must"? We are touching here on a time-honoured controversy. It involves the distinction between the "contingent" and the "necessary": the contingent which can be conceived to be otherwise without contradiction, and the necessary which cannot be conceived to be otherwise without contradiction. And, thence, the distinction between "truths of facts" and "truths of reason", and the part this played in the arguments between empiricists and rationalists.

On this issue, I go with the empiricists. Our knowledge of the actual world, the world which we perceive, in short, nature and natural science seem to me to support a principle which I would like to state in this way: facts are of different orders, and the "necessity" of a fact of a lower order consists in its being an instance of a fact of a higher order, and this whole system, which we discover by scientific research is, at the last, just the inclusive Fact, which we can only accept for what it is; and of which, in the end, we can only say: this is what it is; this is what it reveals itself as being; such, in detail and in general character, is its nature.

Every experience is (reveals itself as) a this-such—a universal here and now realised and illustrated, an instance of a universal. As we grasp the nature of the universal, which may be complex and only partially illustrated in the datum here and now, we claim to "understand" the "particular": we say that we know what it is and thereby why it cannot be otherwise. Why do particular *a*'s behave as they do? Because it is the nature of A, the nature of the kind of thing of which these *a*'s are instances, so to behave. The general fact, the law, the essence, explains the instances. The law (at any rate, when correctly stated) is never broken. The essence is never untrue to itself. The "fact" of the higher order explains the fact of the lower order. The particular is what it is and cannot be otherwise, just because it is an instance of such-and-such a universal or universal connection.

Nature is a system of universals constantly realised and realising itself in instances which, for theory of knowledge, are objects of experience. Knowledge consists in discovering the structure of the system by following (thinking out) the empirical clues offered. It starts with facts the nature of which unfolds itself as enquiry proceeds. Thus from the primary facts with which enquiry starts, facts of a higher order are discovered. But always we remain within the realm of Fact, of absolute *Sosein*. The question: Why? in this context, asked concerning the *Sosein* of any fact, is answered in principle by saying: this is so, because that is so: and this particular nexus is so, because it is an instance of the law that this kind of thing is so, because that kind of thing is so; and if we ask for the Why? of this law, we are led, perhaps through "higher laws", to the ultimate law: It simply *is* so; it is the nature of the Universe, as it reveals itself to us as object of perception and thought, to be so. We may call this "brute necessity": opaque, unintelligible, unsatisfying to our demand for ultimate insight. But I submit, of this sort and no other, is the insight which natural science furnishes. Its "necessities" are factual, not "logical" necessities, if by logical necessities we mean the sort of necessities which we experience when we argue from definitions of non-empirical

("rational") objects, as in mathematics. The law of contradiction applies in scientific thinking, but it applies only to
universals and their connections as revealed in sense-experience
or inferred from such sense-evidence. To suppose that water
should in any given instance behave contrary to its nature is
to suppose the self-contradictory, but the argument applies
only after we have established on empirical evidence *what* the
nature of water is.

In this sense, then, the formula: "Is; must be, cannot be
otherwise" applies only in the context of the self-revealing
Universe: the Universe as we find it to be when we spell out
its total nature from the clues which it offers in our experience
of it.

Fact and Value

ONE of our difficulties is that so many of the words we have to use have shifting connotations. We say glibly that we perceive a certain object, e.g. this desk here, without specifying how we perceive it. Normally by sight, and consequently, to perceive means *par excellence* to see. For science, seeing (vision) is the supreme sense. But other modes of sense-perception, with or without seeing, play their part—not to mention the metaphorical uses of the word, as when we say that we perceive the truth of a remark, or a person's intention (when perceive means infer).

For our purpose the chief difficulty lies, however, not here, but in the question whether perceiving is to be distinguished from judging; or whether we should discriminate between perceiving an object and affirming a proposition concerning that object. Now again, "object" is ambiguous, according as we have in mind such an object as a table or any physical thing, or a colour or coloured shape, whatever is ordinarily regarded as a "quality" of a "thing".

From the point of view here taken, perceiving an object, in the sense of physical thing, includes a judgment, includes the affirmation of a proposition (whether put in words or not) : for the object analyses into data and meaning : the meaning is fused with what is given in sense, and only reflection can artificially divorce them. If, after this divorce, we restrict "perceiving" to having sense-data merely, without meaning, then, to be sure, judgment in the sense of the affirmation of a proposition (e.g. that *this* is a table, or that this colour is the quality of a table; or that in perceiving this colour I perceive this table in so far as it owns this visual appearance) is something more, but still something more which needs the "immediate" sensing as its basis.

The choice here depends on wider contexts, on ultimate assumptions, determining our angle of approach, one *Einstellung*: assumptions which, explicitly or implicitly, we tend to make in the very act of putting and wording our questions.

43

That in every *bona fide* question, the questioner makes assumptions, takes something for granted to which, by means of the answer received, he wants to add; or which he wants to test; or some indeterminancy which he wants to determine one way or the other—this is a commonplace. The "fallacy of many questions", listed in the old logic textbooks, is an extravagant illustration. But what we do not bear in mind as often as we should is that, when we put questions to ourselves and by reflection seek to find answers, we predetermine the nature of the answers, in that we force them to fall into the tacitly-assumed framework of our assumptions. For a philosopher, therefore, although he must begin somewhere, since he cannot take his stand in a void, it is essential to be reflecting always in two complementary directions, viz., forward in the direction of the answers sought; and backward, in the direction of bringing to light and re-examining the assumptions he has made. Here, again, *coherence* is the principle of stability, and of intellectual satisfactoriness, in the result reached *as a whole*.

In a definite sense, *modern theory of knowledge turns on theory of perception*. Many arguments can be adduced in support of this statement.

(*a*) Modern theory of knowledge arose simultaneously with the rise of modern natural science. Modern natural science began with physics (including astronomy)—a science of the physical (material) world, as a world of bodies in motion. Yes, but from first to last, and however "mathematical" it might be, or become, in method and structure, as a science of actually existing bodies it was, and is, a science of bodies and motions perceived by observers. Let theory go on to affirm bodies and motions unperceived and imperceptible—with perceived bodies and motions physics began, and with them it remains always in contact. In short, every natural science is proud to be an empirical science, and the experience to which it appeals is sense experience. The world it explores, whatever else it may turn out to be, is a world accessible to observation, is the world which reveals itself to our senses, in colours seen, sounds heard, and all of the data of touch, taste, smell, and other senses.

(*b*) Perception may itself be treated as an object of perception, in that it may be identified with a commerce or interaction between two bodies (an observer's body and a body observed). Now when perception became an object for the scientist, there arose a scientific, that is, a physico-physiological theory of perception, dealing with physical stimuli, their impact on or contact with sense-organs, the subsequent consequences in the nervous system, including the reaction and response of the perceiving organism (the observer). Within its own context of evidence and interpretation, this theory claims to be well-founded, to be true. This is, it confidently asserts, what happens when an organism perceives its *Umwelt*. The scientific observer who is studying these relations between certain kinds of organisms and their environment, e.g. a dog sniffing at a street corner, can—up to a certain point—study his own body in the same way; and, in principle, he can generalise and say that what is true of other percipient organisms is true of himself as a percipient organism. Now, if perception is a mode of knowledge, this theory of perception will be a contribution to the theory of knowledge.

(*c*) Yet, it has turned out to be a somewhat uncomfortable contribution. For, the scientific observer shares, with lesser mortals, the conviction that scientific perceiving and thinking are affairs of consciousness, intelligence, *mind*. But, here, he has been dealing with perception on a purely physical plane; as, so to speak, a purely physical phenomenon, exhausted in the stimulation of one body by another and the reaction of the second to the stimulation received from the first. Where does mind come in?

Into the various, now generally discarded, speculations about the relation of mind and body (whether in general, or in this special context), we need not go. But one consequence we must note, viz., that this physical interaction of percipient body and body perceived was, in the context of science, naturally construed as a relation of cause and effect, and if the ultimately resulting perception is a mental phenomenon, then as a relation of physical cause to mental effect. Again, into the question of whether such a relation of physical to mental is conceivable or not, we need not go. For us, the important point is contained in the question: What reason, if any, is there to think that perception is true, so that we can say: the object is what it is perceived to be?

(*d*) In short, there comes here into view, a third complicating factor, viz., that the scientific observer, again like lesser mortals, assumes that his perception gives him the truth—at least, the sort or degree of truth which it is in the nature of perception to give. He assumes and believes that, in the absence of definite evidence of misperception, perception reveals the nature of objects—no doubt, only so far as that nature is perceptible; but, within these limits, in principle truthfully. He believes, he cannot but believe (if he is to go on observing, and, by observing to collect data for further theory, for "further additions to our knowledge of nature"), that perception has a cognitive function or cognitive value; truth-value; that the world is what, or as, perception reveals it to be (whatever else it may turn out to be as well).

However, this confidence in the cognitive value of perception is not only not supported, but is severely shaken by the physico-physiological ("transmission") type of theory of perception. For, it makes the "object" of perception a mental image or impression, the end-effect of a long chain of physical and neurological causation. Supposing even the end-effect (mental image) were "like" the original physical cause, what evidence could the percipient mind, confined to images and impressions solely, have to this relationship of "likeness"? Here this generalising transference from percipient organism observed by the scientist to the scientist himself works out with devastating effect. If the percipient organism has nothing but mental images to go on, and I put myself in its place, then I, also, have nothing but mental images to go on. But, if so, what evidence have I that physical things are like my mental images? Indeed, what evidence do I have that there exist any physical things at all? Nay more, in this context do the very words "physical thing" and "material world" have any meaning? Are they not mere meaningless noises? But, on any or all of these consequences, what becomes of science as knowledge of nature, knowledge of the physical world—that it exists, and what is its constitution? The consequences of the "scientific" theory of perception have destroyed the very possibility of science, as knowledge of the real, by destroying the observer's and thinker's right to credit perception with cognitive value, with truth-value, with a reality-revealing function.

(*e*) That, in detail, these fatal consequences took time to be thought out; that, at first, they were applied only in a restricted way by the famous division of the "qualities" of physical bodies into primary and secondary—of all this I wish merely to remind the reader here, as also of all the arguments, born in the same context, denying the legitimacy of this distinction; denying the existence of "matter"; construing the Universe positively as an ordered system of minds (spirits) and their "ideas". What is more to the point—as leading up to the point of view to be adopted in these lectures—is the reminder that, in the midst of the welter of criss-crossing arguments about any and all of the above-mentioned difficulties (and many others not mentioned, e.g., how can two percipients perceive the "same" thing?), there is traceable by selective attention the continuous thread of interest in the real problem of theory of knowledge, viz., the cognitive value, the "truth", the "reality-revealing" function of what we perceive and think. We may instance here Descartes' *Sixth Meditation* with its attempt to justify these distinctions between primary and secondary qualities by means of the distinction between clear and distinct versus obscure and confused ideas, vindicating cognitive value for the former while denying it to the latter. Descartes' treatment is far more acute than that of Locke. Or we may instance the defence of knowledge contained in Spinoza's doctrine of the parallelism of *ideae* and *res*, taken together with his distinction of "adequate" and "inadequate" *ideae*. Even Berkeley's theory of "ideas of sense" as the "visual language of God", through which the divine being gives us the kind of information we need for our practical conduct, may here be listed. No doubt, all these defences of knowledge stand and fall with their several contexts (systems of assumptions): but, at least, they may serve to show us both that the genuine problem is concerned with truth-value, and that the solution proposed depends upon the assumptions made, that is, on the propositions initially assumed to be true. And there is just the paradox: We can discuss "truth" only in a context of "truths" assumed. We can discuss "knowledge" only in a context, or on the basis of, what we assume we know.

(*f*) Lastly, that Kant's *Critique of Pure Reason* is, up to the end of the Transcendental Logic (including the Transcendental Aesthetic) nothing but enquiry into and defence of the

E

cognitive value of natural science as empirical science, and, therefore, of judgments of perception and generalisations from judgments of perception, should be more widely recognised than it is. However, here I shall content myself with the reminders (i) that "Aesthetic" in the combination "Transcendental Aesthetic" refers to sense-perception—to sense-data as ordered in space and time; (ii) that "Transcendental Logic" is a theory of the judgment of perception, as is shown both by the fact that judgment is declared to be the synthesis of "sense-matter" by "forms" of thought: and by the principle: "concepts without percepts are empty; percepts without concepts are blind"; (iii) by the argument that metaphysics as a *science* is impossible, precisely because in this field there is no "sense-matter" to synthesise; (iv) by the rejection of Berkeley's "dogmatic idealism", or, more specifically, the rejection of the theory that perception does not reveal a physical (material) world; (v) by the insistence that the objects, the existence and nature of which science affirms, are not mere images or impressions, but each is a *realitas*, although a *realitas phenomenon*, an "appearance", viz., precisely an empirical or perceived *realitas*.

(g) To come to more recent times, and to take a short-cut across voluminous argumentations let me remind you that, if one of the motives of the various movements of thought which severally claim the title of "realism", was to establish a non-idealistic type of metaphysical theory (in Alexander's phrase, to assign to minds their place in the scheme of things), the other was, largely for this very purpose, to assert the cognitive, reality-revealing function of perception and thought, so as to cut the ground from under the feet of all idealists who, as Ralph Barton Perry claims, have exploited the theory of knowledge in favour of an idealistic metaphysics. To take a typical instance: E. B. Holt's theory of perception as a cross-section of the Universe, defined by an organism's selective responses, here proclaims that the object is what it is perceived to be, or, inversely, that what we perceive is Reality, viz., a cross-section of it, directly revealed, not doubtfully inferred. Holt goes further and extends the principle to all objects whatsoever, perceptible or imperceptible, physical or logical, things or propositions, good or bad, true or false—with a whole-hearted inclusiveness which

makes, so it seems to me, it rather difficult for him to do justice
not only to the concept of knowledge as reality-revealing, but
also to the concept of it as a self-corrective and self-normative
process. At any rate, this is one, and not the least effective,
way of training oneself to apprehend knowledge as reality-
revealing.

So far we have discussed perception much as the word is used
in ordinary life and in science : in science in the sense that when
a scientist, who is unmindful of "scientific" theories about the
physico-physiological mechanisms of perceiving, uses the word
perceiving he speaks, like you and I, of himself as perceiving
this, that, or the other natural phenomenon. We have already
emphasised the fact that, when the word is so used, it includes
judging. To perceive intelligently, to perceive knowing what
we perceive, is to judge that the perceived is, and is so-and-so.

At the same time, so understood, perception, or the judgment contained in perception, and, based on memory of
previous perception and perceptive judgments, can be analysed
into data and interpretation, a logical and, if we like so to say,
an alogical element, or, as I prefer to express it : a this-such, or
a this-here-now instance of a universal. The world perceived
is a world of universals realised in sensuous presentness—not
statically, but in flux and change. It is a Platonic world in the
sense that it is a world of events into which eternal objects
ingress, and yet "event" is itself such an eternal object!

However, it is not its Platonic character that I want now to
stress, but rather that character which, just now, I tried to
denote by "here-and-now-present", or, using now the technical
language of certain thinkers, *the immediate*. In intelligent perception, the immediate is a necessary character : it is basal.
Our perceptive life is an ever-available source of familiarity
with the immediate, for we are perceiving at every moment
of conscious intercourse with one another in our wider *Umwelt*,
and always the Immediate is an "aspect", always there is a
this-such situation.

But perception, so understood, does not exhaust the range
of the Immediate. We are familiar also with the feelings,
emotions, "attitudes" of liking and disliking, which the world
perceived, remembered, and imagined evokes in us. These, too,
contain judgments, these, too, are evidential and they have a

revelatory function. I see here the root of the distinction between fact and value, and that between judgments of fact and judgments of value; the descriptive versus the evaluative or appreciative. Hence, if my perception of X is also qualified affectively, then the nature of X, and the nature of the Universe *qua* containing X, is also thereby revealed. The fact *has* value; value is realised or embodied in the fact. Value-universals enter into (ingress) the stream of actual events like other universals. There is value and there are values, in the Universe. Where? There where they are felt to be. Here, too, the *prima facie* principle holds: the object is what I feel it to be—it has (embodies) the value which my affective experience reveals.

This is the matrix of value-judgments which, like all judgments, "refer to Reality", i.e., reveal the nature of Reality. They are, each taken singly, on the occasion of an affective experience, no more infallible than any other type of judgment contained in immediate experience, indeed, they may even be more fallible: but, as we know from our discussion of truth and error, their fallibility in detail can be discussed only in the context of the assumption that we stand on truth in principle. They have their own logic, and they are subject to the principle of coherence in their own way.

This is more disputed doctrine. Let me try to defend it. And, first, let us face the difficulties.

(*a*) Immediate datum and interpretation seem here less indissolubly fused: Seeing a colour we see a coloured thing. But love and the loved object, anger and that which "makes" me angry, seem, and indeed are, more separable. Values *may* be realised, but *they are not necessarily realised*, in the things which we perceive. These may be "indifferent" (valueless); they may have value sometimes, but not always; they may change value —be valued in opposite ways. Even pain and pleasure seem to be more variable concomitants of things.

(*b*) In this sense alone, then, these experiences and judgments seem more subjective. And, in another sense, too, they are more subjective in that there is more difference between individuals in their affective responses than in their perceptive data. "About tastes there is no disputing", that is about evaluations. Hence, it seems plausible to argue that, if these affects and affective judgments reveal anything, they reveal, not the nature of the "object", but the nature of the "subject", i.e., the percipient's mind and character. *He* is such as to like, love, hate, fear, etc., this or that sort of thing. The *locus* of value is in the human mind, or in the object only *qua* related to a human mind as object of its "interest". Realists, especially, arguing from this assumed Dualism: object with a nature of its own, complete, versus the human mind apprehending and taking an interest in the object, have stated this line of thought in its various possible nuances.

However, this is not the whole story. Let us grant that, when we speak of an object as "pleasant", of an incident as "painful", the implicit judgments are that the object gives us pleasure, the incident causes us to feel pain. But, so far, we are not yet in the genuine realm of values. Pleasure and pain are experienced with evaluating reactions: they are experienced as values, and, thus, mediately, are the objects which bring us these experiences. To think of an object as pleasure or pain-giving is to attribute to it a certain value. "Yes", it may be said, "value for us"; not "value in itself"—value in relation to a feeling mind, no value apart from that relation. Granted, but still the feeling mind is a part of the Universe, and the relations of objects to feeling minds are part of the Universe, so that we are entitled to affirm that under such-and-such conditions, values "appear" (are realised) in the Universe, and the Universe is such that they are so realised.

This is a very simple, too simple paradigm, concerning which it is well to remind oneself that even pleasures and pains are not axiologically unambiguous: to express it plainly—not every pleasure is good, and not every pain is evil, not every pleasure deserves to be sought, not every pain ought at all costs to be avoided. There are hints, even on this plane, of an incipient dialectic of value-recognitions. Value judgments are subject to criticism and revision in the context of more complex value-experiences.

This point is essential when we come to the values revealed to us through our emotional experiences and our desires-aversions. Using "interest" (with R. B. Perry) as a convenient blanket-word for all these, we recognise a duality of direction in interest—attraction and repulsion, a movement of identification with versus a movement of withdrawal from the object;

a towards and an away-from attitude, which latter, in practical
conduct, may take the alternative forms of avoidance, or
destruction (removal), of the offending object. Here is the
empirical evidence for the polarity of values : positive and negative. All positive interest, so far as it goes, contains a judgment
of good ; all negative interest, one of evil.

However, these judgments have their own logic, their own
dialectic, their own conditions of stability. In respect of them we
can, and do, "learn from experience" and from reflection on experience ; in respect of them we are eminently educable, taking
on or discarding attitudes, modifying first by second, simple by
complex responses, under the stimulus and guidance of social
influences of all kinds. Spinoza's teaching that the path to that
wisdom which is also liberty lies not only through the development of intellectual insight but also through the transformation
and discipline of the emotions—a purification and an emancipation of the whole man through the spirit of truth, in the
double sense of truth of fact and truth of value, is here relevant.
Compare, also, W. E. Hocking's chapter entitled "The
Dialectic of Pugnacity" and the whole spirit of his *Human
Nature and Its Remaking*.

I would put it thus : if every pleasurable apprehension of an
object (act, happening), every liking for it, every desire for the
continuance or repetition of an experience contains an implicit
value-judgment ("this, or this sort of thing, is good"), yet this
judgment, although evidentially rooted in the "immediate"
affective experience, is open to challenge : Is this really good?
Does this *deserve* to be enjoyed with pleasure, to be liked, to be
desired? There is the appeal to an inherent standard, which
comes explicitly into play through some *counter*-evidence against
the primary judgment, i.e., through some other affective
experience which, as evidence for a contrary judgment, tends
to throw doubt on the stability of the first. Here conflict, ambi-
valence, dialectic begin. Here the principle of coherence
operates in a new sphere. Here, again, the truth of value-
judgments lies in their stability, based not on a stability of mere
concept-systems, but on a stability of affective patterns of
response. Consistently with the point of view adopted throughout these lectures, "transcendental idealism" goes together
with "empirical realism" : we consider "values", just as, above,

we have considered "objects" or "facts", through value-experiences and value-judgments, on the principle that the Universe here also reveals its nature, that they also are reality-revealing.

The situation has been otherwise analysed by other schools of thought. Some who are realists concerning facts are subjectivists concerning values : making "fact" in itself devoid of value, and treating value as an arbitrary gloss on fact imposed by the feelings and interests of some mind. Other realists speak of "objective values", meaning values that are inherent in things in themselves, as part of their nature, whether appreciated or realised by a mind or not. On the former view, there can be no valuations, and therefore no values, except in minds, or in the "interest" relation of a mind to an object. On the latter view, there can be values, even when there are no valuations. On a third, more sophisticated view, although there may be an objective Reality without mind, it is only with the emergence of mind in the Universe—with the enrichment, so to speak, of the Universe by the evolution in it of mind—that values also emerge and are, as it were, added to the stature of Reality. On a fourth view, Reality always and essentially is in-and-for mind, and values are, therefore, of the essence of it.

Between these views we are not here called upon to decide, nor to take issue with them, except so far as explicitly or implicitly they deny the reality-revealing, cognitive function of value-judgments. This once conceded, the metaphysical issue of the *locus* of values in a theory of the nature of the Universe need not be raised in theory of knowledge.

However, in the context which we have adopted, and in which we have set ourselves to reflect on values *via* reflecting on value-experiences and value-judgments, it is relevant to draw attention to the fact that these experiences and judgments occur on different planes, or are subject to G. E. Moore's "Principle of Organic Wholes". Here, again, there is a parallel with the perception and interpretation of "object" in the sense of "fact". Object may range from a "this-here-now" item, or detail, to the Universe-as-a-whole *via* a diversified range of intermediate objects, of varying range and complexity. Still, as we saw, the principle holds that in apprehending "this-here-now", I apprehend the Universe *qua* including this, *qua* revealing itself as this-here-now. The same is true of value-experience. My liking this, as an instance of my liking this sort of thing, is a bridge to my liking the Universe as containing this, or this sort of thing. Yet, here again, between "this" and the Universe are intermediate planes of more complex objects, the evaluations of which may confirm or over-ride, justify or correct, the evaluations on lower planes. And thus, in principle, we can, and must recognise the possibility of an evaluation of the Whole, as a whole—an affective experience evoked by pervasive, whole-revealing features of the Universe.

Some thinkers profess to find difficulty here, and certainly there is difficulty: *omnia praeclara tam difficilia quam rara sunt.* But nothing is gained by evasion or by turning back. After all, even we do not, with Spinoza, equate "*Natura*" with "*Deus*", even if we do admit the Universe to be wider than "Nature" as the inclusive object of the natural sciences, nevertheless, we use "Nature" here in a sense which may serve as a paradigm for the sense in which we can also claim to be able to think of the Universe as a whole. For nature means, not merely the natural events perceived by a given scientist, or by all actual scientists, at a given moment. It does not mean merely the aggregate of natural events occurring at any given moment, instantaneous dividing line between a past that is no longer and a future that is not yet. It does not mean merely the aggregate of all natural phenomena throughout all time and space. It means a system of universals, complex in structure, with universals of superordinated levels of generality, and universals pervading and ordering these levels, which system is present in the flux of sensible events. To work up from the clues to be found in the flux of sensible events to the system as a whole is the aim and task of science—of "knowledge" *qua* science, of the "will to truth" in this form of manifestation.

In an analogous sense, the Universe as a Whole which includes Nature can be intended and conceived *and evaluated* on the evidence of affective experiences accompanying this way of thinking—evoked by the Universe thus revealed in thought.

Knowledge and Faith

HERE, again, we enter upon a region in which, through much discussion from varying angles of approach (in varying contexts, or on the basis of varying assumptions), all words have acquired a perplexing load of systematic ambiguity.

Every *bona fide* judgment is characterised by belief. To affirm that "*x* is *y*" and to believe that "*x* is *y*" are the same, just as it is the same to affirm and to believe that "*x* is *y*" and that "it is true that "*x* is *y*". To vary the words: to know that "*x* is *y*", to be convinced that "*x* is *y*" and to be convinced of the truth of "*x* is *y*" comes all to the same. If "faith" is firm belief, conviction of truth, then faith in this context is indistinguishable from knowledge.

The extreme opposite position to this is the view which identifies knowledge with belief, or conviction of truth, on the basis of evidence, of "logically sufficient" grounds or of self-evidence, and "faith" with belief, or conviction of truth, based upon logically insufficient evidence, or on "no evidence" at all in the proper sense, or even in the face of contrary evidence: *Credo, quia absurdum, . . . quia impossibile.* Here belongs, in some of its forms, the antithesis of reason and revelation, although, to be sure, revelation might be regarded as a sort of evidence, though not as "scientific evidence", i.e., not evidence at all by the standards, or rules, of evidence employed in natural science (or in some other context, e.g., a law-court). At any rate, here is a conviction the firmness of which, *prima facie*, not only challenges, but rejects justification by, all rational tests—the affirmation of a truth "deeper than", or "transcending", rational truths. And whether this truth of faith is ascribed to supra-natural inspiration, or—as in an opposite type of interpretation — to natural, but non-rational, infra-rational, "instinct", makes in this context little difference. I mean: however important it may be, in a debate between adherents of these two "Irrationalist" views to argue concerning the true nature of the "source" or "authority" of non-rational

55

conviction as compared with conviction on rational evidence, both are "in the same boat".

It will be noted here—another example of systematic ambiguity—that "rational" evidence in this context, especially if this is taken as equivalent to scientifically admissible evidence, means the same as "empirical" evidence, i.e., the evidence of immediate experience interpreted in the light of the universals and universal connections illustrated in it. It does not mean "rational" as *opposed* to "sensible", "pure thought" as opposed to "experience".

Intermediate positions between these two extremes are plentiful. One of the most familiar is that which identifies faith with courage to act on evidence which does not amount to absolute assurance of success, or even courage to act against the odds, against the rational probability of failure. In this sense, faith is William James's will to believe, the conviction that "where there is a will there is a way"; a refusal to admit that the realisation of one's cherished purposes is *ab initio* impossible, a belief in the situation proving plastic to, and mouldable by, the ruthless, the undaunted, the fanatic, the man of "iron will". It is to this sort of faith in itself and in its *Führer* that the National Socialist Party in Germany ascribes its rise to power. It is this sort of faith which it claims as its chief moral asset. It is to the lack of this sort of faith that it ascribes the "cowardice" and "failure" of the "bourgeois" parties of Germany between 1919 and 1933.

Now, something of this sort of faith is found in all religions, so far as they are soul-moving, will-stirring forces—religions in their aggressive, propagandist, missionary aspects, religions which inspire their adherents to go out and "convert" the infidels and re-mould the world of human affairs according to their scale of values (whether or no they speak of this enterprise as a campaign for the "realisation of the Kingdom of God on earth"). At any rate, it is this sort of faith which naturally leads us over to reflections on religion, and the identification of the antithesis of knowledge and faith with that of knowledge and religion.

Now in this antithesis, "knowledge" tends to shrink to, or to determine its meaning as, "scientific knowledge", and thus to remind us that, if modern theory of knowledge was born with the rise of modern science and scientific theories of perception, so, on the other hand, it was also born of the tensions and conflicts of the new scientific outlook with the inherited religious (Christian) cosmology. Consequently, if one of its problems is, and has been, concerned with the "truth" of Science, i.e., the cognitive, reality-revealing function of perception and thought: its other problem has been the "truth" of religious beliefs, i.e., the cognitive, reality-revealing function of religious experience and its interpretation in Theology.

This is far too large a topic to do justice to in detail within the compass of these lectures, especially when, notwithstanding the various kinds of truths comprised within the edifice of Christian Theology—historical, cosmological, moral, spiritual —the claim is made that the system stands and falls as a whole, and that, if it is untrue anywhere, it is untrue everywhere.

I shall, therefore, concern myself here only with a question of general principle. That religious experience has many forms and is evoked by many aspects of human life and nature, as well as by specific "revelation", is (or should be) familiar to all of us. Among those to whom the Christian religion is a living thing, religious experience is at once stimulated and canalised in form and direction, by certain techniques of worship and by the concentration of attention (meditation, intense inward realisation) on certain events, presented as historical, and their spiritual significance for the redemption and salvation of man from "sin". In many non-Christian religions, we find much more of so-called "Natural" Religion than, as in Christianity, of "revealed" Religion—i.e., religious experience evoked by the critical moments of an individual human life: birth, marriage, death, or critical events in the life of tribe, people, nation—like the transition from childhood to adult membership in society—the death of a ruler, the access of a new one, war, pestilence, famine. In general, the cycle of life in nature, with its seeding (begetting), blooming, fruiting (harvest), dying in the succession of the seasons, and the sense of incalculable forces at work in this order which, for all the orderliness of its large patterns is in detail so variable in its impact on human life, has given rise even in the most primitive minds and civilisations to religious responses. William James's *Varieties of Religious Experience* by no means exhausts the gamut even of the forms of religious experience in the so-called "higher" religions of the *Kulturvölker*.

The problem here is not to describe in details these variations, or to assess their value one against the other; still less to do this for the corresponding interpretations, the religious cosmologies and theologies, but, rather, in the light of the conclusions concerning value-experiences and value-judgments, to ask whether in religious experience *as such* we have not a value-experience which may claim, *in principle*, the benefit of being reality-revealing.

To go into detail would require a series of lectures on the Christian religion alone. The Christian doctrine, omitting all denominational differences, contains, as a body of propositions, the outlines of a metaphysic, of which body and soul, matter and spirit, God, man, and nature are the key-concepts; a cosmology in the story of creation; a psychology derived from moral and religious experiences; an historical element in the record of the life, doings, and sayings of its founder, and, later, of its propagators and churches; a moral element in a scale of values held up before men as an ideal to realise; a "spiritual" element in a theory of sin and salvation from sin, be it through faithful membership in a church or individual "surrender of the soul to Christ". Clearly, these propositions belong to very different planes and contexts, and they raise the question of their truth in correspondingly different ways, let alone the totalitarian claim that all of them hang together, notwith-standing the differences of plane, in such a way that the falsity of one would invalidate all.

However, the deepest and most pervasive, the truly totali-tarian element is, surely, a judgment of value, whether that be expressed in the formula that the whole Universe is the creation, and stands under the guidance of a God, all-good, all-wise, all-powerful, or that God is Love and that his love for all his creatures expresses itself even in that the most sinful of souls is still an object of his solicitude and grace. There is no need to point out the more practical corollaries of this teaching, especially as focussed in the life and death of Christ, the doctrine of the Atonement, etc., and the inward attitude towards the inward realisation of all of these doctrines: or the techniques of religious experience which have been developed to maintain or to revive the realisation of these truths in human minds, and thus to produce that purification, conversion, putting-on of a "new" man, that fresh manner and spirit of living which are the fruits of faith.

From the perspective here adopted, the central truth is a supreme judgment of value—positive value of perfection—on the Universe, a perfection including acknowledged imperfection in itself; and this judgment of value claims to be the interpretation of an experience mediated for, brought to, the individual mind by its membership in a Christian community and its meditation on the teaching, life, and death of Christ.

I will not detain you by trying to show that judgments of value form the core, too, of primitive religions with their belief in superhuman forces, capable of affecting the human group and its members for weal or woe, and with whom good relations have to be maintained by a ritual believed to be essential for this purpose. Nor shall I try to compare primitive and higher religions, to show how much more profound and adequate are the value-judgments contained in the latter. I will, instead, conclude with a final argument on the general principle which I have been trying to commend to your attention and acceptance.

There are those who deny to religious beliefs of any and every sort all truth; who declare them, in principle, to be irrational, illogical, mere wish-thinking under the rule of the "Pleasure Principle" (as Freudians would call it); mere fictions, invented to soften by illusion, or avoid by make-believe, contact with an intolerably hard world; mere weak and cowardly surrender to emotions which have nothing to do with the nature of Reality.

If it be demanded of me that I should refute these views, in the sense of compelling their adherents by arguments unanswerable, to confess their error—I admit that I cannot do it; as little as they could convert me to their side. To convince one another, this way or that, we should need a common basis of argument and this appears to be lacking. I can do nothing more than restate the fundamentals of my own point of view and leave you to think them over and work your way through to your own conclusions. And these fundamentals are briefly summed up as follows:

The principle of the self-revelation of Reality in experience is presupposed in our everyday dealings with ourselves and our environment. In everyday perceiving, thinking, acting we always go, implicitly, on the assumption that the facts are as we perceive and think them to be. If, in detail, we make mistakes, as we do, we discover these mistakes only by a better, corrected way of perceiving and thinking which we accept as reality-revealing. On that basis we act: on that basis such success as we have in dealing appropriately with the things we use and handle, is intelligible. On the contrary assumption, i.e., on the view that the nature of the Universe is indefinably *other* than what we perceive and think, our success in living and controlling our environment would be an unintelligible accident.

A fortiori, the principle applies in that systematic exploration of the nature of Reality, whether in ourselves or in the world around us, which we call science, natural science, in all of its branches. From perception it starts; by perceptions it continues to be fed; to perception it goes for ever fresh data, to set problems or test (verify) theories; in the interpretation of perceptual data, in taking them as *points d'appui*, as clues, for the application of systems of concepts (universals), scientific thought essentially consists. There, and nowhere else, lies its "truth", its cognitive, reality-revealing, value.

I can see no good reason for not extending the principle also to value-experiences and value-judgments. This requires the admission that values "exist", i.e., that values occur realised in "particular" objective facts, as do other universals; that, as so realised, they can be experienced and recognised, and that, therefore, these experiences and judgments are, in principle, reality-revealing no less than the judgments of "fact" on the evidence of perceptions, which lie at the basis of science. And to those who say: values occur only as value-experiences; they are, as such, purely "subjective" and "mental", and are not to be attributed as inherent qualities to objects in themselves, I can only reply that I am unable to maintain, in my own thinking, *this* line between a section of my experience which (they admit) reveals the qualities of objects and a section which does not; and, further, that, even on their view, values still have a standing in Reality, a metaphysical status, in that our minds

are part of Reality, and values, even as merely mental phenomena, are so, too. Only, for me, values are *not* "merely mental"
in this sense.

Lastly, although I might have (and it would have been
easier) made a special application of this general defence of
value-experience and value-judgments in the fields of moral and
aesthetic values (the good and the beautiful), I have, for better
or worse, preferred to apply it where it is most disputed, where
the denial has been, and is, most active in the thought-move-
ments of that portion of humanity which shares in western
civilisation, viz., religion. I do not profess to defend every detail
of the dogma of any given religion: but I cannot think that
religion, as such, is in principle, mistaken in its efforts to
conceive the Universe as realising a value, supreme in that it
transcends and contains within itself the conflicting positive
and negative values of moral and aesthetic experience, whilst
at the same time making human life, so largely occupied with
and distressed by these conflicts, fundamentally worth living.

Notes on Truth

1. THE word "truth" is in use either as a concrete or an abstract noun. We speak of "a truth" and of "truths", meaning true propositions. And we speak of "truth", meaning that quality, characteristic, relation, value which propositions must possess if they are to be called "true".

(The words "quality", "characteristic", "relation", "value" are all key-words occurring in current theories of "truth"). We are concerned, then, with the meaning of the word "truth", i.e., with what is meant when a proposition is said to be "true". The whole enquiry assumes that when a thinker affirms a proposition with conviction (or without doubt), he accepts (believes) and affirms (e.g., communicating it in speech or writing to others) it as true. Or, he may at first merely "entertain" or "consider" it, and so may his hearers or readers, and in that situation it will be a legitimate and significant question: Is this proposition "true"? If the question is answered by the questioner in the affirmative (if he "convinces himself of the truth of the proposition"), he will accept, affirm, believe the proposition. If he decides that it is "false", he will reject, deny, disbelieve it. If he fails to settle the question, he will "suspend judgment" and "remain in doubt".

2. In argument—whether with oneself in ordinary thinking and reflecting, or with others in discussion and debate—propositions are always formulated in words, or "expressed" in words. It may happen that, from lack of vocabulary or lack of skill in the use of words (incl. supporting means of communication, like inflexions of the voice, gestures, etc.), a thinker expresses his thought (his propositions) clumsily: he may not "say what he means". For the purpose of the present enquiry, the difficulty of saying (whether to oneself or to others—note that solitary thinking by means of words is self-communication) what one means (saying it "intelligibly" or "unambiguously") will be ignored. In enquiring into "the nature of truth", i.e., into the meaning of the word "truth", I shall assume that the

words in which propositions, whether true or false, are expressed say what the thinker means. I ask attention, not to the words as words (which would be philology, grammar, syntax, theory of language, etc.), but to their meaning. Certain combinations of words ("assertory sentences" of many kinds), as normally used, whether in solitary thinking or in "inter-subjective inter-course", express propositions, and, indeed, propositions which the thinker-and-speaker believes to be true. Explicitly or implicitly, the truth of the proposition is part of what he normally affirms. A man who says with conviction "A is B" (let this combination of symbols stand for *any* proposition), is rightly understood to be meaning (even if he does not say it in words) "it is true that A is B"; just as his *act* of thinking-and-saying "A is B" also implies the proposition: "I think (affirm, believe) that 'A is B' is true". The present argument does not deal with the whole of this complex situation: it does not attend to the words or other symbols used as means of expressing thought (=what is thought=propositions); nor does it examine the relation between words or other symbols and the meanings they express and convey.

It is concerned with these meanings from the point of view of their being affirmed by a thinker as true or false.

3. Assertory sentences and the propositions which they express occur in many contexts and can be used for many purposes. *The present argument assumes a special context, viz., thinking for the sake of knowing.* Differently put, it considers propositions as affirmed in the effort to satisfy a special interest— say a "theoretical" or "cognitive" interest. Thinking, i.e., conceiving and affirming propositions, is something which human beings do; and whatever they do, they do for the satisfaction of some interest or other. I take for granted a cognitive interest (variously described in the books as "will to truth", "search for knowledge", etc., etc.), and I propose to regard, e.g., the systems of propositions known as the "Sciences" as having been discovered or constructed (the difference in meaning between these two words is not important at *this* point) by the coöperation of successive generations of thinkers, more particularly in the context of European culture (or "Western civilisation"), in the satisfaction of this interest. Of course, propositions so discovered or constructed may then

F

serve other, e.g., "practical" interests and purposes, just as the
occasion for a "theoretical" enquiry may be, and frequently is,
provided by a "practical" need, e.g., a problem of deciding
what is the best thing to do. But, the theoretical interest may,
and in "disinterested" research of "pure" theory (cf. "pure"
versus "applied" science) does, emancipate itself from other
interests and achieves its satisfaction in Knowledge-for-its-own-
sake. "Knowledge", here, = systems of true propositions
affirmed by human thinkers. If the Sciences are "knowledge",
this is the same thing as to say that the systems of scientific
propositions are true; are affirmed as true by scientists; and as
a rule accepted as true, on the "authority" of scientists, by the
non-scientific public. From this angle, an enquiry into "truth"
is the same thing as an enquiry into "knowledge". Instead of
saying "the proposition 'A is B' is true", I can also say: "I
know (or: it is well known) that 'A is B'".

4. Consider the situation from the angle of the so-called
"claim to truth". If, as was said in par. 1, it is possible (we
actually do it) to conceive, entertain, consider a proposition
without being able to decide whether it is true or false, the
proposition can be made an object of thought (as the meaning
of the corresponding assertory sentence), in abstraction from its
being true or false. It can be, as we say, "apprehended" or
"understood", even if we do not "know" whether it is true or
false, i.e., even if we cannot pass on to affirming as true one of
the secondary propositions, viz., that the primary proposition
is true or that it is false. In so far as any proposition entertained
challenges such a decision, it may be said to contain a "claim"
to be true. The most familiar situation in which such a "claim"
is experienced is when another thinker affirms to me a proposition as true and I wonder whether to accept it ("Is it really
true?"). But an analogous situation is not uncommon in
solitary thinking when a proposition "occurs" to me, or "comes
into my mind", and I then wonder whether to affirm it or not.
(Incidentally, situations of this type led Descartes to his
doctrine that assent to, or dissent from, a proposition is always
"an act of will", and that there is such a thing as the right and
wrong conduct of the intellect in respect of assent: error, i.e.,
assent given where it ought to have been withheld or refused,
is an immoral act, is "sin".)

5. Apart from this Descartian line of thought, a number of other lines of thought start from this situation. Let us notice a few:

(*a*) When I entertain a proposition (from whatever source) with a view to "making up my mind" about it, it does not much matter whether I put the alternatives between which I seek to describe in the form: Is this proposition true or false? or in the form: Am I to believe this or not? For, in either case, I want reasons or grounds—and, ideally or in the context of cognitive interest (see par. 3, above), grounds for believing the proposition and grounds for its being true coincide. Grounds for believing the proposition X are grounds for judging X to be true=grounds for believing as true the (secondary) proposition that the proposition X is true.

(*b*) "Ideally", I said; or when I am seeking knowledge (="truth", see par. 3). In actual thinking, men often commit themselves to belief on irrelevant or inadequate grounds (irrelevant: e.g., wish-thinking and other forms of emotional bias; believing what one wants to believe, or what one would like to be true—inadequate: e.g., believing on logically insufficient evidence; affirming as true, as proven true, what is only in varying degrees possible or probable). In such cases, obviously grounds for belief and grounds for truth fall apart. In fact, it might be better to call the grounds which are irrelevant (illogical, unscientific, etc.) merely "causes" of belief, rather than "grounds". Here belongs the whole subject of rationalisation: of A. J. Balfour's epigram—"Scratch a reason (sc. an alleged reason) and you find a cause"; or F. H. Bradley's epigram about "finding bad reasons for what we believe upon instinct". But, on the other hand, good grounds (relevant and adequate reasons), "good evidence", "conclusive evidence", etc., when considered as motives for believing, i.e., for deciding to affirm a proposition as true, may also, in this context, be described as "causes" of belief. Hence, it seems best not to distinguish between "causes" and "grounds", but rather to distinguish between causes (motives) of belief which are logically good (satisfy logical tests) and those which are logically bad (either because they do not satisfy the tests completely, or because they are not relevant to these tests at all). Only the former would then be called "grounds" or "evidence", in the strict sense. On this language-scheme, it will be always right to say, not only that every belief, every affirmation of a proposition as true, has causes (motives), but also that these causes, or motives, can, and must, be examined by logical tests (which examination presupposes the cognitive interest), and will then be found to be either good reasons, sufficient evidence; or inadequate reasons, insufficient evidence: or irrelevant reasons, no evidence at all.

(c) The concept of evidence covers in detail many kinds of evidence, according both to the "matter" and to the "form" of the proposition for which evidence is sought. And, correspondingly, there are a great many techniques for "determining" whether a given proposition is true or false. (I am excluding, here, sentences, which, though in virtue of their grammatical structure they look like expressing propositions, are, in fact, meaningless—adding, however, the reminder that what words, or combination of words, have meaning and thus express propositions the truth of which can be enquired into, is matter of debate between "Logical Positivists" and other schools of thinkers.) The theory of "verification"; of the distinction between "formal validity" and "material truth"; of deductive systems; of inductive generalisation; etc., belongs here. And, if a given set of propositions, e.g., those constituting a Natural Science, like Physics or Zoology, contains many kinds of propositions differing in form and matter, then many different tests or combinations of tests will be relevant—will, in fact, be employed by scientists, though scientists may leave it to logicians to construct a reflective theory of the tests employed (i.e., a body of "logical" propositions about scientific propositions and the tests of truth employed by scientists in deciding what propositions to affirm in the name of "Science", i.e., as "knowledge"). Obviously, the theory of the classification of propositions—itself a well-known subject for philosophical argument—belongs to this context of enquiry. Re techniques for dealing with evidence, it is well to reflect on this subject, not merely in the context of scientific (observational, experimental) procedures, but also in the context of the testing of "evidence" (testimony of witnesses) in law-courts; or, again, in the context of testing evidence in historical researches, or, again, there is the question of accepting propositions as true on somebody else's "authority"—a common and in general unavoidable procedure, but also a dangerous one; least so, when the "authority" is a "recognised expert", but unless I am an expert myself, and can judge the other man's expertness, I have to accept as true the proposition that the other man is an expert, either on his own assurance, or on that of others, who may, in turn, be either experts or non-experts!

(*d*) A point which deserves emphasis, in this context, is that nothing can function as evidence (good or bad), except what is so used by an individual thinker who accepts, or after reflection makes up his mind to accept, a certain proposition (=evidence) as true. This reminder that thinking is done by individual thinkers, that believing and affirming is always somebody's believing and affirming, is not—in this argument—intended to be exploited in favour of a theory of individual subjectivity (*quot homines, tot sententiae!*), but is meant to be compatible with, indeed to be supplemented by, the doctrine that the *trained, competent* thinker employs, or conducts his thinking in conformity with logical principles and methods which secure agreement with the thinking (beliefs, propositions, affirmed as true) of other trained and competent thinkers. (Again, there is implied here the concept of cognitive interest as an interest that can, and does, control the thinking of many individual minds, and imposes its own standards, "objective" and "universal", on these minds.)

6. This last remark (section 5, (*d*)) is a reminder, or a restatement, of the doctrine laid down in section 1, and underlying the argument of every later section, viz., that the *total* context of this discussion of truth is: *individual thinkers believing propositions, i.e., affirming them as true.* This formula, if interpreted according to the narrowest meaning of the words, is still inadequate—mainly, by not stating, and drawing attention to, explicitly that thinking in the pursuit of knowledge ("cognitive interest") is not a *purely* individual activity, in which each thinker, like a would-be solipsist, goes his own way regardless of other thinkers, but that it is a social, coöperative, intersubjective, sharing-thoughts, etc., activity. It is this aspect of thinking which leads to the doctrine that truth is supra-individual; or "once true, always true"; or: what is true for me is true for every other thinker. A solitary thinker could only check, criticise, confirm

or challenge any one of his thoughts (=propositions entertained or affirmed by him) by other thoughts (=propositions) of his own: as a thinker in communication with other thinkers, he is forced to check, etc., his thoughts by those of others, and they by his. Reflected on, this situation yields a proposition of the kind mentioned above: if different thinkers "agree" that a given proposition is true, then not only is it true for each of them severally, but also the further proposition that "proposition X is true for all of us" is itself a proposition accepted as true by all. That is why, in this context, the "for us" or "for all of us", is commonly omitted, and the proposition is affirmed unqualifiedly as "true", on the assumption that, however many other thinkers may join the group, they, too, will affirm it to be true. Such agreement implies the use by each of the same (hence, "common") standards of evidence, techniques of investigation, etc., as can be empirically verified by observing the behaviour of investigators in any science.

7. It may be observed in passing that the doctrine of the preceding paragraph, which attempts to give the context of interpretation for speaking of truth as "absolute", does not conflict with, or exclude recognition of contexts, in which truth can be legitimately spoken of as also "relative", or "subjective", so that we can say: what is true for me is not necessarily true for you, and *vice versa*. Note first that, if you agree with me that there are occasions, or contexts, in which this manner of speaking is appropriate (i.e., for which the proposition, just formulated, is, and is to be affirmed as, true), the proposition is for you and me at once a common one, in the "absolute" sense. If you ignore distinction of contexts, and were, e.g., to say: "Every proposition is relative, in the sense of "is true only for an individual thinker"", you would, on reflection, have at once to admit that *this* proposition, as one to which you invite others to agree, cannot be relative in the sense defined. For short: the proposition, "every proposition is only relatively true", cannot itself be treated as a member of the class referred to by the words "every proposition". Or, if it is, a "contradiction-in-terms" results. The formal technique of avoiding such "contradiction" by a "theory of types" is, so it seems to me, intended to secure the same result which I try to get by distinguishing "contexts". That my technique is not abstractly

formal, but appeals to empirically-recognisable differences of context in the thinking of individual thinkers communicating with each other by a common language, is, in my opinion, an advantage. I suggest, then, that the "true for me-true for you" distinction operates usefully, or significantly, only in the context of two, or more, thinkers communicating their thoughts to each other, "agreeing to differ", i.e., agreeing (=accepting as true, in the *non-relative* sense!) on the propositions, (*a*) that they are both affirming as true propositions about the same object; and (*b*) that what the one affirms as true is incompatible with what the other affirms as true. There are many different sorts of situations of this general type; and the difference is not always resolvable, e.g., when two witnesses, reporting the same event (memory-propositions), contradict each other, and there is no other evidence by which to reconcile their accounts, or confirm one against the other. Another sort of situation of this type gives rise to the maxim: "There is no disputing about tastes." If two men quarrel about whether a given picture is beautiful or not, they may agree to differ by agreeing that it gives aesthetic pleasure to one but not to the other. Note, however, that this solution is satisfactory only if they both wish to avoid further wrangling. On the supposition that there are standards of aesthetic appreciation, and that some men are experts, or better judges than others, it does not follow that the above "solution" should be accepted as the last word of wisdom (as distinct from good manners!). However, this subject can be pursued *ad libitum*, provided always that it is recognised that the true-for-me versus true-for-you distinction requires the context of two communicating thinkers, each of whom accepts as true—in the non-relative sense—that "I think this and you think that about the same subject".

8. Another aspect of the problem of truth, when treated in the context of "individual thinkers believing propositions as true" (see section 6, above), is the distinction between *truth* and *veracity* (or truthfulness). When a witness in court swears "to tell the truth, the whole truth, and nothing but the truth", he is only promising veracity, i.e., to speak what he honestly (*bona fide*) believes to be true, though he may turn out to be "mistaken", i.e., to be affirming as true what is in fact false. Fortunately over large ranges of propositions affirmed by all

of us in everyday life, truth and veracity coincide: what we believe and affirm as true is in fact true. But, they can fall apart; and to be aware of that possibility is the beginning of self-criticism and intellectual caution; of developing an "intellectual conscience"; of being alive to possible grounds of doubt; of not resenting being told that one is mistaken. "Uncritical" minds are apt to treat a challenge to the truth of their assertions as an attack on their truthfulness. Dispute the truth of what they say and they will think you are accusing them of lying. Alternatively, they may resent the implied criticism of their trustworthiness as observers; or of the trustworthiness of their memories; or of the accuracy of their learning; or of their power to reason validly. Granted, then, that truthfulness is no guarantee of truth, and that any proposition which I honestly affirm as true may be discovered to be false by myself, or may be challenged by others and require to be "established" or "confirmed", the question finally calls for an answer: what is meant by a proposition being true? (Or: in what does the truth, the "being-true", of a proposition consist?). Note that the question is put in the context of "establishing", or "confirming" ("proving"), the truth of propositions—no answer is, therefore, useful or relevant which cannot be translated into a technique, or method, of adducing "evidence" for, or against, the proposition being true. Any theory of truth which is not "applicable", i.e., which does not yield operations of "proving", or "bringing forward evidence", must be suspected of being mere verbiage without realisable meaning.

9. Another way of putting this is to say that theories of the "nature" of truth must also be theories of *verification*, theories of how propositions are to be tested, established, proved. (From this point of view, the verbal distinction, made by some theorists, between the "nature" of truth and "criteria" of truth, is a "distinction without a difference"). The "Coherence" theory of truth satisfies this condition; and so does the "Pragmatic" theory, at any rate for the sort of propositions of the verification of which it is a generalisation, at any rate in the writings of William James, viz., propositions verifiable by perceptual experience. The "Correspondence" theory of truth, on the other hand, has *sometimes* been so stated as to make any operation of verification in principle impossible.

(Typical example: Descartes' theory—he had to appeal, *via* an *a priori* proof of the existence of God, to the veracity of God, in order to guarantee that the propositions of mathematical physics are true of the physical world.)

10. Before, however, examining these theories of truth, and in order to provide the proper setting, or context, for such an examination, we must return to a question alluded to in section 3, but there postponed, viz., are propositions "constructed"? Are they results or products of thinking, in a sense that is relevant to the problems of their verification?

Alternative formulations of the same problem are: Is the "discovery" of a "new" truth (=a true proposition not previously conceived or affirmed by any thinker) anything other than the act of for the first time thinking, i.e., constructing in thought (or: as an object of thought), that proposition? And, in what sort of experimental context does such construction take place?—Or, again, if a proposition is, as this language strongly suggests, what Kant calls a "product of synthesis" (never mind here, for the moment, Kant's distinction between *a priori* and *a posteriori* elements in every such synthesis), or what, in the language of B. Russell and others might be called a "logical construct" (cf. F. H. Bradley, "ideal constructions"), what is the difference, if any, between such a construct, or product, of thought and a "fact"?

The philosophical literature on this problem is a welter of dialectics, in which much of the language used is in fact functionless, in that there is no context in actual (human) experience in which it can be significantly employed.

Suffice it here to say that, most commonly, "fact" and "proposition" are used synonymously. Every "It is a fact that . . ." is an emphatic way of affirming a proposition as true. When a scientist says: "I have discovered that . . ." (what follows after "that" may be a generalisation; formally, a "universal" proposition of the form "All S is P"), he is saying that he has discovered (or: constructed) a proposition not previously conceived or affirmed: he has made an "addition to knowledge". In this context, the "fact" and "proposition" are names for the same thing. Or, it might be better to say that "fact" and "true proposition" (i.e., a proposition affirmed as true on the ground of having been tested and found to satisfy all relevant tests of being-true) are names for the same thing. For, we do not speak easily of a "false fact", as we speak of a "false proposition".

On the other hand we affirm as true of "facts" propositions which we would not affirm of "propositions": in other words, there is a context in which "fact" and "proposition" (even "true proposition") are different things. This context would appear to be that in which "fact", and especially "physical fact", ="object", and especially "physical object". E.g., the table at which I am writing these notes is a physical object, "of which", so we say, many propositions are true. The carpenter, in constructing my table, did not construct a proposition: if I destroy this table by burning it, I do not destroy a proposition by fire. A cause-effect between events in Nature is a physical fact, distinguishable from the corresponding proposition. The world of physical things and events, so we affirm, exists whether anyone perceives it or not, whether anyone makes an object of thought of it or not. Propositions, on the other hand, whether or not they be "products", or "constructs", of thought, occur only as objects of thought for individual thinkers. In this context, therefore, the words "fact" and "proposition" stand for different things. (An attempt has been made by certain "Realists" to treat propositions on the analogy of physical things in this context, and to say of them that they "subsist" whether or no anyone thinks or affirms them. To me, this seems "functionless" language, in the sense defined earlier in this paragraph.)

I want to maintain that the attempt to construct a theory of truth in this last-mentioned context turns out on trial, i.e., can be seen by reflection on the trial, to be self-defeating, although some forms of correspondence theory make just this attempt. For, note that the context ,above, consists of propositions about "facts", or "objects", and propositions about "propositions"; and that the whole of it might be summed up in the complex proposition: "The difference between facts and propositions is so-and-so." Now, it is possible, by a suitable manipulation of words, to construct a sentence, suggesting a proposition, viz., that when such-and-such a relation exists (or "holds") between a "proposition" and a "fact", then that proposition is "true".

11. For us, the study of different theories of truth, and my

own reflections on the problem as treated in these theories, culminates in the moral that the success of the enquiry depends on *thinking in the right context.*

This context I take to be human experience in the widest sense—sense-data, feelings, concepts, constructs, etc. In this context, the ultimate distinction is between *data* ("immediate experience") and *interpretation, construction, synthesis* (all synonyms, in this context). Every datum is a this-such: instance of a universal, which is found (interpretation, synthesis) to be connected with other universals in orders and systems of varying complexity: e.g., this—red, here and now, is an instance of a certain shade of the colour red; thereby an instance of red-in-general; but, further, if interpreted as quality of a physical thing, it mediates perception of an instance of that kind of thing. Again, *qua* event, it will be effect of a cause, and thus an instance of a casual connection in Nature; and so forth and so on. A "datum" may, with proper caution (i.e., awareness of relevant context), be called an "object" or a "fact"; but, if so, these words do not function as they do (or mean what they do) in the context in which object, fact, =physical thing. In this latter context, an object or fact is a construct, not a datum, though data are the "matter" for the construct. The effect of interpreting data, or integrating them with other data, in constructs (or concepts) is to turn each into a *sign-fact* ("invest it with meaning"), whereby its occurrence in perception functions as a clue to the presence of a physical object, and, through this, to the whole system of physical objects (or "natural phenomena") of which it is part; e.g., when hearing a noise of a certain sort ("this-such!"), I affirm the proposition: that's the hoot of a motor-car passing in the street outside.

On any given occasion, a given thinker may, of course, mis-interpret the given sign-fact or clue: if so, the error will generally be brought home to him by further experience (further data, functioning as clues to interpretative constructs), commonly in the course of acting on the initial interpretation i.e., on the assumption that the initial proposition is true. The correction, compelled by further evidence, will bring about a re-interpretation, which will now include the original datum with additional data in a construct free of internal conflict.

This is the same as to say that a fresh proposition is affirmed as true, which supersedes the original proposition as "false".

Only one remark in conclusion: the whole theory sketched in these Notes, and especially in the later sections thereof, may be summed up in the following propositions: knowledge is a highly complex set of propositions affirmed as true by individual thinkers (if "thinkers" suggests to you—what it is not meant here to suggest—that perceiving, feeling, acting are excluded, say "subjects" or "minds"). The general character of all these propositions, from the simplest to the most complex, is to interpret the data of sense and feeling by means of logical constructs (concepts, universals). Every such proposition, every such interpretation (of varying scope) which is stable, i.e., which continues, on the one hand, to fit in with other interpretations, i.e., with other logical constructs, and on the other continues to be applicable to fresh data as they are experienced —is "true". It will be affirmed with conviction of truth, because, in proportion as these conditions are fulfilled, there is no reasonable ground left for doubt.

This is, as I understand it, the essence of the *Coherence Theory of Truth*. Incidentally, the propositions which constitute this theory itself affirm logical constructs for which other logical constructs on lower planes of reflection furnish this data. The theory is true in terms of itself: its propositions satisfy the tests laid down by it for all propositions affirmed in satisfaction of the cognitive interest.

A Comparison of the Correspondence and
Coherence Theories of Truth

1. ONE of Bacon's most famous essays, as everybody knows, begins with the words: "What is truth? said jesting Pilate and would not stay for an answer." It is not necessary to be a jesting Pilate in order to ask the same question, but it is necessary to be a philosopher if one is to stay for an answer. Indeed, one is likely to need all the philosopher's proverbial patience, for the answers offered are not only many, but, what is worse, they are conflicting. Perhaps the remedy is, as my colleague, Professor R. B. Perry, would have us do, to distinguish four senses of "truth", each legitimate in its own place.[1] Professor Perry's happy knack of tidying up the philosophical universe by neatly distinguishing, and labelling, and pigeon-holing the embarrassing multiplicity of its features, compels the respectful admiration of everyone who, like myself, is cursed with an incurably untidy mind. Even when I try to distinguish, or to work with the clear-cut distinctions of others my trouble is that things won't stay put. Though distinctions will work for me up to a point, there always is a point where they break down; where some affinity, some continuity of nature, between the things that I am trying to keep apart, asserts itself and wrecks my scheme. I appreciate and envy from a distance the conveniences enjoyed by those who, in their orderly universe, have for every fact its ticketed compartment; for whom say, every judgment is either true or false, every act either good or bad. The blessedness of either-or is not for those who, like myself, grope in these matters painfully among the more-or-less. It is the same when theories clash. If one were able simply to choose either correspondence or coherence as the true theory of truth, with what zest might one not take sides and hurl oneself into the din and dust of the dispute. It is far less exciting to find

[1] Ralph Barton Perry: *Present Philosophical Tendencies*, pp. 203 ff. Longmans, Green and Company, New York, 1916.

that, on examination, the keen points of contrast get, not sharper but blunter; that beneath acute differences there is hidden much common ground; that, as tested by actual truth-seeking and truth-finding, the two rival theories are much nearer together than appears when the so-called "implications" of each are developed with dialectical subtlety and ingenuity. Anyhow, the point of the following paper is to avoid all "Spitz-findigkeiten", as the Germans very literally and very aptly call them, and to examine each theory as empirically as possible in the light of actual examples of the kind of situation on which each appears to be based. Nothing is assumed except that each theory attempts to describe the way in which, i.e., the evidence or grounds on which, we come to recognise and endorse a judgment as true. Each is treated as a generalised statement of the *modus operandi* in actual truth-seeking and truth-finding. Hence any merit which may belong to the comparison of the two theories attempted in this paper will depend on this employment of empirical data to determine the exact point at issue between them.

2. *The Correspondence Theory of Truth.*—The correspondence theory is an old one. It goes back almost to the beginning of philosophy. It has again and again been endorsed by thinkers of high repute. We may be sure, therefore, that it is based upon a type of situation that is frequent, familiar, and plain. As usually stated, it affirms that our thoughts or ideas are true or false according as they agree (correspond), or do not agree, with the fact, or, as it is sometimes put, with reality. My thought or idea that the fact is so-and-so is true when there really exists a fact such as I think it to be. This theory seems to fit in with common sense, and when first presented to beginners in Philosophy is apt to appear too obvious to require discussion or to stand in any danger of criticism. Yet some very puzzling problems lurk in the terms it employs—"thought", "agree", "fact". What is meant here by thought? What is the manner of the agreement? Where are we to find the facts with which our thoughts have got to agree? And how do we apprehend them? One thing, however, is clear. On this theory the agreement in which the truth of the thought consists may be an intra-experiential relation, or, in less technical language, the theory allows that the agreement of thought with fact is something

which, at least in many cases, we can actually observe and establish in our experience. On the other hand, there may be thoughts the trueness or falsity of which cannot be so observed because the relevant facts are not to us accessible. Thus, for example, most of the judgments of which history consists concern facts which are beyond the reach of our observation because they belong to the past. But, of course, our inability actually to observe the agreement of thought with fact has, on the theory, nothing to do with the actual existence or non-existence of the agreement. My thought is true if there are, or were, or will be, facts such as I think them to be. It is false if there are no such facts. In either case, the relation of agreement or disagreement exists whether or no I am in a position to observe that it exists. If I am not in a position to observe the agreement I may have to fall back on other considerations and roundabout methods of argument for determining whether my thought is likely to be true. Some recent advocates of the correspondence theory, like Mr. Bertrand Russell, are willing to admit that the coherence theory is useful in this predicament. Correspondence will then be the nature of truth, coherence one of its criteria in cases where its nature is not directly accessible to observation.

Let us illustrate the theory by some examples taken from everyday life.

Suppose you and I are disputing about the exact wording of a passage in Shakespeare's *Julius Caesar*. You think (affirm, judge) it runs thus: I think it runs differently. We both are relying on our memories; we are both, let us assume, confident of their accuracy, and hence each of us claims to "know" that his version is the right one, i.e., that his judgment concerning the words of the passage is true. We decide to settle the matter by an appeal to the text. I instruct you that you will find a copy of *Julius Caesar* on the desk in my study, and to facilitate your search I describe it as a green octave volume, India paper, with a limp leather cover, lying on the right-hand side of the desk. Again I claim to know all this. I have committed myself here from the beginning to end to a very detailed statement which is now to be put to the test. What are some of the possibilities? In the most favourable case for me you will find the volume as described in the place where I said it was, and on turning up the passage, it agrees with my version of it. But, on the other hand, you may find no volume of Shakespeare on my desk or in my study at all; or finding one in the place assigned, discover it to be, not *Julius Caesar*, but *The Tempest*; or to be not green but blue; or bound not in limp leather, but in stiff cardboard; and so on. Finally, the text may show that neither your version nor mine was correct; we were both mistaken. Thus my thought and judgment about the "facts" may turn out to be wholly, or in some detail, in disagreement with the actual facts, and so far "untrue". The fault may be with my memory. I may, e.g., have confused my blue-cardboard edition with my green-leather edition. Or the fault may be in my not having allowed for possibilities that might falsify it. But the example shows how, forgetting to hedge, I may fall into error, even on matters on which I am most confident.

Another example: sitting in my study I hear the steps of my wife coming up the stairs. I say I "hear" all this; but, of course, strictly speaking, what I hear is only a certain noise or sound; all the rest—that the sound is that of human feet, my wife's on the stairs, coming up—is interpretation. The noise *means or signifies* these things to me. As heard by me, it bears at once this detailed content of meaning. Of course, my ability thus to interpret it, the instantaneous, "instinctive" readiness of my reaction, is the result of past experience. I have learnt to recognise and identify that sound; i.e., this sound, and no other, carries for me (is invested by my thought with) this meaning to the exclusion of any other. We all learn to do this with the familiar sounds of our environment. We learn to discriminate, "by ear" as we say loosely, whether a given sound is that of a footfall at all; if so, whether human or animal; if human, whether man, woman or child; whether walking or running; heavy or light; tired or springy; ascending or descending; etc. We do not all become equally expert in these nice discriminations even of sounds that constantly recur in our environment, and we all fail more or less completely with the strange sounds. But the principle remains that, though the ear must learn to discriminate subtle nuances of sound-quality to give the cue to thought, the meaning of each nuance is a matter of thought-interpretation. Thus, to return to the example, if presently the door opens, and I perceive the person whom, from the sound,

I had expected to see, my thought is true. The facts have corro-
borated it. I may not have put the thought into words at all;
but the recognition of the step, leading me to look up as the
door opens and to experience the sight of my wife as the fulfill-
ment of an anticipation, is equivalent to the judgment, that is
the sound of my wife coming up the stairs, probably to my
study—yes, here she is. If, on the other hand, another person
enters, I am brought up with a startling shock against the fact
that I had mis-heard, or rather mis-taken, mis-interpreted the
sound; that I had judged it to be what the facts show it was not.

Now let us try to elicit the principle from these examples.
In the first example, my thought was a memory judgment. In
the second, it took the form of an interpretation of a sound
actually heard. But the common feature of both examples, the
feature to which the term "thought" refers in the formula about
thought agreeing with facts, is a *promise* or *prediction* of certain
experiences. I promised or predicted that you would see in a
certain place a book of certain shape or colour, that on handling
it you would get the feel of limp leather, that on turning up a
certain page in it, you would see printed there such and such
words. So, again, in the second example, from the sound I
heard I anticipated that I should presently see my wife's figure,
hear her voice, etc. Granted that I should not be able to make
these promises, predictions, anticipations without the help of
previous experience, yet the point is that, in both cases I foretell
experiences which I do not have actually now, but which I
expect to get presently, or hold myself able to have, on per-
forming certain movements; e.g., going to my study for that
book. The starting-points of such predictions may be very
various. Any memory, any observation of some present feature
of my environment, any testimony received from others, may
set me off anticipating and seeking definite further experiences.
And so, again, the experiences anticipated may be infinitely
various. But the general principle always is that my thought
promises, or indicates that I shall have, or on certain conditions
may have, or (referring to the past) might have had, definite
experiences of sight, sound, touch, smell, etc. Thought, as the
theory uses the term, means an expectation of, or at least a
reference to, things visible but not actually seen, things audible
but not actually heard, things tangible but not actually touched.

G

The "facts" which by agreeing with the thought show it to be true are the actual sights, sounds, and other experiences referred to.

To prevent misunderstanding, it may be as well to emphasise once more a point already made above. My thought, on this theory, may *be* true, even though I may not take the trouble, or not be in the position, to obtain the experiences, the facts, in agreement with which its trueness consists. Thus, in the second example, my wife may not come to the study, but go to another room and then return downstairs. If so, unless I ask her afterwards whether at a certain time she came upstairs, I shall never discover whether my interpretation of the sound I hear is true. Still, unless I have some positive evidence for suspecting that I made a mistake, I shall take the trueness of my judgment for granted. Again, if I read an account of a battle by one of the combatants, the truth of that account will mean for me that he actually had the experiences which he now recalls; or, in other words, that if I had been he, on a certain day, at a certain place, I should have seen, heard, done the things reported by him. Suppose the sights, sounds, acts, different, and the account will be false. In Chapter XII of *Problems of Philosophy*, Mr. Russell instances Othello's belief that Desdemona loves Cassio, a belief which is, as readers of Shakespeare know, false. Why false? Because the feelings of affection towards Cassio, which Othello in his thought attributes to Desdemona, have no existence in fact, i.e., are not actually felt by Desdemona. In this case, according to Mr. Russell, it is in the nature of things impossible for Othello to establish in his own immediate experience the agreement of his thought with the fact, for he cannot feel Desdemona's feelings; he can at best only infer them from her actions (and make tragic mistakes in the attempt), or learn of them from her confession (and incidentally run the risk of a lie). None the less the situation is clear. Desdemona either has such feelings as Othello judges her to have, or she has not. In the first case, his judgment is true; in the latter false.

This may suffice to make clear the point of this theory, which, so far, certainly will appear simple and obvious. As a matter of fact, deeper analysis opens up difficulties of interpretation which make it a storm centre of debate in modern philosophy. The following comments may give some inkling of their nature, and of the direction in which they may be found.

(1) In the first place, the "facts" with which true thoughts agree and false thoughts disagree, are on all the usual interpretations of the theory, as also in our examples above, facts of sense-experience, such as sounds, sights, objects touched and handled, etc.; in technical language, sense-data, sense-percepts. As the Desdemona example suggests, we should perhaps add feelings and emotions to our list of "facts". Now this raises the very important philosophical question whether *all facts are of this sensible kind*? Is nothing a fact except what actually is, or at least might be, perceived by the senses or felt as an emotion? Is the range of "fact" co-extensive with, but also limited to, the objects of actual or possible sense-experience? The sting of this question comes out even more pointedly when we take the alternative formula. Thought which agrees with *Reality* is true. Is Reality, then, identical with the objects of actual or possible perception? Is nothing real except what is, or can be, seen, heard, handled, smelled, tasted? Is the whole nature of Reality exhausted in the qualities which the senses can apprehend? Are there not other sides to it—"ideal" sides, sides open only to pure thought? Without entering into the distinction between a "visible" and "invisible" world, or the ramifications of the terms "spirit" and "spiritual", we may at least suggest that some of the most familiar features of our daily environment do not appear to fall wholly within the scope of senses and feelings. Or, to put it differently, are all meanings such as to be fulfilled, "cashed" as it were, in terms of sense-data? What for example of moral qualities, and generally of the whole range of values? Some values, like the aesthetic ones (beauty, etc.), are clearly intimately connected with sense-data. But are moral good and evil visible to eye or audible to ear? The act which is good or evil may, as bodily movement, be open to sense-perception; but its moral quality, if it can be said to be "perceived" at all, seems to require something like a non-sensuous, "intellectual" perception. But "intellect" brings us back to "thought". Is some "thought" then fulfilled in sense-experience, and other "thought" only in further thought? The very agreement of thought with fact, i.e., the

trueness of the thought, is not itself a fact of the senses. For logical values, for the perception of trueness and falsity, once more, it seems, we must call in a non-sensuous awareness. The agreement, according to the theory, is frequently an actual fact, but clearly it is not a fact of sense-perception, as the theory usually understands that term. It would be interesting to know in agreement with what "fact" of sense-perception consists the trueness of a judgment which asserts another judgment to be true.

(2) Secondly, all sorts of intricate difficulties have been raised over the possibility of a "thought" meaning a "fact" which is not at the moment actually given. It is obviously one thing, say, to think of the smell of a rose; it is another to be actually smelling the rose, actually receiving and enjoying its smell. In the former case we say, the smell "itself" is "absent"; in the latter, it is "present". But if, when I think of it, the smell is simply absent, how can I be said to be thinking of *it*? Or how can I recognise the smell, when I actually experience it, as being the *same* I was thinking of? How can a situation in which there is, *ex hypothesi*, no smell, "agree" with one in which there is a smell? Or, again, if the smell itself is absent when I think of it, what is present? Some symbol, or sign, or substitute for it; e.g., the words "smell of a rose", or an image, or whatever else may serve as representative for the smell itself. Representative, did I say? But that stirs up the same problem in a fresh form. For, surely, I must somehow be aware of what the word represents, what the symbol stands for. Yet, what it stands for is, *ex hypothesi*, "absent". How then can I be aware of it? This is the problem of "consciousness of meaning", much discussed nowadays. The attempt to avoid it has driven philosophers to some quaint shifts of language. Thus some distinguish an "ideal" from a "real" smell; or a smell thought of and a smell experienced; or a smell conceived and a smell perceived. Not everyone has Professor Dewey's courage to say boldly: That, when I think of a smell, the smell is "present-as-absent", or present-but-not-in-the-way-in-which-a-smell-smelt-is-present. It is a pretty puzzle how to deal with the manifest difference between the ghost-like smell of my thinking, and the full-bodied odour that I delightedly sniff in when I hold an actual rose in my hand. However the trick is done, whatever theory of the

mechanism employed we hold, the fact remains that we can deal, in thought, with the things of sense-experience, and think of them, on these occasions as not now actually experienced. But this brief discussion may serve as a hint of the curious problems that lie hidden beneath the term "agreement" of thought with fact, or beneath our convenient metaphors concerning thought-promises fulfilled by actual experience.

We may conclude this discussion of correspondence theory by developing what was said above about actual and possible sense-experience. Actual sense-experience means things actually seen, heard, etc. Possible sense-experience means things that might be seen, heard, etc., if a percipient were present. Many things that might be perceived, never actually are perceived, either by ourselves or by other percipients. It is obvious that, at any given moment, even under the most favourable conditions, only a very small part of the total perceptible environment actually is perceived by any one of us. But thought emancipates us from the narrow limits within which the moment's perception ties us down. We learn to think of the present moment as but a link in the chain of time that binds past to future. We think of that small portion of space which our visual horizon bounds as but a section of the total space. It is part of our concept of this world we live in that the few things and persons and events which at any moment are revealed to us by our senses are but a fragment of a vaster system of things, persons, events, most of which we shall never perceive, but many of which will, at some future time, enter into our experience. We thus conceive a world of possible sense-experience continuous with, and extending in time and space beyond, that bit of it which at this moment we actually apprehend. This way of conceiving the world is clearly an application on a large scale of the principle involved in our examples above. It is, as it were, a vast map, worked out by thought, of what we might perceive if only the limitations on the field of actual perception were removed; if only we could be at all times in all places at once. As a scheme of possible sense-experiences it is a gigantic enlargement of the narrow field of present sense-experience— a large-scale promise, prediction or anticipation, only a small part of which will ever be fulfilled for any one of us. So far as the sciences do predict, for example, eclipses, or tomorrow's weather, they are elaborating this picture that thought paints for us, launching out from given facts of sense-experience. It is here, therefore, that we must look for the proper field in which the correspondence theory applies. Wherever in thinking we travel beyond the facts perceived at the present moment, the trueness of this panorama of thought consists in its agreement with the facts as perception, were it within our power to perceive, would reveal them to be. Occasionally, the distinction between the objects of actual perception and the objects of thought is expressed in language of "acquaintance" and "description". We are said to know the former by acquaintance, the latter by description; or as William James used to put it, when we perceive a thing we are directly "acquainted with" it, whereas in thought we only "know about" it. "Knowledge about", then, or "knowledge by description" is true only when it agrees with the facts. And for the "facts" we must go to knowledge by acquaintance which is neither true nor false, for there is no chance in it of any disagreement. In it we have got the facts, as they are, really and in themselves.

Any further criticism of the correspondence theory is most conveniently given in the course of the discussion of its rival, the coherence theory, to which we must now turn.

3. *The Coherence Theory.*—As its name indicates, this theory makes truth consist in the coherence—of what? Of *judgments* with one another. Judgments "cohere"—we might almost as well say "agree"—when they are mutually *consistent*, or, put negatively, when they do not contradict one another. A contradiction arises when the same subject is invested with mutually exclusive predicates; i.e., with predicates which cannot co-exist in that subject unless some principle of distinction is found within the subject, enabling it to accept both predicates without clash. If one man orders me to stand still, and another to run away, we have a plain contradiction or incompatibility. If I do the one I cannot do the other, and *vice versa*. I-running cannot also be I-standing-still. I can do first the one and then the other, but not both at the same moment. Running and standing still do not conflict in the abstract, but they do clash when demanded of me at the same time. If, on the other hand, I am allowed first to do the one and then the other, a principle of distinction is introduced (viz., successive moments) which

makes the two actions perfectly compatible for me. Another example: suppose two men disputing whether the fur of a certain animal is black or white. They have both seen it, and each correctly remembers what he has seen, yet the result is a glaring contradiction. The animal cannot be all white or all black at once. But suppose the explanation is that the animal changes its colour with the season, is black in summer and white in winter, and that the one man's experience of it was exclusively in the summer, the other's exclusively in the winter. At once the contradiction disappears. That the same animal should, with changing seasons, be now black, now white, is perfectly consistent. A principle of distinction has been introduced, and the clash of predicates is dissolved in harmony. Let us note that both judgments concerning the animal are true, and both false. Both are true in so far as both speakers state correctly what the animal's colour was as they saw it. But each speaker *over-stated* his case. The one, seeing the animal white, set it down as always white; the other similarly as always black. Had each been careful to limit and hedge his statement by specifying time and circumstances, no contradiction could have resulted. For they would quickly have found that they saw it at different times, and this might have led to the question why the same animal at different times should have different colours. This question in turn might have led us to the discovery of a satisfactory answer in the changing condition of the animal's life at different seasons.

This removal of contradictions between judgments (and that may mean, as this example shows, between the percepts on which the judgments are based) by the introduction of distinctions and qualifications, is typical of a process of correction and harmonisation which is constantly going on in all thinking, whether in ordinary life, in science, or in philosophy. Now just as the correspondence theory was formulated on the basis of the verification of thought-promises by percepts, so the coherence theory is based on this adjustment of conflicting judgments (and through them of conflicting experiences, feelings, memories, percepts) so as to assign to each the limits within which, or the conditions under which, it is tenable, i.e., is consistent with all other judgments (and experiences) bearing on the same subject. It is a process of critical organisation of judgments, mutually supporting one another. It yields us the systems of judgments which we call the "sciences". The result is knowledge, in the pregnant sense. If we want "facts", we must go to "theory". The "facts" are as stated to be by scientific theory, i.e., such an organised, self-consistent body of judgments. The sciences tell us what things really are. Such a coherent body of judgments may be called "the truth" concerning a certain subject-matter, e.g., botany is "the truth" concerning plants. Any single judgment is "true" in so far as it is a member of such a system, or fit to be a member, i.e., in so far as it is consistent with (not contradicted by) all other judgments on the same subject.

When a judgment is thus safe from contradiction and challenge, when it is so well grounded that it cannot be overthrown, we may call it *stable*. To be true, to be consistent with other relevant judgments, to be logically stable, are thus three ways of describing the same situation. The rough and ready judgments of everyday life, unguarded, unconditioned as they are, thus conspicuously lack this logical stability or trueness. Hence, as they state too much or too little, they ignore their limitations, they are always more or less seriously in error. Measurement, comparison, classification, precise analysis of conditions—by these and other methods do we, in the search for knowledge, shape and reshape our judgments until they come to form a self-consistent system; until no argument, no observation can overthrow them; until every past experience, every relevant consideration supports and re-enforces them. In some sciences we are further removed from a realisation of this ideal than in others. But this, according to the coherence theory, is the ideal operative in the actual progress of knowledge. A judgment is true, or constitutes, so far as it goes, "knowledge" of "fact", or of "reality", in proportion as it realises this ideal, satisfies this principle of logical stability. Trueness and falsity are thus a matter of degree, of more or less, not of either—or.

The agreement of thoughts with percepts which the correspondence theory had elevated into a principle of trueness is, according to the coherence theory, but a special case of consistency; disagreement, a case of contradiction. Thus, in our example above, the memory-judgment, a book of a certain description is on my desk, is contradicted by the judgment of perception that there is no such book, or that the book which is there is other than had been described. Again the judgment, that is the sound of my wife coming upstairs, is contradicted if the person turns out to be somebody else. On the other hand, if I do find the book as described, or if I presently perceive my wife, then my judgments, being consistent with all further available evidence, are thereby shown to possess that stability for which I call them true.

Summing up our account of the coherence theory we may say that its strength lies in its appeal to the logical principle of the self-consistency, or internal non-contradictoriness, of the systems of judgments which we acclaim as "knowledge". The realisation of this principle in any given science is always a matter of degree. The history of science shows that principles and theories which for centuries had been accepted as rock-bottom truth have had to be revised or even abandoned. The exchange of the heliocentric for the geocentric system, and the fate of the atom are examples. At the present day, there are regions of unstable judgments not only at the fringes of a science, but sometimes in its very heart. Consider, for example, the extreme conflict about fundamentals in modern psychology, or even—on this very question of truth and on many other matters —in modern logic. The aim on all sides is to get hold of the "facts", and each side, of course, claims to possess them, and denies the "facts" alleged by its opponents. Everywhere the assertions, It is so—No, it is not so, but thus, clash sharply against one another. According to the coherence theory this conflict illustrates the characteristic process of sifting, criticising, reshaping, through which our judgments must be adjusted to one another, through which knowledge is advanced. The principle operative in this process is that of the self-consistency of knowledge, of its logical stability. "Facts" are the outcome of the process, not its starting-point. If we had the facts to begin with, or could have them for the looking, whence the dis-agreement or conflict? Why the need of argument and inter-pretation? Knowledge of facts is the same thing as logically stable theory.

4. *Comparison of the Correspondence and Coherence Theories.*—We are now in a position to compare the two rivals. Broadly

speaking one's impression is that they emphasise complementary aspects of scientific method and of knowledge. The correspondence theory insists, in effect, on the importance for knowledge of the evidence furnished by perception (sense-experience). To avoid the disputed term "facts", let us call this evidence "data". The correspondence theory points out the importance of perceptual data for corroborating, "verifying" our hypotheses, our interpretations, our theories. It finds its strongest support in the search for the validation of tentative guesses, of provisional assumptions, by observation and, better still, by experiment—a search which is a dominant feature of all sound scientific method. The correspondence theory, then, is right in holding that our theories must fit or agree (why not be consistent with?) the perceptual evidence, that this evidence is part of knowledge, and must be absorbed into its structure. It cannot be ignored. It cannot be left out. Theories which conflict with it are certainly false. But is this all the theory maintains? Or does it not go further and, overstating this sound contention, affirm the perceptual evidence is the only thing that matters? That it is the only source of control over interpretation? The only arbiter between rival theories? The only, the exclusive, the final court of appeal—and this because in percepts alone do we have "reality"?

On the other hand, the coherence theory emphasises the logical nexus of the constituents of knowledge. It does not deny the importance of perceptual data, but points out how little these data contribute to knowledge until they have been correlated and systematised by interpretation and theory. The data are important, not so much for their own sakes, as for what theory makes of them. They are not self-explanatory; they cry out for explanation. To know means not simply to perceive, but to interpret and explain what is perceived. Perception presents, at best, fragments of the universe. To work out from these the whole to which they belong and which enables us to explain them and interpret their meaning, that is precisely the aim of "knowledge". This process of working up our data, whatever in detail its methods or its forms, is controlled throughout by the principle of self-consistency or logical stability.

Putting the antithesis of the two theories as pointedly as we can, even at the risk of some exaggeration, we may say that the correspondence theory looks to the data of perception to solve the problems of theory. Where theories clash and contradict one another, where hypotheses are still in doubt, percepts must supply the evidence which decisively clinches the issue. The coherence theory, on the other hand, looks to theory to solve the problems presented by the data of perception. Where the perceptual evidence is full of conflicts and contradiction, theory must step in to straighten out the tangle, to discriminate with nicety just what the perceptual data severally, and together, mean and prove, and within what limits and under what conditions. According to the correspondence theory, we must appeal to perceptual data to throw light on the perplexities of theory. According to the coherence theory, the perceptual data are an unintelligible chaos until theory has brought order and light.

Are these two views of truth necessarily incompatible with one another?

5. *The Problem of Perception.*—If the above accounts, and the subsequent comparison, of the two theories are correct, it is clear that the issue turns on the status in, and value for, knowledge of perceptual data, actual or possible; of things actually observed ("experienced by the senses") or at least such that they may be, or might have been actually observed.

Pursued into its ramifications, this problem would lead us into some of the most difficult logical, and even metaphysical questions discussed by present-day thinkers. We shall touch only on two of these questions, which are so closely connected that we shall not attempt to separate them in discussion. (1) In what sense can the claim be maintained that "knowledge by acquaintance" of which perception is, if not the only, at least a very prominent example, is neither true nor false? That it is, so to say, infallible, and for this very reason the decisive court of appeal for settling the claims of judgments to be true? (2) What is the difference, if any, between judgments and percepts, between what is judged to be so-and-so, and what is perceived to be so-and-so?

The point of the first question may be brought out by returning once more to our examples. How had the coherence theory dealt with the book example? I judge there is a certain book on my table. If I perceive it there, my judgment is confirmed by its consistency with what I perceive. If I fail to perceive it, my judgment is contradicted and shown to be wrong. As every reflecting reader probably noticed at the time, there is an opening which might well tempt the advocate of correspondence to exult: Now has the Lord delivered mine enemies into my hand! For he might turn on the supporter of the coherence theory as follows: "Granted for argument's sake that there are two judgments here involved, (a) the (memory) judgment, There is a book on my table, (b) the (perceptual) judgment, There is no book on my table, and that these make a flat contradiction. But the mere fact that they contradict one another leaves you simply with a deadlock. It gives you no ground for preferring the one to the other. Yet you abandon the memory judgment as false, and accept the perceptual judgment as true. Do you not thereby confess that perception clinches the matter; that it is master over thought, whether memory, inference, or interpretation? Is it not clear that in the data of perception we have solid, unchallengeable, rock-bottom facts? This is what I mean when I say that they are neither true nor false; they are just what they are, and there's an end of it. That is why all theory must conform to them on pain of failure."

Is the advocate of the coherence theory really caught in the obvious trap? In order to decide this question, let us examine the construction of the trap a little more in detail.

The principle on which it is constructed has been expressed with great clearness by Mr. Russell in the following passage: "So soon as it is admitted that there are things that exist, it is impossible to avoid recognising a distinction, to which we may give what name we please, between believing in the existence of something that exists, and believing the existence of something that does not exist. It is common to call the one belief true, the other false."[1] We have, then, on the one side, the order or group of "things that exist"; and "to exist" covers, we may assume, to have a determinate nature, to have definite qualities, and to stand in definite relations to other things. On the other side we have our beliefs (thoughts, judgments, ideas, or whatever we are pleased to call them), that certain things with such-and-such qualities exist. There is a

[1] Philosophical Essays, p. 144.

fundamental difference between a fact's existing and its being thought (judged, believed) to exist, for I may happen to believe that X exists when, as a matter of fact, there is no X.

It may be as well to add a warning that the term "things that exist" is to be taken widely. It covers not merely facts perceptible to the senses, but also such mathematical facts as 2 plus 2 being 4. Wherever, in short, we have an objective order of entities of definite natures and relations, such as we have in the number system, we have a group of facts in the sense intended; i.e., we have something by correspondence to which our judgments will be "true", by divergence from which they will be false. Except on this assumption of a fixed order of fact confronting our judgments, we can give—so the advocates of this view contend—no intelligible account of the difference between truth and error.

Now, if the trueness or falsity of our beliefs is ever to be known, we must have direct access to the facts, and that not in the way of thought and judgment, but in the way of perception and immediate acquaintance. This is the reason, therefore, why every theory of correspondence is driven to assign to perception a prerogative importance for purposes of knowledge. In perception we not only are in direct contact with reality, but we have reality presented to us just as it is. The presentation may be incomplete, but it is free of distortion or perversion. We may not perceive all things that exist, nor even the whole of any one thing that we do perceive, but so far as we perceive anything at all, we perceive it as it actually is. What we perceive, or the thing as we perceive it, simply *is*. To ask whether it is true or false is meaningless. Hence, in disputes about truth, the appeal to facts "as they are" is always an appeal to facts as they are perceived.

This analysis enables us to understand why perceiving is held to be infallible, and in principle different from judging. It must be so if we are ever to get hold of anything to which our judgments may correspond. Now, what is to be urged against these views?

The infallibility of perception is somewhat of a paradox in the face of its proverbial deceptiveness. Since the sceptics of antiquity first enlarged on the untrustworthiness of our senses, many thinkers have echoed their criticisms. What of dreams, illusions, hallucinations? What of the mis-seeing (e.g., in reading) or mis-hearing (e.g., in listening to another's words) which are common incidents in everyone's life? True it is that in the natural sciences observations furnish the first materials, and afterwards the test of hypotheses; but none knows better than the scientist that some men are much better observed than others, and that a trained eye and a trained mind are necessary for observations of scientific value. Why has almost every treatise on scientific method its section on fallacies and errors of observation? Why is it necessary, e.g., in astronomy to calculate and allow for the characteristic "error" of each individual observer? Is it not the experience of law courts that eye-witnesses of the same event, of equal honesty and equal trust-worthiness of memory, are liable to give flatly contradictory accounts of what they saw and heard? Does not psychological experiment confirm this fallibility in detail?

Thus the experience of mankind speaks with a divided voice on the value of perception. The *demonstratio ad oculos* is recommended as the supreme test, the final court of appeal. Yet, on the other hand, the "facts" of perception may themselves be called into doubt. How can that serve as a test which requires itself to be sifted and tested?

It may be, and is very commonly, replied that we ought to distinguish here between *datum* and *inference* or *interpretation*. There is, so it is urged, no such thing as mis-perceiving; there is only mistaking. We cannot perceive anything falsely, i.e., *other* than it is; but we may, and often do, mis-interpret that which we perceive. The sense-datum, to use Mr. Russell's language, is always a "hard" datum. No criticism can make it other than just what it is. It does not disguise itself, it does not masquerade. The sound I hear, e.g., is just that sound, precisely such as I hear it. There is no opening here for error, no possibility for saying the sound is true or false. But if I go on to interpret or describe the sound as my friend's voice (I call it "hearing his voice"), it may turn out that I have mistaken it. I have made a judgment, and that judgment may be false.

There is undeniably much force in this contention. Every thrill of the sense-experience or of feeling has its own unique and distinctive quality. But this acknowledgment carries us only a very little way towards the solution of our problems.

There are three considerations which profoundly affect the status and function of perceptual data in knowledge—considerations which the advocates of the correspondence theory are apt to ignore, whilst it is the merit of the advocates of the coherence theory to insist upon them.

(a) The first is that a pure datum, a datum in no way expanded and modified by interpretation, is not so much a fact of experience as a postulate of theory. If, with Locke, we could conceive the mind as beginning its career as a *tabula rasa*, we might acclaim the first impressions traced thereon as unadulterated data. To get to the bedrock of pure data, we should have to go *even behind naming*. For we may mis-name. To name, therefore, is to judge. And naming, which is one of the most elementary logical operations, practised (we are told) already by Adam in Paradise, implies discrimination of a datum, comparison with other data, identification, recognition on its repetition, etc. Hence to get at the pure datum, we should have to hold all these intellectual processes in abeyance. When I look, for example, at the blue sky—but stop, this is more than pure seeing. What I see no doubt I see, but to see it as "sky" and as "blue"—though I may use no words at all—is in effect an interpretation and a judgment, and may be mistaken. Seeing, and indeed all perceiving, is in this sense judging, i.e., intelligent perceiving (as it is well called) in which we identify and recognise things for what they are. Perhaps we have the nearest approach to a pure datum when, as sometimes happens, we look at things with an "unseeing eye", staring at them "blindly" without "taking in what they are". But intelligent seeing, which does not need to be accompanied by words, but may manifest itself by giving rise to appropriate behaviour, is equivalent to the judgment expressed in the words, I see so-and-so, or This (which I see) is so-and-so.

(b) The second consideration is that perceptual data, just as they come, are at best the threshold of knowledge. Their connections and relations, such as they are traced for us in the judgments of the sciences, are mainly not simply "given", but have to be searched for and worked out. The organisation of the perceptual material, which is but another name for the interpretation of it, and in which the chief task of the sciences consists (we call it formulating "laws", tracing connections of cause and effect, etc.), is something which, even if we can be said to discover rather than to make it, is certainly not given as a pure datum. It is a long road from the chaotic flux of perceptual data in immediate experience, to the stable, orderly world of our daily lives, to say nothing of the world of our scientific theories. It is not easy to make clear to oneself how chaotic the flux of sense-data really is before we have learnt to sort them out and interpret them correctly. Our responses in this matter have become so familiar that it requires an effort of reflection to realise that the mass of sights, sounds, touches, smells, movement-experiences which, at any moment, makes up the complex and ever-changing pattern of our world as perceived, is habitually analysed and ordered by us, and thus *understood*. Data that occur together but do not belong together, as, e.g., the noise of a street-car outside coinciding with the writing of these words, are discriminated and assigned each to its proper place and meaning. Data that belong together, but do not occur together, are connected, as when the sound of the street-car reminds me of its visual appearance. For an infant, as James said, the world is one "big, buzzing, blooming confusion". Another psychologist has pointed out that to an infant, unable to see the bird singing in a tree, it will be the tree that makes the noise. Primitive experience abounds in false connections of this sort.

(*c*) And, lastly, experience not yet intellectually organised is not merely a chaotic flux, but is full of contradiction. Perceptual data may, in a legitimate sense, be said to contradict each other. This is a point too often overlooked by those who insist that each datum is just what it is. The trouble is that data are not isolated, but belong together, and that, belonging together, they yet conflict. This familiar fact, which was already pointed out by Plato, is rediscovered by every philosopher who deals with the subject. Quite recently it has been restated very prettily by Mr. Russell—forgetful for the moment of his correspondence theory—in support of the assertion that "Any statement as to what it is that our immediate experiences make us know, is very likely to be wrong."[1] Mr. Russell shows in detail how the colour and shape of familiar objects change with the angle from which the spectator is looking, the condition of

---

[1] *Problems of Philosophy*, p. 10.

his eyes, the light, etc. A square table, for example, will look from most points of view, as if it had two acute and two obtuse angles. The sides will look now equal, now unequal, now parallel, now converging, Each such "look" of the table may be treated as a single datum, yet all these data belong together, as visual appearances of one and the same table. But how can the table be this conflicting mass, now a square, now a rect-angle, now a trapeze in shape, etc.? By itself, each datum is just what it is. Taken together as my table they are a mass of contradiction. From one point of view I see and judge the table to have one shape; I move a little, and, behold, I see and judge it to have another shape. How can this be? What is the table's "real" shape?

The only satisfactory solution is to correlate and adjust the data so that the contradiction is eliminated. This requires that, instead of opposing perceptual datum and judgment, we should hold to the principle that perceiving is judging, allowing the datum to be absorbed into the judgment. Seeing the table thus, as from any given angle I see it, is equivalent to the judgment, Its shape is so-and-so. Considered as a judgment, the seeing of the table claims to be true, but also runs the risk of error, precisely because this claim is not guarded by due qualifications, by specifying the conditions under which it holds. The datum is genuine enough—so far as it goes. But at the moment there is no "so far as it goes" about it. It fills the whole horizon, so to speak. It is then and there the table's "real shape". But presently it comes into collision with other data, as genuine, as insistent in their claim to be the table's real shape. Clearly, these conflicting claims can be maintained only if each is duly restricted and qualified. But in the moments of perception the data come each with an absolute, unconditional claim. Hence their collisions, with the puzzling confusions they engender. Perceiving an object intelligently is equivalent to the judgment, This is really what I see it to be. But such a claim clearly over-shoots the mark, if "is really" means "is always", "is under any conditions". For presently the same object may be per-ceived differently. Hence the claim becomes tenable only as it is hedged around with conditions, e.g., "is now", "is from that point of view", "in that light", "to a being with sense-organs like mine", and so on. The datum, then, is what it is,

H

if there is still any point in insisting on that; but it is what it is at any given moment subject to precise conditions. If these conditions are ignored, the claim becomes false, and other data compel us to challenge or deny it. Nothing but specification of conditions eliminates the contradiction, and in this way, here as always, the coherence or consonance of judgments in a system of mutually consistent judgments gives "knowledge" and "truth". Perceptual data are thus ordered and organised by "theory": their claims are adjusted and each is affirmed within its proper limits.

Thus, for the coherence theory, perceptual data play their part in the development of a body of coherent judgments. They have a vividness which challenges attention and compels recognition. They are superior as evidence to memory or hearsay. They confirm hypotheses, or, as "negative instances", overthrow them. They are fatal to loose generalisations. But it is not always the theory which has to give way. Often when a fact perceived conflicts at first sight with a well-established theory, re-examination shows that the observation had been inaccurate, or that special circumstances account for the exception.

In concluding, it may be suggested that the coherence and correspondence theories differ in their estimate of the function of perceptual data in knowledge, because the latter looks exclusively to the use of such data in testing hypotheses, whilst the former includes in its survey the development of hypotheses and interpretations from a basis of primitive perceptual experience. The perceptual evidence to which the correspondence theory appeals is relevant and effective just because it consists, not of pure data, but of data shot through and transformed by interpretation and theory—in short, data of "intelligent perception". Or, to put it differently, the observations with which science begins stand logically on quite a different footing from those in which science seeks confirmation of its hypotheses. The observations at the first dawn of attention and discrimination, the first crude attempts at grouping and connecting data, are far less accurate than observations of the same matters in the course of organised scientific research. That is why observations of the former sort merely put problems, whilst observations of the latter sort are fit to test attempted explanations. In the former case my perception is uninformed, and so far unintelligent. In the latter case, my knowledge, i.e., my theoretical command of all other relevant data, enables me to perceive intelligently and with understanding. The emphasis, and even the very details, of what I perceive will be different. I shall attend less to some aspects, more to others. Possibly I shall ignore very conspicuous features as irrelevant, and seek out inconspicuous details as supremely important. I may notice what I had not noticed before. Guided by a theory to be tested, or by an illuminating question, I shall observe more accurately and more minutely than before. Above all, I shall, if it is feasible, exercise experimental control over the nature and sequence of my data. It is under these conditions that the appeal to perceptual evidence has a high degree of logical value, and may fairly be described as an appeal to "facts". But we have "facts" here, not because we are employing pure perception as opposed to judgment or theory, but because we are employing intelligent perception or perceptual judgments as part and parcel of the development of knowledge towards coherence and stability.

On the Theory of Error in Mr. Bertrand Russell's "Problems of Philosophy"

THE theory of error which I propose to examine in this paper[1] is a theory to be found in a widely-read book of which Mr. Russell is the author, but it is not, or rather it is no longer Mr. Russell's theory. I have it on good authority that Mr. Russell has himself abandoned the theory expounded in *Problems of Philosophy* and, in an earlier version, in *Philosophical Essays*. This being so, a word of justification may seem to be demanded for setting out to examine a theory which may be held to be discredited by its own author's abandonment of it. What good is there, it may be asked, in kicking a dead dog?

The reply is, in effect, that the dog is very much alive. No theory is necessarily killed by the fact that its author disowns it—least of all when the author has not, so far as I am aware, made public either the fact of this disowning or the reasons for it, except in lectures and private conversation. I do not see how we can off-hand put aside even the possibility that Mr. Russell's rejection of his theory is itself mistaken. The theory of error in *Problems* may be sound, and Mr. Russell's present arguments against it may be errors. On that ground alone the theory would still be worth discussing. Again, supposing the theory to be false, yet we shall grant, that no thinker so able and acute as Mr. Russell would for several years have upheld a theory unless there were at least *prima facie* reasons of great strength in its support. Now these reasons which once weighed with Mr. Russell, may weigh with others, especially in the absence of Mr. Russell's own public refutation of them. And, in any case, we know from the history of philosophy that ways of argument once tried and abandoned are always liable to be tried again and thus can never be regarded as finally removed from the sphere of legitimate discussion. This must seem particularly obvious to that school of Realists—Mr. Russell himself, I think,

---

[1] This paper was written in 1914.

was once of their number—who believe in the subsistence of a universe of propositions which are, in themselves, true or false, it being the good or ill fortune of the apprehending mind to fall in with one or the other sort. On this view, the propositions which make up the theory of error in *Problems*, subsist timelessly whether true or false, and if they are false, well then it was just Mr. Russell's misfortune for awhile to keep bad company in his excursions into the land of propositions. What may happen to so clever a man, may the more easily happen to the lesser lights among us.

Hence, any contribution to a *catalogue raisonné* of true and false propositions is always in place. But as good a justification as any is, after all, the fact that, whilst Mr. Russell has not yet withdrawn his former theory in all the publicity of print, *Problems* is in people's hands and spreading daily an erroneous theory of error.

As philosophers, we shall all agree that this is an extremely grave fatality for all the English and American homes in which culture is spread by the Home University Library. And lastly, as I shall try to show, the theory of error in *Problems* is closely connected with other theories which, so far as I know, Mr. Russell is still prepared to maintain.

There is another difficulty which meets me at the threshold and to which I may devote a few words in anticipation. It may turn out that I have failed to understand the theory which I am about to examine. Indeed, it is most likely. Have we not Mr. Russell's own words for it, delivered to so respectable an audience as that which frequents the Lowell Lectures in Boston, that "no two philosophers ever understand one another"? It would seem to be almost necessary for me to misunderstand him, if we are both to be philosophers. For if I did understand him, it would follow that either he, or I, or both of us are not philosophers, and any one of these consequences, though not impossible, is not to be lightly accepted, if it can in any way be avoided.

Assuming then that we are both philosophers, the prospect of mutual understanding is sufficiently desperate, even without raising the much more fundamental doubt whether any philosopher ever understands himself. Even the reflection that, though I have not understood Mr. Russell, neither will he understand me, is a poor consolation. Fortunately, Mr. Russell denies mutual understanding only to philosophers. He does not deny a one-sided understanding of philosophers by ordinary mortals. And on that basis, perhaps, we can argue. Indeed I sometimes doubt whether any philosophical argument is ever conducted on any other basis. We philosophers do not really hope to convince one another—heaven forbid that we, who are paid to be infallible, should ever confess ourselves wrong, but we all hope to convince those who are not yet philosophers. We argue loudly at one another, but we compete really for the understanding of our public. We sit each in his *caverna individua*, and would make the whole world at home there, whilst finding the other fellow's *caverna* distinctly uninhabitable. But the scales between us are held by those who come after. And so to business.

I.

The theory of error is put forward in one of the later chapters of *Problems,* but the preceding chapters contain a good many doctrines which it is advisable to discuss first, in order that the theory of error may appear in the proper light. I shall therefore begin by examining the relation of what Mr. Russell calls "acquaintance with sense-data" to "truths of perception".

But before doing this, it may be as well if I state, in anticipation, the points which we shall find to be at issue, and the principles which are involved. For this purpose I shall take it to be common ground that judgment, or thinking, or, in general terms, that mode of apprehension to which the terms "true" and "false" apply, is based upon, or is developed from, another mode of experience—"immediate", if we like to call it so—in which there is neither truth nor error. The point at issue is whether, and in what sense, truth can be said to consist in a correspondence or agreement, and error in a failure of correspondence or agreement, between what is asserted in judgment and this immediate apprehension of "fact". Or we may put it as a question about "fact": is fact identical with what is asserted in judgment, or is the proposition "about" the fact, and therefore other than the fact? If so, is the fact accessible in a form which permits it to be clearly contrasted with the proposition, so as to establish the correspondence? And what is the nature of the correspondence? Clearly, it is hard to stop the issue even here. Is the correspondence—the "fact" of it— immediately apprehended in a way involving neither truth nor error? Or is it a fact only as something asserted which may, therefore, be true or false? And, ultimately, there confronts us a difficulty which touches all theories alike, viz., whether, and how, the alleged immediate experience can enter into "theory" which consists of judgments, or has to do with propositions, without losing its character as immediate? After all, we have to deal here with what is, *prima facie*, a *theory* of the nature of immediate experience and its relation to judgment. We are offered the proposition that its nature is so-and-so, and with that we are in the region of truth and error. It is to say the least a paradox, not to be accepted without further examination, that truth is to consist in some sort of relation between proposita and facts, when even the fact-term is offered in the first instance, as another propositum.

So much for orientation. I turn now to my first topic, viz., the relation as set forth in *Problems*, between "acquaintance with sense-data, and truths of perception". Acquaintance with sense-data, we gather, is a two-term relation, the one term, the sense-datum being non-mental and always a "particular", the other term, "sensing" or "sensation", being mental, and a species of "acquaintance", this latter being the general term for all forms of awareness in which we apprehend "thing". And "things" in their very nature cannot be true or false.

There are some points in this brief statement which must be expanded in order that their bearing may be more clearly seen. "Things" are of two sorts, particulars (e.g. sense-data) and universals. Of the latter I shall speak below: we note here, provisionally, that they are set alongside of particulars as a distinct sort of "thing". Things are to be distinguished from "truths", which is here a somewhat loose term for what I have called proposita—loose, because not all proposita are truths, for some are errors. A so-called "truth" is, so far, only something of which we can intelligently ask whether it is true or false. It is, to use a clumsy phrase, a *somewhat asserted*, e.g., a statement of what is given in sense, when we are acquainted with a sense-datum.

Now the important point for our present purpose is to

examine the meaning of Mr. Russell's reiterated contention that "acquaintance itself cannot be deceptive". I shall try to show that this phrase is ambiguous; that, on Mr. Russell's own showing, it means at least two distinct, and, as I would urge, disconnected things, and that Mr. Russell had not made up his mind which of these he intended to mean. (*a*) let us look first at the full context from which I quoted just now: "whatever we are acquainted with must be something: we may draw wrong inferences from our acquaintance,[1] but the acquaintance itself cannot be deceptive" (p. 186).

Interpreting this passage, we have to remember, it seems to me, that "acquaintance" is the name for a two-term *relation*. Deceptiveness, therefore, appears to be denied of this *relation*. On what grounds? As far as I can make out, *on the ground that it cannot belong to either term of this relation*. It cannot belong to the object-term for "the actual sense-data are neither true nor false. A particular patch of colour which I see, for example, simply exists: it is not the sort of thing that is true or false" (p. 178). And the same would be said, I suppose, of universals and other objects of acquaintance. On the other hand, deceptiveness cannot belong to the subject-term, for acquaintance means being "directly aware, without the intermediary of any process of inference or any knowledge of truths" (p. 73). Again, sense-data are "things immediately known to me just as they are" (p. 74), so much so that "I know the colour perfectly and completely when I see it, and no further knowledge of it itself is even theoretically possible" (p. 73). This is Mr. Russell's chief account of the matter, which may be summed up by saying that he gives two reasons for the non-deceptiveness of acquaintance, viz., (i) that its objects anyhow are not capable of being either true or false, and (ii) that acquaintance, on its mental side, is non-inferential. Two comments on this seem relevant, both bearing on the theory of error which Mr. Russell subsequently elaborates. One is, that these two reasons seem mutually destructive. At least it would be interesting to know how inference, and, in general, any mental activity, could

---

[1] Apropos of this phrase, I note, in passing, that it again may mean several things. I may, I suppose, draw inference either from the fact of my acquaintance with *x*, or from the nature of the *x* with which I am acquainted, or from both these together. Here Mr. Russell seems to be thinking of inferences drawn from *what* I am acquainted with.

falsify objects which are *ex hypothesi* incapable of being other than they are. To escape this, the reply might be attempted that inference does not deal with the objects of acquaintance at all, but only with objects which, in virtue of its own manipulation of them, may be either true or false. But if so, we should ask how the objects of acquaintance and the objects of inference are related to one another, as well as how acquaintance and inference themselves are related to one another. For, clearly, the problem is not merely to distinguish, but also to connect positively. But, in any event, to take this line is to concede that what makes acquaintance non-deceptive is simply the character of its objects, which could not be apprehended inferentially at all. The other comment is that to make the infallibility (if I may call it so) of acquaintance depend on the fact that truth and falsity cannot be predicated of either of its terms, is a somewhat curious procedure for a champion of "external relations". It is meaningless to apply the terms true and false to sensing as such, for that is immediate. It is meaningless to apply them to sense-data as such, for they are what they are. *Ergo*, it is meaningless to apply them to the sensing of the sense-data. Whatever we may think of the argument, at any rate it is clear that it makes the character of the relation depend wholly on its terms. In fact, the more one reflects on the point, the more one is led to doubt whether we are here dealing with a relation at all, and whether the analysis into terms is anything but a fiction. At any rate, unless it be a mere "togetherness" à la Alexander, I find it hard to say what the relation is supposed to be over and above the sensing on the one side, and the sense-datum on the other. And "togetherness" strikes me very much as a word specially devised to avoid the acknowledgment that we are here dealing with a non-relational whole which cannot properly be treated as terms in relation at all. If we insist on a relational scheme at all, it would be better not to speak of a relation of sensing to sense-data, but to treat sensing as the relation between "I" and "sense-data". But in all this, there is so far no ground shown for preferring this view to others which regard immediacy and relations as incompatible with one another.

(*b*) But there are suggestions of another account altogether. In the passage quoted above we read that "whatever we are acquainted with must be something". It is then the fact of there being "something" whenever e.g., we are sensing, that saves acquaintance from being deceptive. If we were to take this strictly, we should have to conclude that deceptiveness, supposing it possible, would belong to states of mind that had no object-term; it would characterise awareness of nothing. To put this suggestion is to reject it. For in every mode of apprehension there is "something" which is apprehended, and if the presence or absence of some thing is to constitute the difference between truth and error, there will be no error at all. The point has been settled since Plato's day: error is not the same as a blank mind. That which is false is not nothing but something other than what it appears or claims or pretends to be. Following this line brings us back to Mr. Russell's other view, from this fresh angle however, that the question now is whether indeed our knowledge of a sense-datum, "just as it is", is perfect and complete in the bare moment of sensing. But the answer to this question is not possible without the consideration of some further points to which we shall turn in a moment. Meanwhile, we have perhaps learnt to understand why, and in what sense, Mr. Russell acclaims sense-data as the "solid basis" of our knowledge (p. 30), so that "even in dreams and hallucinations, there is no error involved so long as we do not go beyond the immediate object" (p. 172). We may however note, as bearing on the subsequent theory, that the "going beyond the immediate object", which constitutes error, is of a very special kind; "error can only arise when we regard the immediate object, i.e., the sense-datum, as the mark of some physical object" (p. 172).

A general comment may be made on this section of Mr. Russell's theory. In treating sense-experience as a complex to be analysed into sensing and sense-datum Mr. Russell fails to consider various aspects of the experience which do not appear to be irrelevant to its cognitive function. For example, attention does seem to make a difference, bringing with it distinction within a context and thus passing on to identification and recognition. In a recent article in *Scientia* (Aug. 1914), p. 2, Mr. Russell in passing does acknowledge this point so far at least as to allow that what is given at any one time is always a complex, and that a determinate "sense-datum" is something singled out within this complex by attention. He even admits the difficulty of deciding what is to be treated as *one* sense-datum. But even here he does not yet consider whether, with this analysis of the total given by attention, we are not on the threshold of judgment. As this point will receive further elucidation in the next section, I will not dwell on it here. Again, we may ask, what has become of apperception? And how can it be fitted into the simple sensing—sense-data scheme? The facts of Psychology are surely not done away with by simply ignoring them. Mr. Russell's theory takes no account of the psychological commonplace that a pure sensation is not so much a fact of experience as a hypothetically posited starting-point, and that the sensations (or sense-data, in Mr. Russell's terminology) which we actually use in knowledge are what they are under conditions of attention and apperception, and the recognition of this brings us round again to the question whether, herewith, we are not on the threshold of judgment and of the true and false. This implies, of course, a different theory of judgment from Mr. Russell's, and a different theory of truth and error. Meanwhile, it would seem that the only sense-data which could fairly be acclaimed as the "solid basis" of knowledge, are the data which are attended to and apperceped.

II.

We must next consider the theory of sense-data in the light of Mr. Russell's account of particulars and universals. Each sense-datum is as we have seen, a particular, a "this". But in each there is also "exemplified" a "sensible quality" which is a universal (pp. 158-59). We become acquainted with universals by sensing many sense-data of the same kind, and abstracting their common quality. Since this is a mode of acquaintance, there is no deception. The universal is just what it is, and the apprehension of it is direct and non-inferential. The same remark applies, apparently, even though with other kinds of universals the abstraction is more difficult, though one would naturally expect that an operation which may be difficult, would be liable to be wrongly performed and to result in errors of abstraction.

But, waiving this, it seems to me that this bit of Mr. Russell's theory throws a startling light on his failure to appreciate the logical character of the process by which common qualities are abstracted.

In the first place, if Mr. Russell were in earnest about his phrase that universals are "exemplified" in sense-data, he would not maintain that any sense-datum is a mere particular, a mere "this". It is rather—if the clumsy phrase be excused—a "this-such", a τόδε τοιόνδε as Aristotle said. The particular which we sense is, from the first, a particular of a kind, and therefore, from the first, we are acquainted also with its character or quality, which is in principle universal. It would be curious to know what exactly this relation of "being exemplified" is. It cannot consist in the particular being a member of the class of particulars constituted by the possession of a common quality, for it is only the possession of the quality which entitles the particular to membership, hence the membership cannot explain the possession of the quality. In fact, we shall suspect that we are not dealing here with a relation at all. The subject-attribute relation would come nearer the truth than the class relation. But it seems better to say that the union of "that" and "what", to use Mr. Bradley's terms for the same thing, is non-relational in sense-acquaintance. One might clinch this by an *argumentum ad hominen*. The very language which Mr. Russell uses bears witness to the fact that his particulars have universal characters, e.g., "when we see a white patch, we are *acquainted, in the first instance, with the particular patch*" (p. 158; cp. "we see a patch of red", p. 179). "Patch", "white", etc., in this context mean universals. To meet a possible objection, it should perhaps be noted that it is not the use of language which introduces the universal characters into the situation. Language helps to fix them, but it does not make them. If there be any doubt on this point, the objector may be invited to consider language itself, as a complex of auditory sense-data. Every sound is a "this", but it is also a "such", and as a "such" it is repeatable. In fact it would seem to be their own universal character which enables sounds to fix and convey the universals which they mean.

Secondly, we may reach the same conclusion when we consider how the particulars are to be selected from which we are to abstract the universal. What makes some particulars relevant and others irrelevant? Their similarity? But that is only another way of saying: those are relevant which are of the same sort or kind. In short, in the very process of comparison and abstraction, the universal character (disguised as "similarity") is already operative. Whether this process and its result are to be properly called "acquaintance" or "inference" and whether they are to be treated as deceptive or non-deceptive, may seem idle points, so long as we think only of sense-data and sense-qualities. If any difficulty arises, we might perhaps put it down to the possibility of making mistakes in apprehending the relation of particular and universal. But this only shifts the trouble to another point. For relations, as we learn from Mr. Russell, are themselves capable of being apprehended immediately. They as much as their objects are things which we may know by acquaintance, some more easily, others with difficulty. The relations which Mr. Russell instances (pp. 159-161) are instructive here. He mentions relations given within a single complex sense-datum; relations of space and time; relations of similarity between two sense-data with which we are acquainted simultaneously; relations between universals. But he says nothing about the relations of particular to universal. Suppose we say, as I think we must from Mr. Russell's standpoint, that this relation, too, is an object of immediate acquaintance. In that case two comments apply. First, we shall press once more the question whether what is given is ever a mere particular, and not always a particular of a kind, or, in Mr. Russell's language, a relation of particular and universal? In short, is this not the *minimum datum* for any act of immediate apprehension?[1] And, secondly, we must ask whether the attempt to follow up the universal character, or characters of the particular does not very soon lead us into regions where we not only meet with "difficulty", but make mistakes? But if so, what becomes of the non-deceptive, non-inferential character of acquaintance?

To test the matter, let us take an example from another sphere. I do not, indeed, know whether Mr. Russell would consider, for example, his country, state, or nation a "datum"

[1] I am purposely ignoring here the questions (i) whether this datum is properly to be treated as a complex of a particular term, a universal term, and a relation between them, (ii) how the difference between "abstract" and "concrete" universal applies.

—not of course, a sense-datum, but still a "this", a "parti-cular" state or nation, capable of being compared with other states or nations so as to make us acquainted with the "universal" state or nation. I do not know whether he would hold that he is "acquainted" with his state, or that he knows it, and other states, and therefore the universal state only by description. So far as Mr. Russell's statements go, I see no reason why he should not here speak of data and acquaintance. Let us suppose then, that the example is relevant. If so, what are we to make of the notorious conflicts of theory among philo-sophers and sociologists concerning what constitutes the nature of a state? Can we here still say that the universal either in the abstract or in its relation to the particular, is immediately apprehended without any chance of deception or error? Mr. Russell's interest, as the Lowell Lectures and other recent writings show, is so narrowly focussed on the special way in which these and similar logical problems arise in a philo-sophical theory of Mathematics and Physics, that he neglects other regions of reality altogether. His arbitrary restriction of the field of legitimate, i.e., for him "scientific", philosophy to the problems of continuity and change, is of a piece with this narrowing of his outlook, and his logical theories seem to me to suffer seriously in consequence.

To mention but one further point in concluding this section of the argument, a point bearing on the difference between "abstract" and "concrete" universal. Suppose a series of "similar" sense-data, e.g., the recurrent ticks of a clock. Are we to treat these as "one and the same" tick repeated, or as so many different ticks "of the same sort"? Suppose again Robin-son Crusoe, before he has got to know Friday, catching glimpses of him among the trees. Would he not, at first, be in doubt, whether he had to do with the same person repeatedly seen or with different persons very "similar" to one another? Either interpretation is, *prima facie*, possible, and might for a time fit the sense-data equally well. This is a small part of the issue between "abstract" and "concrete" universal. Approaching the question from the side of sense-data, we have a number of "similar" complexes. Nothing that Mr. Russell tells us in *Prob-lems* about the relations of particular to universal, enables us to understand how we come to recognise some complexes as different appearances of the same "individual", others as different individuals of the same "kind". In both cases, whether we are dealing with the "same" individual or the "same" kind, the sense-data are numerically different, whilst qualitatively "similar". The truth, surely, is that "similarity" here means qualitative identity in difference, and that this, in turn, becomes the basis for asserting a numerical identity, which we may follow up either into "one and the same" individual (concrete universal) or "one and the same" kind (abstract universal). I am not convinced that Mr. Russell's recent analysis in Lowell Lectures of the "thing" as an aggregate of sense-data is, as it stands, ready to meet the difficulties of this situation. Distinguishable things of the same kind must be, it would seem, on this view distinguishable systems made up of the same kind of sense-data. Face to face with any given complex of data, we are still left to ask, do these belong to the system constituting a certain individual, or do they belong to different individuals of the same kind? Even in the language of systems of sense-data, we still must distinguish between an individual "thing" in different "appearances", i.e., an individual system, and different things of the same kind, i.e., similar systems. It would be a great help if Mr. Russell were to deal with this point fully. In passing, it may be noticed, that, if the points here urged are sound, Mr. Russell's theory of Induction (*Problems*, Ch. IV) would have to undergo considerable modifications. But that is another story.

III.

Sense-data may not merely lead to acquaintance with a certain kind of universal, but they may also give rise to "truths" of "perception" (p. 177), which, when expressed in language, are called "judgments of perception" (p. 178). The "truth" is something different both from the sense-datum, from which it is "derived", and about which it "asserts", and from the words in which it is "expressed". Truths of perception may be of two kinds, according as they merely assert the existence of a sense-datum, or analyse the sense-datum, if complex, into its constituent elements. They are also said to be "self-evident" in a sense of which Mr. Russell in a later passage (p. 212) says that it means "an absolute guarantee of truth", because we have acquaintance with the fact which corresponds to the truth.

To this passage I shall return below. For the present I am concerned to examine the position stated so far.

First, a point about the function of language in asserting. Above, I have taken Mr. Russell to make a distinction between the assertion (=what is asserted, the *propositum*) and the words in which it is expressed. But there is some doubt as to whether this is really what Mr. Russell means. This doubt turns out to be connected with a difficulty to be discussed below, viz., whether, and, if so, how Mr. Russell would draw the distinction between the *act* of assertion and *what* is asserted. If we were clear on that point, we might be able to decide whether the use of words is incidental to the act, they being its instrument or vehicle, or whether they actually *are* the assertion in the sense of what is asserted. Does this sound absurd? Well, what I mean is something like this. Suppose I see a white patch (=acquaint- ance with sense-datum) and enunciate the words (=judge): there is a white patch. The result would be the addition of this series of auditory sense-data to the previous and persistent visual sense-datum. The whole complex would constitute datum + judgment. Compare "we see a patch of red, and we judge: 'there is such-and-such a patch of red'" (p. 179). Of course this account may be said to omit the characteristic operations of thought, such as fixing upon the datum, analysing it, identifying its elements and their relations, etc. But that the exact function of words in this context is far from clear, may be verified from the account in Lowell Lectures (p. 52), where in distinction from the "fact" which is "objective" and "independent of thought" it is said of the "assertion" that it "involves thought, and may be either true or false". But a few lines on we read: "given a *form of words* (italics mine) which must be either true or false . . . we may either assert or deny this form of words". And again: "a form of words which must be either true or false I shall call a proposition".

I doubt whether even Mr. Russell, let alone anyone else, can extract a consistent doctrine from all this. A form of words could be called true or false only in the sense that the words are correctly or incorrectly used. But in what does correctness consist? Mr. Russell, as we shall see, defines truth in terms of "correspondence to fact". But to what do words correspond in the sense here required? A word as used has meaning, and might perhaps be said to "correspond" to its meaning in the sense that it is an element in the word-meaning complex. Correct use of a word depends on conventionally standardised complexes of this sort. But all this is remote from the problem of truth, which would concern not the relation of words to their meaning, but the correspondence of the meaning (=what is thought or asserted) to the "fact". If to think is something more than to use words, i.e., to make a sequence of noises, then the truth of what I think is something more than the making of correct noises. I shall assume in what follows that this is what Mr. Russell himself holds in *Problems* when he distinguishes between a truth and its expression in a judgment.

Secondly, we must protest against the facile way in which Mr. Russell calls assertions about sense-data "truths", thus prejudging the question whether they are liable to error. If they are genuinely assertions, we must unhesitatingly insist that they may be either true or false, and cannot therefore be declared *vi nominis* to be infallible. At best, they are in the first instance only *claims* to truth. In the language of Mr. Russell's theory of truth, what I assert claims to correspond to fact. Whether it actually does correspond in the way required is another question, and would seem to require an endorsing assertion, declaring the first assertion to be true, or to be a truth, on the ground of its correspondence.

Let us pursue this point a little further. In *Problems* ch. xiii (pp. 210, 212, 214) we are told that assertions (also called "judgments" and even "beliefs") derived from acquaintance with data, are "*self-evident* in a sense which ensures infallibility". And when we ask: how? the answer is: because of our acquaintance with the fact which corresponds to the truth. Yet this beautiful theory of self-evidence and infallibility is framed by statements which whittle it down to a point at which it threatens to dissolve into thin air. For on p. 210 we read: "all our knowledge of truths is infected with *some* degree of doubt", and on p. 214 we are told quite explicitly that, in passing from what we are acquainted with to what we assert or judge, we must analyse the given, and in doing so we are always liable to commit errors. For, though there is no deception in our

I

acquaintance with the fact, "a judgment believed to correspond to the fact is not absolutely infallible, because it may
not really correspond to the fact". We can only say hypothetically : *if* it does correspond, then it *must* be true.

The patient reader may well wonder what sort of grudge
Mr. Russell has against the peaceful homes, for which the Home
University Library caters, to visit them with such an infliction.
In the struggle to understand Mr. Russell, two suggestions
towards avoiding the apparent contradictions of the above
doctrine, have occurred to me. The first came from a passage
which I will quote *verbatim* : "In all cases where we know by
acquaintance a complex fact consisting of certain terms in a
certain relation, we say that the truth that these terms are so
related has the first or absolute kind of self-evidence, and in
these cases the judgment that the terms are so related *must* be
true. Thus this ·sort of self-evidence is an absolute guarantee
of truth. But although this sort of self-evidence is an absolute
guarantee of truth, it does not enable us to be *absolutely* certain,
in the case of any given judgment that the judgment in question
is true" (pp. 213-14). The first suggestion, then, is that the point
of this passage turns on some distinction, which I may have
failed to fathom, between a "truth" and a "judgment". But I
can make nothing of that, except wonder whether for Mr. Russell
the statements "a judgment is true" ; "a judgment is a truth" ;
"a judgment expresses a truth", are or are not equivalent. On
the other hand, the second suggestion of which there is also a
hint in this passage is more promising. It is simply this, that
Mr. Russell wants us merely to distinguish between the *fact*
of correspondence between an assertion and a datum, and our
knowledge of that fact. On this interpretation, all he is saying
is that when the required correspondence actually exists there
the assertion is, self-evidently and infallibly, a truth, but that
it is always a matter of doubt, or that we cannot be "absolutely
certain", whether in any given case this correspondence does
exist, even though we judge in the very moment of acquaintance
with the datum. But if this is all that Mr. Russell means, he has
certainly done his best to obscure his meaning. The reader is
inevitably misled by the discussion of self-evidence and infallibility. For, at bottom, as between a truth and the datum about
which it is an assertion the only question is : is the correspon-

dence actual or not? As between us and the truth in its relation
to the datum the only question is: can we discover whether or
no the correspondence exists? Self-evidence and infallibility are
really side-issues which do not help us here at all. But some of
Mr. Russell's statements read as if he meant that given
acquaintance with a fact, the judgments we make about it must
be true, infallibly and without a possibility of error. I submit, that the passage above quoted, *prima facie* demands this
interpretation, but on the whole I am inclined to conclude that
really my second suggestion represents Mr. Russell's position.

But, thirdly, if this is so, then perhaps the most interesting
question is one on which Mr. Russell does not touch, though it
is, I think, relevant, viz., the question how judgments arise or
are made. Mr. Russell discusses only the two questions: (i)
what is the nature of the correspondence in which the truth of
an assertion consists? (ii) How can we discover that this correspondence is a fact? He does not discuss what we can do in
making judgments to secure correspondence or avoid failure.
The same point might be put alternatively by asking: how can
the datum enter into the assertion? Or what is the relation
indicated by "about" when we say that the assertion is about
the fact? These are difficult questions which I have no desire
to follow up here beyond pointing out their bearing and importance. Mr. Russell treats judging as a mental activity establishing a certain relation between terms. What one would like
to know is how, given acquaintance with terms in relation, the
assertion, then and there made, that these terms are so related,
can possibly fail to correspond to the fact in the way required.
This question would not arise for anyone holding Mr. Russell's
earlier view which distinguished the assertion (proposition) alike
from the "fact" and from the act of affirming or denying it.
On this view, there is no question of propositions being made
by an act, or being derived by thought-analysis from acquaintance with a datum. Now the real interest of this question lies
not so much on the *subjective* side, in the transition from, say,
sensing to thinking, but on the *objective* side, in the transition
from sense-datum to propositum, to what is asserted. There
must be continuity, and in fact identity, yet there must also be
difference, for the datum does undergo some sort of transformation. How this can be so is a problem perhaps unanswer-

able. That it is so, we shall find in the next section, to be implicitly conceded even by Mr. Russell's account of judgment and error. Yet this involuntary concession to the principle of identity in difference on the part of a thinker who is constantly attacking and denying it is certainly remarkable.

Lastly, there is another side to this matter, which I cannot pass by without comment. If I am right in thinking that Mr. Russell would have us distinguish between the *fact* of correspondence in which truth consists, and our knowledge of that fact, it is worth considering how Mr. Russell's account of acquaintance and truth applies to the knowledge of this fact. This is, I suppose, the question of the *test* or *criterion* of truth, as distinct from its *nature*. We ask : how do we become aware of the correspondence? For example, suppose I am acquainted with this white sheet of paper on which I am writing, and I proceed to judge "here is a white sheet of paper". Suppose further that I believe (or judge) this judgment to be true. This means that the second judgment asserts that the first corresponds to the fact. This second judgment, in order to be true itself, must itself correspond to fact of correspondence between the first judgment and the original datum. Now we have learnt already from Mr. Russell that correspondence must exist for any judgment to be true, and that it is a difficult matter to know whether, in any given case, it does exist. Applied to our second judgment this means, both that it is difficult to get the basis of fact from which to "derive" it and again difficult to make sure of its own correspondence to that fact. The tangle is getting complicated. The nature and criterion of truth do not appear to have anything to do with one another. We have a beautiful theory of what truth consists in but no means of making sure when our judgments actually are true. And the best of it is that the *theory* of truth, being itself a set of judgments made by Mr. Russell, cannot even itself be known to be true. Where has Mr. Russell's position here any advantage over Mr. Bradley's idea of the Absolute?

The difficulties of Mr. Russell's position here might be exhibited alternatively in this way. If the correspondence of assertion and fact ever does occur, it can presumably be apprehended. If so, we shall expect to apprehend it either by acquaintance or by inference. If by acquaintance which (we know) cannot deceive, then we should expect to be acquainted with the truth of our judgments whenever we are also acquainted with the fact by correspondence to which they are true. We should, in short, be acquainted, with absolute certainty, with the complex of which fact and assertion are the terms and correspondence the relation. Indeed this acquaintance would be the basis of the evaluating judgment that our original judgment is true, and we should be similarly acquainted with *its* truth. But, if so, how do we ever fall into, or rather commit error? Divergence of assertion and fact threatens to become impossible, at any rate so long as we observe the caution of asserting only where we have actual acquaintance with the fact as a basis. If, on the other hand, we apprehend the correspondence by inference, what are its data, and what is the nature of the argument? We have got a relation of which the fact-complex and the assertion-complex are the terms. These terms must be distinct, else we have no relation; yet they must also be somehow identical, else we have no truth. To sum up this criticism in the form of a dilemma: either we know by acquaintance that an assertion is true, and in that case the whole situation is so plain that the occurrence of false judgments is unintelligible; or we know it in the form of an evaluating judgment and in that case we must promptly ask how we can know that judgment itself to be true.

IV.

We are at length in a position to deal with Mr. Russell's explicit theory of truth and error. "A belief is true when there is a corresponding fact, and is false when there is no corresponding fact" (p. 202).

To appreciate this theory fully, we have to bear in mind that it is wholly dominated by the desire to avoid the assumption of "objective falsehoods, which subsist independently of any minds" (p. 196). It follows that truths and falsehoods are subjective. They are of the mind's own making, at least in the sense that minds "create" beliefs, though not the correspondence to fact which makes the beliefs true, or by its absence, false. Only in exceptional cases can a mind not merely make a belief but also make it true, viz., when it lies in the mind's power to go on and make the fact, by corresponding to which the belief then becomes true (p. 203).

Two comments on this in passing; (i) One would have thought that a mind, having a fact before it in the way of acquaintance, and aiming at creating a belief to correspond to the fact, could adjust the belief to the fact, construct the belief so as to correspond. It is surely something of a paradox that the mind, given the fact, cannot for certain secure truth in the making of a belief. We are not told why or how it fails, indeed this whole side of the matter, Mr. Russell has apparently not considered. (ii) Mr. Russell does not tell us whether truths and errors exist only so far, and so long, as a given mind is actually making a judgment or holding a belief, but that would seem to follow from his view that true and false beliefs are the products of special acts, each act being "the occurrence between certain terms at some particular time, of the relation of believing or judging" (p. 197). Truth and error, thus, are qualities of certain events, happening in time, and depending on the existence and activity of minds.

In any case, it is well to emphasise this subjectivity of truths and errors, for if, as I suggested in previous sections, the sphere of judgment extends further than Mr. Russell allows for, it may go hard with Mr. Russell's Realism.

Some further aspects of the theory emerge when we consider it in the light of the distinction between acquaintance as a two-term relation and judgment as a mutiple relation. However complex the object may be with which we are acquainted it stands over against the mind as a *single* term. Judgment, on the other hand, involves several constituent terms, viz., a mind or subject, and a number of objects which the act of judging relates in a certain way to one another and to the subject. One of these objects, i.e., one of the object-terms in the judgment-relation, must be itself a relation, but not a "relating-relation", i.e., a relation actually holding terms together, "cementing" them, creating a complex whole out of its terms, but a relation which is itself "a brick in the structure" (p. 200), a term in the operations of some other relation.

Now for what purpose is all this elaborate apparatus? I do not find it easy to be sure of Mr. Russell's reasons. Why is it that he rejects the analysis of judgment as a two-term relation

—for that is what it comes to—on the ground that to admit it would involve objective falsehoods? His argument, as far as I can make it out, rests on these two considerations : (i) a thing is true or false, not in itself, but in virtue of a relation to something other than itself. Beliefs claim to be thus related to facts, but the facts (=objects of acquaintance) are not in turn so related to anything else. They are simply themselves. They are what they are. Acquaintance, therefore, is non-deceptive, not because its object is "single" but because it lacks this correspondence, or claim to correspondence, to something other than itself. But (ii) this *motif* is crossed by another, which makes acquaintance non-deceptive because it is non-inferential, because mental activity in its case simply apprehends, but does not analyse or otherwise operate upon, the object. In other words, the rejection, for judgment, of two-term relations and singleness of object is wholly based on the assertion that in acquaintance— if the bull be permitted—the mind's activity is altogether passive, whereas in judgment it is active and destructive of the object as given. Acquaintance simply accepts the object as it comes. It does not kill it by analysis. To put this into the language of relations : we have, say, a complex object with its own relating relation. This object enters into a fresh complex with an act of immediate apprehension, but the relating relation of this wider complex does not destroy the relating relation within the object complex. Hence the two terms the subject-term and the whole unanalysed object-term, which, as unanalysed, retains its relating relation and thus may be called "single". Analysis, we are apparently intended to understand, breaks up the complex, transforms its relations into terms, and binds all these *disjecta membra* into a fresh complex, in which the mental operation is itself the only relating relation. The point, then, that emerges as constituting the difference between acquaintance as a two-term and judgment as a multiple relation is, that we must distinguish between a mental activity which apprehends the object as it is given, and one which analyses, breaks up, reconstitutes, and thus creates judgments and beliefs. It would seem to follow that the proper sphere of Realism is the field of objects of acquaintance. For there we get objects apprehended but untouched by the mind—though by what argument Mr. Russell achieves the leap to the "independent subsistence" of the object from the fact that it remains unanalysed, is far from obvious.

The position might be followed up into all sorts of dialectical refinements. Thus one might ask, granted that the judgment-complex, having a mental act for its relating relation, cannot "subsist independently of any mind", is not the relating relation in acquaintance also mental? If so, there is no obvious conclusion to independence from the mere fact that in the one instance the act analyses and recombines, in the other it does not. We see here how much we stand in need of being clearly told whether in acquaintance there is a unique relation which has an act and an object as its terms, or whether the act is the relating factor and the terms a mind and an object. The whole position is closely parallel to the theories of Mr. S. Alexander, according to which experience is a "togetherness" of mind and object, and error arises through the misplacement by mental activity, of objective elements. Togetherness corresponds to Mr. Russell's acquaintance; misplacement of elements to Mr. Russell's erroneous combination of terms. Again we might ask Mr. Russell, as the chief apostle of external relations, how far the object-terms of the judgment-complex are "independent", seeing that in the form employed they are the products of an act of analysis, and that especially the transformation of a relation from a "cement" to a "brick" can hardly "make no difference" to it.

But enough of this. We conclude, then, that the reason why the treatment of judgment as a two-term relation would involve objective falsehoods is because then its object would be a "single" term, therefore an unanalysed whole, therefore an independently subsisting entity. I may commend this to collectors of logical curiosities as an interesting specimen.

This brings me lastly to correspondence. After all that I have already said, this can be briefly disposed of. The theory amounts to this: Correspondence is a relation between a fact-term and a belief-term, both terms being complex. The fact-complex, we will assume for simplicity sake, consists of two terms and a relating-relation. In the corresponding belief-complex this relation becomes itself a term, arranged in its proper "sense" between its proper terms by the judgment-activity of an additional term, the subject. The fact-complex is "composed exclusively of the *objects* of the belief" (p. 200) ; the belief-complex consists of these plus the subject. The identity of the object-elements and of their order in both complexes, notwithstanding the transformation of the fact-relation into a term, secures correspondence and truth.

Two comments will suffice. (i) The correspondence hinges on identity, and in fact on identity-in-difference, thus revealing another unconscious use by Mr. Russell of the principle which he abhors. Quite clearly, as it seems to me, the principle is involved in the relation which in one complex relates and in the other is a term. That this makes a difference to the terms too, might be disputed, but at any rate it must be conceded that, the recent admission, in Lowell Lectures, of the difficulty of determining what really is *datum* of acquaintance, as distinguished from what interpretation and analysis make of it, makes havoc of the comfortable contention that, e.g., "I know the colour perfectly and completely when I see it". It is a good thing in philosophy to have alternative theories on the same issue. That tends at least to ensure that every side of the matter which can be urged, gets expression and obtains a hearing. And from this point of view, Mr. Russell's theory does a service to philosophy as an experiment in making the strongest case for a clear division of acquaintance and judgment. But when we are asked to affirm that acquaintance, e.g., in the form of sense-perception, gives us "complete and perfect" knowledge of its objects, so that no further knowledge is even possible, we begin to wonder what is the use or function of judgment. And when we are further asked to affirm that into sense-perception no judgment enters, we are tempted to reflect that if this view is to be tenable, sense-perception has to be whittled down until it approaches the "bare sensation" of which psychologists talk as a lower limit and of which the "solidity" has been denied by the consensus of philosophy all down the ages. We might urge here that, in ordinary experience no less than in science—at least in the concrete sciences—sense-data are apprehended as qualities of things or as the medium for the outward expression of minds. This is to apprehend sense-data as significant, and in this apprehension of the datum as an element in a full context, it may come to be so subordinate that it is barely noticed. How little of the sensuous detail are we apt to notice about the persons and things with which we habitually deal. We may read an emotion, a feeling, a thought in another's eye and never notice the colour of that eye. What, in that case, do we really "see"? What are we acquainted with? The analysis of such ordinary experience into sense-data plus an instinctive, but theoretically precarious belief in material things and minds somehow related to them, seems strangely artificial. Or we might urge that on the mere basis of sense-data it is not easy to see how sense-data of very different kinds, experienced at different times, by different minds come to be grouped together as qualities of the same thing or person. On this matter, Mr. Russell's account of acquaintance and judgment throws no light whatever. Weighing these and similar points, we may conclude that Mr. Russell has not succeeded in wholly dispossessing the alternative theory, according to which we must not try to get at pure data, still less treat them as solid basis, but look at their function within the organised world of our daily experience, and then take them as elements in the sustained judgment by which we affirm this world as the context to which every detail of experience belongs. Such a view will lead us to extend judgment over acquaintance with sense-data, in order to make the most of them for purposes of knowledge. And we shall find it worth while to weigh against Mr. Russell's view that of Professor Bosanquet, that seeing is judging, that a man may make a judgment "that is a table" by "the mere glance of his eye which takes in the table as a real object in a real world of space", or again that "the visual picture which each of us forms of this room is certainly an affirmative judgment" (*Essentials of Logic*, Ch. II, pp. 31 ff.).

(ii) The second criticism was in effect a challenge to Mr. Russell's account of particular and universal, on the ground that neither are we ever acquainted with a mere particular, nor is every datum of acquaintance a relational complex, of which particular and universal are the terms, and "instance-of" the relation. That relation may be affirmed as the result of an analysis, but in the first instance particular and universal are not terms, but aspects, and if we speak here of a complex, it is at any rate not relational.

Now both these criticisms may be reinforced by looking at the whole matter from a point of view which so far has been

left out of account, viz., the point of view of *verification*. We have
considered the relation of correspondence between acquain-
tance-with-datum and judgment-that,—, in which truth is
alleged to consist. We have considered also the transition from
acquaintance to the making of judgments which stand in that
relation to the datum of acquaintance. We have not yet
considered the reverse transition when, starting with the judgment (however got), we seek for acquaintance with the datum
which will test and confirm the judgment. Suppose we start
with the assertion that all things of a certain kind behave in a
certain way under certain conditions, we shall by observation
or experiment seek to become acquainted with particular
instances of things of that kind in those conditions. It seems a
problem of recognition or identification. We have to recognise
(whether this would have to be called acquaintance or judgment matters not) the identity of the terms and relations of our
assertion with those of the complex perceived. That sounds
simple, yet there is, neither in principle nor by trial in
experience, any reason for regarding this process as more infallible than the reverse process of formulating the datum in
an assertion. What we have got to account for, either way, is
both the notorious "fallibility of the senses", which sceptics all
down the ages have emphasised and which modern psychology
has experimentally endorsed, and also the acknowledged
superiority of the trained observer. Of course, Mr. Russell may
reply that what is fallible in the first case is not the acquaintance, but the judgment of perception, and that what constitutes
superiority in the second case is just the skill with which
relations given to acquaintance are asserted in judgment. Both
criticisms, in short, he might urge, are sound for the judgments,
but do not touch what lies behind them, acquaintance and its
data. But this reply is countered by the difficulty of deciding
where to draw the line. At the point where judgment ceases to
enter into perception, at that point, perception becomes useless
for knowledge. It can no longer be made available. *Mutatis
mutandis*, we reach the situation of which Kant said "perceptions without conceptions are blind".

Verification, however, is only one side of the matter. What
of judgments which we cannot verify for lack of the data of
acquaintance, e.g., where the data are, from their nature,

accessible exclusively to one person, or where, belonging to the past, they are not directly accessible to us now? These cases are instructive because they illustrate the decisive parting of the ways in our theories on these matters. We may either confine ourselves to asking how we discover what the facts were like, i.e., how we come to believe that the facts were so-and-so, in other words, what evidence, what grounds we have for our judgments that they were so-and-so. Or we may assert, as the basis presupposed in any such search, a *theory* of difference between "facts" and "judgments", and of the mode of immediate apprehension proper to facts. The difficulty, which ought, perhaps, to give us pause, is that it is next to impossible to illustrate this situation convincingly. Suppose we take a fact concerning which we are genuinely in ignorance or doubt. I mean a fact concerning which we have conflicting assertions without evidence sufficiently decisive to establish one and reject the other. Then we can only formulate the object of our search in some quite general formula to the effect that there must have been a definite event happening at a definite time and place, in one determinate way, and in no other. But this is, of course, not only itself a judgment, and as such different from the fact about which it asserts, but moreover our search is concluded not by confrontation with the fact itself but by our reaching the judgment which establishes itself against all competition, which is secure and stable, because all evidence supports and none contradicts it. This could be the case when a jury is trying to arrive at a verdict (*Essays*, p. 155). Or we may take a fact such as that "Charles I died on the scaffold", i.e., an established fact, a fact that we "know". But once more this fact is offered in the shape of an assertion. No doubt an assertion stable and secure, but still an assertion, and that is little help to a theory which insists on the essential distinction of fact and assertion. The judgment "Charles I died in his bed" will be false not because it conflicts with the fact "itself", but because it conflicts with this judgment that "Charles died on the scaffold", and with all the evidence on which it rests. But Mr. Russell may reply: what of the evidence? Does it not go back ultimately to the sense-data of eye-witnesses? Or even to the personal experiences of the chief actors? Of course it does, but along this line we get back only into the tangle of difficulties arising from the inability of the witnesses to apprehend the "fact" adequately. We may put this inability down to the incompleteness of their sense-data. After all, there is no reason why the *whole* fact should have been observed either by anyone or by all. Or we may put it down to their failure to translate data into true judgments. Or we may put it down to both these causes. The net result remains: we do not get the fact, the whole fact, and nothing but the fact that way, for the eye-witnesses and even the chief agents did not have that themselves. But the reply comes back: granted that no one was acquainted with the whole fact, just as it was, yet there must have been a whole fact for these fragments of it to have become data to these witnesses and agents. Certainly, but the fact so alleged is indistinguishable from the Idealist's Absolute, which like the Realist's fact, is both basis or presupposition and goal of knowledge, because it is present in all perceiving and judging throughout. To put it differently: the reasons for asserting facts in the way Mr. Russell asserts them are exactly the same which make the Idealist assert an Absolute, and they arise from reflection on the world as we "know" it through judgment, where all conflict, contradiction, doubt, uncertainty between and about the facts as we assert them to be none the less imply an ideal of stability the attainment of which coincides with the apprehension of the whole "fact". The position is not, in principle, altered if we take a fact with which only one person can be acquainted. Mr. Russell hypothetically instances Desdemona's love for Cassio as such a fact (*Problems*, p. 213). But it is as easy to mistake the character of a feeling as it is to mistake that of sense-data. If that is put down as a reflective judgment on feeling which may be wrong, what are we to make of the cases in which an experienced observer recognises love before the person himself is aware of the character of his feelings. But if one can be in love without knowing it, in what form does acquaintance come in, as distinct on the one side from having the feeling and on the other from reflecting on it? But whether or no to have a feeling and to be acquainted with the feeling one has are one and the same thing, it must again be insisted that acquaintance does not give us "complete and perfect" knowledge of our feelings in their full character.

And so the issue reduces itself to this: it is common ground that immediate experience precedes judgment and is its basis. It is common ground also that judgment, in stating a fact, carries with it, for reflexion, the recognition that reality in the full sense transcends and is beyond the judgment-form. It is disputed, however, that the immediate experience which precedes judgment gives, as we have it, the whole "fact" or that truth consists in correspondence with this fragmentary and spurious kind of fact. Again, whatever may be our decision on this first point, it is disputed that judgment is a manipulation of the given fact which moves as it were away from the fact and is "about" it. Rather it is a movement towards completing the given fragments and re-constituting the whole, though this effort of thought must itself be transcended in a higher immediacy. The fundamental problem is: do we get nearer to reality and fact by falling back on sense-data and feelings or by going on to the organised world into which these enter through judgment and of which they are then seen to be a fragmentary form of appearance.

Logic Notes for a Theory of Truth

(Starting from an examination of the " Correspondence " Theory)

1. IN view of the fact (N.B., Observe the use of "fact" here!) that a very commonly held theory makes "truth" consist in a certain relation, generally called "correspondence", between a "proposition" and a "fact", it is desirable to explore, first of all, the difference, if any, between fact and proposition. (Tacitly, in this formulation, the word "proposition" is limited to propositions which are not purely verbal, or analytic, i.e., it refers to propositions which claim to give information about facts.)

Note, here, (*a*) that two things can be said to "correspond" only if (i) they can be distinguished, i.e., there is some sort of difference between them; and (ii) if the difference is such that it can be the basis of, and is compatible with, the relation called "correspondence", i.e., if the difference is such that the *meaning* of the word "correspondence" can be predicated of the relation of the two terms. We must be able to say: A proposition as such differs from (or: is not) a fact as such, but, none the less, for every "true" proposition there is a fact to which it "corresponds".

Note, here, (*b*) that we have to be very careful about the way we speak of *false* propositions. The obvious verbal formula is to say that a false proposition is in conflict with facts: the fact (scil., the fact to which the proposition claims to correspond) is other than the proposition pictures it to be. This formula takes for granted, not only (i) that there is a difference between fact, as such, and proposition, as such, but also (ii) that between any false proposition and the fact to which it refers, there is a further difference, not identical with the former, which excludes the relation of "correspondence", and may, therefore, be called "non-correspondence", or, better, "conflict".

Note (*c*) that, in the grammar of this language, both true and false propositions, whilst differing as propositions generically from facts, must each of them have to some one

fact (however complex) a relation which can be characterised either as correspondence or as non-correspondence
(conflict).

Note (d) that the falsity of a proposition cannot, in this
language-system, be said to consist in non-reference of the
proposition to any fact whatsoever. We are apt to express the
falsity of a proposition by saying "there is no such fact", or
"there exists no such fact as the proposition asserts". But, the
emphasis here lies on "such": i.e., actually this form of speech
admits, and claims, implicitly, that there is a fact to which the
proposition refers, and that the proposition is called "false" on
the evidence of this fact, because this fact is *other than* ("not
such as") the proposition pictures it. If, *ex hypothesi*, there were
no fact at all to which the proposition referred, it could neither
correspond nor conflict with anything; i.e., it could be neither
true nor false.

2. If this theory is to work, or to be applicable at all, i.e., if
there are to be occasions when, in terms of the theory, we are
to be able to observe the correspondence or conflict, between
a given proposition and the fact to which it refers (for, no other
fact from among all the facts in the Universe would be relevant),
both the fact and the proposition must be severally given to,
or apprehended by, the thinker who is testing the proposition
by comparing it with the fact. If facts were, *ex hypothesi*,
completely inaccessible to any human mind, no propositions
dealing with facts could be tested, and either verified or falsified.
We would then be in the position which G. E. Moore once held
(and, perhaps, still holds), according to which we "know"
what truth is (or what the word "truth" means), viz., correspondence of propositions to facts, but can never actually compare any proposition with the relevant fact, so that we can
never decide whether any fact-proposition is true or false. Our
"knowledge" of truth, here, is knowledge of the definition, or
concept, in the form of a verbal, analytic proposition; no
instances of the concept being identifiable.

3. The only theory I am aware of which tries to meet all the
conditions here laid down for the applicability of the theory of
truth as correspondence of proposition to fact is that given by
Bertrand Russell in his *Problems of Philosophy*. It is instructive to
study if for this very reason.

Verbally he illustrates the difference between a fact and the proposition referring to it by using "this white wall" as the verbal rendering of the fact, and "this wall is white" as the verbal expression of the proposition which refers to, and is true by correspondence with, this fact.

Next, he takes the words rendering fact to be used by one perceiving the fact, i.e., treats the fact as an object of perception, and declares perception to be in two-term relation, viz., object perceived and mind perceiving (or: mental act of perceiving). Whether *all* facts are objects of perception, actual or possible, he does not here enquire.

Thirdly, he declares the proposition to be an object, not of perception, but of thought. It is—though this language is not used in the *Problems of Philosophy*—a logical construct, produced by analysing the object of perception and re-combining the elements yielded by the analysis in the new object which is the proposition.

Let us look back on this and take stock. There are two objects here: an object of perception (=fact) and an object of thought (=proposition). It is, apparently, assumed that the object of perception, though complex (for it can be analysed; and must be analysed to be transformed into the object of thought), is perceived, *globularly* as it were, as an *unanalysed whole* (although the verbal description of it—e.g., "this white wall"—clearly presupposes analysis, and indeed the very analysis embodied in the proposition "this wall is white").

Next, we must note, but need not make a difficulty of, the transformation of fact (=object of perception) into proposition (=object of thought) taking place whilst the perceiving of the fact continues: the demonstrative "this", in "this white wall" and "this wall is white", bears witness to the continuance of the perceptual situation. The thought-analysis and synthesis operate on the perceived object here and now present. *The fact enters into the proposition itself, but analysed and re-synthesised.*

The whole transformation is a case of identity in difference. The identity is to be found in the *same* elements constituting both fact and proposition: the difference is to be found in that the elements co-exist in the fact unanalysed, whereas in the proposition they are discriminated and re-combined.

Fundamentally, Russell repeats Bradley's doctrine that every

K

judgment of perception is at once analytic and synthetic. The "correspondence" which makes a proposition true consists in this sort of identity-in-difference relation to the fact.

The important question, of course, is whether *all* facts are objects of actual or possible perception and whether *all* propositions distinguish and put together again the elements of a complex perceptual whole. If there are other sorts of facts, and other sorts of propositions, does this concept of correspondence still apply? And, if so, how?

4. Russell seems to have felt that the simple example by which I have, so far, illustrated the theory, does not bring out the full force of it: the distinction between the two objects, fact and proposition, is a precarious and, as it were, vanishing one. Better, therefore, take an example illustrating the transformation of a fact into a thought-construct (=proposition) more strikingly. He chooses for this purpose the proposition believed by Othello that "Desdemona loves Cassio". If this is true, there must be a fact, viz., "D's love for C." He then proceeds to point out that the proposition and the fact contain the same three elements, viz., Desdemona, Cassio, and loving as the "relating" relation, in the direction from D. to C., which connects D. and C. The proposition differs from the fact only in this that the relating relation now is Othello's thinking which combines D.-loving-C. in this order—only, loving in this thought-construct is now one of the *relata*, no longer the relating relation.

It is not without significance that Russell here takes an example, not from actual life and experience, but from a work of fiction. Thereby, we as readers know the "fact" (sc. the fact within the total context of the fictitious tale) through the propositions which the poet gives us: we do not "perceive" it for ourselves. We are told in the play that there is no such fact as "D.-loving-C.", and that Othello believes a false proposition when he believes "that D. loves C.". But, if it were a true proposition, how would it differ from the fact by correspondence to which it is true? Not merely by the fact being an unanalysed whole whereas the proposition is that same whole analysed and re-synthesised, but by a subtle change in that the relating relation of the fact-whole becomes an additional relation (term) in the whole which thinking, as relating relation, constructs out of the elements of the original whole. (This doctrine of thinking as the relating relation in the construction of a proposition is, of course, in principle equivalent to Kant's synthesis, but with the omission of Kant's doctrine of categories.)

Let us pass by the awkward question, how in actual life we perceive, or otherwise apprehend, wholes of this sort, so as to have a factual basis for our propositions. In any case, once more, correspondence turns out to be a species of identity-in-difference. Once more the globular object: elements in a certain order (=fact) becomes the articulated object (or thought-construct): same elements in same order, but now distinguished from each other and from the combining relation, and simultaneously affirmed as actually existing in just this relation (=proposition).

5. Under the pressure of criticisms from Wittgenstein, Russell is said to have abandoned this theory: not having read his latest book, on *Meaning and Truth*, I do not know what theory he there expounds. Whatever it may be, I would still maintain that the theory above examined, regardless of its author's abandonment of it, is the only theory which attempts to fulfil the conditions which a workable (applicable) theory of truth as correspondence between proposition and fact must satisfy. Its defect is that it is plausible only for the field of perceptual propositions: it cannot be generalised for other facts than objects of sense-perception, and other sorts of propositions (excluding purely verbal propositions). And, even in this field, where its applicability is, *prima facie*, most plausible, it is open to criticism: is it true that all perceiving is globular, i.e., non-analytic? (N.B., If the proposition contained in *this* question is true, how do we apprehend the fact by correspondence to which it is true?) Is it true of the *selective* perceiving of the scientific observer? Or merely of ordinary intelligent perceiving in everyday life—the perceiving which is one with correctly recognising and identifying the objects perceived; with "knowing what one perceives"?

A sophisticated student of philosophy will note at once that in this last question it has been assumed (as the "white wall" example assumed) that the objects of perception are physical bodies. But, what if we distinguish in such an "object" what is pure sense-datum from what is interpretation or construction? What if we limit the "objects" of perception to bare sense-data? What unanalysed whole is then left? To what can the propositional construct correspond? How can this reduction down to sense-data be applied to the "D.-loves-C." example? In fact, is Russell's own theory of physical bodies being logical constructs reconcilable with the correspondence theory, as stated above?

Again, if we begin with a proposition and seek to verify it by perceptual evidence: must not the verifying fact (=object perceived) be perceived as having the elements thought of in this proposition, and these elements in the order, or relation, in which they are thought of? How can non-analytic perceiving of a complex fact verify the analytic-synthetic thought-construct corresponding to that fact?

6. To sum up: We have found that "correspondence", as a working principle for testing the truth of propositions, turns out to be a case of identity-in-difference; and that when we apply and use the principle, we do not so much compare two objects, respectively, "fact" and "proposition", but one object apprehended in two different ways, which ways may succeed each other in one of two orders, viz., (a) apprehension of fact first, followed by construction and assertion of proposition, or (b) starting with the proposition, as the meaning of an appropriate sentence, we seek to verify it by an appeal to fact, i.e., we seek to give ourselves a perceptual experience in the object of which we can claim that meaning to be realised and embodied. If we call these two orders, respectively, the "order of discovery" and the "order of verification", then the former illustrates identity-in-difference in the transformation of the unanalysed "fact"-whole into analysed and re-integrated "proposition"-whole, whilst the latter illustrates the same principle in the assertion that the object of perception has the character and structure of the proposition to be verified.

A Note on Philosophy and Language

THERE are few philosophers who have not, at one time or another, felt hampered by the language which they had at their disposal. Yet the philosopher's complaint that the resources of current speech are often inadequate for the thoughts which he is struggling to express is matched by the complaint of his public that thoughts and matters of common and indeed fundamental, human concern should not be hidden behind an array of unintelligible technical terms. A man of science may be as technical as he likes. To him is readily granted the right of speaking as an expert to experts in a dialect which only the initiated can understand. But of the philosopher it is expected that he speak the language, if not of the market-place, yet at least of great literature—a language which at least every educated man can understand. He is warned—indeed he warns himself—not to mistake obscurity for profundity, or technicality for truth. It has become as axiomatic that when the language is not clear the thought cannot be clear either, as it has become fashionable in many quarters to abuse the great German philosophers, a Kant, a Fichte, a Hegel, for their mystifying style, with the innuendo in the criticism that what the critic cannot understand is nothing but an inanity dressed up in solemn terminology. Yet, allowing that a great thinker need not be a bad writer, it must be clear that the intelligibility of language depends not merely on the logical clearness of the meaning which the thinker is trying to express, but also on the reader's power of grasping the meaning. Unless we are prepared to deny that new meanings may be discovered by philosophical reflection, we can hardly deny either that the resources of existing speech may prove inadequate, or that the apprehension of an unfamiliar meaning however expressed, may require much training and effort on the reader's part. When language has to be adapted to new uses, the choice lies between inventing new terms—perhaps a whole new language, like the symbolic language of the logisticians—which leads to technicality or else using current terms in new senses which tends towards confusion and ambiguity. The difficulty is least where the new meaning is in the main but an intensification and sytematisation of meanings with which every thoughtful reader is familiar. Thus the speech of daily life, especially when re-enforced by that of great literature, suffices commonly to express the philosopher's deeper insight into the matters of morality and religion. Yet even here a limit is reached sooner or later. We all know arguments in which, for example, the word "God" survives with but little, if anything, of its current meaning. However, these are not the most troublesome cases. The linguistic handicap is felt most acutely when familiar meanings have to be examined from unfamiliar points of view. It is then that current terms come to be used in forced and artful senses, and that language has to be twisted and tortured to get the effect desired. Paradoxically enough, the most unfamiliar approach to a familiar meaning is provided by the simple demand to state to ourselves clearly what that meaning actually is. We are in the habit of assuming that because we use a term every day of our lives therefore we "know" what it means. But as Socrates showed more than 2500 years ago, familiarity with a thing may go hand in hand with that ignorance of it which leaves one helpless before the demand for a reasoned and logically tenable account of what it really is. "Account"—but that is a call for more words! We are asked to "define what we mean", and we become voluble with a further flow of language. But how is the meaning of one word "made clear" by the piling of words on words? The new words can be effective only by their meanings, but what if we are challenged to give an account, in turn, of their meanings, and so on in infinitum? Is there any escape from the mesh of language? Is it not a common experience that when we are put to it to say what exactly we mean by a word, we are at a loss for words? We feel as if a bluff had been called. Or rather, we were not aware that we had been bluffing and with amazement we find ourselves empty-handed. In much philosophical analysis we are engaged in calling our own bluffs, or at least in taking careful stock what exactly the hands which experience deals to us amount to, before we play them for more than they are worth.

In the last resort there is only one way of such stock-taking.

This is not the way of definition, though many present-day philosophers show a pathetic faith in the value of definition. No definition, we may bluntly say, can take the place of insight. As a formula, composed of further words, it must itself be understood in order to be effective. This presupposes that the meaning of its words are understood, and thus but pushes the problem a stage further back. It is only by taking it for granted that the meaning of the defining words is understood that we can distinguish between a "verbal" and a "real" definition, between an agreement that, within a given context, a certain set of words (or other symbols) is to be always equivalent to, and therefore capable of substitution for, some other words or symbols, and a genuine insight into what the word or symbol means, i.e., stands for. A verbal definition makes symbols stand for one another. A real definition interprets one meaning by others. But even such interpretation presupposes that the meaning which is used to interpret another is *known*, and the problem to which the argument has led us is precisely this—how a meaning is apprehended or, better still, *realised*.

The way, then, which we are seeking is the way of realisation what a word, or other symbol, means. It is the way of becoming acquainted with what the traditional logic calls "indefinables". Only we shall find reason to extend the range of the indefinable considerably beyond what the traditional logic has customarily recognised as such. If we do not know what "green" means, the only way to learn is to be *shown*. We must have an instance of it pointed out to us. Something in the field of what we experience must be indicated or somehow singled out as that which the word "green" means. One point here deserves special notice. We are made acquainted with meaning of "green" by having our attention directed to *this*—this specific something which here and now by its characteristic quality differentiates itself from that and that and that, i.e., from other items in the field of present experience. And, further, *this* (not yet, so far as our experiment has gone, known to be an instance of a "sort" or "kind") both *is there*, i.e., exists, has being and *is such*, i.e., has quality. If we may here borrow technical language from a much more sophisticated level of analysis, we can distinguish *that* it is, and *what* it is, shortly its "that" and its "what", its "existence" and its "quality". And the symbol or word, we note, means both these aspects. It *denotes* "this", it *connotes* "such". Or, again in technical language, it denotes the "particular", it connotes the "universal". But we must note that particular and universal are given together, as a "this-such" and that we become acquainted with them together. It is only by subsequent reflection on further experiences of greens that we learn to distinguish "this (particular) green (thing)" from the "greenness" (of this and other green things), i.e., learn that "this" is an instance of a kind, a member of a class.

For all the technicality involved in stating it—and the experiment may serve as an example incidentally of how one becomes acquainted with the meanings which technical terms are needed to fix and express—this has been a simple case for illustrating what is meant by "realising" the meaning of a word. Meanings in the field of sense-data are among the easiest to realise for normal human beings, though a person congenitally blind is cut off from realising the meanings of any term expressing colour or an aspect of colour, just as a person congenitally deaf can never "know", in the way of acquaintance by realisation, what a sound is like. Sense-data are vivid, impressive, easily distinguishable, relatively simple; and our familiarity with them and exploration of them goes back to the very beginnings of our knowledge of anything whatever. But when we come to meanings which are complex, and which are not thus realisable in sensuous form, the task of realisation becomes much more formidable. Attention to a characteristic item in the tissue of sense-data no longer suffices. We need, by all the resources of reflection and analysis, to train ourselves to perceive—if not by the eye of the body, then by the eye of the soul (let the metaphor pass)—characteristic unities as wholes: to realise them, to explore them, to make ourselves thoroughly acquainted with them, by a process of which the reality cannot be doubted, and to which it matters little whether we call it "thought" or "intuition". Now here language, skilfully used, may render a new service, acquire a new power. It is necessary as an instrument for directing our attention, for pointing out the thing and the character to be seen (or thought). Often much argument is needed for this sort of pointing *out*, where in the sphere of sense-data a direct pointing *at* suffices. The main function of language as a vehicle of philosophical analysis is to put oneself and others in position to *see*: to help us realise a new meaning. There is one last observation which must be made to complete this preparatory argument. To realise a meaning is to understand a *theory*, and to understand it in a way which allows the theory to be appreciated in respect of its truth or falsity. To ask, in philosophy, for the meaning of a word is to ask for a theory of what the thing, or kind of thing, is to which the word refers. Theory, in short, deals with universals, but being very literally a way of seeing, it requires, if it is not to become "abstract", to retain that immediate contact with the universal concretely embodied in the particular which we have proposed to call "realisation".

There is no subject to which these general observations apply more neatly than the one in which we are now about to do a little exploring—the subject of the *self*. . . .

A Note on the Meanings of "Mind"

1. NO student of modern philosophy needs to have pointed out to him the extent to which our disagreements and difficulties are due to the different meanings given to the term "mind", and to certain other terms, like "consciousness" and "experience", which are commonly used as synonyms for "mind". The same remark applies to the adjectives, "mental", "conscious", "psychical", and "subjective". In theory of knowledge and metaphysics, Idealists dispute with Realists about the nature and function of mind. In psychology, the adherents of introspection confront the behaviourists, and the reality of group-minds is challenged by those who admit only individual minds. The theories of Freud, Jung, and other psycho-analysts introduce a further complication in the large part they assign to the "unconscious". Minor differences and nuances might be distinguished within each school or tendency, but an exhaustive catalogue is no part of my argument. The brief survey above will suffice to remind us all how widespread the trouble is.

2. What are we going to do about it? The purpose of this note is to suggest, not a standard theory and terminology of mind which shall hereafter be used in every context and for every purpose, but a method of studying these differences and minimising their conflicts without, for the present at least, abolishing any of them. For myself, I am doubtful whether it is possible or profitable to define or construct *the* one and all-sufficing meaning of "mind". At any rate, this note is devoted to the humbler task of pointing out a method by which we may to some extent escape from the disturbing ambiguities and barren disagreements at present besetting philosophy.

3. The suggestion I have to make is based on observation of a fact which needs only to have attention drawn to it, in order to be, as I believe, acknowledged by every student whose reading has at all sampled the different branches of present-day philosophy. Open any philosophical or psychological text and you find yourself, as soon as the author gets to grips with his subject,

introduced to what is both a point of view and a terminology. There may or may not be explicit "definition"—the main point is that the author introduces his readers to what is nothing other than a *technical dialect* in terms of which he is going to express the rest of his argument. Take, e.g., a few sentences from the two opening paragraphs of Berkeley's *Principles of Human Knowledge* :—

> "It is evident to anyone who takes a survey of the *objects of human knowledge*, that they are either *ideas* actually imprinted on the senses; or else such as are perceived by attending to the passions and operations of the mind . . . And as several of these are observed to accompany each other, they come to be marked by one name, and so to be reputed as one *thing* . . . But, besides all that endless variety of ideas or objects of knowledge, there is likewise Something which knows or perceives them. . . . This perceiving active being is what I call, *mind, spirit, soul,* or *myself.* (Para. i, 2. Berkeley's italics.)

This is a particularly clear example, but something analogous will be found in every treatise whatever its subject. It will be noted that it is far from "evident" that all objects of human knowledge are "ideas", or, rather, it is evident only to those who have already through the study of Locke and Descartes habituated themselves to the use of that language. At this point, Berkeley's language is determined by his philosophical scholarship ; he talks the dialect of a school and tradition. When, on the other hand, he goes on to the distinction between ideas and the "Something which perceives" we may suppose him to be inviting us to notice a distinction analogous to that which Professor Alexander and other Realists offer us as an "intuition", viz., the distinction between the act of perceiving and the object of that act, the only difference is that Berkeley passes from the act at once to the agent, the "active being" who "exercises diverse operations, as willing, imagining, remembering" (l.c., para. 2)—a transition too metaphysical for the taste of many Realists.

But whether the terms are chosen from everyday parlance, and in harmony with its usage, to express the findings of an intuition or direct inspection of the facts, or whether they are already technical and loaded with the associations of previous theory—in any case, every great thinker makes and imposes on his readers his own distinctive language. That language will have its characteristic vocabulary for the terms, relations, activities, events, etc., with which the thinker's theory is concerned. As the argument progresses, the vocabulary will be expanded by the addition of fresh terms. Good examples of this may be found in the introduction of fresh terms at the opening of each of the five books of Spinoza's *Ethics*, or, in a less systematic way, throughout the progress of Kant's three *Critiques*. It is, however, very important to notice that the bulk of a philosopher's vocabulary is not technical at all, but composed of the language in which we express our everyday experiences, this language being used in the ordinary non-technical way. The whole "effect", so to speak, of philosophical argument lies just in this interpenetration of ordinary and technical language, in the transformation of the meanings of ordinary life into the meanings of philosophical theory. Thus Berkeley translates "houses, mountains, rivers" into "things perceived by sense", and thence into "our own sensations or ideas", of which it can finally be said that they "cannot exist" "unperceived" or "without a mind". Thus Kant translates every physical thing, *qua* object of sense-perception, into the product of a synthetic activity of which the factors are sense-data, schemata of the imagination, and categories. Thus Professor Alexander treats even "images" as "non-mental" and "physical", because they are objects "contemplated", not acts "enjoyed". It makes, in introspective psychology, all the difference in the world whether, at the outset, we elect to express ourselves in the language of agent and activity, and talk, as James Ward does in his *Psychological Principles*, of an "experient" or "self" who perceives, thinks, feels, wills, or whether with William James in his *Principles of Psychology*, we talk the language of the "stream of consciousness" in which feelings, thoughts, and volitions occur as "processes" or "events". Other languages, now more or less out of fashion, have "conscious state" or "mental faculty" for their key-words. The famous dispute between F. H. Bradley and James Ward about "mental activity" was, from this point of view, nothing but a dispute between men using different dialects. It was, very literally, a dispute about words. Either dialect, consistently used, had its merits. But nothing except confusion resulted from Bradley's attempt to forbid Ward the use of the term "activity" because

there was no room for it in Bradley's own psychological vocabulary. An even extremer case is found in the attitude of certain
behaviourists, like John Watson, formerly of Johns Hopkins
University, Baltimore, towards introspective psychologists
generally. According to Watson the programme of Behaviourism is, in effect, to substitute for the language of Psychology
the language of Physiology, and ultimately of Physics and
Chemistry. He would eliminate all the terms which have a
meaning in the context of introspection and talk only the language appropriate to an external observer. He hopes that the
behaviour-language will supersede the mind-language as the
language of astronomy has superseded that of astrology, and
the language of chemistry that of alchemy.

4. But enough of examples, which anyone can multiply *ad
libitum* for himself. The starting-point, then, of the method
which I suggest, is the frank recognition that we are, as a
matter of fact, confronted by a *variety of philosophical languages*,
and that the first duty of a student of philosophy is to learn
these languages—learn them, that is as much as a child learns
his mother-tongue, viz., learning the words and the meanings
together. As a rule, as we all know to our cost, this needs a lot
of practice, for most of the time we misunderstand one another
simply because we are unfamiliar with each other's language.
With each philosophical language, as we practise it, we shall
acquire the characteristic point of view or "set" (Einstellung)
which that language is fashioned to express. And more, we do
not really master the meanings of any of the terms of a philosophical language except by mastering the whole language in
application, using it as its author uses it. For no term in a
philosophical language has a meaning in isolation. Its characteristic meaning depends on the *context* in which it is used. This
is to say, it depends partly on the way in which a technical
term is applied to the non-technical terms in the philosopher's
vocabulary, and partly it depends on the propositions or
sentences in which technical terms are related to, or predicated
of, each other. Each philosophical language has, as it were, its
vocabulary and its syntax, but these, in abstraction, do not
carry us far : we get the full meaning only through the use and
application of it, i.e., through experiencing (thinking out for
ourselves) the transformation of ordinary meanings by technical

meanings. Just what "mind" means in the mouths, respectively, of a Realist or an Idealist can be learnt only by practising the use of the Realistic and Idealistic languages. Such practising need not commit us to believing or accepting as true, but it is essential to understanding. In this sense, Professor Alexander is quite right in saying that the main function of the use of words in argument is to bring the hearer or reader to the point where he will see a thing as the author sees it.

The student who practises a philosophical language will, of course, "think for himself", that is, he will experiment with the language and explore. He may apply it in fields to which its author did not apply it, and thus discover new ranges of power in it. Or he may discover in his experimenting that there are regions of facts which lend themselves at best but awkwardly to expression in that language. This appears to have been, to some extent, the experience of Professor John Laird, in his *Study of Realism*. Ambiguities arise when the same *word* belongs to the vocabulary of two or more philosophical languages. For, by the principle of context, just stated, it will have a different meaning in each of these languages. Its connotation will certainly be more or less different and its denotation may be so, too. For the range of application may differ in languages which have the word, as sound symbol, in common.

I repeat, then: there are different philosophical languages, which have to be learnt by practice and without, in this note, raising the question which language is better or truer than the rest. Moreover, these languages have to be kept strictly apart, for nothing but confusion results if the identity of sound symbol in both languages occasions an intermingling of them, or if a problem stated in one language and legitimate in terms of it is disputed or answered in terms of another.

PART II
REPRINTS OF PUBLISHED ARTICLES

Image, Idea and Meaning

WE are all familiar with the terms "image", "idea" and "meaning" from their prominence in psychological and philosophical discussions. And one would naturally expect that their technical use had resulted in investing these terms with a definite sense and in determining accurately their relations to each other. Personally, I must confess, that I have found the very reverse of this to be true. I have found not only that different writers use these terms in very different senses, but—what is more perplexing—I cannot help thinking that the same writer often employs them in different senses. And thus from a good deal of philosophical reading I have carried away the general impression that much confusion prevails in the use of these terms—a confusion of which the users themselves seem for the most part to be blissfully unaware. No doubt, it is but fair to acknowledge that after all the confusion may be due to myself, and to my failure to understand what to others is plain. However that may be, I can but give voice to my trouble, in the hope that if the fault should be mine, it may be pointed out to me. But if, as I suspect, others have been perplexed as I have been, they may welcome an attempt to point out the root of the confusion, and to insist on some distinctions which ought never to have been neglected.

To prevent a misunderstanding of my purpose, I would have the reader bear in mind that I am concerned with the sense which the terms image, idea and meaning bear in Psychology and Logic, but that I am not concerned with more ultimate problems of Epistemology or of Metaphysics. I shall, therefore, without scruple use the language of ordinary Dualism and speak e.g., of experience and reality as distinct, of objects as "independent" of our ideas about them, of past and future as "real" though we only deal with them through the medium of present ideas, and so forth. In short, I shall hold myself free to speak dogmatically of many matters which, from another point of view, would legitimately be treated as problems.

A.

There is a well-known theory which distinguishes the image as psychological idea from the meaning as logical idea. Its usual statement is: In every idea we can distinguish three aspects—(1) existence, (2) content, (3) meaning or significance. In other words, (1) the idea exists, i.e. it occurs as a psychical fact within the conscious experience of an individual mind. (2) The idea has a certain character or content which distinguishes it from other ideas and other modes of consciousness, along with which it may happen to occur. (3) The idea has a certain meaning, i.e., it is an idea of something, it refers to some object or aspect in the real world. The first two aspects of the idea are psychological, the last is logical. Psychology is concerned with the occurrence and the character of an idea regarded purely as a mental event in an individual mind, and its various relations to other events in the same mind. Logic, on the other hand, is concerned with the idea in so far as it has a meaning and is referred to reality, i.e., in so far as it is used as a "sign" for something other than itself. In thinking, our attention and interest are wholly centred in the meaning of our ideas, not in the ideas themselves as psychical occurrences. We are concerned with the objects, not with the "signs" which represent the objects "in our heads". As a rule, we are more or less unaware even of the existence and character of these signs, and it requires a special effort of introspection to bring them before consciousness. But in thus making objects of these mental signs, we must, it seems, employ another set of mental signs, and so on *in infinitum*. In short, in Logic we have to do with what may be called objective thinking, i.e., thought in its reference to objects, thought as a medium of knowledge. In Psychology, we study thought in abstraction from this objective reference as a mere process in an individual consciousness. Psychologically the idea is an image, logically it is a meaning. Thus in thinking of a horse, I must distinguish on the one hand a psychical image, i.e., a present modification of my consciousness consisting in a more or less vivid and complete "revival" of the visual perception of a horse, and on the other hand, the horse itself, as a real creature in the real world, which consumes so much food a day, which I can ride, for which I have paid much money, and which will finally be made up into sausages for the East-End. In other words, I think of the real horse by means of my horse-image.

All this seems beautifully clear. And I have spent so much time over an elaborate statement of a theory with which most students of philosophy will be familiar because it is the most consistent of which I am aware, and will therefore supply the best possible basis for the criticisms which I have to make.

I must say at once, that there is not a single point in the above theory which is satisfactory, or can be accepted as it stands. Indeed, the difficulties by which it is beset and the problems which it raises are so numerous that the critic is almost embarrassed to know where to begin.

In the first place, we must discuss the relation of the image to the meaning as represented by the theory. I have spoken above as if "meaning" and "object" were interchangeable terms. That, no doubt, would be the simplest assumption. The image, in that case, would be the mental event "in my head", and the meaning would be the "real object". I may illustrate this by a quotation: "A lion is the symbol of courage, and a fox of cunning, but it would be impossible to say that the idea of a fox (=fox-image) stands for cunning directly. We mean *by it first the animal called a fox*, and we then use this meaning to stand as the sign for one quality of the fox".[1] The words which I have italicised plainly imply a distinction between the psychical image and the real animal which we mean by means of the image. This, of course, suggests a question as to the nature of this link between image and object, and as to its recognition by the mind. The explanation offered, if I understand it right, is that *part of the content of the image*, set apart and fixed by the mind, *is itself the meaning*. Such at least appears to be the sense of the following continuation of the above quotation: "Just as the image or presentation of a fox is *taken by us in one part of its content*, and referred away to another subject, so this meaning

[1] Bradley, *Logic*, p. 5. I wish it to be understood that I am quoting this and other passages merely as illustrations. I am not to be taken as criticising Mr. Bradley. For Mr. Bradley, by refusing to have his *Logic* republished, has indicated that he has in important respects changed his views. And the theory which I am criticising therefore may no longer represent what he really holds. It is for me simply "a" view which happens to be found in one of Mr. Bradley's books; but it is not Mr. Bradley's view. I should like to refer the reader in this connection to Mr. Bradley's footnote in the last number of *Mind* (N.S., 60, p. 446), which I have seen since writing the above.

itself suffers further mutilation : one *part of its content is fixed by the mind* and referred further on to a second subject, viz., the quality in general, wherever found". And again, "that connexion of attributes we recognise as horse, is one part of the content of the unique horse-image, and *this fragmentary part of the psychical event is all that in Logic we know of or care for*".[1] The words in italics, if taken literally, are so astounding that one would fain believe them to be a mere slip. Granted even, that in judgments about a horse we make use of a more or less complete horse-image (which is by no means the case), it is surely nonsense to say that merely a fragment of an image, itself fragmentary, is used as meaning. On the contrary, it would be truer to say, that our meaning is far *fuller* than anything contained in the image. But one can see how the mistake arose. An image usually contains much that is irrelevant, and not, therefore, "used as meaning". Thus, if we think of death by means of an image of a "withered flower",[2] it is clear that we do not wish to ascribe to death *all* the characteristics of the dead flower, but only its deadness. And this is said to be (*a*) singled out and "fixed on" by the mind and (*b*) "referred away to another subject". These seem to be the two stages of the mysterious process of meaning one thing by means of another. But I doubt whether this gets us any further. Suppose I want to think of the colour "red". I may have an image of a circular red patch, or a red flower, or a drop of blood. But, of course, I do not mean these images as wholes, I mean merely the quality of red in them. That I "fix on". But how does that help me? The redness of the image is not the colour red-as-such which I mean. It is a particular quality of a particular image. No amount of analysis of the image, or of fixing one's mind on the redness of the image, will make that redness universal. It is, and remains, the redness of that image, and the more we fix on it, the more we succeed merely in meaning that particular red, and not redness as such which we want to mean. The meaning lies beyond the image, and no operation on the image will get us to the meaning. And, in any case, it is unintelligible how this particular element of a particular image should lose its particularity by being "referred away to another subject". Berkeley and Hume were no doubt mistaken when they

Bradley, *Logic*, p. 6. Italics mine.   [2] *Ibid.*, p. 9.

attempted to define a universal as a "particular idea with a general signification". But I fail to see that our metaphors about "fixing on" part of an image and "referring it away to another subject" are any more successful. There is no way of deriving a universal meaning from what, as a mental occurrence, must always be particular. And there are other difficulties. According to the theory I can think of a horse as actually seen with the bodily eye only by means of an image of the horse. But the image manifestly lacks many of the qualities of sense-perception. Yet I succeed in meaning by the image not the horse as imaged but the horse as seen.[1]

But there is no need to go into details. The theory derives such plausibility as it possesses from the fact that it considers only that class of mental "signs" which is composed of images in the strict psychological sense of the word, i.e. "revivals" of visual, tactual, auditory sense-perceptions. Except for this arbitrary restriction, the identity (partial or total) of content in sign and thing signified could not be maintained. Yet it is made the corner-stone of the theory, when the mind is said to "fix on" part of the content of the image and refer to it another subject; or to put it in plainer language, when the content is treated not as a qualification of the image but as a qualification of the real object which we "mean". We have nothing to qualify reality with except the contents of our minds, our imagery, which we "divorce" and "cut loose" from its existence in the mind so as to weave a garment for reality out of it. That this identity of content, even so far as it exists, is wholly insufficient for the purposes of the theory, I have shown above. Now I shall have to mention a far more serious difficulty. How, on this theory, are we to explain the thought of all those persons who are defective in imagery, and think mainly with the help of words? And indeed, how are we to deal with language, with all those cases in which words are used as "signs" for meanings? We can surely not say that the content of the word (or verbal image) is "fixed on" and "referred away to another subject". As Professor Stout[2] says: "It is, of course, sheer nonsense to say

---

[1] For further examples and a fuller criticism of the theory that there must be identity of content between the psychological and the logical idea I may refer to an extremely interesting article by Prof. Stout on "Mr. Bradley's Theory of Judgment" in *Proceedings of the Arist. Soc.*, N.S., iii., 1902-3, pp. 8-13.

[2] *Loc. cit.*, p. 12.

that the specific nature of what we think of, when we thus think in words, is constituted by partial features of the content of the words themselves considered as auditory-motor or visual-motor complexes". And, finally, what imagery can be suitably suggested for highly abstract terms, such as "unity", "difference", "spontaneity", "reciprocity", etc.? For such meanings words are the only signs, but in what sense the content of the word and the content of the sign can be said to be identical, it is impossible to see.[1]

However, even if I assume all these difficulties not to exist, I am unable to convince myself that the theory gives a true account of what happens when we think. And as the conclusion to which I have come on this point differs somewhat from those usually accepted, I must be permitted to set it forth at greater length. In the first place, an idea or image which is not an idea or image *of* something, is not, even psychologically, an idea at all. Indeed, I should be prepared to uphold the paradox that there is no idea, or combination of ideas, which is wholly meaningless. An idea always carries with it a relation to something other than itself. Thus, I should say, even "square circle" is not meaningless. Each element of the complex has its own definite meaning. And though they refuse to join into a harmonious whole of meaning, as e.g., "equilateral" and "triangle" do, the whole signified by square circle is a whole characterised by extreme inner conflict of its elements, and this conflict, this refusal of the elements to be joined, is an experience as distinct and definite in its way as the experience of the blending of "equilateral" and "triangle". And hence the words "square circle" cannot be called meaningless, as if the words conveyed nothing beyond their own sound, and left the mind a sheer blank but for their own presence.[2] There is then, even for

---

[1] James, *Principles of Psych.*, i., p. 417 ff., also criticises the view that "ideas, in order to know, must be cast in the exact likeness of whatever things they know".

[2] The nearest approach to a blank would be constituted, I suppose, by a string of "meaningless" syllables, e.g., by a word from a foreign language, of the meaning of which we are wholly ignorant. But even here, there is observable a continual *tendency* of the mind to pass beyond the mere word, to some other content which might be its meaning, though this attempt is continually baffled, and the mind driven back on the mere sound. By the way, would a "pure" sensation, if such a thing existed, be a sensation of anything? Strictly speaking such a sensation would be, e.g., a blue sensation but not a sensation of blue. The objective reference presupposes an act of distinction, turning the content of the sensation into its "object".

psychology, no idea or image which does not carry with it a meaning. Our consciousness of the idea involves our consciousness (more or less explicitly) of its meaning, and the ideas with which Psychology deals are not mere signs without signification. In other words, ideas are understood, and, as I have already mentioned, in ordinary thinking our attention is not directed always or even mainly to the ideas, but primarily to their meanings. And it is only when we fail to understand, that the idea itself (the word or image) becomes prominent in consciousness. In short, no idea is a "mere" idea, the cognitive function, i.e., the relation to something which it means, is essential to its very being.[1]

Both the idea and its meaning, then, must be present to consciousness. Or, perhaps, it would be more accurate to say that they form together a complex psychical whole, a "psychosis" of which the different elements, however, enjoy different degrees of prominence in consciousness, or draw upon themselves different amounts of attention. To use the convenient phraseology of Professor Lipps, the whole is "perceived", but only some parts of it are "apperceived", or as Mr. Bradley would say, "fixed on". Normally we apperceive merely the meaning, and the image or sign remains in the background, in the shade, as it were. But, of course, we can make the image or sign the special object of attention; we can "apperceive" it, and correspondingly the meaning falls into the background. But it does not disappear, it remains in consciousness. Even when the psychologist studies the character and behaviour of his own images he is always conscious that they are images of such and such an object. It is their image *of* a breakfast table which Professor James' pupils describe.[2] Thus the distinction between image and meaning would seem to be mainly one of the emphasis with which attention is directed now to one element, and again to another, of a complex psychic whole. And it is not at all essential that there should be, as in the case of the present example, and indeed of all images, a relative identity of content between image and object. Complex wholes of sign and meaning may be formed without any such

---

[1] I shall amplify this statement lower down, more particularly with reference to the "ideas" of imaginary objects and their meanings.
[2] *Principles of Psych.*, ii., pp. 56-7.

identity whatever, as the use of words clearly shows. The sound of a word, and the sensations of throat-, lip-, tongue-movements in pronouncing it, have no identity of content with the object meant, and yet the word and its meaning can form a psychic whole, in which either the meaning or the word can be more prominently "apperceived".

And here I must be permitted a short digression. Psychologists have not, I think, sufficiently observed that the complex of word-meaning is *not formed by mere association*. The understanding of a word, i.e., the use of the word as a "sign" for its meaning, is something altogether different from the associative passage of the mind from one to the other, even if such passage should be regular and uniform. This is beautifully illustrated by the account of the way in which Helen Keller learned to understand that words (in the manual alphabet of the blind) have a meaning, and to use these word-signs to convey her own meaning. Of course, she used signs, such as gestures and screams long before she learned to speak. And, as she was thus familiar with signs, it is the more curious that for a long time after she had learned to imitate various word-signs and to associate them with the right objects, she did not understand that these signs *meant* the objects. Miss Keller's teacher, Miss Sullivan, used to spell into her hand the names of things which she might be handling at the time, succeeding thereby in forming associations, but not succeeding at first in producing understanding. Thus she tells[1] how on one day she spelt "c-a-k-e" and then gave the child a piece to eat. On the next day, when the child was busy over a sewing-card, she began spelling "c-a-r-d", but when she had got to "c-a" the child impetuously pulled the teacher's dress and pointed downstairs, obviously wanting her to fetch some cake. The "c-a" revived the "cake" of the previous day, and that led to a demand for the article. But the process was purely one of association, and there was no understanding that "c-a-k-e" *meant* cake. This is shown clearly by the following quotations from Miss Sullivan's letters: "Helen has learned several nouns this week. 'M-u-g' and 'm-i-l-k' have given her more trouble than other words. When she spells 'milk' she points to the mug, and when she spells 'mug' she makes the sign for pouring or drinking. . . . She has no idea yet

[1] *Helen Keller, The Story of My Life*, p. 305 ff.

that everything has a name".[1] And again we get this glimpse of a daily lesson: "I gave her an object, and she spelled the name . . . and made the sign for cake (it did not occur to her to spell the word)".[2] What is characteristic is that she uses *her own* signs to convey her meanings, and not the word-signs which she has learned to associate with certain objects. The thing might suggest the word, and the word the thing, but there is no consciousness that the one means the other. This is Helen Keller's own account of how she discovered that words have meanings:[3] "Some one was drawing water and my teacher placed my hand under the spout. As the cool stream gushed over one hand she spelled into the other the word *water*, first slowly, then rapidly. I stood still, my whole attention fixed upon the motions of her fingers. Suddenly I felt a misty consciousness as of something forgotten—a thrill of returning thought, and somehow the mystery of language was revealed to me. I knew then that 'w-a-t-e-r' meant the wonderful cool something that was flowing over my hand". This occurred a considerable time after she had learned to spell the names of certain objects, and even to connect the right names with the right objects. The understanding of the meaning of a sign, therefore, implies more than an association between two distinct mental elements; the elements must be fused into a new psychic whole, in which they are simultaneously present though with different degrees of prominence.

This view of sign and meaning as forming a psychic whole enables us to dispose of a difficulty which was a great puzzle to an older generation of psychologists. Turning round upon their own minds to discover what was really present there when they thought of anything, they were much astonished to find there merely signs, and *nothing beyond the signs*. All trace of the meaning, the object, seemed to have vanished. More particularly was this the case where the signs consisted of words. Images seemed at least to carry with them something of the substance of their objects, however attenuated and shadowy, but words apparently brought before the mind nothing but their own sound and look, and if you asked for their meaning,

---

[1] *Ibid.*, p. 312.
[2] *Ibid.*, p. 315. The cake was the child's reward for obedience.
[3] *Ibid.*, p. 23.

other words were all that you could find. Did you think of "love"
—what were you conscious of except the sound of the word, or
perchance the words of some definition that might occur to
you? Where was the thing itself and how were you conscious of
that?

The mistake which Hobbes and Hume and Dugald Stewart
and many others made in putting the question in this way,
was that they broke up the psychic whole of sign and meaning,
and fixing their attention purely on the sign, tried vainly to
convince themselves that this miserable remnant was itself the
whole. Instead of holding fast to the patent fact, that in ordinary
thought they did succeed in giving meanings to their thoughts,
they asked themselves the absurd question, what are we really
conscious of when we are conscious of meaning something?
And having forced themselves by the very formulation of their
question to look for something other than the meaning, they
could of course find only the empty shells which had contained
that meaning. They proceeded, as Professor Stout wittily says,
like men looking for spectacles which are on their noses all the
time. Signs are always sensational in nature, whether they are
actual sensations (as in sense-perception) or ideas (images or
"revived" sensations). Words are nothing but complexes of
kinaesthetic, auditory, and visual sensations and images, and
the same applies to all other signs. But the fact that a significant
psychic whole contains as a subordinate factor these sensational
elements, and that such a whole apparently cannot be present
in our consciousness without the help of such elements, in no
way entitles us to treat them as the only solid and substantial
factor, the only objective content, as it were. I have exposed
this fallacy due to a misuse of introspection at some length,
because even psychologists who in one direction have recognised
and avoided it, have fallen victims to it in another. Thus it
appears to me—if I may digress once again—that Professor
James' theories of Emotion and of Mental Activity both involve
the fallacy of taking the sensational elements of complex
psychical wholes as constituting those wholes. When Professor
James identifies an emotion with the various organic sensations
and feelings arising from the symptoms of its bodily manifestation,[1] or again when he identifies our experience of activity

with the muscular sensations that accompany it,[1] he is un-doubtedly guilty of not accepting the first-hand evidence of his own inner experience, but offering to us instead a mangled extract of sensational elements. Says Professor James: "It is difficult for me to detect in the activity any purely spiritual element at all. Whenever my introspective glance succeeds in turning round quickly enough to catch one of these manifesta-tions of spontaneity in the act, all it can ever feel distinctly is some bodily process, for the most part taking place within the head". Yet in speaking of "meaning" the same Professor James had wisely said: "The sense of our meaning is an entirely peculiar element of the thought. It is one of those evanescent and "transitive" facts of mind *which introspection cannot turn round upon*, and isolate and hold up for examination, as an entomologist passes round an insect on a pin".[2] Is an emotion or a feeling of activity in any way less a "peculiar element" of our experience? Or does Professor James really think he has succeeded in pinning these experiences down, and walking round them introspectively? The consciousness of an emotion is no more the same as the consciousness of "quickened heart-beats", "shallow breathing", "trembling lips", "weakened limbs", "visceral stirrings", than the consciousness of the meaning of a thought is identical with the consciousness of the word or image or other sensational element which serves as its "sign".

I hope this digression has served to make clear the sense in which I have spoken of a sign and its meaning as forming to-gether a psychic whole. But, unfortunately, this account is itself beset with difficulties. The distinction between sign and meaning is usually not regarded as merely a distinction between different aspects or elements of a whole, but as a distinction *between distinct and separate existences*. And, as a rule it is even implied, that these existences belong to different orders of being, that the sign is always psychical, but the thing signified material.[3] Thus Professor Stout distinguishes in cognition two elements: (i) A thought-reference to something which, as the thinker means or intends it, is not a present modification of his

[1] *Ibid.*, i., p. 299 ff.   [2] *Ibid.*, i., p. 472. Italics mine.
[3] For the sake of simplicity I put this down without qualification. Of course, when we think e.g., of an emotion, both sign and thing signified belong to the psychical order of being.

individual consciousness; (ii) A more or less specific modification of his individual consciousness, which defines and determines the direction of thought to this or that special object. . . .
In the perception of a tree the reference to an object is circumscribed and directed by a plexus of visual and other presentations. The object . . . is a material thing, not a mental occurrence. . . .[1]

This is a good statement of what is commonly implied in
cognition. The simplest perception is on the one hand *my*
perception and on the other hand my perception *of a certain
object*. Every idea is on the one hand *my* idea and on the other
my idea *of something*. Every act or process of cognition contains
these two aspects inseparably within itself, and it is perhaps the
greatest and most difficult of all philosophic achievements to
keep the unity of these two distinctions steadfastly in view. The
difficulty emerges as soon as we attempt to give a more detailed
account of the way in which the two aspects are related one to
the other within the single cognitive act. Do we look first at the
perception or idea *qua* being mine? Then the object appears at
once merely as a part or qualification of this particular modification of my consciousness. It serves to give that content and
character to the perception or idea by means of which we
distinguish it from every other perception or idea. Do we look
next at the object? And lo, it seems to owe all content and
character to perception, thought, consciousness. Do we try to
define them so that they may be distinguished? Then we are
in danger of making knowledge inexplicable, and being left
with the insoluble problem, how an idea which is a "modification of an individual consciousness" can mean an object
which is not a modification of consciousness. The only way to
escape these puzzles is to take one's stand resolutely on what
may be called the self-transcension of consciousness, i.e., on the
fact that we are and can be conscious of objects whose nature
and existence we do not regard as simply identical with the
nature and existence of our own states of consciousness. If there
is a problem here, it is a problem for Metaphysics. But in
Psychology and Logic to take one's stand on anything less than
that, ensures from the very start the failure of every attempt to
deal with the relation of sign and meaning.

[1] *Anal. Psych.*, i., p. 47.

I do not feel sure that the attempt of Professor James to solve this problem by means of the conception of a "psychic fringe" wholly escapes the dangers which I have indicated. The considerations which led to the conception, if I understand them right, are these. When we think we are conscious not merely of an idea, i.e., of a present modification of our consciousness, but we are also conscious of meaning something by the idea. There is therefore not only the idea, but something *more*; and this something more must on the one hand be in consciousness (for else we should not "understand" anything by the idea) and again it must transcend consciousness, for else there would be no objective reference. To meet this situation the conception of a "psychic fringe" is offered.

It is, of course, impossible to deny that this conception describes indubitable psychological facts, and I fully agree with Professor Stout's admirable account of "acquirement of meaning" in his *Manual of Psychology*.[1] It is perfectly true that, e.g., in listening to a tune or to a sentence, we are not merely conscious of the particular tone or word which we may be hearing at the moment, but that each tone or word carries with it the accumulated after-effects of all previous tones or words, and at the same time predisposes us to anticipate the continuation of the tune or sentence in a particular way. If each word or tone dropped completely out of consciousness, as its successor entered, without leaving any traces of its presence, we should never be able to take in a sentence or tune "as a whole". We should be confined to the mere sound of the word, and we may well doubt that sound would carry with it any "meaning" at all. If this be the meaning of "fringe" no one can doubt that it represents psychical fact. But what I am reluctantly compelled to doubt is that the conception supplies an adequate solution of the fundamental problem of meaning, viz., the relation of sign and thing signified, the "objective reference" of the sign. There are passages in Professor James' *Psychology* in which he says explicitly that the objective reference of the sign *consists* in its psychic fringe. I am very reluctant to assume that he really means what he says, but his language is so emphatic that I am forced to protest. "Each word", says Professor James, "is felt, not only as a word, but as having a meaning. The 'meaning' of a word taken thus dynamically in a sentence may be quite different from its meaning when taken statically or without context. The dynamic meaning is usually reduced to the bare fringe we have described of felt suitability or unfitness to the context and conclusion. The static meaning, when the word is concrete, as 'table', 'Boston', *consists of sensory images awakened*; when it is abstract, as 'criminal legislation', 'fallacy', the meaning *consists of other words aroused* forming the so-called 'definition'.[1] In other words, the meaning of "Boston", "fallacy", etc., consists of the "fringe" of images and words which are more or less subconsciously present, whenever the words themselves are present. Normally this fringe remains in the background of consciousness, but it can be called up explicitly if need be. Now in the first place, this account is wholly untrue as regards our ordinary consciousness of meaning. For what normally occupies the focus of attention is the meaning, the objective reference, whereas *the sign forms the fringe*, of which we have but a more or less shadowy consciousness. Professor James exactly reverses the true state of affairs, for according to his theory, the sign should occupy the centre of attention, and the meaning form the vague background.[2] Whether I have images or not, and whether I know the exact definition of a word or not, in ordinary thinking what looms large in my consciousness is the meaning and not the word. And this meaning does not consist in images or in other words. And this brings me to the second and even more important point which I have to make against Professor James' account. As the account stands, it *would be fully applicable to a solipsistic experience and to extreme subjectivism*. And that, I take it, is the last thing that Professor James intends. On the contrary, I take it, he would heartily agree with the passage from Professor Stout's book which I quoted above: "In the perception of a tree the reference to an object is circumscribed and directed by a plexus of visual and other presentations. The object . . . is a material thing, not a mental occurrence. . . ."[3] But the images which according to Professor James are meant by "Boston", and the words of the definition which are meant by "fallacy", are, in

---

[1] James, *Principles of Psych.*, i., p. 265. Italics mine.
[2] Professor Stout, *Anal. Psych.*, i., ch. iv., brings the same criticism against Professor James, but there are one or two passages where he seems to have slipped into the same mistake. See below, p. 157 *n*.   [3] *Cf.* p. 80.

the context, mental occurrences, and they are nothing else. So long then as the fringe is merely a psychical fact or occurrence, it seems nonsense to say that *it* is the meaning of another psychical occurrence. It amounts to saying that the meaning of a sign is to be found in other signs. But where, then, is the "thing signified"? The meaning of Boston is emphatically not the images of this or that person, nor even the images of all persons together. Even for myself the meaning of Boston consists not of my images of Boston (supposing that I have any images at all), but of a certain town in America, to which those images themselves refer, and of which they themselves are merely "signs". Hence to explain the meaning of an image or word by reference to its "fringe" and to make this fringe consist of *other* images and words, is not to solve the problem of the objective reference of signs, but merely to put it one stage further back. For the fringe itself, when it is made explicit, is seen to consist but of signs, which would have their own meaning in turn beyond themselves. The only reason why Professor James is content to accept certain images as the meaning of "Boston" and a certain definition as the meaning of "fallacy", is that these images and words are not mere images and words, but themselves carry meanings with them, and these meanings are not again other images or other words but are the things signified themselves. The images are of value to him, not because they *are* Boston, but because by means of them he can *think of* Boston itself, and connect the word "Boston" with the actual city. And again the words of the definition of fallacy are important to him not as words, which can be substituted for the word "fallacy", but because he can bring before his mind by means of them the real nature of fallacy. Professor Stout's language in respect to the same problem is far more careful than that of Professor James: "It seems certain that the mental state which we call understanding the meaning of a word need not involve any distinction of the multiplicity of parts belonging to the object signified by it. To bring this multiplicity before consciousness in its fulness and particularity would involve the imaging of objects with their sensory qualities, visual, auditory, tactual, etc."[1] This passage implies, that both words and images

---

[1] *Anal. Psych.*, i., p. 79. However, there are other passages in which Professor Stout seems to have been betrayed into the mistake of which I complain. Thus on p. 83,

being signs, involve a reference to objects other than themselves, and it avoids the mistake of saying that because the
meaning of a word can be made clearer by *means of* other words
and images, therefore the meaning of the word *is* those words
and images. The phrase "psychic fringe" contains a great
temptation to commit this confusion. And it may be as well to
lay bare the root of the confusion. As I said above, sign and
meaning form an indissoluble psychic whole. Yet, on the other
hand, when we introspectively analyse that whole, we seem to
discover only those sensational elements which constitute the
sign. What, then, could be more tempting than to assume that
the meaning is present only as a more or less indistinct, subconscious "fringe"? And what easier than to confuse this non-
existent and imaginary fringe with a very real and existing
fringe, viz., the fringe constituted by all those words and images
with which a given word is associated? *It is an utter mistake to
think, that when a meaning is unanalysed and implicit, it is present
merely as a "fringe".* There is, indeed, a "fringe", but it consists
of other words and images. And though we must use these to
make explicit our meaning, they help us to define it, only
because they themselves are signs referring to that meaning,
not because they *are* the meaning. The advance from an implicit
to an explicit meaning, implies as its instrument the development of the "fringe" which surrounded the original sign, but
this fringe never loses its character as sign, and is in the apprehension of the explicit meaning *always subordinate*, as signs
normally are. And the character of the meaning as implicit or
explicit, unanalysed or analysed, undeveloped or developed, is
not a character of its mental signs at all. These signs, *qua* signs,
are neither implicit nor explicit. These adjectives are quite
meaningless as applied to signs. Otherwise, we should have to
say, e.g., that one man's very full and complete visual image
of Boston means Boston more "explicitly" than the fragmentary, scrappy image of another, whereas experience shows
that a person wholly lacking in visual imagery can mean a

we are told that the sight of an orange involves more than merely the "modification
of sentience directly traceable to the play of light on the retina"—which is right.
But then Professor Stout proceeds: "The thing, as a unity in multiplicity, is present
to consciousness as a psychic fringe"—which seems to me wrong. The recognition
of the yellow patch which we see as an orange, possessing all the other qualities
of an orange, is not a matter of "psychic fringe" whether we explicitly run over
those other qualities in our minds or not.

thing as explicitly as another person with a very highly developed visual imagery.

I have laboured this point at what, I fear, must seem excessive length. My excuse must be that the confusion is widespread, hard to detect, and hard to guard against. And I may now sum up what I regard as the positive results of the discussion up to this point. Sign and meaning are inseparable, both for Logic and for Psychology. Neither knows anything of a sign which is not a sign of something, of an idea or a perception which is not an idea or a perception of some object, whatever order of being that object may belong to. Every idea is a concrete whole of sign and meaning, in which the meaning, even when unanalysed and "implicit", is what is essential and prominent in consciousness. The sign, on the other hand, which we saw reason to identify with certain sensational elements in this complex experience, is normally subordinate. And I have called this concrete idea a "psychic whole", not with any intention of suggesting or implying that the "thing signified" is itself necessarily psychic, but simply to express the fact that "to mean something" is after all a conscious act, and that what I have called the self-transcension of consciousness inherent in all objective reference is something *experienced* by us. The fundamental fact which, at any rate for the purposes of this paper, we may not question or doubt, is that in experience we are conscious of reality. It is but a special case of this consciousness that our ideas have meaning, i.e. refer to reality. But we must now turn to a class of ideas which apparently have no meaning and lack all objective reference.

However, before I pass on, I ought, perhaps, briefly to notice one possible objection. I may be told that by speaking of sign and meaning as a "psychic whole" I have committed the very same mistake for which I have been criticising others, and that my "psychic whole" is as much a mere mental event, distinct from the object, as the "sign" of the theories criticised by me. To this objection I can reply only that, in my view, the moment we come to deal with the relation of sign and meaning we are beyond "mere" psychical events altogether. And, therefore, if anyone chooses to say that my phrase "in experience we are conscious of reality" implies subjectivism, I reject the interpretation and cheerfully leave the objector to make the best of his

M

own mess. Of course, I am not denying that our signs, i.e., our images, verbal and otherwise, may be studied in abstraction from their objective reference, and that such an investigation belongs properly to Psychology and not to Logic. But I hold it to be manifestly absurd to say that the individual mind, with which Psychology is supposed to deal, is conscious *of signs only* and not of their meaning.[1] On the contrary, I regard the consciousness of meaning as primary and fundamental, and the distinction of sign and meaning as a product of reflection. And if it be admitted that sign and meaning thus belong together and form in everybody's experience a concrete psychic whole, I do not much care whether the study of these wholes be included in Psychology or assigned to Logic. But what I do contend for is that, if a psychologist deals with meaning at all, it is an appalling mistake to make the sign primary and fundamental, and to degrade the meaning to a more or less subconscious fringe. Or, what is but a more elaborate form of the same mistake, it is absurd first to represent objective thinking[2] as a procession or stream of signs, and then (from an uneasy consciousness that signs must have meanings) to make their meaning consist in other signs, i.e., in those parts of the stream which have not yet come into the focus of consciousness. This is the sum and substance of what I have been contending for so far, and with this restatement I think I have earned the right to proceed.

B.

The result of the previous section might also be expressed by saying that the distinction between sign and meaning, in the sense in which we saw reason to maintain it, is by no means coincident with the common distinction between idea and reality. And this is the second main point with which I wish to deal. There is a widely spread view according to which the distinction between idea and reality is a distinction between "mere" ideas and facts, or, to put it differently, between ideas that have no meaning or objective reference and ideas that have. When, e.g., we speak of a view which is in conflict with

---

[1] This assertion, as we have seen, is implied in the view with a criticism of which I began this paper. *Cf.* p. 144.   [2] I.e., thought referring to objects.

the facts as a "mere idea", or when we contrast dreams and imaginations with reality, we mean according to this view that these ideas are mental occurrences and nothing more, that they refer to no objects, that they are, as it were, mere pictures in somebody's mind without counterparts in the real world. This view seems to me radically false. A careful analysis of an imaginary idea or a dream-picture will reveal in it exactly the same three aspects which characterise our ideas of real objects. My idea of a centaur, a sea-serpent or an angel is characterised by (1) existence, (2) content, (3) meaning, as much as my idea of a horse, a snake or a human being. And the imaginary events of a novel are as little events merely in the author's head or the reader's head, as any historical event like the Battle of Salamis or the French Revolution. To a child the events of fairy-tale are as "real" as the events of ordinary life; to the primitive mind a myth is a tale of "fact" as much as to us a historical or scientific statement. These facts suggest, indeed, that at a certain level of mental development the distinction between a "real" and an "imaginary" world has not yet arisen. But they suggest *also* that real and imaginary experience are made *of the same stuff*, as it were, and that whatever the principle of distinction between them may be, it cannot be that in the one case our ideas have objects and in the other they have not. The golden mountain of fairy-tale is as little identical with my image of it as the real mountain is identical with my image of it. In the one case, as in the other, there is a "thought-reference to something which as the thinker intends it is not a present modification of his individual consciousness". And since, then, all ideas, imaginary no less than others, involve an objective reference as part of their very nature, we seem driven to say that there are objects which are real and *objects which are unreal*.[1] We must frankly admit that we can be concerned with unreal objects, and that those ideas which deal with unreal objects do not deal

[1] I must beg the reader to remember that I am not talking Metaphysics, but maintain throughout this paper the point of view of "ordinary common sense". In the metaphysical sense of reality *all* kinds of experience go to make up the material of reality. *Cf.* Mr. Bradley's *Appearance and Reality*. I would add also that he above was written before I had seen Mr. Bradley's delightful article on "Floating Ideas and the Imaginary" in the last number of *Mind* (N.S., 60). Though my phraseology differs considerably from his, I hope I am right in thinking hat my view, though much more crudely and shortly expressed, does not in ubstance differ very seriously from his.

with no objects at all, i.e., are not ideas without any objective reference whatever.

It is not my business here to investigate the principles on which we distinguish real from unreal object, or again different kinds of unreal objects[1] from each other. But I will try to enforce my view by indicating some of its implications. In the first place, all unreal objects have a tendency or claim to be accepted as real. It is only because they have come into conflict with, and been rejected by, my real world that I am compelled to think of them with the mental proviso "unreal". Except for that conflict there would be no distinction between them, for, as I put it above, they are of the same stuff. I do not mean, of course, that we accept every day-dream as real until it comes somewhere into violent conflict with reality. Mature minds are so familiar with the distinction that it is made almost automatically. But everyone will be able to recall sad occasions in his childish days on which he discovered that some beloved figure of fairy-tale could have no place in the real world, and would henceforth have to be labelled "unreal". This experience could not have come to the child but for his firm belief in the reality of the fairy-figure and the subsequent conflict of that belief with "facts".[2] One might express this tendency towards reality of imaginary objects by calling them "possible" rather than unreal objects. And one might suggest that there are degrees of such possibility according as the content and character of the imaginary objects is less or more at variance with the content and character of real objects. And from this point of view one might say art and the creations of the artistic imagination that the highest art is not that which most faithfully copies what one may call historical actuality, but that the objects of which possess the highest degree of possibility in

[1] Such as, e.g., dreams and creations of the imagination, and again hallucinations and illusions and hypnotic suggestions.

[2] My point is that in many cases it is essential to the child's enjoyment of the imaginary that it should *not be recognised as imaginary*. To most children, I think at a certain time of life, the events and persons of fairy-tales are *real* events and *real* persons, and when this illusion is laid bare, interest in this now discredited type of the imaginary is apt to vanish. It is but rarely replaced by conscious make-believe. Thus, to give an instance from my own experience, I believed, like most German children, at one time firmly in the existence of the Christ-child as a bringer of presents at Christmas, to whom a letter setting forth my wishes had to be duly despatched. This practice ceased to interest even as "play" and "make-believe" when its foundation was discovered to be imaginary.

the above sense. We may embody more or less of the spirit and essence of reality in the products of our imagination, and the more we embody the more will the unreality of our imaginations seem a mere accident. Indeed, it seems necessary to the full enjoyment of a novel or a play that we should get the "illusion" of its reality, i.e., that we should, for the moment, abandon ourselves to its claim to be real, and forget its conflict with our real world. But this illusion of reality would be impossible unless imaginary objects had a tendency towards reality which is checked only by their conflict with reality, and asserts itself as soon as we disregard that.

In the second place, I may support my contention by an illustration from the nature of wish. A wish (as against a desire) involves the presence of an imaginary idea, i.e., an idea which is not objectless, but which is so disconnected with our real world, that we regard its object as "unreal" or rather as incapable of realisation. Yet a wish, as Mr. Bradley and others have well shown, "entails logically, and it *continually in fact tends to pass into,* an actual desire".[1] In desire we have an idea regarded as capable of realisation, so that we have here a strict parallel between the tendency of a wish to pass into desire, and the tendency of the idea of an unreal object to pass into the idea of a real object. And again, just as we can maintain a wish only by suppressing the collision of its idea with reality, so the abandonment to a work of imagination implies forgetfulness of its unreality.

And I may repeat now the positive contribution of this section to our discussion. The distinction between idea and reality is not a distinction between a mental fact which has meaning, and a mental fact which has no meaning. All ideas refer to objects, and the division of these objects into "real" and "imaginary" has no basis in the character of the ideas as mental events.

C.

But there is another problem concerning the relation of ideas to reality which is of the utmost importance, and on which

[1] F. H. Bradley, "The Definition of Will" (iii), in *Mind*, N.S., 49, p. 17. Italics mine.

considerable confusion seems to prevail. We are all familiar
with a view, often explicitly expressed and yet more often un-
consciously presupposed, according to which the "ideal"
character of an experience *ipso facto* disqualifies its content from
being real. An ideal content, it is said, by its very nature lacks
reality; it cannot stand on its own legs as it were; it is abstract,
whereas reality is concrete, etc. In short, in so far as our
experience works by means of ideas we are removed from contact with reality. Whatever we apprehend ideally cannot as
such be real. I cannot attempt here to follow out in detail all
the developments to which this principle has led in the history
of philosophy, such as the view that only particulars are real,
whereas universals, relations, laws of Nature, etc., are "merely"
ideal, and therefore not real. I will discuss only two applications
of the principle. 1. In the first place, the contrast between idea
and reality is taken to be a contrast between present reality
and something which in one sense or another is "not present".
Thus the past and the future are usually said to be "ideal" as
against the reality of present experience; and again in volition
we have the opposition between my present state and an idea
of change, the "realisation" of which would satisfy me. 2.
Secondly, reality, as contrasted with idea, is more particularly
identified with sense-perception.

These two distinctions, of course, frequently coincide.
Present reality generally manifests itself, in part at least, to our
senses; and again the realisation of an idea in volition must be
directly experienced by us. But the distinctions do not necessarily run on the same lines,[1] and for our present purpose it
will be more convenient to keep them apart.

I proceed, then, to deal with the first distinction, viz., the
distinction between idea and *present* reality. The problem here
involved is this: the past, as past, is no longer present; the future,
as future, is not yet present. Yet, in so far as I am conscious of
either, I am *now* conscious of it. And thus it would seem that
past and future must be somehow present, if I am to be conscious of them at all. And we solve the problem by saying that
past and future are present "in idea", but not "in reality".

---

[1] E.g. my present condition which in volition is opposed to an ideal modification of it, is by no means confined to what I apprehend of myself in present sense-
perception.

The idea, i.e., my thought of past or future, is present now to
my consciousness; the past or future to which I refer and which
I "mean", are not present now. Thus we get the seemingly
paradoxical result that a present idea can mean a reality which
is not present. And yet this reality cannot lie wholly beyond the
reach of our present consciousness, or else we could not "mean"
it. Now, in the first place, we must observe that the word
"present" is here used in two senses. The first sense is purely
temporal. The memory of a past event is the thought of an
event of which I think as "not-present". The event is characterised for my thought by this temporal element which forms
part of the very content of which I think. And the same applies
mutatis mutandis to the future. It is purely a question of the
temporal localisation of contents. It is part of the objective
reference, the meaning of our ideas. In short, we must distinguish between the date of the object to which an idea refers,
and the date of the idea itself regarded as an event in our
mental history. We have here two entirely different sets of
temporal distinctions, or rather temporal distinctions made
from different points of view and dealing with different objects.
In the one case we have the temporal localisation of the objective meaning of our ideas, in the other we have the temporal
localisation of the idea itself in the succession of our conscious
life. And here I would recall to the reader the conclusion of
the first section. We found there that signs and meaning formed
a whole, in which the weight of attention fell normally on the
meaning, not on the sign. And hence we are conscious, as a
rule, *only of any temporal determination that may belong to the meaning*,
but we are not at all conscious of the fact that the meaning is
present to us *now*. We think, e.g., of the past as past, but we do
not at the same time think of this thought of the past as being
our present thought now. An event receives its date from its
temporal relations to other events, but not from the fact that
in dating it, it is the object of my present thought. This thought
is itself dated as "present" by means of the fact that as an event
in my mind it has an aspect of immediate feltness, and not at
all with reference to its meaning. And, even then, the explicit
recognition of an idea as "present" involves an act of reflection,
and it is, strictly speaking, always the idea which is *just past*
which is called present, even as introspection would be more

appropriately called "retrospection", because to make an object of one's own states of mind involves a new state of mind which is not itself an object, so that the object is always the state of mind which is just past. To sum up, then, we must distinguish between the time-determinations that are part of the meaning of an idea, and the time-determinations of the idea itself, i.e., of *my* consciousness of that meaning. There is a temporal element both on the objective and on the subjective side. The sign has its place in my mental life, just as the thing signified has its place in the whole scheme of meaning of which it is a part. And these two sets of temporal determinations are not confused, because we are never simultaneously conscious of them. When I am conscious of the past as past, or the future as future, I am not conscious of them as present, though my consciousness of them itself is a "present" consciousness.[1] But it is "present" only when it becomes itself the object of a fresh act of reflection, which in turn possesses no temporal determination, until yet another act of reflection has again made an object of it. I do not think that I can make this point any clearer by labouring it further, and I will pass on to the second meaning of present.

This second meaning has nothing to do with time at all. Hence, in this case, when I say that something is before me in "idea" and not in "reality", I do not mean that the reality is localised in a different moment of time from the idea. I am wholly indifferent to the question whether the reality belongs to the past or the future or, indeed, to any time at all. What I refer to is, on the contrary, a *qualitative difference* between two ways of experiencing the same content. The one way of experiencing gives me merely the idea, the other gives me the reality. Before attempting a general statement of this difference, I will try to make it clear by instances. A revived sensation differs from an actual sensation as idea from reality. Yet a colour as seen, and a colour as imagined, a tone as heard and a tone as revived, remain the same colour and the same tone. Indeed the example is particularly instructive in showing

---

[1] It would be false to say, that in thinking of the past as past we are "abstracting" from the fact that the thought of the past is a present thought. We can abstract only from something of which we are explicitly conscious, but as I have said, we are not conscious of the time of an idea when our attention is wholly fixed on the time of its meaning.

clearly that the difference in the two modes of experience is not
a difference of objects. One can only say that it is a difference
of *mode*, not a difference of content. It is a qualitative difference,
but not a difference that affects the qualities of the objective
content, but a difference in the quality of our experience of the
content. The intensity, saturation, etc., of the imaged colour
are the same as the intensity and saturation of the colour as
perceived. The image of an electric light has greater brightness
than the candle-flame which we actually see.[1] The revived tone
of an organ is louder and more voluminous than the actual
tinkle of a bell. As Professor Stout expresses it, the actual colour
and the actual tone "strike the mind" in a different way from
their images. To take another example, when we think of a
horse, we mean the real living creature with all the qualities,
etc., which we know it to possess, whatever the nature of the
image or other mental sign may be by means of which we think
of it. Yet, of course, thinking of the horse, and actually
experiencing and dealing with the living creature, are for us
two different things. And they differ, to put it quite roughly, in
that the process of thinking, even whilst it is concerned with the
object, can yet go on without the coöperation, as it were,
of the object, whereas the experience of an object as real
involves the presence of the object as a contributory factor in
the occurrence of the experience. At the same time, this difference is for certain purposes irrelevant and may be neglected.
More particularly, this is the case where our attitude towards
the object is purely theoretical. In theory, memory not only
can, but often must, take the place of the immediate experience
of the actual object; and it can do so because our ideas (whether
in the shape of images or otherwise) are able to revive and red-
integrate the objective content of the original experience,
although the subjective character of this experience of the
redintegrated content differs from the subjective character of
the original experience.

Perhaps the best way of expressing this qualitative difference
between two ways of apprehending the same content is to
speak, as I did just now, of the difference as one between an
original experience and the "memory" of that experience.

---

[1] *Cf.* on the difference between images and sensations Professor Stout's chapter
on "Ideas and Images," *Manual*, p. 393 *et seq.*

There is, surely, no objection to this manner of statement, provided we do not give too narrow a sense to memory. As I have used the word above, it is equivalent to *retentiveness in the widest sense*; in other words, I have not confined it to the recalling of particular events in all their particularity and with an explicit temporal qualification referring them to a definite place in the series of my *past* life or in the wider series of historical events. On the contrary, I have assumed that any kind of experience and any kind of objective content can be retained and recalled, and that a temporal qualification is found only in a relatively small number of cases. Any other view seems to me in open conflict with facts, and to make any account of the important part played by retentiveness in our intellectual life impossible. Whenever we "think of" or "about" something, and whenever we rely on acquired knowledge, we make use of memory, though we need not in recalling, say, a scientific theory, recall the occasion when it was first discovered or when we first learned it.

In this connection, I can best explain why I said above that the difference was for certain purposes irrelevant. It is irrelevant for Logic, but not for Psychology. Or, as I might also express it, it is a difference which affects our practical rather than our theoretical interests. For the purposes of knowledge, if the problem, for instance, be some point about the nature of the horse, we can establish it either by actual observation on some particular "real" horse, or we can "think of" a horse. In both cases, of course, we take the individual instance as typical of its kind, and what we are interested in is not some particular attribute characteristic of that horse only and of no other, but some universal property that shall be true of all horses. In other words, as we have all, I suppose, learned from such logicians as Mr. Bradley and Professor Bosanquet, in aim and intention all scientific knowledge is knowledge of universal connections of content, and from that point of view it makes no difference whether we find the material for our universal constructions in immediate or in retained experience, in direct apprehension or in memory. It would, perhaps, be more accurate to say, it makes no difference *in principle*. For in practice, of course, we have to consider (*a*) the trustworthiness of memory, and (*b*) the fact that the value of memory, even when trustworthy, depends largely on how *organised* it is. And this, in turn, depends primarily and mainly on the direction of our interest, which determined what we should attend to in the original experience or experiences now recalled. But the place of memory in cognition is too large a subject to be adequately treated here. At any rate, it is clear that without it we could have no universals, and this shows that it would be false to confine memory to the recalling of highly particularised experiences carrying with them a temporal qualification. On the contrary, highly generalised and abstract thought-contents, without any temporal determinations whatever, are retained, and without such retentiveness all more highly organised knowledge would plainly become impossible.[1] And whether, in a given case, we recall an object in all its particularity (as a "this"), or for the sake of its universal nature (as typical of its kind), depends on the direction of our interest at the moment.

So much for the logical importance of the distinction between original experience and memory or retentiveness, which, as we have seen, is relatively small. But psychologically the distinction is of the utmost importance as necessitating a different principle of explanation. We can explain memory by speaking of traces left behind by the original experience, or of a disposition which under given conditions (association, etc.) leads to the "revival" or "ideal redintegration" of the original experience. On the other hand, for the explanation of the original experience we have to go in the last resort to the real object itself, the "coöperation" of which,[2] as I put it above, is necessary to the production of the experience. This way of putting it may be metaphysically objectionable, but it is convenient, if not indispensable, for the purposes of psychology, besides being in accord with common-sense views. And I have at the beginning of this paper warned the philosophically-minded reader, who will be content with nothing short of Metaphysics, that I had no intention of giving him Metaphysics. And the point which I now wish to emphasise above all is this. Wherever the co-

---

[1] It will be seen from this—and I emphasise it to prevent misunderstanding—that by speaking of retentiveness I do not mean *bare* repetition (if indeed such a thing exists) and that I do not deny intellectual constructiveness, but rather lay stress on the fact that without retentiveness such construction would be impossible and our mental life lack continuity.

[2] Psychologists call it the "stimulus".

öperation of the object is necessary to the production of an experience, we have an experience of the object *as real*. And whenever we have once experienced an object as real, it never after loses its "Realitäts-character",[1] even though all our subsequent experience of it should be through memory. In other words, we remember it as real, and in all further intellectual analysis of, or construction about it, even though we should have nothing but our memory to rely on, we think of the object as real and regard our theories about it as revealing to us its real nature. This then is the general principle. Whatever we have once experienced as real remains real for us in all our subsequent dealings with it. Thus we can explain the reality of the past as we remember it, and, further, the reality of that wider past with which History deals. And, again, this explains the derived reality of all results got by legitimate inference from data themselves characterised as real. When once I have experienced an object as real, I henceforth remember it, think of it, speak of it, etc., as real, even though that original experience should never be repeated. Every idea of the object is henceforth an idea of it as real.

I hardly know whether to say anything more on this subject, for to some I shall seem to have been labouring a truism, whilst others will think me guilty of something worse than paradox. Hence I can do nothing but repeat that the distinction which I have been trying to make accounts for one of the senses in which we oppose idea to present reality. Our state of mind in such cases is complex, containing, as a rule, some elements which we apprehend directly "as real", and others which by contrast are merely ideal. And when we speak of the former as "present" reality, the adjective "present" refers not to any temporal determination, but primarily to that "Realitäts-character" of the experience which I explained as due to the coöperation of the object in the production of the experience. A temporal reference may indeed be intended besides the "Realitäts-character" in all cases where, as in volition, the ideal element in our complex experience is characterised, not as real now though out of reach of my experience, but as cap-

---

[1] This, of course, is merely the general principle. I have omitted qualifications for the sake of simplicity. Any reader of the second section will be able to supply them for himself.

able of realisation in the future. This, however, is a special case, which I have space only to mention and not to explain.

After all that I have said there is little that I have to add on the second distinction between idea and reality, in which the latter is identified with sense-perception. It is clear that this distinction is but a special (though by far the most obvious and frequent) case of the distinction formulated in the last paragraph. For a large part of our "ideal" experience is, of course, redintegration of an original sense-experience. But the contrast between idea and sense-perception brings out very clearly two points on which I have insisted in my account above. (1) It shows that the difference is not one that affects the object, but the subject's relation to the object. We say that the idea of an object is less real than the perception of the object, but we do not mean that the object itself loses any of its reality because of the change from perception to idea in our attitude towards it. Both perception and idea are "of the object", and whatever difference there is between them does not, we take it, affect the reality of the object. (2) Secondly, it shows that for the original experience, on which the idea is based, the coöperation of the object is necessary. For sense-perception normally, of course, rests on a physical relation between the real object and myself, or rather my body with its sense-organs. It clearly requires the "external stimulus" proceeding from the object, whereas the memory-idea (taking the word in the widest sense) is stimulated from within. And again it is clear, as I mentioned above, that the distinction is important for practice rather than for theory. By which I do not mean that in theory we could get on without sense-perception, which would be obviously absurd, but that the results of observation, preserved either directly in memory or recorded in writing, etc., can take the place of direct perception for theoretical purposes. But practically it is otherwise. No memory-experience can take the place of the direct experience of the object. No recollection, however complete and vivid, of a sumptuous feast will allay the pangs of a hungry man. The idea of a horse will not serve a man to ride on, nor imaginary clothes to cover his nakedness. What he requires are those experiences which only the real object can give him, and for which no images and ideas can form a substitute. It is always in some kind of sense-experience that practical processes terminate. In theory, emancipated from directly practical interests,[1] that is not the case. Sense-perception is necessary as a starting-point and again for verification, but it is not the terminus and goal of the process. Knowledge, even as an ideal, is not the simultaneous presence of the whole universe in the form of sensation.

And now there is only one point on which I have to comment. Sense-perception is a term which bears an evil repute among many philosophers owing to the disputes which have raged about its relation to thought. These disputes were largely nourished by a confusion as to the meaning of idea. As I have used the word in the above discussion it means in the widest sense the revival, redintegration, reproduction of the content of an original experience. We have ideas where, and so far as, we have the working of retentiveness, and the difference between the idea and the original experience is, as I have emphatically pointed out, a difference in their *subjective* character as experiences. It is not, so far as meaning or objective reference are concerned, a difference of content. There are, of course, *also* objective differences, or differences of content. And of these differences of content the most important is the difference between the sensational element and the thought element in experience. Now unfortunately the term "idea" has been used not merely to describe the retention and redintegration of *any* content, whatever its nature, but also to describe the special thought element in experience as distinct from the sensational element. It is impossible to gauge even approximately the amount of confusion which has arisen out of this double use of the word idea, as describing (*a*) a qualitative difference in the contents of experience, (*b*) a qualitative difference in the mode of experiencing a content, whatever its own qualitative nature might be. Now, if we choose to call the content "red" or the content "blue" sensational and the content "colour" (as such) ideal, there is no objection provided we do not proceed to call the latter content less real because it is ideal, or the former more real because it is sensational. The distinction has nothing whatever to do with the reality of the contents. All contents, whether "sensational" or "ideal", can

[1] I do not, of course, mean to suggest that there is no interest or purpose or striving in theory at all.

alike be redintegrated. But idea, in the sense of redintegration, is *not identical* with idea in the sense of "ideal content". I am inclined to think that most thinkers who opposed sense-experience and thought to each other, whilst identifying thought with idea, confused these two senses of idea. They were never clear whether they were opposing idea in the sense of revival to some kind of first-hand experience of the content as real (which might involve sensation, but might also be "pure" thought), or whether they were opposing to each other different contents of experience. It is one thing to contrast the idea of a horse with the real horse, when the contrast is really between the revival of the original experience of the real horse and that experience itself. It is another thing to analyse that experience of the real horse itself and to distinguish in it those elements which are sensational from those which are ideal (thought-elements). It is this analysis which shows us that what we ordinarily call sense-experience is a highly complex thing, in which thought-elements far preponderate over the sensational ones, giving structure and form to the whole, without prejudice, in spite of their "ideal" character, to the "reality" of the object. In the further development of this process we get the "real world" of Science with its "ideal" laws. However, I need not go into details which all who are curious may find in Kant's *Critique of Pure Reason*!

D.

Finally, I will attempt in a few words to apply the results of the three previous sections to the "realisation of an idea" which is the feature of volition. In the first place, the idea has objective reference or meaning. We are concerned not with an image or mental sign, but with a definite content of experience which we "mean". But, secondly, our consciousness of this content is in the nature of a revival; the realisation of the idea, therefore, demands the repetition of the original experience.[1]

[1] I am here speaking, for the sake of simplicity, only of those cases in which the end of volition is the repetition of some former experience, and I am neglecting the far more important cases in which our constructive intelligence has been at work, and the idea to be realised, therefore, goes beyond what we have met with in former experience. I must beg the reader to observe, that in these final remarks I am not trying to do more than give a rough, and necessarily inadequate sketch, of the way in which the general theory of the foregoing pages might be applied to volition.

Thirdly, this repetition involves the coöperation of the real object. In some cases, the willing individual himself is this real object, as, e.g., where the idea to be realised is the idea of a movement to be executed by himself. In that case the idea passes at once into its appropriate reality, i.e., the kinaesthetic images pass into the corresponding kinaesthetic sensations. But behind this whole process of realisation lies as the condition of its possibility the real individual, regarded as a unity of body and soul, a psycho-physical organism. In other cases the realisation of the idea involves the coöperation of some of the other real objects amongst which the individual finds himself placed. And in that case, his judgment of the possibility of the realisation of his idea, and of the steps which he must take towards it, depends on his knowledge of the nature and behaviour of the objects concerned. And the realisation of the idea takes place not merely through his own efforts, but also through processes in the environment with which he has to deal.

I have used above the phrase "the idea passes into its appropriate reality". It remains to explain this a little further. It is often said, and said rightly, that we can will *only our own experiences*.[1] It would seem then that the reality of an idea must always be found within our own experience. This is true, but it must be rightly interpreted if it is not to give rise to serious misunderstanding. Quite generally, the statement merely means that the realisation of the idea must be experienced by me, if my volition is to terminate and to be satisfied. Should my

[1] I am aware that this statement is at variance with the doctrine which Mr. Bradley has laid down on this point in his admirable articles on Volition in recent numbers of *Mind*. Cf., especially, *Mind*, N.S., No. 44. Mr. Bradley refers to testamentary dispositions as clear cases of volition not realised in the agent's own experience. I have no space here to defend my adherence to the more usual view. But I should say that no theory of volition can do justice to the facts without admitting that the process of realising an idea (1) need not be due exclusively to the agent's own activity; (2) and need not wholly fall within the agent's immediate experience. In other words, I see no reason to exclude inferences. Thus, e.g., if my volition be to communicate some news to a friend by letter, the realisation of this idea, up to the dropping of the letter into a pillar-box, falls within my immediate experience, and takes place by my agency, whereas for the further realisation I have to trust another agency. Normally, I have no reason to doubt that even then my volition is being realised, although receipt of my friend's answer alone would be complete evidence of realisation. And any failure on his part to reply would naturally lead me to infer loss of letter and consequent non-realisation of my volition. Just as in this case I infer the realisation of my volition, I should say, that in Mr. Bradley's example of testamentary dispositions, the agent infers the realisation of his idea, and accepts that inference instead of the direct experience of realisation, from which by the nature of the case he is excluded.

idea be realised without my knowledge, I remain in a state of active conation and continue my efforts towards the realisation of my idea as if nothing had happened. My volition, then, must terminate in some definite experience of my own. But this experience need not be *in itself* that which I willed and desired. *It may be the end of my volition not for its own sake, but in so far as it is evidence to me of the realisation of my idea.* In other words, in the majority of volitions I am assured of the realisation of my idea only *through inference* from certain immediate experiences. An example will make this clear. When I will to make another person happy, my idea is realised by the occurrence of a certain experience in another person, and not, apparently, in myself. I do not will my own happiness, but that of the other person. Yet, even if I succeed in making that person happy, my volition does not terminate, unless I am also explicitly aware of my success. And in this sense I must experience the other person's happiness, if my idea is to be realised *for me*. The experience which assures me of the realisation of my idea may be no more than a smile or a word of thanks, but these are not in themselves the realisation of my idea, nor are they what I wanted to experience for their own sake; they satisfy me merely because they are signs of the other person's happiness, and, therefore, in experiencing them I experience the realisation of my idea. I have an experience of the *reality* of the other person's happiness, and though this experience is largely inferential in character, it is quite different from the mere idea of it which I had before.

This example illustrates at the same time how an idea may be realised in an "ideal" content. But it may be as well in conclusion to give yet another example on the same point. When a man desires, e.g., to realise his idea of goodness, and under the influence of this idea acts in an appropriate way, the act, taken barely as a psycho-physical process, is not a realisation of the idea of goodness at all. But, of course, the act is more than a psycho-physical process. The agent's total experience of his act includes as an element the recognition of the act as "good", i.e., as the realisation (so far as it goes) of an idea of goodness which inspired the act and determined its character. The act is real and is really good, and its goodness is an ideal (i.e., thought-) element in the total fact. The agent's idea is thus realised in an experience which itself contains ideal elements.

N

Concerning Universals

1. IN various passages of my *Studies in Contemporary Metaphysics*, published in 1920, a certain view about universals is briefly sketched, with a promise to give a fuller explanation in a further volume of *Studies* then projected. During the intervening years, in response to demands and opportunities which I could not anticipate in 1920, my literary plans have changed, and most of the materials gathered for that further volume have been, and will be, absorbed into other books. The problem of universals, however, lends itself to separate treatment. Hence, I venture to offer the following paper by way of fulfilling my promise, so far as it is now possible to fulfil it.

Moreover, there is a further reason for dealing with the topic of universals. During the past five or six years, a number of English and American thinkers have made contributions to the discussion of the nature of universals and their relation to particulars. In England, the interest in this topic, stirred up in 1911 by Mr. Bertrand Russell in his Presidential Address to the Aristotelian Society on "The Relations of Universals and Particulars", has revived after the interruption of the War. The work of Professor E. Husserl, in his *Logische Untersuchungen* and in the various volumes of the *Jahrbuch für Phaenomenologie*, has begun to exercise its influence on a number of thinkers, both in England and in the United States of America. Mr. George Santayana has given us his doctrine of "essences", most recently in his *Scepticism and Animal Faith*, and a number of "Critical Realists" support, in their several ways, the same general type of theory. Professor A. N. Whitehead's highly original theory of "events" and "objects" cuts across all other treatments of the topic, raising in its agreements and differences tantalising problems of comparison. Professor G. F. Stout, in his Hertz Lecture to the British Academy on "The Nature of Universals and Propositions", has put forward a theory of the universal as the "distributive unity of particulars", which has been met with vigorous criticism by Dr. G. E. Moore and others.

This catalogue is far from being exhaustive, for every recent writer, either on Metaphysics, like the late Professor J. McT. E. McTaggart in his *The Nature of Existence*, or on Logic, like Mr. W. E. Johnson in the three volumes of his *Logic*, has had something to say on universals. Any student of philosophy who wished to take stock of how the problem of universals stands in present-day discussion, at least so far as that discussion is carried on by thinkers using the English language, would have to pay attention to the thinkers and theories above enumerated.

The purpose of the present essay, however, is one at once different from, and less ambitious than, a complete survey of this field. What I propose to do is to develop a line of thought about universals which is, so far as I can see, not represented in present-day discussions at all. I shall try to present this line of thought with a minimum of polemical reference to the problems and terms of other contemporary discussions. For my chief purpose is, in the first instance, to develop it as fully as I can, so that its nature and importance may be estimated. I want to remind students of sides of the problem of universals and particulars of which they find hardly any hint in contemporary philosophical literature. Yet, they are sides which we dare not neglect if we desire a synoptic treatment of the problem as a whole. It is as a contribution of materials for such a synoptic treatment, that I offer the following argument.

2. My most convenient starting-point is the same from which, explicitly or implicitly, most other discussions start, viz., the "general name", or "class-name", of the *Logic* books, with its two kinds of meaning, "extension" (or "denotation") and "intension" (or "connotation"). The general name, it is usually said, "applies in the same sense to many objects". Let "man" be our example of a general name, then all the objects in the world, past, present, and future, of each of which we can say, "this is a man", will be the many objects to which, in the words of the formula, "man", as a general name, "applies in the same sense". We will leave aside here the special difficulties which are raised for this formula by classes which have only one member, or even no members at all. Though these difficulties have received attention especially from the mathematical logicians, far more commonly the interest of recent discussions

has been in two other directions. Following the one direction, the intension, as "universal", has been distinguished—one is tempted to say "divorced"—from the extension, as "particular", thus leading to the question, whether there is a fundamental division of objects into two classes, particulars and universals. One basis for such a division has been sought in the supposedly different relation of particulars and universals to human cognition: particulars are "perceived", universals are "conceived". Another basis has been sought in relations to space and time: a particular exists in space and time, but cannot be in two places at once, a universal is in itself indifferent to space and time, and independent of them, but, as appearing in (realised in, embodied in) many particulars, it can be in several places at once. A third basis has been sought in different modes of being: particulars "exist", universals "subsist". Finally, a fourth attempt at defining the difference has taken its clue from the analysis of the categorical proposition into subject and predicate (the latter term being understood to include both qualities and relations), and has declared particulars to be entities which can only be subjects of predicates, or terms of relations, but never themselves predicates or relations, whereas universals are entities which can only be either qualities or relations.

This fourth attempt, taken by itself, is at the same time identical with the second of the two directions taken, as I said just now, by recent philosophical discussions of universals. It leads in its developments, as is obvious, into questions of the correct analysis of propositions, of the function of symbols, of the relation of thought to immediate experience, of the relation of substance to attribute, of the category of thing-quality, of the nature of relations, and what not. All these questions, though they can, perhaps, be distinguished, can hardly be separated in the end. Hence it has been a common experience, though one which has not always been reflected on, that a thinker who has begun with some *prima facie* view of the correct answer to one of these questions, has been compelled, as the other questions opened up before him, to have recourse to all sorts of ingenious devices, in order to maintain his original position intact against the pull of these questions in a very different direction. However, I have mentioned these different paths of enquiry only in order to put them aside for the present, and to make it quite clear that the path which I shall try to follow is other than any of these.

I go back, then, to the initial formula: A general name "applies in the same sense to many objects". Certainly, in understanding and accepting this formula as the starting-point of our discussion, we are taking it for granted that "the world is full of a number of things"; that these things fall into classes, or are of various kinds; that it depends on the "qualities", or "nature", of a thing what classes or kinds it belongs to; that the possession of these qualities or nature, and, therefore, the membership of a class or kind, can be predicated of a thing in a judgment or proposition. In short, to "apply" a general name to an object is to judge that the object is a member of the class which forms the "extension" of the name, because it has the qualities which form the "intension" of the name. The qualities, of course, must have been attended to, and distinguished from, other qualities, before they could receive a name to themselves. But, thereafter, the name may be given, or "applied", to any object in which these qualities are found or recognised. The intension, as it is said, determines the extension. Is a thing to be called this or that? Is it to be put into this class or that? Is, e.g., an act of killing to be called murder, or culpable homicide, or justifiable self-defence? The answer will depend on what we mean by "murder", etc.; that is to say, it will depend on the "intension" of these terms, as defined. The definition of murder, in stating "what murder is", lays down the conditions, so to speak, which an act of killing must fulfil if the name "murder" is to be applicable to it.

All this is commonplace, of course, but nonetheless it is useful to rehearse even elementary commonplaces, in order to make clear, beyond all danger of confusion, the total *context* in which attention is to be focussed on a special problem.

This problem lies in the words "in the same sense". If a general name is applicable to many objects "in the same sense", this would, *prima facie*, mean that the same qualities are to be found in every one of the objects to which the name can be given. Yes, but in what sense the "same"? Does it require that every member of a class is an exact replica of every other? That they are "exactly similar"? That, like the "identical twins" of popular parlance, they are indiscernible but for what is called their "numerical difference"? That, in other words, in respect of their class-character there is no difference between them by which any one might be distinguished from any other?

It would be possible, no doubt, to set up as a logical ideal this concept of a class, the members of which should be indistinguishable, one from the other, except for their numerical difference. It would be possible, then, to grade actual classes according as their members were, or were not, "as like as two peas". The class of newly-minted pennies might serve as an instance from practical life, or, with theoretically even greater perfection, in mathematics any number defined as the class of all classes which are similar to a given class. On the other hand, the class of all human beings, or its countless sub-classes, e.g., all schoolboys, or all spinsters, or all politicians, would be by this standard vastly imperfect, by reason of the endless differences between their members.

On this ideal of exact similarity two remarks may be made which will carry the argument forward. The first is that it plays no part in the thinking of the Natural Sciences, where the discriminating of classes and the working out of the inter-relations of classes in classificatory systems form so essential a part of our knowledge of Nature. No Natural Science expects the members of its classes, e.g., the specimens of a species of plant or animal, to be all exactly alike, and to exhibit only numerical difference, nor does it regard this fact as a logical imperfection. Indeed, it might be argued that where the inherent individuality of the members of a class is at a minimum, there also the concept of class becomes most precariously applicable, just because the differences between the members are either accidental or arbitrary. Is a chemical element a class? And, if so, what are its members? Assuming that the quantity of a chemical element in the universe is, if not measurable, yet at any rate, limited, and imagining it as chemically pure, are we to conceive it as a class which has at any moment as many members as there are separate amounts of the element in different places at that moment? Or are we to think of it as a class with only one member because, conceivably, all there is of that element might be assembled into a single lump? Clearly, the instances of an element, which would be the members of the class, are either arbitrary (amounts taken for human purposes) or accidental (amounts found occurring in Nature). Moreover, additional members can, at will, be manufactured by subdividing any given amount, just as the number can be reduced by lumping different amounts together. By contrast, the members of a class in Botany or Zoology have each an individuality of its own, which tempts one to say that it is only in the animal and vegetable kingdoms (including, of course, man and all his works) that the class comes into its own. The objects in Nature which lend themselves most successfully to classification—so successfully that we ought rather to say that they *demand* classification by their very nature, i.e., because they actually exist as classes—are to be found in organic, not in inorganic, Nature. Yet in the study of organic Nature classes that have the above proposed character of perfection, viz., exact similarity and merely numerical differentiation of their members, are neither found, nor required. This reflection does not, I think, prove the ideal under discussion to be theoretically false. But it does show that there is an alternative preference open for a Logic which, finding that the facts range from classes with members exactly similar at one pole, to classes with members differing as individuals and not merely as numerical units at the other pole, prefers to take the latter type of class as its standard because its field is the concrete.

I used above, speaking of plants and animals, the phrase they "exist as classes". The defence of this phrase against possible criticism brings me to my second remark. Classes, it may be said, are fictions of the classifying, literally class-*making*, mind. Nature has only particulars or individuals. It is the human mind, the scientific mind, which collects and groups the particulars into classes. The answer to this argument depends on whether, for science at any rate, we accept the distinction between "essence" and "accident", and the correlative distinction between a "theoretical" and a "non-theoretical" (often called "practical") interest in things. No doubt, if pressed, these distinctions break down and give rise to dialectics. But that is no reason for not using them as far as they will carry us. And here, at any rate, they enable us to insist that, so far as the interest of theory (or knowledge) for its own sake is an interest in the essential nature of things for their own sakes, classes are not made but found. The groupings are determined by the essential natures of the objects grouped, and by their affinities according to their essential natures. A classificatory system exhibits, in Mill's language, a "connection of attributes": it embodies on a larger scale the principle that "intension determines extension". The particular, or individual, has a place in one of the pigeon-holes of the system, because the nature of the particular has just these determinate relations to the natures of other particulars. This argument becomes stronger still if we remind ourselves here of the well-known point that a perfect classificatory system is, logically, of the type of a complete disjunction, in which the alternatives are exhaustive and mutually exclusive, and in which successive levels, or stages, are more specific determinations of the general character, or nature, on which the system is based. If, now, we consider, in the light of this concept of a classificatory system, the purely "numerical difference" which, on the ideal under discussion, will alone separate the "exactly similar" members of a class, it becomes clear that two members of a class, A_1 and A_2, if they are absolutely indistinguishable in respect of their class-character, can be "numerically" distinguishable only in virtue of some character which has nothing to do with their class-character at all, e.g., occupying different positions in space, or being marked by ribbons of different colours, like twins. Their numerical difference, in short, will not consist in a differentiation of their class-character, but be "external" to it.

This brings us face to face, at last, with the crux of our problem. To say that a general name is applicable "in the same sense" to many objects, meant, as we saw, that these many objects each possess the same quality or character. But we have just seen reason to reject the view that this sameness of character implies that the many objects need be exactly alike, and therefore indistinguishable in respect of the same character, and distinguishable only in respect of some other quality, not connected with their class-character. Can we, must we, then—this is our problem—understand the phrase "in the same sense" so as to allow for, nay include, a range of differences?

Now, if we look at the facts, i.e., at the objects covered by any classificatory system, especially in the Biological Sciences (the sciences of organic Nature), it is obvious at a glance that for two specimens of a species, even, say, for two dogs of the same sex in the same litter, to be indistinguishable in respect of the qualities which constitute their species- and genus-characters, is the rare exception, not the rule. Individual specimens differ from each other, very largely, if not wholly, by differences which are, in fact, particular modifications of their species- and genus-characters. Following the prevailing usage, which calls a character "universal" and the instances in which it is realised "particulars", we may express the facts by saying that *a universal is realised "more or less" in its particulars*.[1] Furthermore, it seems to me that there are two ways in which a universal may be realised "more or less" in its particulars.

Firstly, the universal may be a simple quality ("simple", at any rate, for our perception). In that case, I propose to say that it may be realised in its particulars in varying *degrees*.

Secondly, the universal may be a compound, or complex, of qualities more or less closely inter-related and mutually dependent. The more complicated variations in the realisation of such a universal in its particulars I propose to express by saying that the universal is realised in its particulars in varying *modes*.

There is not, I think, any profound difference in principle between these two kinds of universals, but the distinction is none the less convenient for purposes of exposition. A few examples will illustrate it :—

That qualities may differ in degree is, of course, a familiar fact. Now, whenever a quality is made the basis of classification, the "many objects" classed together as possessing that quality will be found to exhibit it with differences of degree, varying from instance to instance. This occurs equally in natural objects and in artefacts. The flowers of a certain kind of plant have all the "same" colour, but compare single blooms with each other, and the "same" colour appears in each with slight differences of shade or nuance. The occurrence of instances "exactly alike" is the exception rather than the rule, and, if we choose, we can

---

[1] I am not using "realised", here, as a technical term, and to raise technical problems here about the meaning of "realisation", or about the subject-predicate relation, or the thing-quality relation, would be to miss my point. I am concerned merely to draw attention to certain facts with which we are all familiar, without prejudice to different theories about these facts.

always suppose that with acute powers of discrimination a difference would even here be found. But it is enough for my argument if it is conceded that "exact similarity" is the exception, not the rule. We might suppose that artefacts would exhibit less variation in degree. And, it is certainly true that, if we take great care, e.g., in colour-mixture, we can, if not eliminate variation completely, at least greatly restrict its range. Yet even here variations occur, and may become important, as every stamp-collector knows. The stamps of a given issue have all the "same" colour, yet the scientific collector is not satisfied until his collection contains items illustrating the range of shades of that "same" colour found in that issue. Further, this variability of the universal in its instances is far from being merely a curiosity, without intrinsic practical or theoretical importance. On the contrary, if there is any truth in the traditional view of the role played in evolution by "accidental variations", any one of these oscillations of quality around the average, or norm, may be the starting-point of the development of a new variety, or even species. The efforts of the breeder of plants or animals certainly begin with the selection of instances relatively free from a quality to be "bred out", or possessing, in more than usual degree, a quality to be "bred in". Thus, if we wish to be true to the facts, the "same sense" in which the name of a quality is predicated of all the members of a class, must certainly be elastic enough to cover the variations of degree in which that same quality is found in the several members. If "sameness" here is to mean "exact similarity", and to exclude all "differences" of degree, then certainly the classifications of the Natural Sciences are strictly unscientific, or, at least, illogical. But we do not need to choose this alternative, so long as there is open to us the other alternative of framing our logical ideals on the actual procedure of scientific thinking, instead of setting up standards which the sciences do not acknowledge because the facts reject them.

So much for differences of degree; now, for some illustrations of differences of *mode*. Let us take "rationality" as the distinctive characteristic of man. It is irrelevant to the point of our argument whether, as a matter of fact, rationality, or the possession of reason, is to be found only in man, or also in other animals. If we take it abstractly as a simple quality, it illustrates, of course, the principle of degrees: one man is more rational or reasonable than another; the same man may be more rational at one time of his life than at another. Yet, in spite of these variations, men are still "men", and still "rational". The "sameness of sense" may be strained by extreme fluctuations, but even when we call a man, or his actions, "irrational" and "unreasonable", we do so only because he has fallen away from his true nature. We do not mean that he has ceased to be a man, and that he should be classed with some non-human species of animals. At any rate, such reclassifications are indulged in only by way of abuse; they have no place either in the language of Science or in that of Ethics. In other words, if, by way of criticism, we call "unreasonable" a being whose nature it is to be "reasonable", we are neither saying what is false in fact, nor contradicting ourselves flagrantly, but we are expressing an extreme fluctuation in the quality of reasonableness—a diminution of it to the point of disappearance, as when we say that someone is "bereft of his reason", or has "lost his head".

However, with all this, we have not yet come to differences of *mode*. These we can illustrate, still taking rationality as our example, if we interpret the term, not abstractly as meaning a quality, but concretely as meaning the habitual performance of, or participation in, that complex of activities and interests which constitutes what Santayana has called "the life of reason". After all, when we look for the fundamental differences between man and non-human animals, we shall not find them in that human beings "reason", whereas non-human animals do not, but in that human beings have created in art, science, religion, philosophy, in their forms of government and social organisation, in their discoveries and inventions and the industries and commerce based on them, a complex civilisation and culture to which, as a whole, we can find no parallel or analogue in the animal kingdom outside *homo sapiens*.

Now, if we define "being rational" as participating in these activities, it is obvious that one man will differ from another, not only in degree, but also in mode. That is to say, one man will specialise in one kind of activity, another in another, e.g., artist, scientist, politician, priest, will each, in his own way, carry on the life of reason. Not that all these ways are necessarily incompatible, in principle, with each other, but there are practical limitations to the extent to which they can be successfully combined even by those who have aptitudes for more than one. The fact is that there is both differentiation of aptitude and division of labour, and either, or both together, give us differences of mode. A musical composer's *mode* of being rational will be different from a poet's or a painter's, and the mode of all three of these, as artists, will be different from that of a mathematician, a geologist, a biologist. Yet, the work of all these, on the view here taken, consists of rational activities, and in each kind of characteristically human work we have, therefore, a characteristic mode of being rational.

Within each mode there will be differences of degree: one musician will be more or less of a musician than another; one scientist's thinking will be more or less scientific than another's. But, as between mode and mode there is not, in general, any such comparison possible. It would be groundless to assert, e.g., that art is more or less rational than science. Yet all these modes of activities make up the "life of reason" in the concrete—the historical reality of human civilisation.

Of course, if we conceive rationality in this way, as meaning, concretely, the whole network of activities which constitute human civilisation, and each of these "at its best", or developed to its fullest degree, it is obvious at once that this type of universal, even less than the previous one, is realised in its fulness in any one of its instances or members. Indeed, it is possible here to raise the question, what are the members of the class determined by this universal? Is the human race, as a whole, the subject of which the life of reason, as concretely realised in the activities constituting civilisation, is to be predicated—thus forming a class with one member? Or are we to distinguish civilisations according to nation, or race, or perhaps even merely according to geological epoch (e.g., human civilisation in the quaternary epoch)? Or, lastly, are we to take as our class not civilisations, but civilised men, and the individual human being as the instance in whom the activities, in which being civilised consists, are present in varying modes, and each mode in varying degrees? Fortunately, for our present argument it does not matter which of these alternatives we adopt. For, on any view, the whole of civilisation is not realised, as a whole, in any one or all its instances. No single man, even in a "complete life" (as Aristotle might have said), no single national, or racial, or epochal type of civilisation, not even the human race as a biological unit, realises civilisation in all its modes or in the fulness of each mode at any one time. What then becomes of "in the same sense"? If, striving for sameness to the exclusion of difference, we cut down our concept of being rational (in the concrete sense of our present definition) to that range of degree and mode which we can predicate "in the same sense" of the primitive savage and the cultured European, we leave out the bulk of what constitutes rationality If, on the other hand, we construct as full a concept as we can, we pass beyond anything which is anywhere realised in actual fact.

Is there any escape from this choice between an empty minimum and an unrealised and unrealisable maximum? The only way out would seem to be that we should give up the prejudice in favour of conceiving universals with a hard-and-fast sameness, which would forbid, not only the recognition of differences of degree and mode in the instances of their realisation, but also any evolution, any history of development from lesser to fuller realisation. If the use of general names "in the same sense" of many objects forbids all this, it is a useless use, and the wise man will adopt a use which enables him to do justice to the facts. Flexibility is a virtue of thinking, no less than fixity.

Or, to put this differently, rationality is an example of a universal which is realised in its instances, not as a standing possession, but rather as a variable achievement. Being reasonable is a task, but a task laid upon human beings by their very nature as human. Hence, it is at once something which we are, which we strive to be, and which we ought to be. This is a point to be further elaborated below (section 4). Here it is mentioned only in order to support from a fresh angle the thesis that we shall do well to reject any interpretation of the demand for self-identity, contained in the phrase "in the same sense", which disables us from recognising universals as variable in the degree and mode of their realisation. If, on the contrary, we do conceive universals in this way as "identities in differences", we can not only expand our classes so as to include instances belonging to different levels of an evolutionary series, but we can go on to specify the conditions under which a given mode and degree of the universal is realised. And, from this study of conditions we may perchance learn further how to achieve a yet fuller realisation of the universal than any with which we are at present acquainted. Surely, it is no mean thing so to conceive universals as realised in particulars that we do justice at once to the classificatory, the evolutionary, the causal, and the purposive points of view. Any theory of the universal which does not, at least, attempt to provide such a synthesis, or which does not furnish a basis for these four ways in which universals determine our thinking, can hardly claim to touch the centre either of knowledge or of reality.

Some of the advantages of this way of looking upon universals may be emphasised even at the expense of a certain amount of repetition.

(a) If once we admit degrees into our concept of the realisation of a universal in instances, the possibility of measurement suggests itself. Not many qualities can be measured, directly or indirectly, but wherever measurement is possible, there we can give precision to the relation between variations in degree of quality and variations in the conditions under which the quality occurs, or in response to which it is displayed. But, with or without measurement, degrees invite the application of that most fruitful of all inductive methods—the method of concomitant variations.

(b) Again, where the common nature by which objects are classified together is complex and permits of analysis into its elements, it may happen that an object has all the elements but one. Its dominant nature, therefore, points to its inclusion in the class, and certainly forbids its inclusion in any other class. Yet its deficiency in one quality may seem to go against the definition and thus compel its exclusion. Here the concept of degrees varying with varying conditions opens a way out. For, the disappearance, or non-appearance, of a quality may be regarded as the extreme lower limit of variation. In other words, we may assign the quality to the object, but put down its value as zero. An example from Professor R. M. MacIver's analysis of the "foundations" of nationality may serve to illustrate the method.

Professor MacIver enumerates the following "chief qualities

or interests in the recognition of which, either as common or as exclusively common, the foundations of nationality must be sought:—(1) Race; (2) Language; (3) Territory, as occupied effectively (cf. (7c) below); (4) Economic interests; (5) Culture, i.e. characteristic standards and modes of life; (6) Religion; (7) Political unity; (7a) Political Tradition; (7b) Political Subjection; (7c) Political Domination. Applying these tests to a number of the most prominent states and peoples, he gets the following result:—

	(1).	(2).	(3).	(4).	(5).	(6).	(7).	(7a).	(7b).	(7c).	Pure Determinants.
British	O	X	X	X	X	O	X	I	O	I	(7a), (7c).
U.S.A.	O	X	X +	X	X	O	X	O	O	O	none.
French	X	X	X +	X	X +	O	O	I	O	I	(7a), (7c).
Italians	X	X	X +	X	X	O	O	O	O	O	none certain.
Russians	X	I	X	X	X +	O	X	I	O	I	(2), (7a), (7c).
Germans	X	X	X +	X	X +	O	X	O	O	I	(7c).
Jews	I	O	O	O	X	I	O	I?	I	O	(1), (6), (7b).
Japanese	I	I	I	X	X	O	I	I	O	?	(1), (2), (3), (7), (7c).
Spaniards	I	X	I	X	X	X	I	I	O	O	(1), (3), (7), (7a).
Swiss	O	O	I	X	O	O	I	I	O	O	(3), (7), (7a).
Poles	I	I	I	X	X	X	O	I	I	O	(1), (2), (3), (7a), (7b).
Czechs	I	I	I	I	X	O	O	O	I	O	(1), (2), (3), (4), (7b).
Magyars	I	I	I	X	X	O	X	I	O	I	(1), (2), (3), (7a), (7c).

Explanation of Symbols: I=factor *recognised* as exclusively common; X=factor recognised as common but not exclusive; O=factor in respect of which there is no community co-extensive with nationality; X +=factor nearly approaching I. The last column recapitulates the "pure determinants" (I).[1]

---

[1] This table is quoted from Professor MacIver's article on "Foundations of Nationality", in the *Sociological Review*, July, 1915. Many of the details, of course, would have to be changed, if the Table were to be redrawn in accordance with the results of the Peace Treaties of 1919-20.

Whether all Professor MacIver's details are correct is irrelevant to my argument. What is relevant is only the method, which not only recognises the principle of degrees (X+), but acknowledges factors in some nationalities which are non-existent (O) in others.

What saves the procedure from the charge of bare-faced fiction-mongering is precisely that it enables us to apply, or extend, a classification to objects in which a character is absent by atrophy, or because special conditions have led to its repression, or, at least, have given no opportunity for it to be evoked or developed. Once more, an immense gain in elasticity of thought, enabling us to follow the track of identity in difference where a rigid insistence on abstract "sameness" would erect an insuperable barrier.

(c) Thirdly, we need the concept of the universal here proposed to deal with objects which, whilst exhibiting a common character (and "common", here, means "same"), yet differ among themselves in that some exhibit this character in a "simple" or "rudimentary", others in a "complex" or "highly developed", form. Such objects may, of course, form an actual evolutionary series, but they need not do so. And whether they do so or not, the whole grouping of them together, the whole treating of them as instances of the "same" must seem to be logically illegitimate, unless we credit the "same" with differentiating itself under different conditions.

3. So far, the argument has treated the universal in the main as simply a class-character, common to, or identical in, many objects whose membership of the class is thereby determined.

We have next to point out that this is not the only function of the universal, either in theory or in practice. The universal is not only a class-character, it is also a standard or norm. Its function is not only classificatory, but also normative. Recognition of the universal in the particular enables us to judge, not only that the particular is of such and such a kind, but also that it is good or bad of its kind.

This function belongs to the universal equally whichever of the two chief senses of "norm" we adopt. We may mean by "norm" the "best"—the ideal standard of perfection for that kind of thing. Or we may mean by it the "average"—the normal as determined by the majority of instances. In either case, it supplies a measure of excellence. We may judge a thing to be either better, or worse, or equal to the average of its kind. And, again, we may judge it to be a perfect specimen or example of its kind—as good as it is possible for that kind of thing to be. Thus, the universal makes possible, not only judgments of fact, purely descriptive and classifying, but judgments of value as well.

The term "value" may be challenged on the ground that value is meaningless except in relation to desire. And it certainly seems far-fetched, especially in the context of Natural Science, to attribute to animals and plants, let alone to inanimate objects, a conscious desire for, or even merely an unconscious nisus towards, either the perfection of their own kind (an excellence above the average), or conformity to the average of their kind. However, not only do I not know any better word to use, but I am also inclined to challenge the whole theory which would make value relative to desire, so that "good" can mean only "what is desired", or, at most, what is "such as to be desired". This is not the place to argue this point on its merits, and I must, therefore, be content to ask for permission to use the term "value" without any reference to desire. To mark this independence of desire, I shall speak of "intrinsic" (or "objective" value), meaning that terms like good and bad, better and worse, perfect and imperfect, can be used of things significantly, with reference to a standard supplied by the nature itself of the things in question.

Now, the recognition of this intrinsic standard, and the making of comparative judgments of excellence, is possible only if the instances of a certain kind (or "nature") are not all exactly alike, but differ from each other in degree and mode precisely in the way described in the preceding section. If objects which are all of the same kind yet differ among themselves in the way in which their common character is realised in them severally, we have sufficient grounds not merely for judgments of more or less, but for judgments of better or worse, more perfect or less perfect.

It is not relevant to my purpose to investigate, at this point, what Kant would call the "possibility" of such judgments. That we *do* so judge, will be, I think, conceded. That we have a *right* so to judge may be disputed. I am here going to assume

o

that we have a right to do what we are doing, and that the same processes of thought which, by comparison and discrimination, enable us to recognise divers particulars as having the same character and being of the same kind, enable us also to discern where that character is most fully and perfectly realised, and to do this by a standard intrinsic to the character itself. Of course, such judgments are as liable to error as are purely descriptive and classificatory judgments. And, equally of course, do we learn in this matter by experience, if only because a limited and non-representative collection of instances is a poor guide to the discrimination of the intrinsic standard. There are contemporary thinkers who declare our right to generalise by inductive reasoning—and classifying particular objects as being of the same kind is one kind of generalisation—to be logically questionable. No doubt, these same thinkers will challenge even more vigorously our right to elicit from the same data which yield classificatory generalisations, a standard by which the degree of intrinsic excellence of these same data can be judged. To me, on the contrary, both kinds of thinking and reasoning seem to stand or fall—seem, in fact, to stand—together. And, without pursuing the *quaestio juris* into polemical by-paths, I am content to appeal to the fact that such judgments of intrinsic value are regularly employed even in the most severely scientific thinking. This is true, at any rate, of the biological sciences, in which the expert's distinction between a good and a bad, a better and a worse, specimen of its kind is a familiar thing. The selective judgment of the breeder of plants and animals is but an extension of the same principle, though here a definite reference to human purpose, utilitarian or aesthetic, may enter in.

At any rate, the points of our argument so far have been two. (*a*) In section (2), it has been argued that if it were really a logical pre-requisite of classification that every member of a class should possess the "same" character without differences of degree or mode, we should not be able to classify at all as we do, especially in the biological sciences. And (*b*), in the present section (3), it has been argued that the very differentiation of the "same" character in its instances enables us to rank them by an intrinsic standard of excellence—the standard of being, so to speak, "true" to the character of their kind. This standard reveals itself to the discerning mind through the very acts of comparing and distinguishing by which the lines between classes are traced.

4. But, we can now carry the argument a step further still.

Above, we said that to ascribe to the individual object, or to Nature as a whole, a desire for perfection would be fanciful. We may permit such language to poetic licence; we banish it from the rigorous speech of science. We refuse to say that every living thing, or Nature in every living thing, aims at the utmost perfection which, under the given conditions, is possible for that kind of thing. Yet, if we compare the dwarfed and stunted pine near the tree line on the upper slopes of the mountain with its majestic brother in the forest of the valley below, we are not false to the spirit of science, if we correlate the perfect growth of the one with the favourable conditions of the valley, and the thwarted growth of the other with the handicap of unfavourable conditions on the heights. We can hardly avoid saying here that each living thing "does the best it can" under the conditions, even if we check ourselves from saying that it "seeks" to do the best it can.[1] But when we come to beings that are *conscious*, and above all to beings which are *self-conscious*, some, at any rate, of these scruples may be laid aside. And so our argument about universals enters upon a fresh stage when, to the factors which we have considered so far, we add now the *consciousness* of their own kind, of their own characteristic nature, which human beings, at least, possess.

With the facing of this fact our argument swings into familiar tracks and allows us to travel fast and far.

First, with consciousness comes knowledge. True, this is not yet "reflective" knowledge, distinguishing self and not-self, nor even, at the start, amounting to explicit judgment. And yet, the most rudimentary form of consciousness, however we conceive it—e.g., a flux of sensations, peripheral, organic, kinaesthetic, shot through with pleasure and pain—is already an awareness in germ of self and world. Whatever language we use about this pre-linguistic stage of knowledge must, of course, be taken in a Pickwickian sense. For, taken literally, it imports meanings

---

[1] Spinoza's *conatus in suo esse perseverare* (*Ethics*, Part iii., Prop. 6) should be interpreted as an endeavour on the part of each thing to *realise its nature to the utmost* under the conditions of its existence.

which are not yet there; it assumes distinctions as yet far from being made. But, if we are to speak, hypothetically, of these things at all, we can do so only by giving them, in anticipation, the character which it is their destiny to acquire in the course of evolution. In this sense, we can say that the earliest glimmerings of peripheral sensations constitute a rudimentary awareness of what concerns the creature for good or ill in its environment, the lesson of good or ill being taught at this stage by pleasure and pain. And, similarly, the earliest organic and kinaesthetic sensations are the creature's way of being aware of its own bodily condition and movement. The steps by which, from some such beginnings, the evolution of mind may be supposed to have travelled to man's articulate knowledge of self and world, we need not trace. Enough for our argument that we can, and do, not only distinguish the various kinds of things which make up our environment, but also that we know, more or less adequately, the kind of thing we are ourselves as a class, and, indeed, the kind of thing each of us is in himself as an individual.

Self-consciousness, in short, brings self-knowledge. Or, lest we be reminded that we know all too little about ourselves, both individually and as a race, and that much which passes for self-knowledge is really illusion and error about ourselves, let us rather say that self-consciousness brings *self-objectification*. We make, quite literally, "objects" of ourselves. We can, if we choose, study human nature and behaviour in ourselves and our fellows as we study the nature and behaviour of non-human kinds of animals and plants. We can identify our place in the object-world at large, and trace the manifold relations which indissolubly bind us to it, conditioned and conditioning. We can do for our own kind what we can do for all other kinds of objects; we can trace how the "same" nature differentiates itself in infinite variety of degree and mode in the members of the class *homo sapiens*. We can discriminate, too, between these differentiations, sorting the better from the worse, the more human (or the more truly human) from the less human. And so, here as everywhere, the universal functions at once as *fact* and as *ideal*—as "nature" or "character" actually embodied and realised, and yet also as a standard by which the degree of perfection of each realisation can be estimated, and which ever confronts the actual with an unrealised, or not-yet-realised, better.

Thus, human nature is what makes us men. But it is also a norm by which we can judge how far we succeed or fail in being men. We are self-conscious; therefore, self-knowing or, at least, self-objectifying; therefore *self-normative*. Knowing human nature in ourselves (or having at least some concept thereof), we also know (or have some concept of) the standard or norm intrinsic in human nature. A norm known, and known as the norm of our own nature, becomes an object of desire, of aspiration, of endeavour. We can, even if the rest of Nature cannot, aim at making ourselves more perfect than we are— more perfect as human beings. Human we are: humaner we must strive to become.

For, the norm, or ideal, of our own nature is not merely an object of theory, nor merely an object of desire: it imposes also an obligation, it defines a *duty*. What we are, that we may desire to become more perfectly: but, whether or no we desire this, we recognise that we ought to attempt it. The ideal may attract, but it certainly also binds and obliges. If it is an end sought, it is also a task to be shouldered with effort. And being the ideal of our own nature, it is always, in principle, both.

Familiar paradoxes, which yet are among the fundamental verities of man's spiritual life, flow from this situation. The distinction between the "actual" self and the "ideal" self (in the sense of the "true" or "perfect" self, the self, "at its best") is a traditional topic of philosophical dialectics. But the facts of normal human living, of daily experience, which lie behind the dialectics, are undeniable. The dialectical antitheses are no artificial figments of theory: they do but put into technical language the ambivalences and oscillations of human conduct and judgment. Only one who is a man can fail at being a man. For, to fail is to fall short of the intrinsic demand and standard involved in "being a man". Being a man, such a one is yet a "poor specimen of a man". And, in facing this double-edged fact, if, indeed, he does honestly face it, it is brought home to him at once that he wants to be, and that he ought to be, a better man than he is. So, again, only an artist can be a "bad" artist, only a doctor can be a "good" doctor. But what boots it to multiply examples? Throughout the whole range of human nature, whether we look to innate endowments or to acquired skill, knowledge, character, the principle holds good: what a man is, that he can be either better or worse. His nature is at once actual and ideal. And being "true" to it, or to himself, does not cease to be either an aspiration or a duty, for all that he may succeed in it more often than he fails. It is only a "man" who can be reproached with "being a beast": just as it is only a man who can be bidden to become "like unto God".

But I do not want to labour this point. Rather do I want to conclude this section by glancing once more at the controversy about objective value and value relative to desire, which was touched on above. If there is anything in the argument of this section, it follows that we must regard the values of human desire as derivative from the values intrinsic to human nature. We may, of course, *define* "good" as the object of desire, and "bad" as the object of aversion, but we cannot abolish facts by a fiat of definition. If we adopt this definition, we must find other words in which to state the facts. For, the facts are there for us to see, after the definition no less than before it. Perhaps we may put the matter thus: needs, wants, desires, are part of human nature. To begin with, we desire food, not because food is judged to be good, but because we are built that way. Indeed, our earliest desires (if this term is applicable at all at this early stage) involve no awareness of their "object", of what would satisfy them. The object is learnt later, by experience and re-collection of satisfactions provided by those who knew what we needed better than we did ourselves. In *this* context—and this insistence on *context* is an essential qualification—we may concede that "good" is relative to desire; that for a thing to be good means for it to be desired on the ground that it is known from previous experience of one's own, or inferred by analogy with the experience of others, to bring satisfaction. But desires, and their objects and satisfactions, may be considered also in *another*, and wider, context. As parts of human nature, they fall under the principle above elaborated, viz., that human nature involves an intrinsic standard or ideal. To desire certain things, to seek certain satisfactions in certain ways, is to be human, is to realise human nature. But, for this very reason, the question applies: Is it to be rightly and truly human? Does this way of life realise human nature at its best? Thus, an objective standard of value can be brought to bear on desires and their objects, as on anything else in which a universal nature is realised in particular instances. The standard can be brought to bear, because it is itself but the universal nature in one of its aspects.

In short, human desires and human satisfactions, in their different degrees and modes (cf. section (2)), are some more, some less, human in the sense that some represent a higher level of human nature than others. Nor does the phrase "higher level" tell the whole story. For, in the first place, it is characteristic of the development of human nature to higher levels by self-objectification and self-judgment (self-criticism), to give rise to desires of a higher order, i.e., to desires for, or aversions from, certain kinds of other desires. Such a desire of a higher order—a desire for a desire, so to speak—is possible only at the level of self-conscious reflection where desires and their satisfactions can be compared and a choice, if need be, made between them. Usually we call such a desire of a higher order rather a "rational preference", or a "principle of conduct". But the terms do not matter so long as it is agreed that in such choices, or preferences, there is operative, in principle, an intrinsic standard of excellence, an ideal of human nature and of human life as a whole. Moreover, in the second place, such a preference, in proportion as it is an effective determinant of conduct and does not remain merely a pious aspiration, embodies itself in a habit of cultivating certain desires and their satisfactions, and of subordinating, nay even repressing, others. It thus acts as an *organising* principle in human conduct. We have, each of us, his own "economy of desires", his own system or hierarchy of interests, his own scale of values, in accordance with which our lives are more or less consistently ordered. And, if the comparison, above, of desires as more or less human has still seemed strained to some, in spite of all previous argument, it may be easier for them to recognise and admit the principle when the comparison is between whole lives—types of lives—in respect of the order (economy) in each life of various kinds of desires and satisfactions. Here, surely, it cannot well be denied that not all human lives are equally ("in the same sense") human, and that some achieve a much higher level of humanity than others, and come nearer to what a human life can be at its best, and ought to be. Such judgments as these on human lives pervade our practice. Such judgments—this is the whole point of the argument—are justified in theory. And on what other ground can they be justified, or, at least, justified so successfully, as on the present theory of the function of universals as intrinsic, or objective, norms?

Morality, lastly, from this point of view, may be regarded as man's consciousness of the intrinsic ideal inherent in his nature (which term we must here expand to include his relations to his world), and as his effort to realise that ideal, to achieve, so to speak, the maximum of humanity. Moreover, the fact that morality has so often been construed under the antithetic concepts of "happiness" and "duty" becomes intelligible from our point of view when we recall that the ideal of our own nature at once exercises an attraction and imposes an obligation. These two sides of the ideal have often been divorced from, and opposed to, each other in theory, because they often conflict in life. But, in principle, they are compatible with, and indispensable to, each other. We might almost construct a Hegelian triad, and say that desire and duty are "moments" in the love of the ideal.

5. Mention of morality, however, suggests yet a further line of thought. For, the fact that morality is not a purely individual, but a social phenomenon, may serve to remind us of an important limitation which has characterised our whole point of view so far. From the moment when we began by investigating the sameness of sense in which a general term is applicable to many objects, we have been thinking of members of *classes*, not of members of *organised groups* or *wholes*.

In order to make my point as briefly as possible, I shall omit here from consideration all non-human groups or societies, the adult members of which we may credit in varying degrees with leading self-conscious, self-knowing, self-normative lives, in the sense given to these terms in the preceding section.

The point of principle here to be made is one familiar from Plato's *Republic*, where its theoretical importance was, so far as we can tell, for the first time explicitly recognised. It is simply this that such differences of degree and mode as we have shown to exist among members of the same class, make possible that kind of *ordering* of these members in a social group which we call *organisation*. The differences of degree and mode in the way in which the common class-character is realised in the multitude of members, become positively significant when they are made the basis of differentiation of function within the structure and life of a society. True, we have no philosopher-kings charged with the task of ascertaining what every member of society is best fitted for, and of assigning him to that work. We leave the selection partly to the accident of opportunity, partly to the individual's judgment of his own abilities, partly to the conflict of his own interests and ambitions. But this does not affect the principle, which is, perhaps, most easily appreciated when stated in negative form. No whole of differentiated parts, no structure with organs specialised for their several functions, can be constructed out of parts each of which is exactly similar to every other. Such parts could only do exactly similar work in exactly similar ways. They could not coöperate with each other by contributing, each in its own way, to a common achievement.

It is unnecessary to labour a principle so familiar as this, though it was necessary to mention it for completeness of exposition. Only one minor point may be added. A class-character is, as such, indifferent to the number of instances ("extension") in which it is realised. Of course, the larger the number of instances, the greater the possible range of differences of degree and mode. But, to fix for the membership of natural classes either an upper or a lower numerical limit would be a futile undertaking, in the absence of any rational grounds for such a determination (unless we fix the minimum at one individual of each sex, for purposes of propagation). On the other hand, when we come to organised groups, the numerical aspect tends to assume positive significance. According to the purpose for which the group exists, and the differentiation of functions necessary for the realisation of this purpose, there may be both minima and maxima, below and above which the group ceases to function effectively, if it does not cease to function altogether. *Tres faciunt collegium* prescribes a traditional minimum for an academic lecture group. "Two is company" excludes the unwelcome third from a group of lovers. Small executive committees are found to be better for discussion of details and for administrative decisions than large committees and conferences in which it takes long for singleness of mind to be achieved. Yet, for discussions of principle large gatherings are generally indispensable, in order that every one of many relevant interests or points of view may have its representative and advocate. Groups for the purpose of law-making (parliaments, legislative assemblies, etc.) invariably have a fixed numerical limit, however it may be determined from case to case, e.g., by population, by constituent states, etc. It is noticeable that among primitive peoples the loss of a member from a sib or tribe, e.g., by marriage into another sib or tribe, or by death, is generally felt acutely, and that special rites or ceremonies are practised to re-affirm the stability and solidarity of the group. With larger groups, like nation-states, the tendency for the organisation to embody itself in a definite number is no longer so marked. If the membership becomes very small, the state will no longer be able to maintain itself against the pressure of other states. If the membership becomes too large, the internal unity of the state may be strained to breaking point. But to pursue the ramifications of this subject lies beyond the scope of the present argument. Enough if we have shown how the extensional aspect appears in a different light, when number is considered in relation to organisation. For, an organised group is an embodied universal: it exists as a common principle, or purpose, in the relations and activities of the members of the group. These members as particulars are enumerable, and it may matter to the embodiment of the universal what their number is, or, at any rate, between what numerical limits in a given case it falls.

6. So far I have developed my argument without using the terms "abstract" and "concrete" universal. The omission has been deliberate: I wanted to state my argument, if possible, without the help of these terms, not because they are in themselves inconvenient, but because they have become catchwords of controversy. Not that I want to shirk debate on fundamental philosophical issues, but the avoidance of controversial terms has sometimes this advantage that it facilitates a re-consideration of the facts on their merits. The mere mention of a term round which there has been a well-known clash of opposing views is an invitation to take sides and settle the question with

habitual judgments *pro* and *con* instead of looking at it with fresh eyes.

I make these remarks by way of preface to the attempt, now to be made, to connect the argument of this paper with the brief statements, in my *Studies in Contemporary Metaphysics*, about universals. The view taken in my *Studies*[1] may be summarised as follows. Every datum, every bit (so to speak) of reality that comes to us in experience, is a "this-such". It is emphatically *this*, and no other, and so far "particular"; but it is also "*such*", and so far "universal"; that is to say, it has a nature, character, quality—a "what", as F. H. Bradley would have said—which makes it just what it is, and in thus constituting its identity also differentiates it from every other "this-such" in the company of which it may happen to appear in the context of experience.

It will be convenient to interrupt my summary here to explain, and, so far as I can, defend this first step.

This concept of the minimal datum as a "this-such" has been questioned, and I confess I do not know how to demonstrate my view. We are here in a region beyond the reach of argument, if by "argument" be meant a process of reasoning which proves a conclusion from premises accepted. No, the function of all so-called "argument" in matters of this sort is simply to *point out*—to induce the reader so to look at the subject under discussion that he sees, or intuits, the datum in such a way as to perceive the description of it as a "this-such" to be appropriate. I may fail in this endeavour for lack of skill in the use of words, just as conceivably the reader may fail through bias of other theories to adjust his vision to what I would have him see and acknowledge as self-evident. At any rate, if our minds do not see alike in this matter, what follows will have been written in vain.

But it may assist the reader in reaching the desired adjustment, if I guard against one or two possible misunderstandings. Language, in its theoretical use, bears the stamp of "discursive" thinking—of thinking which analyses and distinguishes, no less than it synthesises, relates, identifies. To speak of "a" datum already implies discrimination, selection, isolation of this from that, of this from others. To speak of the datum as

[1] See, especially, pp. 131 ff., 183 ff., 208.

"this-such", at once makes explicit in the wholeness (so to speak) of the given the distinction between two aspects—this and such. The very concept of data is possible only at a level of thought at which data are actually only an element in the tissue of knowledge, and, when distinguished and isolated, are clearly "abstract". But, whether we consider the datum thus abstracted, or whether we posit hypothetically a level of immediate experience or pure awareness, prior to language, prior to thinking; whether, with Mr. Russell and others, we analyse the universe ultimately into "atomic facts", or whether, with Professor Whitehead, we conceive of it as a flowing continuum, a tissue of events; whether our datum be thought of as a simple *quale*, or as an ever-changing complex of *qualia*— on any of these alternatives, it seems to me that whatever is, is "this-such". Whether we talk of experience, or perception, or acquaintance; whether we believe that what we experience, perceive, or are acquainted with, is the real or merely an illusory appearance of it; and whether the object of our awareness be the whole, or only a part of it, large or small—that which we are aware of here and now exhibits always indissolubly conjoined in fact, though distinguishable by reflective analysis, the two sides, or aspects, which I express by the compound term "this-such".

If I have failed to convince, I can say no more. But, if this first step be granted, then—and here I resume the summary of the view put forward in my *Studies*—I go on to say that the development of knowledge, the apprehension of reality as an intelligibly ordered system, whatever fragment of it may be datum here and now to a particular mind, proceeds by following the clue of the nature or character (the "what") of the given—the "universal".

Here I must interpose that, from this point of view for which "this" and "such", particular and universal, are inseparable, though distinguishable, aspects of the real, the central question of much modern discussion, viz., whether particulars and universals are two fundamentally (i.e., metaphysically) distinct classes of *objects*, is full of mistaken assumptions, especially when the answer given to the question is affirmative. For an affirmative answer hypostatises the products of abstraction, and those who adopt this answer pay the inevitable penalty in losing themselves in the maze of problems which centre around the "existence" of particulars and the "subsistence" of universals, and, further, around the relation of these two classes of objects, each with its own mode of *being*, when an object of the one class is predicated in a proposition of an object of the other class.

The more logical ingenuity is diverted in this direction, the more is the basis of all these fine drawn theories lost from sight, viz., the union of "this" and "such" in every bit of the real which we at any moment immediately apprehend.

But to return from this polemical digression. The programme of "following the clue" (as I called it just now) of the universal may lead us in any one of several different directions, all of which, however, are contributory to knowledge, all of which reveal the real to us as an ordered, and so far intelligible, whole. From any "this-such", however it comes to be singled out, we may, by way of "another such" and more other suches (if the solecism be permitted), i.e., by way of others of the same sort, reach classes. Or, again, by correlating one sort of *quale* with another sort of *quale*, we may reach causal laws and generalisations to the effect that one kind of event is necessarily connected ("functionally correlated") with another kind of event. Or, yet again, from any this-such we may, by way of "this again" (even if it be, as it generally is, "this again with a difference") reach *individuals*. To illustrate the point crudely: Robinson Crusoe, believing himself alone on the island, catches, for the first time, a momentary glimpse of a dark figure among the bushes. Later, he perceives again a dark figure. Two distinct perceptions: two distinct objects, each a "this-such". Question, both practically and theoretically of immense importance to Crusoe: "This again" or "Another such"? Two groups of data, certainly; but whether they belong to one and the same individual or to two different individuals only further experience can settle. Anyone of the several possible types of order may attract to itself a theoretical interest of its own, yielding classificatory science, causal science, biography and history. But, because each contributes to knowledge and helps, in its own way, to reveal the nature of the real, each may also subserve the others, and help them more completely to achieve their purpose. However, this is not the place to pursue this topic of *types of order*, which are different kinds of universals, into all its ramifications. Whatever has been urged in previous sections of this essay, belongs here. What I have said in this section is enough, I hope, to show how the view taken of universals in my *Studies* underlies, and is completed by, the account given of them in this paper.

As the first glimmerings of experience expand into articulate knowledge, the "this" of the first datum expands into the world, the universe, the real as a whole, and the "such", distinguished from, related to, identified with, other "suches", expands into the variegated system of systems which is what the real is for us—which is what we mean when we say, "*Such* is the nature of reality: *Such* we perceive and think it to be".

Neo-Realistic Theories of Mind or Consciousness[1]

INTRODUCTION

SINCE the beginning of this century the philosophical world has been full of movements of unusual interest and promise. First, the academic calm was stirred by the *Pragmatism* of William James with its off-shoot, the *Humanism* of Mr. F. C. S. Schiller. Then came the discovery of Bergson, who, after having for many years thought and written in comparative obscurity, suddenly experienced a meteoric rise to international fame. Whatever value we may put upon his theory as a whole, some of his profoundest ideas will, I am convinced, have an abiding influence on philosophical speculation long after he has ceased to be the fountain of wisdom for soulful ladies of fashion. Like all fresh and original minds, Bergson is hard to fit into the pigeon-holes of our traditional classification of philosophical systems, but, if he is to be fitted in, he must be called an Idealist. Yet, at the same time, the other and older forms of *Idealism* have by no means lost their vitality or their fruitfulness. It is enough, within the English-speaking world alone, to point to the recent Gifford Lectures of Professors James Ward and Bernard Bosanquet, and in America, to the writings of Professors Josiah Royce and Hugo Munsterberg. And, lastly, within quite recent years we have been able to welcome in

[1] In order to reduce the references in the body of the following paper to the indispensable minimum, it will be best to give, at the outset, a list of the chief books and articles which I have had in mind in writing. They are:

(1) For the Oxford School of Neo-Realism: Mr. H. A. Prichard's *Kant's Theory of Knowledge*.

(2) For the Manchester School: Professor Alexander's articles during recent years in the *Proceedings of the Aristotelian Society*, in *Mind*, and in the *British Journal of Psychology*.

(3) For the Cambridge School: Mr. Bertrand Russell's *Philosophical Essays* and *Problems of Philosophy*; and articles by him and by Mr. G. E. Moore in *Mind*, and in the *Proceedings of the Aristotelian Society*.

(4) For the American School: Professor R. B. Perry's *Present Philosophical Tendencies*, and the volume entitled *The New Realism*, containing essays by six American Realists.

Neo-Realism a vigorous movement, which has already split up into several different schools, and which, aggressive in its challenge and ambitious in its constructive programme, bids fair to play a far more important part on the philosophical stage than either Pragmatism or even Bergsonianism.[1] Its challenge is directed against Idealism in all its forms. By its very name it claims to champion *reality*, to re-assert the existence of an independent object-world against what it takes to be the theoretical denial of that world on the part of Idealism. Now, in the clash of philosophical arguments, as in other battles, the dust is apt to fly, and a condition results such as that which made Berkeley complain that "philosophers first raise a dust, and then complain that they cannot see". The points of issue become confused, and the arguments on both sides correspondingly irrelevant. This is what I believe to have happened to some extent in the recent controversies between Idealists and Neo-Realists. Hence there is, I conceive, a real and pressing need for a precise definition of, and orientation about, the points of issue. The time has come for a laying of the dust, and it is a contribution to this humble, but necessary, work that I propose to offer the following discussion of *one* only, but that the most fundamental of the problems in dispute, viz., the problem of Mind or Consciousness in its bearing on the theory of the nature of reality. The issue may be, briefly and provisionally, stated thus: Idealists of all shades agree in construing the universe as, in last analysis, mental; as a mind or a system of minds. Realists of all shades agree in holding that reality is different from, and independent of, mind; or, more accurately, that mind, which is, in some sense, undeniably real itself, is only a part of the total reality, and, moreover, a part which is not necessary to the existence and nature of the rest. This, then, is the problem which forms the subject of this paper.

[1] If this estimate of the importance of Neo-Realism be challenged as an exaggeration, I should reply (1) that Realism is the natural reaction against the apparent paradoxes of Idealism, and that attempts to maintain it, in some form or other, will therefore continue to be made as long as Idealism holds the field; (2) that modern Neo-Realism, in particular, is important as introducing into philosophical speculation many of the recent results and theories of Natural Science, Mathematics, and the Logic of Relations; (3) That a movement led by such thinkers as Mr. Bertrand Russell and Professor Alexander in England, Professor O. Kulpe (the first volume of whose *Realisierung* appeared last year) in Germany, and a vigorous band of young philosophers in America, is bound to have a considerable influence.

PART I.—GENERAL SURVEY

Nothing, at first sight, may well seem more in keeping with commonsense than the position of the Realist, nothing a wilder paradox than that of the Idealist. The distinction between minds and bodies, as the two chief constituents of what we ordinarily call the "real world", is one which the very words of language teach us to make, and which constant use has made so familiar that, ordinarily, we have even ceased to reflect upon it. Most of us, if not versed in philosophy, may even discover a sneaking tendency in ourselves to look upon the body, because it is solid and substantial and space-filling, because, in short, it is material, a thing to be seen and felt and handled, as somehow *more real*, more securely *there* (as it were), than a thing invisible, intangible, immaterial, "abstract", like the mind or "soul". Religious motives may lead some to reverse this valuation, to put the body low in the scale of reality because it is perishable, and the soul high on the ground that it is immortal. But when we approach the question from the scientific point of view, we tend to be impressed rather by what I will call the *continuity* of the body with the material universe and the *discontinuity* of the mind, both within itself and in its contact with other minds. The body, though subject to dissolution as an aggregate of elements, none the less, just through these very materials of which it is composed, shares in the stability and permanence of the physical universe as a whole. This stability, of which the law of the conservation of matter is the most general formula, has found expression in the scientific concept of the material world as a closed, self-contained, mechanical, material system; a system in which minds have no share or place, which was before ever a mind had evolved, which will be long after all minds are extinguished, and which behaves according to its own laws, independently of the presence or absence of minds. We need but go one step further, and either deny the existence of minds altogether, or treat them as mere idle, ineffective by-products of the bodily machine, to have the theory of reality which is called *Materialism*. In the continuous material system which this theory assumes, minds seem but like discontinuous sparks, kept flashing, here and there, by bodies of a certain structure—sparks which glimmer for a brief space and then are

P

gone for ever. Not only do they seem to have no continuity with each other: even within their own short span of existence they are subject to constant interruptions by sleep and unconsciousness. What tides us over these intervals, these breaks in our mental life, except the continuity of the material frame, the body? Reflections such as these almost inevitably lead one to ascribe a higher reality to the body, and in general to the material universe, than to the mind—to call the material universe "reality" par excellence, and to treat it as complete in itself, and independent of mind.

This was the position of the *Old Realism*, which was thus, in effect, more or less deliberately, more or less outspokenly, *materialistic*. We shall recognise it wherever, in any philosophical theory, we find these two orders of existents asserted, a material order and a mental order, with the implication that the former is fundamentally more real than the latter, and therefore the latter dependent on the former, but not *vice versa*. It is a view which we can easily identify by asking the *fundamental test-question* which I propose to address to all Realisms: supposing there were no minds at all, supposing them all annihilated, how much would be lost out of our universe, how much would remain? Whatever we take as remaining after the subtraction of minds—*that* will be our "independent reality", and the exact character of our Realism will vary according to the way in which we conceive this independent reality.

Neo-Realism differs from the older forms, not in the fundamental principle of asserting a non-mental reality, but in refusing to regard this reality as exclusively material. Material objects are to it only one kind, and perhaps not even an ultimate kind, of reality. There are *non-material objects*, which, for all their non-materiality, are yet non-mental, i.e., are in character and existence independent of mind in the sense required by Realism. True, the different forms of Neo-Realism in England and America differ widely from one another in the extent to which they go beyond Materialism. The *Oxford Realists*, led by Mr. Prichard, are nearest to the Materialists: in fact, their independent reality is just the material system of the Physicists, a universe of molecules, atoms, electrons, etc., a universe without sound or colour or taste or smell, in short, a universe stripped of its *secondary* and reduced to its *primary* qualities. Again, the *Manchester* school, represented singly but mightily by Professor Alexander, is materialistic in temper, for it speaks of real objects as "physical" and as "bodies". Its Materialism, however, is, like Sam Weller's knowledge of London, "extensive and peculiar", for it treats the objects of dreams, hallucinations, imaginations as no less "physical" than the things of our waking perception. Only when it comes to *numbers* does it confess itself puzzled. For they are clearly not physical, and yet are "real" and "independent". The last of the *English* schools, viz., the *Cambridge* school, led by Mr. Bertrand Russell and Mr. G. E. Moore, is very much less materialistic than the previous two,[1] largely because, through Mr. Russell, it has been profoundly influenced by modern mathematical and logical theories, and among the latter, more especially by the writings of Meinong.

Now, it is just here that, as it seems to me, we come quite clearly upon the decisive break between the Materialism of the older Realists and the fresh conception of reality of the modern Realists—the fresh conception which justifies the epithet "New". The decisive point, in principle, is the recognition of *reals* which are *non-material*, without thereby becoming "*mental*", which are, therefore, both non-material and non-mental. For want of a characteristic word we may call them, with the *American* school of Neo-Realists, "neutral". It is to be set down to the credit of the American Neo-Realists that they have recognised the character of the new principle more clearly than the English schools. Yet even they do not all seem to have appreciated its significance or scope. Many even among them tend to gravitate back towards too exclusive a preoccupation with reals which are material. But the principle itself is clear enough. It is nothing but the recognition that every form of apprehension has its "object" and that the "existence" or "subsistence" of this object can be distinguished from the occurrence of the apprehension. The principle might perhaps be called the *principle of the independence of the cognitive object*. It posits as fundamental the "objectivity" (=the "Gegenständlichkeit" of German logicians) of whatever we are aware of.

---

[1] A good test of this is Mr. Russell's attitude on the question of the reality of *universals* (*Problems of Philosophy*, ch. ix.), or again, his theory of Sense-data (*ibid.*, ch. i.-iii.).

To be aware "of" something implies that there *is* something of which we are aware. The exact status of this something in the realm of being may be matter for discussion, but its being there, as that which we apprehend, is guaranteed by the apprehension itself. Anything whatsoever, then, which we can in any way apprehend at all—any object in this wide and inclusive sense—is real (i.e., exists or subsists), and is independent in the sense required by Realism. That is what the principle claims, or would claim, if all Realists fully appreciated its significance. Within the general "universe of being" which is thus posited, we can make what distinctions the character of the objects appears to demand. We may class them as material and non-material, as facts and fictions, as appearances and realities, as abstract and concrete, as truths and errors. But, in so far as they all are objects, they all alike exist or subsist independently of the mind, i.e., of apprehension, thought, knowledge.

This seems to me the really important principle in Neo-Realism—important, both because it frees Realism from the fetters of a Materialism which had become a mere effete prejudice, and even more because it affords, as we shall see, a basis for fruitful discussion with every kind of Idealism which calls itself "Objective". To be sure, Realists themselves are often still very far from appreciating this fully, partly (as I suggested just now) because they have not yet shaken off the old habit of assigning to the problem of the material world a prerogative place, partly because the application of this principle with ruthless consistency to all objects whatsoever runs counter to many other established habits of thought, e.g., it involves "objective falsehoods". It is sufficient, however, merely to think of the whole range of mathematical entities to have an example of objects which may be said to subsist, and therefore to be real and independent, without being either "material" or "mental" in any sense ordinarily attached to these terms.

At this point we shall be well advised to take a fresh breath, for the next big wave of the argument is about to rise up and smite upon us.

Those with a keen ear for dialectical over-tones will have noticed, that in the course of the last argument the relation of real object and mind has transformed its character. Such terms as "object", "cognitive", "apprehension", "knowledge" were repeatedly used. But with these very terms the problem has been put in a fresh form. We had begun by considering the current distinction of "minds" and "real things" *without reference to* the special feature that "things" are said to be "known" by "minds". But from the moment that we began to treat "things" as "objects" which, through perception and thought, are "apprehended" or "known", the whole problem shifted under our hands. The question is no longer how to distinguish in our universe non-mental realities from minds, both being admitted to occur, to co-exist, and even to co-öperate as, e.g., in the "psycho-physical" human personality. The question is now the much narrower, but also much profounder one of *the relation of realities, regarded as objects of knowledge, to the minds which are said to know them.* In short, we have broached what has often been declared to be the central problem of modern philosophy, viz., the *theory of knowledge.* We are dealing with the cognitive situation or relation : minds know objects, objects are known by minds. This apparently commonplace and harmless situation gives rise, as is well known, to some of the most puzzling problems of philosophy. We can now re-define the issue between Realism and Idealism in a preciser form. Idealism, according to the interpretation of its Realist critics, holds that to be real is to be known, to be object of a mind, that this relation to, or dependence on, a knowing mind is essential and constitutive alike for the existence (or subsistence) and for the nature of the object known. Idealism, on this view, extends Berkeley's *esse est percipi* to judgment and inference : it is the thorough-going and consistent elaboration of a monstrous initial assumption, viz., that things are "real" or "have being" only when and as long as some mind perceives or thinks them. That the language commonly employed by Idealists lends colour to this interpretation, is undeniable, cp., e.g., the phrase "reality is our intellectual construction". But I shall try to show below that the interpretation is, none the less, misleading. However, for the present, the point to note is that Idealism is held to identify reality and mind in the sense of dissolving our stable, systematic universe, e.g., the world of nature, into the dream-like tissue of the flux of perceptions and thoughts. There is nothing real, Idealists are understood to say, except what minds perceive and think when and so long as they

perceive and think it. Truly this may seem a reduction of reality
to mind which dissipates reality, and which, instead of real
things, leaves nothing but mental states in our hands. No
wonder that the Realist rises up in defence of reality and proclaims its independence of mind, in the sense that it exists and
has a definite nature of its own, whether it is known or not.
Thus Professor Perry declares that Realism "means that things
may be, and are, directly experienced without owing either
their being or their nature to that circumstance".[1] Professor
Montague states the same view more fulsomely: "Realism
holds that things known may continue to exist unaltered when
they are not known, or that things may pass in and out of the
cognitive relation without prejudice to their reality, or that the
existence of a thing is not correlated with, or dependent upon,
the fact that anybody experiences it, perceives it, conceives it,
or is in any way aware of it".[2] The English Realists speak in a
similar strain. Thus Mr. Prichard says: "Knowledge un-
conditionally presupposes that the reality known exists independently of the knowledge of it, and that we know it as it exists in
this independence".[3] And again: "We can no more think that
in apprehending reality we do not apprehend it as it is apart
from our knowledge of it, than we can think that existence
depends upon our knowledge of it".[4] Professor Alexander
declares the "vital question" to be whether objects "are independent of mind", and proposes to use the terms "non-
mental" or "external" to express this independence.[5] These
quotations may suffice to illustrate the insistence with which
Neo-Realists of all shades uphold the conception of a universe
which shall be "real" in the sense of "independent of mind",
where "mind" means knowledge or the processes (or activities)
of knowing (perceiving, thinking, etc.) and where "independent" means that these processes make no difference[6] to the
nature or existence of the real.

Now, in order to deal with the issue in this form, we must

[1] *Present Philosophical Tendencies*, ch. xiii., § 6, p. 315.
[2] *The New Realism*, appendix, p. 474.
[3] *Kant's Theory of Knowledge*, ch. iv., p. 118.   [4] *Ibid.*, p. 119.
[5] "On Sensations and Images," *Proc. Arist. Soc.*, 1909-10, pp. 5, 6.
[6] Professor Perry protests against the phrase "making no difference" (*New Realism*, p. 104), but it seems a fair paraphrase of the view expressed in the quotations
given, and it has the authority of Professor Royce (*The World and the Individual*,
First Series, pp. 118-123), and Mr. Joachim (*The Nature of Truth*, pp. 33, 58).

once more take a survey for orientation. And our best clue will be to put the question: *What do we mean by a mind?* What does it do? What is it made of? What are its constituent elements? To guide us to the answer, let us again apply the test-question suggested above: What would disappear from our universe if minds were wholly to disappear out of it? That is, in effect, the subtraction which the Oxford Realist, Mr. Prichard, asks us to make when he lays down the principle that we must treat as mental everything in the universe which would disappear with the disappearance of minds. Very well, let us make the subtraction.

(*a*) Minds are commonly said to feel, to think or know, and to will, or to consist of feelings, perceptions, and thoughts and volitions. Rough and ready as this threefold division is, it has well-established philosophical tradition in its favour, and it is, moreover, endorsed by most modern psychologists. It will serve sufficiently well for our present purpose, and so we shall conclude, in the first instance, that the disappearance of minds from the world would mean the disappearance of every kind of feeling, thought, and will—in short, of "consciousness"— but would leave everything else as it is.

(*b*) But *is* there anything else? That is just the point at issue. Let us try further. Leaving aside feelings and volitions, on the ground that the dispute is concerned only with "knowledge" of real objects, we shall say that to "know" is to perceive and think. It might be objected that this is too unqualified a statement. To know, it may be said, is to perceive and think *truly*, to perceive and think things *as they are*. Not all perceiving and thinking satisfies this test. We mis-perceive, we mis-think. Mistakes and errors are not "knowledge". But this distinction, again, we may neglect, for even when we think falsely, we do undeniably think *something*: our minds are not an empty blank. There is, cognitively speaking, an *object*—misconceived and distorted if you will, but still an object. For this reason, we shall take knowing in this wide sense of "apprehending", by perception or thought or imagination or in any other way, any "object" whatsoever, and we shall ask again: what disappears when knowledge or knowing is subtracted from the universe?

And here we are at the parting of two ways. "Knowledge", I said, or "knowing". That suggests the distinction between "knowing" as the mind's *activity*, and "knowledge" as *what is known* (=the object). The conclusion, paradoxical in language, would be that, though knowing disappeared, knowledge would remain. And, further, it would follow that what is known and what is real are, in principle, one and the same, and Idealism is on the point of being justified. But the solution, alas, is not so simple. We are forgetting that this simple distinction between the activity of apprehending and the object apprehended, though defended by recent theory, runs counter equally to everyday thought and to much authoritative philosophical speculation. For example, when we dream or indulge in the play of imagination, we do not merely regard the activities of dreaming or imagining as mental, but the dream-objects and imaginations as well. In a word, we recognise *objects* which are "mental" and would disappear with the disappearance of minds. And these "mental" objects we class as "unreal" by distinction from those which, though equally capable of appearing within the field of apprehension, are "real". And of these "real" objects we tend to say that, in becoming objects, they do not become "mental"—in short, that they are non-mental, or at least not merely mental, not such as to depend for their existence and character on the activity of the mind.[1] Our conclusion would then seem to be that for these unreal objects,

[1] In this passage, the terms "mental", etc., have been used in their current, "commonsense", meaning. But to a critical reader it is obvious that this sense is full of ambiguity; and where there is ambiguity, there the situation is full of dialectical possibilities. For example, the current distinction of minds and bodies, and the identification of bodies with material=non-mental=real objects, is a piece of naïve metaphysical dogma which takes no account of the paradoxes of the theory of knowledge. It does not reflect that bodies and minds, in order to be distinguished, must both be thought of, i.e., must both become objects, must enter into cognitive relation to a mind. But this means that the mind is capable of apprehending both itself and what is not itself (its "other"), and of distinguishing itself from its "other".—Or again: we distinguish with illusory ease in popular theory between "things" and "thoughts", and since the mind thinks or has thoughts, we tend to identify the distinction between things and thoughts with the distinction between objects (non-mental) and minds. But thoughts are "of" or "about" things. What, then, exactly is the distinction between a thing and the thought of that thing? Or between the thing in itself and the thing as thought?— And yet again, as we found just now, a mind can make an object of itself, i.e., form a thought of itself. But if so, the distinction does not lie simply between non-mental objects ("things") and thoughts. There is a *double* distinction, viz., (1) between "things" and "minds", both alike regarded as *objects*; and (2) between all objects, mental or non-mental, and the *thoughts* of these objects. This is the distinction involved in the cognitive relation, "object" and "mind" being the terms related, and "knowledge", "apprehension", etc., the names for the relation. Or we may push the subtleties still further and ask, whether we ought not to distinguish between a mind and its thoughts, as well as between its thoughts and

these creatures of dream and imagination, the Idealistic theory holds good: for them *esse est percipi*. On the other hand, real objects are thought to have an "independent" existence *per se*. They pass into and out of the cognitive relation, in principle without modification. The status of being apprehended which they may temporarily occupy makes no essential difference to their character or existence. On this view, then, the total universe of our consciousness—the universe which is co-extensive with the range of mental activity—is made up of real or non-mental and unreal or mental objects, of which the former would survive, and the latter perish, with the disappearance of minds. It is also implied that, while the universe of consciousness contains much that is unreal, it is very far from containing all that is real. The real objects which at any one time are within it are only a fragment of a vaster non-mental universe of independent entities.

Very well, let us see whither this view leads. What objects are mental in this sense? Dreams and imaginations we have mentioned already. Hallucinations and illusions are an obvious addition. In general, all errors and mistakes and "mere", or "subjective", ideas belong to the mental group. And why only false ideas? Why not all ideas whatsoever? Does not truth, after all, belong to the mind as well as error? Commonsense will hardly object, and there is good philosophical authority from Descartes onwards for treating all ideas as mental. Indeed, if an

the objects of these thoughts, even though one of them be the mind itself? And whether, in the end, a mind can think anything at all but itself? All these dialectics and plenty more, are to be found in the literature of the subject, and very pretty sport they make for those who care to exercise their ingenuity in this way. As the net result for our present purpose we may perhaps carry away this moral: that we must distinguish between (*a*) the grounds on which, within the totality of possible objects of thought, "mental" may be differentiated from "non-mental" objects without any reference to the cognitive relation; and (*b*) the ground on which, in analysing the cognitive relation of a thought to the object "of" which it is said to be the thought, *any* object whatsoever is discriminated from the thought of that object or from the mind that thinks the object. The issue between Realism and Idealism, at least as interpreted by Realists, arises wholly under (*b*), being based on the cognitive relation. The decisive question is whether that relation is essential and constitutive for the existence and nature of all objects whatsoever. Most Realists hold that there are objects for which the relation is temporary and accidental and which are, therefore, "independent" and "real", and other objects which are "mental" in the special sense that they occur only in this relation. In this form, the issue involves the logical character of *relations*; a problem with which I am not concerned in this paper. But an examination of some other arguments concerning the "mental" character of objects will be found below in the "Conclusion". In this context, the paradoxes about "ideas", alluded to below in the text, should also be noted.

"idea" is not mental, what is? But "Achtung!" as the toboganists cry at Swiss winter-sports. What in the world is not idea or capable of becoming idea? For an idea is the thought of an object, and even the most realistically real object can be thought of. It *must*, in fact, be thought of, else how could the Realist theorise about it? It thus can assume the status of an idea. But does it not hereby become "mental", an element in some mind? With the disappearance of mind will not then the universe *qua* idea, *qua* object of mind, disappear? If you eliminate minds, so it would seem, you eliminate their ideas, and thereby the universe so far as it is "object". But, if so, is there any universe left at all? Once more the Realist, if rashly tempted to commit himself to this line of thought, finds himself in dire peril on the precipitous edge of Idealism. He can save himself only by abandoning the identification of real with non-mental, and of unreal with mental objects, and falling back on the broad principle that "activities"[1] of apprehending are mental, and that nothing else is. All objects, therefore, will be real *qua* objects. We return, in short, with fresh appreciation to the *cognitive* sense of these terms, the recognition of which, as I said above, is the characteristically new feature in Neo-Realism.

The ambiguity of the terms "mental" and "real", and the instability of the current distinctions between them, may be illustrated by another line of thought. Among the objects which are mental, and which would disappear with the disappearance of minds, there are, according to a well-known view, all colours and sounds, all tastes, smells, touch-qualities, temperature-qualities, in short, what philosophers have called the "secondary" qualities of things. The argument in support of this view is almost too familiar to need re-statement. Real and non-mental are the physical disturbances, the air-waves, the ether-oscillations, the chemical processes in nose and tongue;

---

[1] "Activities" is used in a quite general sense, being a term employed by all schools of Neo-Realism. But among themselves they differ widely as to the character of the cognitive activity. To some American Realists it is apparently identical with the selective reaction of a nervous system to stimuli. Professor Alexander treats knowing, thinking, perceiving, etc., as so many "conations". And to him, as to most English Realists, these activities are ultimate, unanalysable modes of being conscious, modes of awareness. Similarly, "relation", as applied to knowledge, is a word common to all Realists, though the nature of the "cognitive relation" is very differently interpreted by different schools. On both these points see below, Part II of this paper.

real also are the effects of these agencies in the nervous system—
the nerve impulses started in the sense-organs and propagated
to the brain. Only their ultimate results, the "sensations" of
colour, etc., are mental. A pleasing, but in spite of much
scientific support, alas, an unstable view. For, clearly, from the
point of view of knowing, we have to begin with these mental
objects, and by an effort of inference we have to reach the non-
mental causes that lie beyond them. These are not, therefore,
directly apprehended. They are matters of inference, that is of
theory; they are assumed as *hypotheses*, whose maintenance
depends on the somewhat precarious factor of their "working"
value. No doubt, many scientists, being—perhaps excusably—
little interested in the philosophical aspects of their procedure,
take atoms, and electrons, and electric vortexes, and ethers and
rays of all sorts, as so many solid facts. But those with a taste
for speculation soon realise the *hypothetical*, the often almost
fictitious, character of these entities. I need not quote Helm-
holtz, Mach, and other leading authorities, in support of a view
which I may assume to be familiar. The more science goes
beyond the direct matter of fact, presented by the senses, and
builds up its theoretical edifices with hypothetical bricks, the
more does it deal with "things of the mind". The universe
which is "real" in the naïve sense, cannot well, it is thought,
be the abode of things which are fictions and whose existence
depends on the maintenance of hypotheses. If the objects of all
imagination are mental, and therefore unreal, how can the
objects of the scientific imagination be exempt? But behold the
paradoxical conclusion to which we are driven. The world of
the physicists, so far from being through and through "real"
and non-mental, is through and through mental and "unreal".
For whether we take it as colours and sounds, etc., or as electrons and energies, in either case arguments for the "mental"
character of their universe can be brought forward, which
scientists themselves have endorsed. There are only two
remedies: either to revise the whole loose conception of
"mind" and the loose distinction of "mental" and "non-
mental", and the loose identification of this pair of terms with
"unreal" and "real" respectively,[1] or to cease regarding the

---

[1] Some further observations on these points will be found in the "Conclusion"
of this paper.

"mental" character of objects as fatal to their "reality". In a sense, these alternatives are not exclusive, but, *prima facie*, Realism adopts the first and Idealism the second.

We may perhaps summarise the net result of this first and longest part of our argument by saying, (1) that we have found all the current distinctions between reality and mind, however convenient in their own context, to break down under pressure of philosophical criticism; (2) that we had better say, with the Realists, that any and every object of apprehension has "reality" or "being" in the most fundamental logical sense of "objectivity" or "Gegenständlichkeit"; (3) that, on this common basis, the issue between Realism and Idealism is whether, over and above this sense of reality, there is a further sense in which all objects (or perhaps only some of them) are "independent" of apprehension and therefore of mind,[1] and what is meant by "mind" in this context.

PART II.—NEO-REALISTIC THEORIES OF MIND

The general survey, undertaken for the sake of orientation, which we have just completed, will now enable us to appreciate the exact bearing of the Theories of Mind, offered by modern Neo-Realists. We must say "Theories", for it is just on this central point that Neo-Realists differ most strikingly from one another. In order to keep this paper within reasonable limits, and not to blur the points which I shall try to make, I shall neglect all minor variations and go straight to the fundamental cleavage which ranges the English and the American Realists in opposite camps. To state their difference at once in technical language: the English Realists are *Dualists*; the American Realists profess an "Epistemological *Monism*". In other words, for the English schools *minds or consciousnesses are a distinct kind of entities or things*—*subject*-reals, if I may use the word, as against all other entities which are *object*-reals. They hold that there is something distinct from all objects, having (as it were) a substantial existence of its own, and this something, the activities of which we call sensation, perception, thought, memory, imagination, etc., is mind or consciousness. The Americans, on

---

[1] This is, of course, the same issue as that mentioned at the end of the footnote on p. 215, viz., whether there are objects which are "real" in the sense of having an existence apart from their occurrence as terms in cognitive relation.

the other hand, hold what they describe as the *relational theory* of consciousness—a theory at first sight much more difficult and paradoxical than the English theory, yet containing, as I believe, the truer principle. On this theory, which has as yet been stated only in fragments, *a mind is simply a selected group or class out of the total universe of things which subsist.* My mind, e.g., at any given moment, is just that limited range of objects, whether perceived or thought or imagined, etc., which at that moment lie within, or constitute, the field of my consciousness. "Consciousness" is merely a demonstrative term; a "field of consciousness" is just an inclusive phrase for that fragment of the universe which is at any given moment an "object". It means the relation or principle of grouping which, from moment to moment, out of the totality of reals in the universe, brings just this miscellaneous lot of odds and ends together which I see, hear, think, doubt, etc., etc. The explanation of the grouping is to be found in the selective action of the nervous system which responds only to certain elements in the total environment.

Let us trace the difference between these two views more in detail.

The English Realists—we may take Professor Alexander as a clear example of this line of analysis—start from the "cognitive situation", e.g., I perceive a tree. Direct inspection of this situation reveals the fact that we have here the "compresence" or "togetherness" of two things, viz., a physical thing, the tree, and a mental thing, viz., the perception or act of perceiving. The Dualism of this view is obvious. The function of the perception is to reveal the tree just as it is; hence it is, or ought to be, infallible; there ought to be no room for any mistake; it cannot falsify or distort. For consciousness is a quality-less, transparent medium, which, having no character of its own, cannot alter or modify the character of that which it reveals. When steeped into this medium, as it were, things are said to be apprehended, but it is not necessary to their existence or to their nature that they should be so steeped. They are what they are, whether or no consciousness envelops them wholly or partially, for a longer or a shorter time. Only in one respect does Professor Alexander indicate the character of these quality-less, transparent acts of consciousness a little more fully. He describes them as "conations",[1] with reference, it would seem, chiefly to the element of attention to, or direction upon, an object. A "mind" thus is a system of "conations". In part, the point of this view is polemical, and directed against much current Psychology, which, by means of the ambiguous phrase, "content" of mental processes, places within the mind all kinds of elements which, like the so-called "qualities" of sensations and "images" and "ideas", are for Professor Alexander part of the objective reality, strictly to be distinguished from the mental processes or acts which are transparent conations directed upon these "objects".

Now, this view is not nearly itself so transparent as it looks. We can ask several awkward questions about it.

(1) In the first place, if consciousness has no character of its own, how can we recognise it or identify it at all? How can we distinguish it, when present, from the thing which is its object? What is the difference, except in words, between the tree by itself, and the tree enveloped in this translucent medium? In short, does the word "consciousness" stand for anything at all?

(2) If consciousness has no character of its own, how can we distinguish between different forms or modes of it? What is the difference, e.g., between perceiving and thinking and imagining? Clearly, there is only one way out—the way which Professor Alexander is compelled to take—viz., to connect apparent differences of consciousness with genuine, qualitative differences of its objects, to correlate sensing with "sensa", perceiving with "percepta", thinking with "cogitata", and so on. But this, I submit, may save the situation verbally, but is in effect a confession of the breakdown of the attempt to distinguish consciousness as a separate "somewhat" from its "objects".

(3) Suppose we grant to Professor Alexander that every item of perception or thought or memory, etc., is in itself directly apprehended, such as it is, there yet remain to be accounted for all the operations of synthesis and analysis, of interpretation, of inference—in short, all that is usually described as the work of "constructive intelligence". For example, I do not simply

---

[1] See his paper in the *British Journal of Psychology*, vol. iv., 1911, entitled "Sketch plan of a Conational Psychology".

"see" a tree. On the contrary, visual perception, stripped of all inferential interpretation and reduced to the actual visual datum, presents me merely with a variously coloured patch of a certain size and shape in my visual field. That this, which is all I strictly "see", is or means a tree, is more than sight, it is inference. But, supposing it were all sight, I should not ordinarily stop there, but go on to think about the tree, to recall other things connected with it or bearing on it, e.g., that it illustrates certain botanical principles, or that I climbed it as a boy, or that it is to be cut down for firewood. The chief function of what is ordinarily called "mental activity" is just this expansion and amplification of the "given" object. We do not merely apprehend passively, but we elaborate actively. We add, we modify, we analyse, we interpret. True, it is through these processes that error is apt to enter, but it is also no less true that only through these processes do we achieve knowledge. How can the theory of a quality-less activity account for these facts? A conation, such as Professor Alexander describes, might conceivably be directed upon a given something. But how could it add to it? Or go beyond it by memory or inference or imagination? Clearly, the nexus which makes the additions relevant, and the whole spring of the movement which leads to the additions, is to be sought *in the nature of the objects*, not in that of the supposed transparent conations.[1]

In principle the same distinction between an object and a transparent mental act is drawn by Mr. G. E. Moore, of the Cambridge School of Realism. To reduce the problem to its most elementary form, he takes the example of a "sensation of blue",[2] which he analyses into the object-element "blue", the mental element sensation, and a unique and not otherwise describable relation between these two. The sensation is "a case of 'knowing', or 'being aware of', or 'experiencing' something". The blue is not a mental "image" or the quality of anything mental at all. It is a real, independent feature of the universe, standing momentarily in this unique relation to a sensation or act of sensing. To reflect on one's sensation of blue is to be "aware of an awareness of blue". Mr. Moore goes

---

[1] This is really the feature on which "Objective Idealism" insists. See below in the "Conclusion" of this paper.

[2] See Mr. Moore's article, "A Refutation of Idealism", in *Mind*, N.S., No. 48 (Oct., 1903), p. 449.

on to point out that there is this difficulty about the analysis, viz., that to fix one's attention on the "consciousness" apart from the "object", is apparently to focus on mere emptiness, on something so "diaphanous" that nothing seems to be there at all. Most students will agree with Mr. Moore in this, but they will draw the opposite conclusion from that which Mr. Moore has drawn. They will conclude that consciousness is not distinguishable, in the sense required, from what are called its "objects". But Mr. Moore sets out with the determination to find such a distinction, or if he cannot find it, then to manufacture it in the name of Realism. Thus he is driven to invent a diaphanous consciousness to fill the gap. But there is, as I shall try to show below, another way.[1] Meanwhile, suffice it to say that Mr. Moore has not, so far as I know, extended his analysis to other modes of mental activity. Hence, whilst his view is open, in principle, to the same objections as Professor Alexander's, we have even fewer data for inferring how Mr. Moore would deal with the difficulties.

Now, the American Realists, as I said above, recognise no such mysterious, diaphanous "consciousness" existing alongside of independent "objects". They take their cue from an article, written by William James in the last years of his life, which is entitled: "Does Consciousness Exist?"[2] It is interesting to note here that, whilst never abandoning Pragmatism, James was the author of articles which make him unmistakably the forerunner of American Realism. In the paper just mentioned he says of "experience" that "it is made of *that*, of just what appears, of space, of intensity, of flatness, of brownness, of heaviness, of what not. . . . Experience is only a collective name for all these sensible natures. . . ." In short, he unmistakably identifies experience with the objective context, with the world, the universe. Now this is just what "objective" Idealism also does. Perhaps the point becomes clearest by asking: what, after all, is the character of seeing as distinct from the colours seen, of hearing as distinct from the sounds heard, of thinking as distinct from thoughts, i.e., from what we think, of consciousness or awareness as distinct from what we call its objects? James replies: There is no such distinction. Seeing means

[1] See the "Conclusion" of this paper.
[2] See *Essays in Radical Empiricism*, pp. 26-27.

colours occurring, hearing means sounds occurring, thinking means thoughts occurring—all these in a certain context, described as a "field of consciousness". We have, in short, the relational theory of consciousness: a mind is a selection, a fragment out of the total mass of "being". On this basis, a Realistic theory can easily be built up. We need merely assume that the selection or grouping is, in a manner, accidental to the elements thus brought together, that these elements have a nature of their own, and stand in relations to one another, and to other elements not included in the selection, which nature and relations are independent of this special grouping, so that they may be taken to exist, whether or no they happen to be grouped together as a mind—we need merely assume this to get straightway a realistic conclusion.

If my account is sketchy, I must excuse myself with the fragmentary and tentative statements of my authorities. The most important of these are Professors Perry and Holt, of Harvard, who both, as I read them, hold such a view as I have attempted to outline, except that Perry appears to lay undue stress on the physical environment as the totality, out of which the response of a nervous system selects the items which, at any given moment, constitute a "mind". This seems to me unduly narrow, to lay too much emphasis on objects of perception, and to neglect the ranges of objects with which we deal in Mathematics, Logic, Ethics, Religion and other branches of thought. Holt, more soundly, makes his "universe of being", within which minds are subordinate groups, all-inclusive.[1]

By way of rounding off this sketch of the Neo-Realistic theories of mind, let us once more apply our test-question. We

[1] Perry (see, e.g., *Present Philosophical Tendencies*, ch. xiii., § 10) seems to take a too narrowly biological view in treating consciousness as a "species of function" exercised by an organism upon an environment. This tends to restrict the environment to physical, i.e., ultimately to material, nature. At any rate, there is no hint of the environment being, e.g., moral or social or æsthetic or religious, and of the organism reacting to these characters as well. Holt (*New Realism*, p. 372), on the other hand, says: "The picture I wish to leave is of a general universe of being in which all things physical, mental, and logical, propositions and terms, existent and non-existent, false and true, good and evil, real and unreal *subsist*. . . . A mind or consciousness is a class or group of entities within the subsisting universe, as a physical object is another class or group." The whole passage should be read: it puts the important points with great clearness.

I ought to add that, in singling out Professors Perry and Holt as the spokesmen of American Realism on the subject of mind, I am omitting Professor Montague's view (*New Realism*, p. 281). Not feeling sure that, in its present form, I understand this view, I think it safer not to comment on it.

Q

then find: (1) That for English Realists the world would by the disappearance of minds lose only a transparent something-or-other which leaves the rest exactly as it is; and (2) that for American Realists there disappears only a special grouping or relationship of the objective elements of the universe. The universe, composed in the last analysis of simple, unanalysable entities, would remain what it is, notwithstanding the elimination of minds. It would only cease to be carved up, here and there, into a special kind of temporary aggregations of selected elements. On either view, reality in its own character is indifferent to the presence or absence of minds—that is what makes these views realistic.

CONCLUSION: THE MAIN POINT FROM THE REPLY
OF IDEALISM

Throughout this paper I have had occasion to emphasise the issue between Realism and Idealism. Hence it will not be inopportune if I conclude by outlining, briefly, the main point of the Idealistic theory concerning the nature of mind.

I said above that Idealism construes the universe, in last analysis, as a mind, the so-called Absolute Mind, or as a system of minds. Fortunately, it is not necessary for our present purpose to go into the difference between these two—the Absolutist and the Pluralist—views. Questions of considerable technical difficulty are involved which lie outside the proper limits of this paper. It will suffice if we concentrate on the principle which is common to all forms and varieties of Idealism, viz., the identification of reality in its full character with the nature and life of mind.

Now, thus boldly stated, this theory may easily seem the wildest of paradoxes, but the paradox soon disappears when we frankly and fairly face the issue: what does "mind" mean? What features of the universe does the term stand for or point to? And are these features so fundamental that we have a right to acclaim the universe, in its final constitution, as mind?

This problem is purely one of *Logic*—of Logic in the sense in which its task is to trace out the conceptual structure of the universe, or, in other words, the structure which the universe must have, on the assumption that it is a single self-consistent

whole. In the technical language of Idealism, it is a problem
of the adequacy of certain "categories" for metaphysical
theory. All difficulties and misunderstandings which divide
Idealists and their critics arise from the fact that the meaning
of mind is ambiguous, that the word is variously used to point
to features of the universe which stand on widely different
levels in the scale of categories, which are, in other words, of
very different degrees of adequacy to the nature of reality *as a
self-consistent all-inclusive whole*. I will point, in support of this
contention, only to two meanings of "mind", neither of which
is that of the Idealists, but each of which has been attributed
to them by their critics, and made the ground for a complete
rejection of their theories.

(1) The first is the *psychological* theory of mind as a flux of
perceptions and thoughts—the "stream of consciousness", in
William James's picturesque phrase. This theory may be adequate for Psychology, but it is agreed on all hands that it is
inadequate as the basis for a theory of the universe. Its category
is that of ceaseless, unstable, temporal sequence. The mind is
the variegated sequence of all the feelings, sensations, ideas,
memories, etc., that follow one another in rapid change from
moment to moment. No one can consistently suppose—though
Hume tried to do so—that this flux is the last word, the ultimate truth, about the reality which we claim to perceive, think,
recollect, etc. To have shown the inadequacy of this view is the
achievement of Kant in his reply to Hume. And Kant succeeded
because he took his stand on the nature of *judgment*, and through
it on the *logical structure* of our universe which is expressed and
affirmed in our judgments.

(2) The second misleading interpretation of mind is one
which, borrowing Professor Perry's convenient phrase, we may
call the *ego-centric*.[1] The term calls attention to the fact to
which all the language inevitably used by us bears witness, viz.,
that minds, at any rate in their mature human form, are *selves*.
Each of us says: *I* think, *I* feel, *I* will, etc. Each of us speaks
of *my* perceptions, *my* ideas, *my* world. There is no object, no
element, in the universe which, as perceived, thought, spoken
of, does not thus come within the "field of consciousness" of

[1] See *Present Philosophical Tendencies*, ch. vi., § 10, p. 129, on the Ego-centric
Predicament.

a thinker, a self, an Ego. But, argue the Realists, these temporary associations of real objects with Egos (=English Realists), these temporary aggregations of real objects into ego-centric fields of consciousness (=American Realists), are not the ultimate truth about the universe. Minds, as Selves, are transitory forms. The range of reality which they cover, whether at any given moment or in the ideal sum of the moments of their lives, is a mere fragment of the infinite totality. The parts of reality that a Self at any time apprehends are mere isolated, selected, abstracted bits of the whole, and these aggregations are unstable and constantly dissolved and re-constituted. Again we see that the criticism, in its fundamental logical motive, turns on the inadequacy of the categories employed. There is again the challenge on the ground of the transitoriness and instability which is inseparable from *time*; there is the challenge to the inadequacy of *fragments* isolated from the *whole*; there is the challenge to the largely *chaotic* and *accidental* nature of these fragmentary selections from the whole, as against the *orderly* and *systematic* character of the whole; there is, lastly, the challenge to the *dispersion of reality* into an indefinite multitude of finite minds, which between them may not cover the whole.

And so, on all these grounds, the Realists reject the Idealistic identification of reality and mind: they labour to discriminate between the nature of reality and the nature of mind. But, in all this, they are really fighting for a *logically adequate* conception of reality: they are fighting against inadequate categories. And, therefore, they are in the paradoxical position that, *at bottom, they are fighting, not against Idealism, but with it*.

For the Idealists, as I understand their theory, entirely and whole-heartedly agree with the Realists' criticisms of mind understood in either of the above-mentioned ways. In fact, they have urged these very arguments themselves. But they reply that the Realistic theories overlook altogether certain all-important features of the universe, and that it is just these for which Idealists use the term "mind".

Perhaps I can best make this Idealistic conception of "mind" clear by saying at once that the Idealist has no use for the English Realists' conception of an indescribable, diaphanous consciousness. On the other hand, he can make some use of the American Realists' conception of a mind as a selection, and therefore a fragment, out of a wider objective totality. For this is exactly what the Idealist calls a "finite mind". But the Idealist does not stop at this point. For if this were the whole truth about our minds, we could not possibly know it. If my mind were nothing more than a selection out of the totality of real objects which compose the universe, I should never be able to discover the fact, unless I were in some way aware of this very totality from which I select, of the ranges of fact lying beyond the circle of my selection. We have, in short, to think the whole, in order to distinguish ourselves as parts within it. And, in order to *think* the whole of which it is a part, a mind has, in the measure of the completeness of its thought, to *be* the whole. If our minds are selections out of the totality of reality and, at the same time, recognise themselves as selections, then in this recognition they affirm themselves to be the whole, focussed in fragmentary form. A mind, which *ex hypothesi* were no more than a fragment, could not recognise itself as such, and therefore could not distinguish itself from, or within, the whole. This is the paradox of the "logic of self-consciousness"—yet it does no more than point out the logical nexus of our thought in this act of distinction and recognition of the self within its world. It is also the paradox of what Idealists of the Hegelian school have called the "finite-infinite" nature of mind, which is nothing but an attempt to formulate the plain logical situation which consists in a mind, conceived as a fragment of reality, differentiating itself from the whole reality, and yet at the same time acknowledging itself as a part of that reality. To do that, it must be more than "finite": it must be a "finite" form of the "infinite".

Now, whatever we may think of this paradox when thus baldly formulated, it is at any rate possible to point out some features of our universe which support it. These features are *logical*, and are revealed in the transformation which the real, as given, undergoes (in the form of what we call judgment, inference, science, knowledge) under the pressure of the demand for consistency—a demand which is an ideal to be achieved just because it expresses the inherent and fundamental character of the real in its "true", i.e., logically stable, form. The whole drama of the universe, we may say paradoxically, is thus in its core a struggle towards logical completeness. The fragments, from the friction and contradiction of their isolation, strain back to the self-consistent completeness of the whole. It is this *movement or nisus towards logical stability* which runs through all that we perceive and think. These terms, perception and thought, stand, as we have seen, for no bare, featureless activity or consciousness: they stand for the "objects", for *what* is perceived and thought *and* (we must now add) for the ceaseless processes of supplementation, combination, differentiation, interpretation, "construction", which transform any given elements in the direction towards a logically stable form. Take the world at the beginning and at the end of a process of thought, say the solar system as it was conceived by primitive man, by the Ptolemaic astronomers, by Copernicus, by twentieth-century science—it is the *same* in one sense throughout, yet what a transformation! It is not merely that we know more about it, but that we have re-arranged it all. I say "we" have re-arranged it, but the nature of the facts demanded it. They re-arranged themselves. In fact, however paradoxical the language, it makes little difference whether we say: we think the world so-and-so, or: the world thinks itself so-and-so in us. As Spinoza would say: "deus sive natura, quatenus humanam mentem constituit".

In conclusion, I will summarise the positions which I have tried to maintain in this paper. In Part I., in addition to a general survey for the sake of orientation, I showed (i) that the New Realism does not, like the Old, conceive reality as exclusively material, but tends to think of it as comprising all objects of any kind which can in any way be experienced or apprehended; and (ii) that it thus starts from an analysis of the cognitive relation between mind and reality, and that the antithesis of these two terms dominates Realistic thought throughout.[1]

[1] It should be noted in this connection that, for reasons both of space and of clearness, I refrained from touching on all those arguments of the Neo-Realistic schools which are built up on the axiom that relations are external to their terms, and that these terms are ultimately simple, unique, and unanalysable. All Neo-Realists seem to be agreed on this axiom of "External Relations", though some make more use of it than others. The questions involved are exceedingly technical and difficult, and at bottom the issue lies between two Theories of Logic, the Idealistic Theory on the one side, and modern developments of Symbolic Logic on the other. Thus the problem of relations is another point of conflict between Idealism and Neo-Realism. In fact, they give battle to one another on a good many points, of which the problem of mind is only one, though one of the most

In Part II. I contrasted the English and the American Realists' theories of the nature of mind or consciousness, and showed (i) that the former tend to think of mind as a transparent something, distinct from the object, though directed upon it: and (ii) that the latter identify mind with a selection from the totality of what is objectively real.

In the Conclusion I argued (i) that, whilst the theory of the English Realists has no common ground with the Idealistic theory of mind, the theory of the American Realists offers a basis for discussion. For the identification of mind with the objective field of what is perceived and thought, and the recognition of this field as a fragment of a wider whole, is common to both Idealism and American Realism. But (ii) I tried to show that both forms of Realism fail to take account of the one feature of reality which, for Idealists, is more fundamental than any other, viz., the logical striving of reality, in the form of finite minds, from its fragmentariness in this form towards supplementation and self-completion. Hence the "true" nature of fact is not to be found except in terms of stable and logically consistent theory; all perceiving and thinking, with their progressive stages of intellectual interpretation and construction, are but the self-revelation and self-transformation of the real from more fragmentary and less stable to less fragmentary and more stable forms. The details of this view have to be, and have been, worked out in systems of logic, which, guided throughout by the clue of self-consistency or logical stability, trace in detail the structure of the real world of our knowledge.

important. It is clear that, if the principle of External Relations were established beyond dispute, and if it were also established that knowledge is correctly construed as a relation, then the Realistic Theory of the independence of reality on its relation to minds which know it, would follow by a simple syllogism.

A Plea for a Phenomenology of Meaning

§ 1. *The Need for a Phenomenology of Meaning.*—The purpose of this paper, as its title indicates, is a humble one. So far from having a definite theory of meaning to offer, I am only groping towards one. Indeed it is part of my thesis that all current theories of meaning, so far as I am acquainted with them, are, for one reason or another, inadequate. They are either too general to make intelligible the facts in their concrete diversity, or else they are based on some selected group of facts, and thus do not cover the ground. Moreover, they reflect the general philosophical presuppositions of their authors, and as a result they are either simply incommensurable or even actually conflicting. The chaotic terminology which prevails in the theory of meaning is symptomatic. The very term "meaning" is nearly as ambiguous as the term "idea". The need for further study is, therefore, incontestable. It is the chief purpose of this paper to urge that, before constructing further theories, we require more of the humble discipline of patient and exhaustive phenomenology, by which I mean the collection and unprejudiced examination of all types of empirical situations in which signs function, in which meaning is present. It is remarkable that the prominence of signs and symbols in our lives—in religion, in art, in science, in business—has not attracted attention more persistently to this field of enquiry. Yet "brain-work" is eminently sign-work—sign-using, sign-interpreting, if necessary sign-inventing. In every society, the educated and "governing" classes are mainly symbol-mongers. They deal with realities indirectly. Think of the apparatus of maps, reports, statistics, orders, through which the G.H.Q. of an army in the field conducts operations. Its knowledge of the facts on which its decisions are based comes mostly not at first-hand, but through signs, and through sending out signs it initiates and controls the marching and digging and fighting of the troops. Without signs we should have neither social organisations, nor the systems of science and philosophy, nor religion, nor art. Yet the problem of signs and meanings has been neglected by most philosophers, except when irritation at the ambiguities of language has aroused a passing interest in the functioning of words.

§ 2. *Review of the Literature.*—Having brought against current theories of meaning the accusation of inadequacy, it will rightly be expected of me that I should substantiate my charge. I can do this best by critical comments on a select few, and I shall begin with the theories which were offered at the Oxford Congress[1] in September 1920:—

(*a*) Dr. Schiller's theory that meaning is "essentially an *activity* or *attitude* taken up towards objects by a subject", that it is "personal" and, indeed, "relative to the *whole* personality", seems to me in his presentation of it to suffer from a failure to distinguish between phenomenologically different situations. The theory, in short, is too general: its application to different situations is not worked out. We are told that meaning is all-pervasive; that we look for a meaning in everything that happens to us; that meaning, like value, resembles an "atmosphere" through which all objects are observed. But mixed up with this meaning of objects is much argument about the meaning of words and images. For a phenomenology of meaning, I submit, these are different cases. The interpretation of the meaning of objects and events, as I shall try to show below (§ 3), is different from the interpretation of words. There is a corresponding difference in the senses of "expression". A man, I agree, "expresses" his personality in the way he takes the things which happen to him—optimistically or pessimistically, as due to chance or as due to God, as causes and effects or as omens and signs of good or evil spirits. He expresses himself in the meanings he entertains, affirms, acts on. But if his meanings are thus expressive, they are themselves expressed, in another sense of the word "expression", by the signs, verbal or other, which he uses. In Dr. Schiller's remark "the commonest meaning of 'it is a fine day' is 'let us talk'", the two senses of meaning and of expression for the distinction of which I am pleading, are very obviously run together. However, the general direction of Dr. Schiller's theory seems to me right. His emphasis on the "standpoint of the agent", of "the person who

[1] See *Mind*, N.S., vol. xxix., No. 116.

means", is, as we shall see, a contribution of central importance for the theory of meaning.

(*b*) Mr. Russell has made various contributions to the problem of meaning which it is far from easy to reconcile with each other. In his Oxford Congress paper and in the relevant passages of his address on *Propositions* before this Society, he appears to have written mainly as a psychologist. On the other hand, in his paper *On Denoting*,[1] and in certain passages of his *Introduction to Mathematical Philosophy*, he deals with a rather technical problem of logic. Whether there is any connection between these two modes of treatment for Mr. Russell, or whether he is conducting his arguments in watertight compartments, remains obscure. The psychological treatment is both phenomenologically too narrow and biased by theoretical preconceptions. It is too narrow, because (*a*) it restricts itself to the meanings of words and reduces this further to the meaning of images, on the ground that "images resemble what they mean, whereas words, as a rule, do not"; and (*b*) because it restricts the function of words to that of stimulating us "to act with reference to an object which is not present". The whole context and language of Mr. Russell's theory make it a fair inference that the only type of situation of which he is at the moment thinking, is that in which some sense-datum or image, generally verbal, functions, by association or "mnemic causation", as a cue for appropriate behaviour towards further sense-data to come. But does no scientist ever use language significantly in recording what here and now he, for the first time, observes? Or can any of the language of Mr. Russell's mathematical treatises be brought under his formula? And there are plenty of other negative instances. As for imagery—the view that images are, in last analysis, necessary to meaning has been so often and so completely discredited, that Mr. Russell's attempt to renew it without any reply to its critics, is somewhat surprising.[2] Mr. Russell's rejoinders to Dr. Schiller's strictures

---

[1] Cf. *Mind*, N.S., vol. xiv., No. 56.

[2] Some of these arguments are forcibly stated by Dr. Schiller (*loc. cit.*); others were urged years ago by Dr. G. F. Stout in a paper before this Society on "Mr. Bradley's Theory of Judgment" (*Proceedings*, N.S., iii., 1902-3). The fullest discussion of them in English, with special reference to Bradley and James, is still, I venture to think, to be found in my paper on "Image, Idea and Meaning" (*Mind*, N.S., xvi., No. 61, pp. 70-86). The arguments against the image-theory of meaning, as there given, still seem to me sound, though in some other respects I

ignore the main point, viz., that we can and do mean lots of things which no image can possibly "resemble". It is irrelevant to urge that words may function in the place of images once present, now forgotten. What images does, or did, Mr. Russell use for the objects and relations on which he discourses in his books on mathematical logic? The fact is that, alike in selecting his data and in framing his theory, Mr. Russell is dominated by a theoretical bias. Meaning, he postulates, "is an observable property of observable entities, and must be amenable to scientific treatment", and by "scientific treatment" he appears to mean the analysis of all entities into complexes of sense-data and images, e.g., "sensations and images, suitably related [are] a sufficient stuff out of which to compose beliefs". In the same spirit he defines the "essence of meaning" as lying "in the causal efficacy of that which has meaning", though this definition, as it stands, seems manifestly too wide.

The logical discussion on "denoting" raises, incidentally, one point of phenomenological interest. As will be recalled, the problem concerns proper names or other denoting phrases when they occur in propositions which manifestly have an intelligible meaning, and which may be true or false, whilst yet there exists no real person or thing to whom the proper name belongs or to whom the denoting phrase descriptively refers. To say that the denoting phrase has a meaning but denotes nothing, leads to certain difficulties with which we are not here concerned. To avoid these, Mr. Russell proposes to say that the denoting phrase has *per se* no meaning at all and must be analysed away so that a technically correct expression of the proposition no longer contains it. Now Frege, from whom Mr. Russell differs on this point,[1] holds to the view that denoting phrases have a meaning even when there is nothing which they denote, among other reasons because it is only when our interest is cognitive that the existence or non-existence of the denoted object matters, whereas when our interest is aesthetic, the denotation is irrelevant. If we read *Hamlet* as a work of art, not as a work of history, it does not matter whether

do not now hold either to the language or the doctrine of that paper.—In German, E. Husserl, *Logische Untersuchungen* (2nd Edit.), Vol. II, Part I, ch. 2, §§ 17-20, says briefly and clearly all that is necessary.

[1] See *Zeitschrift für Philosophie und phil. Kritik*, vol. 100, p. 33. Mr. Russell originally held a closely similar view, cf. *Prin. of Math.*, ch. v.

"the Prince of Denmark" ever existed. But we cannot enjoy the drama, unless "Hamlet" "the Prince of Denmark", etc., have a meaning. Now, it seems clear that if we analyse the denoting phrases in the drama according to Mr. Russell's prescription, the basis of the aesthetic enjoyment disappears. Meinong's concept of *Annahme* offers the most plausible solution, but unless I am mistaken, even an *Annahme* requires the meaning which Mr. Russell proposes to deny to denoting phrases. This is precisely one of the cases which show the need for a more comprehensive phenomenology.

(*c*) Lady Welby's *What is Meaning?* and F. Toennies's Welby Prize Essay on *Philosophical Terminology*[1] offer little that is directly relevant to a phenomenology, being mainly focussed upon the improvement of language as an instrument for the expression of meanings. Lady Welby would ascribe to every sign three kinds of meaning, viz., sense—meaning—significance, which she correlates respectively with denotation—connotation —suggestion, with signification—intention—ideal value, and even with the instinctive—the volitional—the moral. But these suggestions are not developed or tested, for her interest is not in phenomenology, but in the problem how best to use metaphor and analogy for expressing spiritual truths. From her, however, we may take the hint that one of the most important topics for a phenomenology is the interpretation of sensible signs as expressions or revelations of invisible (non-sensible) realities, be their name mind, spirit, value, or what not. This may serve as a corrective to Mr. Russell's way of narrowing the meaning of signs to "objects not now present", i.e., to objects perceptible but not at the moment actually perceived. We have no right to rule out *ab initio* the possibility that sensibles are signs for supra-sensibles, especially when we all use precisely this relation in our interpretation of bodily gestures and vocal sounds as expressive of mental processes or activities.[2]

(*d*) The articles on Sign, Symbol, Sign-making function, Intent, and allied topics in Baldwin's *Dictionary of Philosophy and Psychology* were mostly written by Charles S. Peirce and Dr. G. F. Stout. They are valuable as being the only conveniently

---

[1] *Mind*, N.S., vol. viii., Nos. 31, 32, vol. ix., No. 33.
[2] Royce's discussion of interpretation in *The Problem of Christianity* (vol. ii., chs. xi.-xiv.) is relevant in this connection.

accessible source for a study of Peirce's theory.[1] To Peirce's
definition and classification of signs I shall return below (§ 3).
Here it is enough to note, as symptomatic of the terminological
chaos, that whilst Peirce defines a "symbol" as a "sign which
would lose the character which renders it a sign if there were
no interpretant", and cites speech as the most obvious example,
Stout contrasts symbols as "substitutive" signs with words as
"expressive" signs, on the ground that whilst the latter serve
to direct attention to the object signified, it is the explicit function of the former to dispense with attention to the object. In
addition, Stout distinguishes three other classes of signs, viz.,
demonstrative, discriminative, mnemonic, but it would be
hard to say to which of these five classes would belong, say, an
omen, or an example of plant-signature, or a flag, or a cross,
even when we distinguish different sorts of uses of such signs as
flags and crosses.[2] Stout's definition of symbol as a "sign provisionally substituted for the thing symbolised" raises an
interesting phenomenological question, viz., whether algebraic
symbols are rightly conceived as marks meaningless in themselves, for which yet concrete objects can be substituted in such
a way that operations on the marks hold good for the objects.
Husserl's discussion of this familiar view is worth pondering, it
seems to me. Undoubtedly there is a simplification and
economy of labour. The operations may be performed almost
"mechanically". But is it not an exaggeration to say, or imply,
that for the cognitive interest of the mathematician the signs
are just meaningless marks? If so, what of the variable and of
other mathematical concepts? The symbols eliminate irrelevant
diversity but retain a minimum of meaning, defined by the
rules of operation.[3] The joint article of Stout and Baldwin on
Intent adds a phenomenological point not previously touched
on. Recurring to James's phrase, "what intelligent consciousness means or intends", they contrast the "content" of consciousness with its "intent", and inserting this distinction into

[1] For a list of other references, see Royce, *loc. cit.*, p. 114.
[2] In his definition of the "sign-making function" as "The selection or construction of certain objects in order that by mentally operating with these, results
may be obtained applying to other subjects", Dr. Stout seems momentarily to
have forgotten all kinds of signs except the kind which he calls "symbols".
[3] See Husserl, *loc. cit.*, § 20, pp. 68-70. Husserl's view supplies, too, the correct
interpretation of the amusing *quids* and *quods* game in which C. I. Lewis's examination of "mathematics without meaning" ends. See his *Survey of Symbolic Logic.*

the context of cognitive endeavour, identify "content" with
that fragment or aspect of the object which the mind actually
apprehends, "intent" with the "total object, considered as
goal of conscious endeavour". It follows that the "intent"
is "what the mind consciously means or intends but does not
yet contain". This whole doctrine seems strictly identical with
Royce's distinction, in *The World and the Individual*, between the
"internal" and the "external meaning" of ideas, except that
Royce's turn towards the Absolute is left out.

(*e*) Meinong's brief, but clear statement,[1] has, from the point
of view of phenomenology, the defect of confining itself exclusively to speech. Within these limits, however, all that
Meinong says is valuable. He does, indeed, offer the general
formula that we have the relation of sign to significate[2] wherever, given A, we can infer the existence or non-existence of B.
In short, the sign is *causa cognoscendi (Erkenntnisgrund)* for the
significate. To the question of the adequacy of this account, we
shall return below (§ 3). In application to words, it compels
Meinong at once to distinguish what words *express*, viz., the
speaker's mental acts or processes, from what they *mean*, viz.,
the objects of his acts. It follows that words always mean the
object of the thought which they express. It follows also that
there are words which express a state of mind, but do not mean
anything, viz., when the state of mind is not cognitive, is not a
praesentierendes Erlebnis. A word means an object when it
expresses an act which presents that object to the mind. Artificial as this terminology is, it marks distinctions which are important. These are, however, worked out with much more
detail by—

(*f*) Husserl, whose *Logische Untersuchungen* seem to me to contain the best work yet done in phenomenology. The relevant
chapters,[3] though difficult to read, are, in the very laboriousness
of their detail, extraordinarily valuable. His treatment of *Bedeutungsintention* and *Bedeutungserfüllung*, leading to a *Phaenomenologie
der Erkenntnisstufen*, provides, it seems to me, a basis for dealing

---

[1] *Über Annahmen*, 2nd Edit., §§ 3, 4; to Meinong's other writings I have not
had access in writing this paper.
[2] May I venture to suggest this term as the equivalent of *das Bezeichnete*? We
need a simple term for the circumlocutions "thing signified" or "that which is
signified".
[3] Esp. Vol. II, Part I, Section 1, *Ausdruck und Bedeutung*, chs. 1-4: and Part II
(1921), Section vi., ch. 1, *Bedeutungsintention und Bedeutungserfüllung*.

fruitfully with the tantalising contrast between perception as presenting actual, concrete reality, but yet only a fragment or aspect of its full nature, and thought, which can present that nature more comprehensively, but yet not concretely possessed or fulfilled. From among points of detail, I may be forgiven for singling out one which is of special interest to me personally and illuminates a problem commonly ignored. Drawing attention, in my *Studies in Contemporary Metaphysics*,[1] to a peculiar and, as it were, essential ambiguity in the meaning of the personal pronoun "I", I have recklessly committed myself to the statement that "I" is the only word exhibiting this ambiguity. From Husserl[2] I have since learnt that there are several classes of such words, and what is the generalised theory for them. It is the more a pleasure to acknowledge this, because my own independent discovery of part of the facts is amply confirmed by Husserl's comprehensive treatment, which, in its turn, may perhaps gain some little support from my testimony. In general, I have only one criticism to urge against Husserl, and one misgiving. The misgiving is whether he is not beginning to over-multiply the "acts" of many diverse sorts which he needs to restore the concrete unities, after his subtle analysis has broken them up into their last, often almost vanishing constituents. The criticism which I urge with much more confidence is that Husserl, too, though perhaps excusably in the context of "logical" enquiries, limits his phenomenology to signs and meanings in the service of theory or cognition. But knowledge is only one of the autonomous ends of life, and to other autonomous ends it may stand in an instrumental relation. The use of signs or symbols is as wide as the field of mental activity, and it is to be expected that a study of signs and meanings in other forms of activity will react on, and help towards, a better understanding of them in the context of science and philosophy.

§ 3. *A Sample of Phenomenological Study.*—The title of this section is, perhaps, over-ambitious, yet having exhibited, as strikingly as I could, the inchoate state of current theory of meaning, it is "up to" me at least to make an attempt at illustrating the kind of phenomenological study for which I am pleading. For this purpose I shall single out a prominent theory

---

[1] P. 256.   [2] *Loc. cit.*, Vol. II, Part I, §§ 26-28.

and test its adequacy against as varied a range of facts as I can bring forward in the limited space at my disposal.

The theory selected is one which, in one formulation or another, is advocated by several of the best authorities. We have met with it above in Meinong's statement that one thing (A) is the sign of another thing (B) when, given A, we can infer the existence (or non-existence) of B. In vaguer terms Toennies says the same thing: "We call an object (A) the *sign* of another object (B), when the perception or recollection A has the recollection B for its regular and immediate consequence." Mr. Russell's formula, "the sensible (or imaginal) presence of A, which is a sign of the present or future existence of B, enables us to act in a manner appropriate to B", obviously combines two things, viz., (1) what Mr. Russell also calls "the causal efficacy" of the sign, i.e., its functioning as stimulus for appropriate behaviour, and (2) its indicative (*anzeigende*) function, which latter is what Meinong and Toennies exclusively emphasise. Husserl gives the most careful statement: We have the actual functioning of a sign, "when any object or matter-of-fact of the existence or subsistence of which someone is actually aware, indicates to him the existence or subsistence of certain other objects or matters-of-fact, in the sense that his conviction of the being of the former is experienced by him as a motive (to wit, a non-intelligible motive) for the conviction or supposition of the being of the latter".[1] It is important to notice that Husserl explicitly restricts this formula to one kind of sign which he calls *Anzeige* (index), whereas the other three authorities impose no restriction on the scope of their formulae. We shall find below that Husserl is right here, and the others wrong. Somewhat apart stands Peirce's formula for all signs, viz., a sign is "anything which determines something else (its interpretant) to refer to an object to which itself refers (its object) in the same way".[2] I have never felt sure that I understand precisely what Peirce means by this formula, even when "interpretant" is further illuminated by the subsequent phrase, "an interpretant idea having been determined in an individual consciousness". I take the meaning, however, to be that something functions as sign when it makes someone think of an object, which object is

---

[1] *Loc. cit.*, Vol. II, Part II, § 2, p. 25. My translation.
[2] Baldwin's *Dictionary*, *s.v.* Sign.

then called the sign's object, i.e., the thing signified. A glance at Peirce's classification of signs suggests that his language may have been deliberately general to the point of vagueness, because neither association nor inference suffice for explaining the functioning even of those signs which alone are taken account of in Peirce's list. This, however, is a guess, for Peirce's classification is inspired by other interests. He distinguishes *icon*, *index*, and *symbol*. An *icon* is "a sign which would possess the character which renders it significant, even though its object had no existence", e.g., a pencil-streak meaning a geometrical line. An *index* is "a sign which would, at once, lose the character which makes it a sign if its object were removed, but would not lose that character if there were no interpretant", e.g., a bullet-hole meaning a shot. A *symbol* is "a sign which would lose the character which renders it a sign if there were no interpretant," e.g., speech means nothing if it is not understood. Judged on its merits, this classification is, surely, one of Peirce's least successful experiments. It neither covers the ground, nor touches the essence of those signs which it includes. But, at any rate, it suggests that the way in which a sign "determines" our "idea" to refer to its object is neither necessarily inference nor necessarily association. Inference is excluded in the case of icons and symbols, and association is excluded in the case of icons. It is surely not by association, in the usual sense of habitual conjunction due to experience, or "mnemic causation" (as Mr. Russell calls it), that a dot means a mathematical point. Indices, on the other hand, fit the inference formula best, though it is easy to adduce examples in which the nexus of index and indicatum is certainly, as Husserl says, and Meinong grudgingly concedes, *uneinsichtig* (non-intelligible). As a matter of fact, even where the nexus is *uneinsichtig*, it is doubtful whether "association" fits the facts. The connection of a word with its meaning is usually called associative and ascribed to habit formed by repetition, but I venture to call attention to the evidence which I have brought forward in my article on *Image, Idea, and Meaning*[1] for thinking that more than association is involved. This "more" I should now describe by saying that whilst association may cover the *indicative* function of the sign it does

---

[1] *Mind*, N.S., vol. xvi, No. 61, pp. 77, 78. See above, pp. 143 ff.

R

not cover its *expressive* function.[1] In any case, it seems to me Husserl is right in saying that association is not merely mechanical, but also creative; that it effects not merely conjunctions but connections which further effort of thought may transform into intelligible or logical coherences. This view has obvious affinities with Bradley's "association marries universals".

Let us review the situation: We are confronted by a general formula for the nexus of sign and significate, which claims to be applicable to all signs, but which varies in its description of the nexus all the way from clear inference (Meinong's sign= *Erkenntnisgrund*) to habitual association (Russell's mnemic causation). We find in Husserl explicitly and in Peirce implicitly the recognition that the formula applies, not to all signs, but only to those which Husserl and Peirce agree in calling indices (*Anzeigen*).

Can we now clear up this situation further, and develop it, by experimenting with these theoretical suggestions upon as large and varied a body of facts as possible?

The most obvious instances of things functioning as indicative signs, i.e., as ground of inference to the existence of other things are, of course, to be found in the system of nature, more especially so far as the mutual implications of things within it have been scientifically traced out. A certain formation of clouds is a sign of approaching storm; certain anticlines are signs to the geologist of the (at least probable) presence of oil; coal and fossil bones are signs of a prehistoric flora and fauna; certain markings on Mars are signs of canals and of their makers; certain dreams are to the psychoanalyst signs of repressed complexes; diseases are recognised by their symptoms.

But now take another group of examples, in which natural objects and events once more function as signs, but not in ways endorsed by science. A comet is a sign of impending war; entrails of animals, according to their condition, presage victory or defeat in battle; so does the flight of birds and many other kinds of omens and portents; dreams reveal the future; lines in the hand are signs of character or of coming good or ill fortune; "plant-signatures", i.e. resemblances between parts of plants and parts of the human body, are signs of a divinely

---

[1] This distinction will be explained presently.

appointed affinity, making parts of plants effective, as medicaments or aphrodisiacs, for the healing or strengthening or stimulating of the corresponding parts of the body;[1] and so on *ad infinitum*. Inference again? Yes, but resting on quite other premises than in the former group. In many, if not all, of the examples of the present group the major premise of the inference appears to be the belief in a God, or gods, or spirits, who, as it were, signal through certain events or natural arrangements, who give hints to man for his guidance, or at least reveal their mood or their attitude towards his undertakings. In short, the inference treats the signs as *indicative* of other natural events only because they are first interpreted as *expressive* of non-human or supra-human powers, the existence and purposes of which they reveal.

Let us test this distinction further.

So far we have taken our examples from signs which were in no sense man-made, man-produced—signs commonly called "natural" as distinct from "conventional" or "artificial",[2] signs by which man seeks to guide himself in his adjustment to his environment. But the clear-seeming distinction is none the less a tricky one. For, in the first place, human beings themselves may be regarded as parts of the system of nature, and all their actions—whatever they do, whatever they make, whatever they say—may be studied, like the automatic processes in their bodies, as purely indicative and not as expressive at all. Of any observable event in a human body we can, in the spirit of natural science, ask: What other observable events does it indicate (where "observable" refers not only to future events which may, or will, be observed, but also past events that have, or might have, been observed)? Husserl and Meinong, unacquainted with our ultra-behaviourists, are a little precipitate at this point. They go on at once to distinguish between what the actions indicate, viz., that certain psychical processes of

[1] The belief in plant-signatures and, similarly, in animal and mineral signatures, was once widespread, and elaborate treatises, setting forth the facts and recipes authoritatively, were written by reputable scientists even in post-renaissance times. Many common names of flowers, e.g. lungwort, are survivals of the theory. Anyone who has hunted with a French Canadian guide can testify that French Canadians as firmly believe and as regularly act on the theory as the most up-to-date scientist believes in and acts on his theory. In China, too, I am told, the theory is widely held.

[2] *Cf.* Martinak's distinction of "real" and "final" signs, in his *Psychologische Untersuchungen zur Bedeutungslehre*.

perceiving, thinking, willing, etc., are going on in the speaker's mind, and what the words express or mean, viz., the object perceived, thought about, willed. And Husserl further analyses this expression into denotation (what is named or referred to) and connotation (the character, relation, activity, etc., predicated of the object, its *Sosein*).[1] A strict behaviourist, like John Watson, keeping rigidly to what is observable from a spectator-standpoint, is bound to disallow the inference to unperceivable mental processes. For him the sounds of language can be indicative only of other sounds to be heard or movements to be seen. They cannot be treated as expressive of "metaphysical" or "mystical" mental processes. The behaviourism which is ever becoming more fashionable among present-day biologists conforms, of course, strictly to this pattern. The moral, I suggest, is that we can treat human speech and behaviour (I omit the sign-making of non-human animals for simplicity's sake) as indicative of mind, and therefore as expressive, only if we have first made up our minds, in the teeth of a pronounced tendency in modern "science", to believe in the existence of minds and in their expressing themselves—*äussern*, as the Germans are able to say neatly—in visible, audible phenomena, which are for this reason expressive, interpretable signs, signs which, so to speak, make the invisible visible. For this belief we have only one ground, but surely sufficient:—Descartes' *cogito*, or, in the common teminology, which Dr. Schiller in his Congress-paper, too, employs, and which Mr. Russell, in his reply, so strangely fails to understand, the "inner" point of view of the "agent",

---

[1] There are interesting minor differences here between Meinong and Husserl, which unfortunately increase the terminological chaos. When I say, e.g., "That dog is angry," they agree: (*a*) That a hearer can infer from my words that I am looking at and judging about the dog; (*b*) That the hearer, without normally attending to (*a*) at all, will himself be led to look at the dog and to entertain (*annehmen*), if not also to confirm, my judgment. This is for him to "understand" my words, to "know what I mean". Husserl says that the words *indicate* (*anzeigen*), or more specifically, *communicate* (*kundgeben*), my mental processes, but that they *express* (*ausdrücken*, with synonyms *bedeuten*, *meinen*) what is the object (including Meinong's "objective") of my thinking. Meinong says the words *express* (*ausdrücken*) my mental processes, and *mean* (*bedeuten*) their object. It follows, as we saw above, that for him purely emotional ejaculations express but do not mean. Husserl, following a different track, denies of gestures, play of features, etc., that they "express" in his sense of the word, on the ground that there is no intention to express or communicate or make manifest anything. Presumably, he could treat Meinong's emotional ejaculations similarly. Of course, all such utterances or actions may serve to another as indices for inference. Clearly there is room for much subtle detail work here.

as distinct from the "outer" point of view of the spectator. It is because we are acquainted with what expressing is by doing it most of the time, that we are entitled to use sensibilia, not merely as indicative signs for other sensibilia, but, rising above this phenomenalism, to interpret them also as expressive of other minds. Of course, such interpretation should be experimental, and subject to methodical tests. It is not to be understood off-hand as justifying those extravagances of animal psychology against which our behaviourists are in revolt. Nor is it a plea for pan-psychism, or even for Berkeley's interpretation of nature as the visual language of God. The abuse of a principle, if it has been abused, is a good argument for caution in its use, but not for its abandonment.

The position tentatively reached now may be summarised as follows. With hardly an exception, everyone who has written on signs and meaning has begun from the spectator's point of view. He has thought of himself, not in the first instance as expressing himself, or his meaning, through signs, but as confronted by signs which put to him the problem of discovering their meaning. Everyone has begun at the periphery and worked to the centre, though in expressing his findings he was at the centre all the time. If we begin from the centre, it is likely that, as Dr. Schiller says, meaning precedes expression, though "precedes" must not be taken too literally, for meaning is hampered in development where means of expression fail.[1] At any rate, from the outsider's point of view, the first question is how to recognise a sign as a sign. Fortunately, this question *solvitur ambulando*. As Toennies says ,"a sign is what functions as a sign", i.e., what makes us perceive, think, feel (as the case may be) something other than itself. But this formula covers two types which few thinkers have clearly distinguished. The question, what does this sign mean? covers the two questions: (*a*) what does this imply, or what can be inferred from this? (*b*) what does this express? This gives us the distinction between the *indicative* and the *expressive* function of signs. It is the expressive function which gives rise to the most interesting and subtle phenomenological problems, which I can here only indicate. Thus, e.g., when we analyse what is expressed, we are led to

[1] I regret that I am not well enough acquainted with Croce's work to say how far his theory of expression would fit in with these suggestions,

distinguish between mental acts which have, or present, objects and mental acts which are non-presentative. Any other person to whom, intentionally or not, we communicate ourselves through our expressions, may, if he pleases, so interpret them as to learn of our mental acts, but as a rule he will be so wholly interested and absorbed in their objects, that he attends neither to his own thinking (which is yet involved in his understanding us) nor to ours—only to *what* we think in expressing ourselves and what he, too, thinks in understanding us. So it is, too, with the solitary thinker. He expresses himself, he uses signs (whatever their nature in detail may be); we may even say that he is communicating with himself. Yet he attends to his own signs and his own processes of thinking as little as he does to another's in reading or listening. He, too, is as a rule wholly absorbed in *what* he is experiencing in thinking: he "lives in" his objects, as almost every writer on meaning justly reiterates.

All this touches but a small corner of the subject, though it is the corner which, as nearest to their own work, philosophers have most often sought to explore. But beyond it lies a large field which is almost virgin soil. Let me, in conclusion, only indicate, at random, groups of facts by which our initial theory must be further tested and perhaps transformed.

(i) The combination of indicative and expressive functions in the same sign offers many problems. Husserl and others treat mnemonic signs (e.g., knot in handkerchief), discriminative signs (e.g., a brand on cattle), and such signs as national flags or monuments as purely indicative. But it might well be argued that any arrangement purposely made to serve as a sign has an expressive function, too; especially when, like a flag, it may be an excitant of intense emotions and actions. To restrict these signs to the indicative function is to keep too closely to the outsider's standpoint. Should we not ask also how much of ourselves we can express through such signs as these? Take, e.g., badges of rank, signs of office, professional garb, like a military uniform, a cleric's cassock, a scholar's gown. They obviously serve as indices to others, but may they not help the wearer to be more effectively what they declare him to be, to play more fully the part among men for which he is dressed?

(ii) The problem of the proverbial "thoughts too deep for words" has all too rarely led philosophers and psychologists to explore the expressive value of non-verbal symbolic actions, indeed, the need of expressing in action what cannot be said in words. Human life is full of such actions, especially where deep affection is involved. And thence open vistas upon ritual in religion (and elsewhere), for which I must be content to refer, as an illustration, to Miss Dougall's essay on *The Language of the Soul* in Canon Streeter's book on *The Spirit*.

(iii) Lastly, there is the symbolism of art—a field of meaning and expression of meaning almost unexplored from the side of phenomenology. No one will say that the sounds of music are "mere" sounds: no, they are expressive, they are charged with meaning, though what they mean can hardly be translated into, or expressed in terms of, any other language, unless it be dancing. Inference and association here leave us in the lurch as explanatory principles. Even the distinction of the indicative and expressive functions of signs becomes almost an irrelevant artificiality when applied to music—a reminder of the wholly tentative character of the results we have so far reached. But this itself is but another argument for the plea: More phenomenology!

The Absolute

THE Absolute is the Universe, the All.

In denotation, the words "the Absolute", "the Universe", "the All", and likewise "Reality" (*la réalité, die Wirklichkeit*), are different names for the same thing. They are synonyms for the object of Metaphysics.

Every metaphysician, thus, in taking the whole Universe for his province, is an Absolutist. Every metaphysical theory is an attempt to give an account of the nature of the Absolute. Spinoza's theory of one all-inclusive substance is no more and no less a theory of the Absolute than is Descartes' two-substance theory or Leibniz's Monadology. Whether our metaphysical theory be materialistic or spiritualistic; whether it interpret the All in terms of matter, or life, or mind, or God; whether it find in thought, or will, or imagination, or the unconscious, or the *élan vital*, or even in Herbert Spencer's Unknowable, the clue to the nature of the Universe—it will always be a theory of the Absolute.

Metaphysical theories differ, not in their object, but in their renderings of its nature. The battle is not for, or against, the Absolute: it is between rival versions of the nature of the Absolute. A philosopher need not be an Idealist in order to be an Absolutist.

Yet, on the other hand, it is undeniable that, owing to the use of the word "the Absolute" by the post-Kantian Idealists, it has become associated with idealistic Metaphysics and acquired a specialised meaning. It stands for an idealistic interpretation of the nature of the Universe. However, even this statement is still too wide. For, not all Idealists are Absolutists in the most special sense of the word. Among Idealist Metaphysicians, there are those who are Monists and those who are Pluralists (or Monadologists). For the latter, the Absolute Idealist goes wrong in giving too monistic an interpretation of the Universe. That is the point of William James's attacks on the "block universe" of Josiah Royce. There lies the sting of

James's declaration: "we must always experience the Absolute as if it were a foreign being". He did not mean that the Universe is foreign to us, but the nature of the Universe as interpreted by Absolutists is foreign to us, i.e., is utterly different from what in common experience it seems to be. And when Bosanquet replies to James: "we experience the Absolute better than we experience anything else", he asserts that, if we interpret what experience reveals of the nature of the Universe, we are led to the theory of its nature which is summed up in the concept of the Absolute. Thus, "the Absolute", giving the word now its fullest technical meaning, stands, not merely for a metaphysical theory in general, nor merely for an idealistic metaphysical theory, but for a special type of idealistic metaphysical theory.

In the mazes of contemporary philosophical controversy, the situation thus schematically outlined often fails to be recognised. Non-Idealist thinkers attack the theory of the Absolute because it is idealistic, but also because of other features in it which are not specifically idealistic at all, but which, occurring in this context, come falsely to be regarded as specifically idealistic. Non-Absolutist Idealists attack the theory of the Absolute because they regard it as a false rendering of the common principles of Idealism. In either case, the argument may be conducted on any one of many different planes and be directed against any one of the many different aspects of the theory. Thus, it may move on the most abstract logical plane in dialectics about the One and the Many, or about Identity and Difference. Or it may centre in the concept of Relation:—are relations internal or external in their nature; and can the all-inclusive Whole, for all that it has distinguishable parts, be conceived as relational in its ultimate nature? Yet again, granted —and who can refuse to grant?—that the Universe contains many different things, numerically many, qualitatively diverse, are these many constituents and kinds of constituents barely conjoined in chaotic togetherness, or are they connected in systems and orders? If so, what are these systems? Are they themselves ordered? Is there a supreme, all-inclusive order? And, if all is gripped in pervasive system, is not everything necessarily determined? If so, what room is there for chance, spontaneity, freedom, novelty, evolution, creation? Again, what of time?

If the Absolute is timeless or super-temporal, what becomes of the time-process, what of change, activity, distinction of past and future, of planning and realisation? Once more shifting the plane of argument, we may ask: what of the place in, and the bearing on each other in the Whole, of the phenomena which we sum up under such blanket-labels as "matter" (physical bodies), "life" (organisms), "mind" (whether as feelings, perceivings, thinkings, etc., or as souls, selves, spirits which feel, perceive, think, etc.)? Yet again, what of Morality, with its distinction of Good and Evil: what becomes of these in a Universe conceived as beyond good and evil, as perfect even with evil in it? Or what of Religion with its concept of God, especially if it be the concept of a personal God?

These riddles have been selected to illustrate, not to exhaust, the area over which the debate concerning the Absolute ranges. No category, no *cadre de l'intelligence*, no Platonic "form", but is somewhere drawn into the orbit of the argument; as, indeed, it must be if it truly represents an aspect of the Universe.

The historian of philosophy readily recognises here the ruins of Hegel's edifice. No modern philosopher, even though he be a "Hegelian", would at the present day venture to defend Hegel's system in detail, or to construct an alternative system in which, rising plane upon plane, each category, each universal, considered as an aspect of the nature of the Universe, has its appointed place, revealing in its own nature something of the Whole, even whilst its own nature is itself more adequately revealed when it is considered, not by itself in abstraction, but in its place among other aspects of the over-arching Whole. Yet, the inspiration of Hegel's dazzling construction, the example of his magnificent effort at synoptic thought, seeking to be at once severely logical in its rigour and also exhaustively responsive to the whole range of human experience, has remained, and will remain, an undying part of our philosophical heritage. Every metaphysician, with the Universe as a Whole before him as at once his object and his problem, has, according to his powers, explicitly or implicitly striven to realise in his theory the twin ideals of comprehensiveness and intelligible connection. He has aimed at a theory which should set out the systematic order of the Universe in its main ramifications, whilst including, at the same time, in that order the whole range of phenomena found in human experience. But, no thinker has in the same measure as Hegel impressed on us the vastness and the difficulty of the task. It is true that these two ideals, as such, do not compel an idealistic metaphysic. They may be honoured by Realists (like S. Alexander in his *Space-Time and Deity*), or even by thinkers who, professedly rejecting "metaphysics", seek to work out a positivistically oriented phenomenology. But, it is also true that absolute Idealists have been in a distinctive sense the heirs of Hegel's inspiration. For, they derive from him, not only these two ideals, but also the conviction that only within the context of an idealistic interpretation of the Universe can these ideals be realised, so far as the limitations of human thought permit their realisation at all.

Obviously, the topic of the Absolute is too vast to be adequately dealt with in a short paper. Hence, I shall confine myself to selecting, out of many possible lines of argument, one which will, I hope, prove a fair sample of the kind of reasoning which culminates in the metaphysical edifice of Absolute Idealism. I shall present this line of argument in three sections, dealing,

(1) with the nature of thought in general, and of metaphysical thought in particular;

(2) with certain considerations which make for an idealistic interpretation of the Universe; and

(3) with the issue between Idealists who accept, and Idealists who reject, the Absolute.

(1) Thinking is a response, not to a stimulus which, by definition, lies *outside* the thinkers' experience, but to a problem which presents itself to him *in* his experience. E.g., a novel object, for the first time met with, may arouse curiosity: "What is this?" The question initiates a seeking for further evidence, whencesoever it may be got—from further perceptual exploration, with or without manipulation and experiment; from comparison with other objects on the basis of memory; from imagination; etc. The result, if thinking is at all successful, will be an enriched apprehension of the object, a fuller revelation of its nature, enabling the thinker to say: "Now I know what this is". Or, again, the problem may take the form of some contradiction or conflict between thoughts: thinking this and thinking that, we find we cannot affirm both this and that together.

As a problem-solving activity, thinking has direction and aim. It aims at—what? We can say only: "at what will, when it comes, be found to satisfy", or "to answer the question". What in detail the answer to any problem will turn out to be, we cannot know in anticipation of the finding. We know only that, when we discover it, we shall recognise it as being what we are seeking. For, it will bring with it a distinctive intellectual satisfaction which enables us to say of the answer: "it is so; it must be so; it cannot be otherwise". In so far as what the thinker thinks possesses this character, his work is ended. He has reached the acme of insight. There is no evidence more complete than this: indeed, this is self-evidence—when what he thinks, summing up in itself the whole process, from putting the problem through considering the evidence as it comes in (testing, sifting, modifying, putting together, etc.) to formulating the conclusion—when all this guarantees, as it were, its own outcome.

We can speak of such thinking, which is problem-solving or, at least, solution-seeking, as the expression of a "will to truth". Or we can describe it as moulded by an "immanent compulsion"—a compulsion rooted in *what* we think. Whether we choose to speak of seeking and finding the truth, or of the truth revealing and imposing itself irresistibly on us—in either case we describe the same experience from opposite, but complementary, angles. To say of what I think: "it is so; it must be so; it cannot be otherwise" is but another way of saying: "I think so; I must think so; I cannot think otherwise". The most fundamental principle of all thinking, so we find on reflection, is that the object is what we think, and cannot help thinking, it to be.

The point is important enough to be put another way. Everything, it is said, is what it is. This, surely, is self-evident; the law of identity, in fact. But, if we want to make any use of this law, we can apply it only to what we experience, in the widest sense of that word. To nothing else can we apply it. Thus, in actual application, "everything" means "everything we experience", and can mean nothing else.

It follows that what we feel, perceive, think, desire, etc., has always in it something *absolute*. Every object as we experience it, or every experience with its object just as that object is there revealed, says, as it were: "whatever else may be, I am, and am what I am".

More, this is not a mere brute absoluteness of fact, but an absoluteness of self-justifying value. Every perception, feeling, desire, taken within its own four corners (so to speak), not merely says: "I am what I am", but also: "Being what I am, I am right just so". Self-approval is the companion of self-evidence. In cognition, i.e., in perceiving, thinking, reasoning as Universe-revealing, this self-approval, this being "right", is called "truth". What I perceive and think is just so, and must be affirmed by me as being just so, unless I have grounds (evidence) for doubt. Hence, every judgment carries with it the implicit affirmation of its own truth. In that sense, "X is Y" is equivalent to "it is true that X is Y" (or "X is Y is true"). No doubt, we shall not ordinarily use the second formula except after having reflected on whether there is any evidence for X being other than Y (or—it comes to the same thing—for thinking X to be other than Y). Finding no such evidence, we then reaffirm our original judgment with the added emphasis of "it is true". But, though the second formula belongs to a further stage of reflection, it merely makes explicit what was by implication already affirmed on the primary plane.

Similarly, every feeling, every desire, taken by itself, affirms implicitly its own justification, and in this character we have the root of aesthetic and moral values, as in the corresponding character of perceptions and judgments we have the basis of truth. This, surely, is the meaning of the familiar principle that whatever we desire, we desire as good or *sub ratione boni*.

We know, of course, that this absolute character of every experience does not prevent it from coming into conflict with, and being challenged by, other experiences. Its absolute character then weakens to a mere claim to absoluteness—a claim which needs to be re-enforced and sustained, or which may be rejected and denied. Yet, even as a mere claim the fate of which is still to be decided, nay, even as a rejected claim, the experience in question still is; and it must be included in, and provided for, in any genuinely comprehensive theory. Even rejected, it is still in the Universe and of it. Error, intellectual, moral, aesthetic—believing what is false; desiring what is evil or wrong; feeling otherwise than we ought—is still part of the

Universe and may not be omitted in a complete theory of its nature.

The application of these conclusions to metaphysical thinking is plain. The problem of such thinking, viz., the nature of the Universe, presents itself only at a high level of reflection, on the basis of much previous exploration of special aspects of the Universe which arouse cognitive interest more urgently and directly. In any case, it is a problem the full range and ramifications of which come into view only when a rich and many-sided civilisation, with highly-developed special departments of thought (e.g., History, the Sciences, Theory of the State, of Morals, of Art, Theology, etc.), offers abundant materials for the synoptic task of the metaphysician. But, whatever be the resulting theory, and whether it offer itself with the assurance of an unquestionable intuition (like Bergson's *élan vital*), or be squeezed painfully out of laborious dialectics and remain beset by self-confessed "ultimate doubts" (like F. H. Bradley's *Absolute*), it will still be affirmed with the conviction that so it is, so it must be, and other than so it cannot be. And what, above, was called the "absolute" character of every experience, will be for the metaphysician evidence of its metaphysical relevance. For, in that character he will recognise precisely the Universe-revealing function of every experience. It may reveal little: it may reveal much. In any case, it will reveal something and must be taken into account. The metaphysician has no data or materials for a theory of the nature of the Universe other than those which the Universe itself offers through experience in all its forms.

Moreover, some forms of experience are more revealing than others; hence for the metaphysician more significant. How select and grade these? Where find the standard to be used? Once more, the question *solvitur ambulando*: the standard, too, is immanent in the nature of a self-revealing Universe. Let all-inclusiveness and coherence (or non-contradiction) together with the "spiritual" values of truth, goodness, beauty, be the standards: it is still the nature of the Universe which imposes these standards and demands their recognition. They are no mere arbitrary human fictions or inventions imposed *ab extra* and thus falsifying the picture. They represent no mere subjective bias of minds which, standing outside their object, the

Universe, can make a theory of it only in their own image, whilst its own nature remains ever beyond them.

In short, the metaphysician, even less than any other thinker, may abandon the principle that the object—even the Universe —is what he thinks it to be; or that what he experiences is, so far as it goes, the Universe revealing itself just so. And, if he chooses to distinguish between subject and object, between thinker and what-is-thought, between mind and what mind knows, he must at once remind himself that this distinction, taken as absolute, divorces him from his object, by denying the Universe-revealing character of all experience, thus making the Universe unknowable and his so-called knowledge no better than illusion. He can escape this devastating conclusion only by reflecting that subject, thinker, mind, still remain part of the Universe, and if the Universe is their object, then they are its *organs for self-apprehension.* In short, in the end, a self-revealing Universe can reveal itself only to itself. This is how the meta-physician must think of the nature of thinking, if the phrase "theory of the Universe" is not to be a meaningless jumble of words. Not every metaphysician may have explicitly acknow-ledged the view of thinking here set out, but all have acted on it. To deny it would be to stultify the whole enterprise of Meta-physics, make of it verily a fool's game.

Beyond the agreement of metaphysicians on this point which we may thus claim, their common interest in the same object has secured at least a minimum of further agreement among them. For, any thinker who takes the Universe for his object knows that he is dealing with what is, in some sense, a One-in-Many (or a Many-in-One). That there are differents, endless in number and variety, in the Universe, his experience tells him. No less surely, if a little less obviously, it tells him also that these differents belong to a single Universe. Indeed, this double-edged insight, like the concept of the Universe in which it is expressed, precedes philosophical reflection and is but re-enforced and confirmed by it. The familiar dialectical veri-fications of this point need no repeating here. Even the multi-plicity of Leibnizian monads still forms a unity through pre-established harmony. There is no monad, nor anything else, outside the system of harmoniously corresponding monads. In this ultimate and fundamental sense, so-called Monists and so-called Pluralists are alike "Monists". And, when they debate whether the Universe be One or Many, they are really debating the nature of the unity (or system) in which the Many have their being. Even if we entertain the concept of "possible" Universes, i.e., of possible Universes other than this actual Universe, they must still have the same general logical pattern, and, what is more to the point, there is only one actual Universe and only one conceivable as actual. For, even if we try to suppose more actual Universes than one, we cannot help conceiving, at once, also the super-ordinate Universe which includes all lesser actual Universes.

(2) The view, just put forth, of thought and experience as being essentially Universe-revealing, leads by a natural transition to an idealistic interpretation of the Universe.

Much might be said under this head. But, to cut a long matter short, it may suffice to say simply this:—Granted that there is experience; and granted that experience is, as we have taken it to be, essentially Universe-revealing: it seems that such self-revealing must be a self-revealing of the Universe to itself, and that it must be essential to the Universe's own nature. If we accept this at all, we must accept it as fundamental to metaphysical theory.

This position involves no "ego-centric predicament", illegitimately exploited. Even if for "ego" we substitute "experience" as such, there is no predicament. Rather, this self-revelation of the Universe—without which, if it is indeed essential to the nature of the Universe, the Universe could neither be nor be known—is our supreme opportunity. There could be no Philosophy and no Science without it. This insight is at once the first and the last thing in philosophising—the last, because reflection culminates in it and, after repeated trials, confirms it; the first, because once achieved, all else is thereafter considered in its light.

This does not mean, however, that the effort to reach, to maintain, to recapture, this insight does not meet with serious difficulties, which to many critics of Idealism have seemed insuperable and fatal.

Speaking generally, these difficulties arise from the fact that when we apply this metaphysical concept of experience to our actual, everyday experience, it comes into conflict with other concepts of that experience—concepts belonging to other contexts. Now, if we fail to recognise these different contexts (perhaps overlooking the metaphysical one altogether, because of its unfamiliarity), or, if, recognising them, we fail to keep them apart or falsely identify them, the result is sheer confusion and antinomy. Certainly, the bulk of "realistic" criticism of Idealism rests on taking statements concerning experience (or "mind", as a synonym for "experience"), which are meant to be understood in a metaphysical context, and applying them in some other context. Inevitably, so misunderstood or misapplied, they seem fit only for rejection.

The metaphysical context is defined by the principle that the Universe is self-revealing and that experience is its self-revelation; also, that on this principle must rest all theory of the nature of the Universe, and all theory of the knowledge of the nature of the Universe. In all other contexts, on the other hand, this Universe-revealing character of experience is either ignored or else it is treated as not of the essence of mind or experience. No wonder, then, that critics, viewing mind and experience in one of these other contexts, fail to verify what is said of them in the metaphysical context. The cause of the trouble is, in part, unfamiliarity with the metaphysical context, and, more often, the absence of a context-indicating adjective when we speak of "mind" and "experience".

Thus, e.g., mind (in the metaphysical, Universe-revealing, sense) may not be treated as a phenomenon among other phenomena. It can be viewed only as the matrix, so to speak, or field of all phenomena whatsoever. Of experience or mind in the metaphysical sense it is meaningless to ask: What is its relation to "matter", or to "body", or to anything else whatsoever? Such questions have meaning only in contexts in which experience or mind are contrasted, as phenomena of a distinctive kind, with phenomena of other kinds. But, so understood, mind has not, and cannot have, the metaphysical or Universe-revealing function. So understood, it is an object among objects —not the revealing of any object.

As a positive science, therefore, Psychology omits, or abstracts from, the metaphysical character of mind, and so do all other "scientific" theories of mind, especially those which treat mind in a biological context as a product of evolution, as response to

s

a non-mental environment, as a function of a certain kind of animal body. In none of these contexts can the metaphysical function of mind be recognised or dealt with. To say this is not to find fault with scientific Psychology, or with Science in general, as if they were failing to do something which they ought to do. But it is a warning not to make Science the basis of Metaphysics. It is a reminder that the conclusions of Science must be re-interpreted by Metaphysics, not Metaphysics be tied down to the conclusions of Science. Epigrammatically, we might say: There is Metaphysics of Science, but there cannot be scientific Metaphysics. In other words, Metaphysics, as the theory of the nature of the Universe as a whole, has among its data the theories of the Sciences concerning their limited and selected aspects of the Universe. Moreover, the metaphysician must bear in mind, not only that the Sciences are selective in their subject-matter, but also that their treatment of their subject-matter may be determined by the deliberate and exclusive use of only such categories and concepts as are considered by the prevailing fashion to distinguish uniquely what is genuinely "scientific" thinking from what is "unscientific" (cf., mechanism in biology). For the metaphysician to accept results got in this way as final and absolute, and to squeeze his own theory of the Universe as a Whole into a scientific bed of Procrustes, would be to betray his proper task. And, as regards experience and mind, we must repeat without hesitation that any theory of them in a scientific, naturalistic, positive context—any theory of mind as a "natural phenomenon" distinguishable from body and other natural phenomena—cannot do justice to, and will, in fact, be bound to ignore, the metaphysical nature of mind.

Out of many other possible applications by which this argument might be illustrated, I will add but one more. It might be claimed that the analysis, made by many Realists, of cognitive experience into act, object, and relation of act to object, is not "naturalistic" or "scientific" in the sense just criticised, but that it is purely "phenomenological"—an analysis performed directly on experience itself and thus, surely, revealing its nature as it is and as Metaphysics must accept it. But this is an illusion due to the use of words as if an analysis had been performed, whereas, in fact, the words have no verifiable meaning. This may be tested by applying the alleged analysis to any actual experience as it is actually lived through (*erlebt*). In perceiving, thinking, remembering, etc., if we set on one side what is perceived, thought, remembered, have we anything identifiable left on the other side to be the natures of these various acts? *A fortiori*, have we anything left to be the relations between these acts and their objects? No wonder Dr. G. E. Moore, attempting just this analysis, was moved to comment on the "diaphanous" character of the acts! If, further, we exploit the analysis and claim that the object is what it is, whether or no there be any act to which it is thus related, or that it pass into and out of such relation to acts without alteration in its nature —the whole affair being entirely accidental to the object—our argument will seem plausible only so long as we fail to remember that by "object" throughout we mean, and can mean only, the object-as-we-preceive-it-to-be. Yet, at the same time, we insist on treating this essential qualification as irrelevant. How impossible this is should become clear when as our object we take the Universe which includes these very acts. Here, at any rate, the acts cannot be accidental or nonessential; and if they cannot be so here, how can they be so for any part or aspect of the Universe, except when, by deliberate make-believe abstraction, we ignore the presence of the Universe in its parts and treat the parts as if they were complete in themselves?

Another way of reaching the same result is to place oneself "within" (so to speak) an exploring and problem-solving process. There is here nothing of act, object, relation—there is only the kaleidoscopic content-change through which, however, there runs, as definite pattern, the nisus towards a fuller revelation and display of the nature of the object. We find here, in short, precisely that Universe-revealing character which belongs to all experience and of which every actual experience of individual human minds is a more or less adequate instance.

(3) We pass, lastly, to a brief discussion of the issue between Absolutists and non-Absolutists among Idealists themselves.

For this purpose, neither those aspects of the concept of the Absolute which are common ground to all metaphysicians, nor those which are common to all Idealists, are relevant. The issue is narrowed down to one on which Idealists take opposite sides, for all that they start from the same fundamental premises, viz., that a Universe which is self-revealing is a Universe which is Experience through and through.

This general formula is elastic enough to permit within itself a variety of developments, like variations of the same musical motif. Most of these developments, though they differ from, do not necessarily contradict each other, and may therefore be accepted as emphasising, each in its own way, the richness of the common theme. But, two of them are so different, and diverge on so fundamental a point, that they do split the Idealist Movement into two major schools: the Absolutists and the Pluralists (or Personalists), respectively.

At any rate, this is true of the Idealist Movement in the English-speaking world. Nowhere else, so far as I am aware, has the argument between Absolutists and Pluralists been so keen and so alive, though anyone not familiar with the technical language of metaphysicians would perhaps hardly suspect a soul-stirring argument to be hidden behind the question: Do Finite Individuals Possess a Substantive or an Adjectival Mode of Being?[1].

It is common ground among the two parties to the debate that experience at the human level, occurs in, organises itself into, individual foci or centres. Experience, we might also say, occurs as experiences; and experiences hang together in clusters, each cluster distinct from all others, whatever linking identities there may be. Mind occurs as minds. The Universe appears to have a monadic structure.

The problem is:—How fundamental is this appearance of monadic structure? What is the function of this individualisation of experiential foci—of this self-direction or self-differentiation, of the Whole into a multiplicity of minds (souls, spirits) of each of which, however much it may have in common or share with others, it is none the less true to say that it is itself and no other?

Moreover, the problem, so stated, is so general that it permits special interpretations in a variety of directions.

Thus, e.g., we may ask whether the individual minds are

[1] *Aristotelian Society Proceedings*, N.S., vol. xviii (1917-18); reprinted by the Society in *Life and Infinite Individuality* (1918).

temporary and transient existents, coming into being and then again annihilated, to be replaced by others; or whether they participate in the timeless existence of the Universe itself. Applied to minds such as ours, this leads to speculations concerning survival of death and pre-existence before birth, where timelessness is envisaged under the image of existence throughout all time.

Again, minds are not all of one kind or type. Whether or no we choose to speculate about minds of plants, or even of atoms (if so, why not of electrons and protons?), or, at the other end of the scale, about superhuman minds (e.g., angels)—even within the *bona fide* empirical range of minds, there is evidence enough of difference of degree and kind, enabling us to construct scales and gradations. From the abstract formal individuality of mere self-identity ("I am I") which characterises all minds alike, we can pass to higher forms of individuality, to "selves" (in various degrees of selfhood), to "persons" (on various levels of personality). Starting from this basis, we can ask how individualities as such, and, again, individualities of different degrees and types, can, without detriment to their individuality, be related to each other within the single Universe which they all help to embody and which exists in and through each of them. Indeed, is not the very "in-and-through" relation to the Whole a diminution of their self-contained individuality? Can individuals be conceived as parts, or constituents, of a higher individuality, without loss of selfhood? Can different minds be expressions of a single mind which includes them all? Can persons be, and be conceived, as included in a greater person? Can the Universe as a Whole be conceived as a single, all-inclusive, mind or self or person?

Questions of this sort can be combined with questions of the previous group:—Are all kinds and degrees of individual minds timeless and eternal, or only the higher kinds of minds: selves, persons, rational souls?

And, as if this interlacing of various strands were not enough, we find all these questions debated on various planes, from the purely dialectical argument on the plane of abstract logical principles (the "I am I" plane, so to speak), through the plane of Empirical Psychology (with its description of minds, animal and human, infant and adult), of Social and Political Science (dealing with the inter-relations and inter-actions of minds as members of social groups), to the moral and religious planes where arguments about the immortality of Man and the personality of God have their proper place. Obviously, within a field of such range and complexity, there is ample room for thinkers, none of them omniscient, each limited in outlook and experience, each conditioned by the influences in his age which have moulded him, each with his bias, his preferences, his special knowledge, and his special ignorance, to attempt widely diverse syntheses.

Yet, broadly, all these syntheses tend to fall into one or other of two groups. There are the Theories of the Absolutists who stress the dependence of the individual mind on the Absolute, the Universe as a Whole. And there are the Theories of the Pluralists who defend the selfhood and energy of individual minds against undue absorption into the Absolute.

In the brief space which remains to me, I cannot attempt to marshal, let alone discuss, all the ramifications of this debate. All I can usefully do is to select a few salient points to illustrate the spirit in which, and the method by which, Absolutists conduct their side of the argument. Their watchword may be taken from Bosanquet:—"the best of logic and the best of life". Or, as I have attempted myself to express it elsewhere: "What is the reasoner to reason with except the materials which human experience, in the widest sense of that word, puts at his disposal? What he is to think on any given problem, and ultimately on the Universe as a Whole, is bound to depend on what he has to think with. There is nothing else on which it can depend. Reasonings differ partly, no doubt, because some minds are more logical than others, but partly, and especially so on philosophical issues, because as between one mind and another there are differences in the range, kind and quality of the experiences which are their material for reasoning, and even more because out of the same sort of experience one mind can elicit more insight than another".[1]

For the upholder of the concept of the Absolute, the problem is how to interpret the admitted *prima facie* individuality and self-existence of our minds in the light of their being organs of the self-revelation of the Universe through them, and how to

[1] *Studies in Contemporary Metaphysics*, pp. 68-9.

use our experiences, in their various degrees and kinds, for that purpose.

On the negative side, he tries to trace the plausibility of the Pluralist view to its source and exhibit it as illusory.

The Pluralist view rests, in the first place, on the privacy of each mind: its experiences are its own—on their felt side exclusively so. But, the Pluralist, here, not only exaggerates the actual degree of privacy, but allows it to blind him to the extent to which individual minds have experiences in common and know that they have them in common.

Next, the body plays an important part. Practically and legally, it supplies, if not the actual standard of individuality, yet its most convenient defining mark. On the principle, one body—one mind, individual minds are identified as the minds of individual bodies. Once more an exaggeration: there may, as the phenomenon of multiple personality shows, be more than one mind to a given body. Or what of the mediums through whom departed spirits claim to communicate?

Moreover, the spatial distinctness of human bodies, and their four-square isolation and self-containedness to the outside observer (barely qualified by occasional contacts, in coöperation or physical conflict), suggest a similar isolation and self-containedness of the minds that go with these bodies. We certainly do not, in the mutual positions and behaviours of bodies towards each other on the perceptual plane, get much evidence of "the spiritual structure which lies behind the visible scene". If we omit spoken and written language, how much would the observer from the outside know of the relations of minds to each other, of their nature as members of social organisations, of their nature as organs of a self-revealing Universe?

In fact, when we approach the individuality of the mind through the individuality of the body, which at best reveals so little of the full nature of the mind and which can so easily be studied as if it were not an organ of mind at all, our theory is readily deflected, first, into generalisation about (physical) "things" and, next, into a further thinning down of the concept of *thing* into the abstract logical concept of *substance* as the bearer of predicates. When we have reached this level of abstraction, neither are our reflections checked any longer by the specific experiences in which mind has its being, nor can these in their turn be adequately interpreted by this abstract concept. At this point, therefore, theory can run riot in speculations about individual minds whose self-identity is in no way affected by the relations in which they stand to others, and whose nature need in no way be conceived as expressing the nature of any Whole to which they belong. The only question we must avoid asking, or at least pressing home, if we would not bring the whole edifice tumbling down, is whether these concepts fit the facts as we actually experience them.

A simple experiment in reflection about one's own mind helps to bring home what is meant by testing such concepts in respect of their fitting the facts. If I suppose all the "objects" of the experiences which, together, constitute my mind, to be other than they are, a different mind results—not my mind, not I.

If I abstract from all objects which actually make my experiences what they are, and try to see myself as a bare centre of mental "acts", once more the result is not I as I find myself in the concrete to be. As a unity of experiences, I am a microcosm (as Leibniz rightly saw), a cross-section of the Universe (as E. B. Holt and other Realists of his type express it), in many distinguishable dimensions.

On this basis, then, of taking my mind as a cross-section of the Universe, a world which is at the same time a fragment of the total World, I may note, as significant for an adequate theory of individual mind, four things.

First: the gamut of fluctuations, from shallowness to depth, from blindness to insight, from thoughtless impulse to thoughtful purpose. Yet, through this gamut, actual and potential, there is recognisable, though often defeated and often missing its way, a *nisus*, a striving for a form of experience in which my fragmentariness shall be made whole, my inadequacies and defects made good. "*Im Ganzen, Guten, Schönen resolut zu leben,*" as Goethe phrases it, that seems to be the fulfilment which mind craves by its own nature. Its actuality falls short of its intention and destiny, yet its nature is incompletely conceived without these.

Secondly: there are not only fluctuations from more to less adequate and satisfying experience, but actual disharmonies, contradictions, conflicts; and in striving to overcome these, once more the *nisus* towards harmony and wholeness manifests itself, which is the nature of the Absolute working in the individual mind.

Thirdly: I never know myself fully and as a whole, because I never am, though I always would be, a whole. Whatever I am, when I try to think it out, points me beyond myself to the Absolute of which I am a part. Hence, there is nothing in me, nor does anything come out of me, that I could claim as "mine" in detachment from the Universe or in opposition to it. In all that I feel, think, desire, the Universe communicates itself to me and thus makes me what I am. *My* nature is *its* nature specialised in this unique way: *Deus*, as Spinoza says, *sive natura quatenus humanam mentem constituit.* This applies no less to human minds in contact with each other: if love, for instance, glorifies them and lifts them on to a higher plane, and if the joint life founded on their love is a finer thing than either partner, separately, could have lived, are the lovers not instrumental to a greater reality? Are not their energies drawn from sources beyond their private being?

Fourthly: if we consider individual minds as members of organised communities, with which they are, and experience themselves to be, identified, is it not clear once more that, as functioning in such contexts, their natures are what they are only as moulded by the natures of these superordinate wholes? Divorce individual minds from such contexts, i.e., leave such contexts out in your study of their natures, and large tracts of their natures (i.e., of what they actually feel, think, do) become unintelligible, or else escape notice altogether. If an analogy can help to drive home the point, let this of Bosanquet's serve: "Our minds, if they could be visualised, . . . would not look like self-contained shapes, each repeating the other side by side like our bodies set in a row. They would look like bits of machines or organs of organisms, fragmentary and incomprehensible till the whole were supplied to which they respectively belong, each with its driving-bands or nerves or wireless aerials hanging loose around it, all senseless and self-contradictory apart from the inclusive structural system. . . ."[1]

To these four sets of considerations we may, not inappropri-

[1] *Life and Finite Individuality*, p. 82.

ately, add that, if it is hard to conceive a mind of this sort as one of the abiding purposes of the Universe, co-eternal with it, yet, on the other hand, there is no good reason for limiting its effective existence to the period between the birth and the death of the body. "Their works, their thoughts", we say of great minds, "live after them". It is part of the nature of every mind to influence and mould other minds, just as in turn it is moulded by them. And, this effectiveness is not restricted to minds contemporarily "in the flesh". If I study works of the great thinkers of the past, their minds affect me now and will affect the minds of students yet unborn in years to come. On the theory of minds as expressions and revelations of the Universe this is not unintelligible, for the Universe, the Absolute, is the living identity which differentiates itself into individual minds, and is effective in each according to the degree and kind of the self-expression which the Absolute has there achieved.

Absolutism, or Absolute Idealism, we may briefly sum up, is the theory that the Universe is Experience, being at once all experiencing and all that is experienced; and that individual minds (or centres of experiences) at once have their root in the Whole for the total self-revelation of which they are, each in its own way, essential, whilst at the same time, as each but a fragment of that total life, they point and strive ever beyond their actual selves to their completion and fulfilment in the Absolute.

Neo-Realism and Religion

NEO-REALISM, we shall all agree, has come to stay. Though the most recent of philosophical movements, it has already made an abiding impression on contemporary thought. Less noisy than Pragmatism, less fashionable than Bergson's Intuitionism, it has yet quietly won over to its side a far larger number of the younger students of philosophy than one would suspect from the comparatively small amount of Neo-Realistic literature. What is even more striking, its criticisms of Idealism have had at least this effect, that many thinkers who are commonly labelled "Idealists" have hastened to dissociate themselves once more in the most explicit terms from that sort of Idealism of which the watchword is Berkeley's *esse est percipi*. The so-called "Objective Idealists" have become noticeably more objective. To have compelled this realignment is in itself no small achievement to the credit of Neo-Realism.

By calling itself "new", contemporary Realism rightly emphasises its profound difference from the older type of Realism which was synonymous with Materialism. When the tide of reaction against the "speculative philosophy" of Fichte, Schelling, and Hegel was at its height, and the age demanded a philosophy in harmony with the concepts and theories of physical science, then to be a Realist meant to analyse the Universe exclusively in terms of "matter" and "force".[1] The world was regarded as a large-scale mechanism, and minds, together with all they stand for, as an insignificant and ineffective by-product ("epiphenomenon"), comparable to the noises or sparks of a machine. Philosophy was little more than physics exaggerated to metaphysical dimensions. Whatever facts in the Universe cannot be dealt with by the methods and concepts of physics were depreciated, if not ignored. The modern Neo-Realist knows better than that. He is no longer preoccupied with the problem of matter and mind. He is no longer concerned to proclaim matter as the ultimate substance

[1] Cf. Buchner's *Kraft und Stoff*.

265

or to treat life and mind as accidental and irrelevant. He knows that "science is not all of truth, nor physical nature all of being".[1]

There is another important difference between the old Materialism and the new Realism. The former inevitably inclined towards a pessimistic philosophy of life. It depreciated moral effort on behalf of ideals on the ground of its being doomed to ultimate defeat. It depreciated religion as unscientific superstition and make-believe, intellectually false, morally mischievous. Morality was regarded as nothing but man's misguided attempt to stem the tide of nature, to assert his pigmy self against a hostile world, to impose moral ideals on natural forces wholly indifferent to good and ill. Religion could claim scientific warrant neither for the facts on which it pretended to be based, nor for its optimistic estimate of the significance of human values in the scheme of things. From all these prejudices, too, the Neo-Realists have shown themselves to be emancipated, whenever they have dealt with these problems at all. There is nothing in the position of modern Realism which precludes the attempt to provide an adequate "philosophy of life".

In fact, some of the spokesmen of Neo-Realism appear to claim that it is the only type of philosophy which can successfully make this attempt. It is put forward as the only genuine reconciler of science and religion, the theoretical and the practical interests of men. To achieve such a reconciliation has, not with justice, been regarded as one of the most persistent problems of philosophy. But in all previous solutions, so Professor R. B. Perry declares on behalf of Neo-Realism, philosophy has taken sides. It has either, as "naturalism", capitulated to the aggression of science, or it has, as "romanticism", made itself the champion of religion, even at the price of cherishing illusions. Neo-Realism alone, so we are told, combines disinterested respect for the facts of the world with loyalty to moral ideals. Compared with romantic illusions about the "perfection" of the universe, it is a "philosophy of disillusionment".[2] But the disillusionment is wholesome, for the courageous acceptance of a hard truth is a source of power. Neo-Realism "re-

---

[1] R. B. Perry, *Present Philosophical Tendencies*, p. 108.
[2] *Ibid.*, p. 331.

moves illusions only in order to lay bare the confronting occasion and the available resources of action".[1] The world is not perfect, but perfectible. To perfect it so far as in us lies is morality. To have confidence in its perfectibility and in the efficacy of human endeavour—this "hazard of faith" is religion. Realism is "opposed equally to an idealistic anticipation of the victory of spirit, and to a naturalistic confession of the impotence of spirit. In this sense all bold and forward living is realistic. It involves a sense for things as they are, an ideal of things as they should be, and a determination that, through enlightened action, things shall in time come to be what they should be".[2] Thus Neo-Realism goes with science in its detached, dispassionate respect for facts, regardless of their present conformity to human wishes and ideals. It goes with morality in encouraging the effort to leave our world better than we found it. It goes with religion, at least if religion is adequately summed up in the belief "that what is indifferent will acquire value, and that what is bad will be made good".[3] On this reconciliation of facts with values and ideals, of nature with spirit, Neo-Realism bases its claim to be the only philosophy which allows us to combine science and religion without sacrificing the one to the other.

In these ways, then, Neo-Realism is genuinely new as compared with the old Materialism. Of course, it has affinities, especially in its treatment of religion, with other modern movements. It shares the belief in the perfectibility of the world ("meliorism") with the Pragmatism of James, and the Instrumentalism of Dewey. In eliminating from religion all supernatural elements and identifying it with the hope of, and endeavour for, a more glorious future for mankind, it presents the same marriage of Naturalism and Philanthropy which was characteristic already of Comte and Mill and the "religion of humanity".

At any rate, it cannot be charged against modern Realism that, like Materialism, it is hostile to the claims of man's spiritual life. A Realist may be zealous for righteousness, for his philosophy may encourage activity on behalf of all good causes. Thus it is because Neo-Realism challenges Idealism, not merely on the technical ground of the *esse est percipi* principle, but on the ground of its philosophy of life and of religion, that it is

---

[1] *Ibid.*   [2] *Loc. cit.*, p. 347.   [3] *Loc. cit.*, p. 344.

worth while to examine critically what positive alternative Neo-Realism had to offer. How in detail does Neo-Realism interpret religion? To what facts of experience does it appeal in support of this interpretation? How does it define the relations to each other of knowledge and conduct, of theory and practice, of science, morality, religion and philosophy? It will but add doubly and trebly to the importance of our investigation that we shall ultimately find the whole issue to be turning on the problem of evil.

The course of our argument thus demands, first, a brief survey of the main types and varieties of Neo-Realism with special reference to their bearing on religion (Section I). Thence we shall pass to an examination of the only available Neo-Realistic account of the difference between and relation to one another of the theoretical and practical attitudes in life, our main purpose being to determine, in the light of this distinction, how philosophy ought to interpret morality and religion (Section II). Lastly, we shall find ourselves involved in nothing less momentous than a discussion of the problem of evil (Section III). The melioristic thesis that there is no problem of evil except the practical one of how most efficiently to do away with evil, stands confronted by what seems the gratuitous paradox of the thesis that the world is perfect and that the evil in it is a necessary constituent of its perfection. We shall have to ask ourselves whether meliorism is really as plausible and reasonable, and its rival as unreasonable and self-contradictory, as either appears to be on first inspection. It may be we shall be driven to the conclusion that, for a deeper insight, the paradox of perfection disappears, whereas in meliorism contradictions come to light which make it untenable as an ultimate basis for a philosophy of life.

I.

To make a Neo-Realist, very little is needed; least of all any excursions into the realm of religion. Whether a thinker is to be classed as a Realist or not depends solely on his attitude towards two somewhat technical problems. Has he renounced "epistemological dualism"? Has he, once and for all, forsworn the heresy of *esse est percipi*? If so, he is a Realist. The recipe for making Realists may thus be summed up by saying: Be an "epistemological monist" and affirm the "independence" of reality and knowledge. Both requirements are combined in Professor R. B. Perry's "cardinal principle of Neo-Realism", namely, "the independence of the immanent".[1]

Let us translate these forbidding technicalities into simpler language. A familiar way of expressing the fact that somebody *knows* something is to say, he has an *idea* of it. Similarly, to be ignorant of a subject is to have no ideas of it. Thus knowledge would seem to consist of "ideas" which are "in" the mind of the knower and "of" the object which is known. But what is an idea? A moment's reflection shows that there is nothing to which we can apply the term unless it be what we have in mind, i.e., what we are conscious of, when we perceive and think. As Locke said, an idea is whatever object is before the mind when it thinks. Thus then of the things which I am now perceiving—pen, paper, table, books, etc., I shall have to say that they are ideas in my mind; so also are Neo-Realism, and the theory of knowledge, and all these topics with which my thoughts are occupied as I write these lines. But if so, what of the real world? What of the things themselves, "of" which I have ideas, that is, to which my ideas refer? These clearly must form a separate order of existences, distinct from the ideas in my, or in anybody else's, mind. Strange as this transformation of everybody's world into ideas in his mind referring to real objects "outside" may seem, are we not committed to it by saying that to know is to have ideas of objects? And where else can ideas exist except in minds? Ideas are mental and to be sharply distinguished from real objects which are non-mental. The familiar distinction of body and mind appears to reinforce this analysis of knowledge. And to clinch the matter, we may remind ourselves how commonly we speak of certain sorts of experiences, for example, dreams, as consisting of "mere" ideas, that is, ideas to which no objects correspond in the outer world. How can we get on without the distinction between ideas which have objects corresponding to them and ideas which have none?

To argue thus is to be an epistemological dualist, that is, to construe knowledge as a relation between two factors, ideas

---

[1] *Present Philosophical Tendencies*, p. 313.

in, and objects outside, the knowing mind. From the difficulties of this theory, which are too obvious and well-known to require recapitulation, our Neo-Realists have happily shaken themselves free. As sound "epistemological monists", they insist that it is reality itself which we apprehend, not some substitute for, or representative of, it in the shape of an "idea". The object, as Perry puts it, is "immanent" in knowledge. If we still choose to speak of "idea", we ought to mean by the term the *status* of the object in its relation to the knowing mind. Thus, for example, my idea of the table is not a mental fact duplicating and referring to an extra-mental fact; it is the table itself considered as an object of apprehension for me, the table so far and so long as it figures in my field of consciousness. On this point all Neo-Realists appear to be agreed, however they may otherwise differ from each other. The English Realists (S. Alexander, B. Russell, and others), for example, have a very different theory of what a mind is from that of the Harvard group of American Realists (R. B. Perry and E. B. Holt). But when Russell declares that "the faculty of being acquainted with things other than itself is the main characteristic of a mind", and that "acquaintance with objects essentially consists in a relation between the mind and something other than the mind; it is this that constitutes the mind's power of knowing things"[1]—he eliminates ideas as the *tertium quid* standing between a mind and its objects as decisively as S. Alexander does when he analyses all knowing into a relation of "togetherness" or "compresence" between a mental act of apprehension and a non-mental thing.[2] And in a different way the same "monistic" effect is achieved by Perry and Holt when they treat knowing as a "specific reaction of the central nervous system", and knowledge as the peculiar complex of objects defined by this reaction and by it selected from the objective universe at large.[3] Knowledge, in Holt's striking phrase, is a "cross-section" of the Universe. What a given mind knows and what it ignores, what is in that mind and what lies beyond it, depend simply on what the nervous system at a given moment specifically reacts to. Here again there is no room for "ideas".

[1] *Problems of Philosophy*, pp. 66-7.
[2] "The Basis of Realism", *Proceedings of the British Academy*, vol. vi., passim.
[3] Cf. R. B. Perry, *Present Philosophical Tendencies*, chs. xii., xiii.; E. B. Holt, *Concept of Consciousness*, ch. ix.

But this is not all. To eliminate "ideas" from the theory of knowledge is not the same thing as to overthrow the *esse est percipi* principle. For it might still be true that objects cannot exist except in relation to some mind which apprehends them, or some nervous system which reacts to them. Hence it is as essential a part of Neo-Realism to insist upon the "independence" of the object, as it is to insist upon its "immanence". "Things may be, and are, directly experienced without owing either their being or their nature to that circumstance,"[1] declares Perry. To be is one thing, to be experienced is another, says Holt; a thing must be before it can be experienced, hence its being cannot depend on its being experienced.[2] In general, things may pass in and out of the relation to a mind or a nervous system, in virtue of which we say that they are known, without being thereby affected in existence or character. As an English Realist puts it: "We can no more think that in apprehending reality we do not apprehend it as it is apart from our knowledge of it, than we can think that existence depends upon our knowledge of it."[3] In the light of these quotations, we may claim to have made good the point that the minimum which is required to make a Realist is the affirmation of the "independence" of the object of knowledge and the denial of "representative ideas".

Has all this any specific bearing on religion? Clearly not. So far we have found Neo-Realism to be narrowly preoccupied with a technical problem in the analysis of what it has taught us to call the "cognitive relation", and the conclusions reached by it carry no obvious consequences for other fields of investigation. Indeed, the Realism of many Realists seems to begin and end here. Where it does so, it is only by guess-work that we can apply the Neo-Realistic conclusions to the problem of religion. Alexander, for example, would probably not object to saying that in religion we are "compresent" with God; and he does speak of the highest stage of knowledge as "seeing all things in God". Russell's theory of acquaintance would, if applied to religion, suggest the question whether, as a matter of fact, we are acquainted with God. And if the answer should be in the affirmative, and if we further remember that acquaint-

---

[1] *Loc. cit.*, p. 315.   [2] *Loc. cit.*, pp. 20 ff.
[3] A. H. Prichard, *Kant's Theory of Knowledge*, p. 119.

T

ance can never be mistaken, the conclusion should satisfy even
the most orthodox. But actually Russell's discussions of religion
do not follow this line at all. In fact, they have no point of
contact whatever with his Realism in theory of knowledge.
Instead, he is concerned with the status of morality and
religion in a world of which he conceives the nature and
future fate on the lines of scientific materialism. How on this
basis he reaches the conclusion that ultimate extinction awaits
the human race and the ideals for the realisation of which it
struggles, has been discussed in a previous article in the
Harvard Theological Review.[1]

But there is, of course, no reason why Neo-Realism should
remain thus narrowly *epistemological*, why it should not explore
the wider vistas which beckon and tempt every philosopher to
adventures in speculation. Hence it is not surprising that some
of the most powerful thinkers among the Neo-Realists should
have responded to the opportunity, and enlarged their vision to
the dimensions of a *metaphysical* theory. Nor again is it surprising
that through all their differences there should run a common
strain, which we can describe only as a naturalistic or, more
specifically, *biological* bias. When the history of philosophical
thought at the beginning of the twentieth century comes to be
written, the adoption of the biological standpoint will, we may
safely predict, be recorded as one of the outstanding characteristics of that thought. Having analysed the nature and function
of mind in knowledge, the Realist is naturally ambitious to
paint the picture of the Universe and assign to mind its place
within the cosmic scene. Alexander puts the point prettily.
"The temper of realism," he writes, "is to de-anthropomor-
phise: to order man and mind to their proper place among the
world of finite things; on the one hand to divest physical things
of the colouring which they have received from the vanity and
arrogance of mind; and on the other to assign them along with
minds their due measure of self-existence."[2] In a similar spirit,
Perry accuses Idealism of being anthropomorphic and "bio-
centric", and consequently unable "to survey the totality of
things dispassionately", or "to treat them in a spirit of free and

[1] Cf. an article by the author on "The Religious Aspect of Bertrand Russell's
Philosophy", in the *Harvard Theological Review*, vol. ix., April 1916.
[2] *The Basis of Realism*, p. 1.

critical enquiry".[1] Pronouncements such as these may seem to
accord ill with the statement that Neo-Realism exhibits a biological bias. But it is precisely biology, and more generally the
theory of evolution, which have led Neo-Realists to look upon
life and mind as phenomena in a context of varied other phenomena, as late-comers in the order of evolution, and as confronted on arrival by a determinate and pre-existing environment. It was an easy transition from the independent object of
knowledge to the pre-existing environment. It was a fascinating
task to seek a place for mind and knowledge within the detailed
context and structure of this independent universe, once its
independence had been established by epistemological analysis.
The biological importance of the central nervous system could
then be recognised, and it could be fitted into the pattern in its
proper place. Mind and knowledge could be brought under the
concept of "behaviour", and treated as identical with, or at
least as dependent upon, specific responses of the organism to
its environment. It was but a step further to ask how far increase of knowledge might extend man's control over his environment for the satisfaction of his needs, how far nature might
prove plastic to the realisation of his ideals and be made the
tool of his progress. Not all Neo-Realists, however, are interested
in this latter question. Indeed, we can at this point discern
something like a parting of the ways. Our Realist metaphysicians divide themselves into two groups—the *cosmologists*
and the *moralists*, as we may conveniently label them. The
former are interested mainly in the diversified spectacle of the
Universe, which they are content to analyse and describe in
detail. The latter are interested above all in "moral causality",
in "the operation of moral agents on a pre-existing and independent environment". They seek knowledge which shall
"illuminate things in order that action may be invented which
shall make them good".[2] Cosmological Realism is represented
by Alexander and Holt, though in widely different ways,
Moral Realism by Perry. Alexander, so far, has given us little
more than fragments and sketchy outlines of his universe.
Roughly we can discern that he arranges its manifold consti-

[1] *Loc. cit.*, p. 107.
[2] These phrases and sentences are quoted from R. B. Perry, *Present Philosophical Tendencies*, ch. xiv., "A Realistic Philosophy of Life".

tuents in an ascending order, which appears to be both an order of temporal evolution and an order of perfection. Each fresh step or level in this order is as real and "self-existent" as the rest, but each also introduces some new quality and is thus more perfect than its predecessors. The "secondary qualities" (colour, sound, etc.) are apparently regarded by Alexander as one such level of perfection; life is another, consciousness in animals and men a third. But man is not the apex of this hierarchy. Above man there are higher levels of more perfect beings, for example, angels, and we may fairly conjecture that the hierarchy somehow leads up to and terminates in God. Each level of existence, as Alexander quaintly says, "enjoys itself" and is "contemplated" by the more perfect beings above it. All this, however, is as yet tentative and shadowy, though no doubt it is being more fully developed in the Gifford Lectures which Alexander is now engaged in delivering at one of the Scottish Universities. It is a strange mingling of echoes from early Christian and Talmudic literature with highly modern psychology and biology. But though this Realism is without any explicit philosophy of religion, it is clearly in temper religious. Though its account of the levels of perfection in their relation to each other provides rather for man's contemplation by God, than for God's contemplation by man, yet it is eager to have us realise "both mind and things to be fragments not merely of something larger than their own salient momentary existences but of an infinite whole". In this sense it invites us to "see all things in God".[1]

The other of our two cosmological Realists, Holt, is even more silent on religion. His universe is a "neutral mosaic"[2]— "neutral" in the sense that the ultimate elements which analysis can distinguish within it are neither mental nor material but logical. It too has an ascending order, embodying a kind of logical evolution from simple to complex. It is a universe "graded in a strict and inalienable order of complexities". As his clue for a tentative sketch of this order, Holt has apparently used the system of the sciences. His universe begins with the simple entities of logic and mathematics. Soon after come the

[1] S. Alexander, The Basis of Realism, p. 19.
[2] The following account is based on certain passages of ch. viii., "The Neutral Mosaic", in E. B. Holt's Concept of Consciousness.

secondary qualities; then space (geometry); time, motion, mass (mechanics); matter (physics); the chemical elements; the "larger aggregates, such as clouds, rivers, and seas, mountains, plains, continents, and planets". Thence, passing from the inorganic to the organic, we get plants and animals. To this level of complexity too belongs mind or consciousness. Last in the ontological series comes the level of values, to which correspond the normative sciences, for example, aesthetics and "ethics, including perhaps theology".[1] Clearly, this is a meagre result for the philosophy of religion, unless we are willing to squeeze what comfort we can out of the assurance that the beautiful, the real, the true, and the good, though the least fundamental in the ontological system, are "the very most important for us as human beings".[2]

The only type of Neo-Realism which is directly interested in religion and which attempts to offer a definite "philosophy of life" is the Moral Realism of R. B. Perry. Negatively this shows itself in its unsparing attacks on Idealism (or "Romanticism") as a philosophy of religion which declares the world to be perfect and the good to be fully realised here and now. Positively it shows itself in its plea for the cosmic efficacy of moral efforts, and in its demand for a religion, not of resignation and endurance, but of vigorous aggression upon evil and devoted labour in the cause of human progress. To the examination of this theory of religion we must now turn, considering first its general account of the relation of theory to practice (or "belief"), and secondly its plea for the perfectibility of the universe.

II.

Belief and theory, so we may summarise Perry's argument,[3] are both forms of knowledge, and "knowledge furnishes the illumination and guidance of all conscious action". In order to do so, knowledge must of course be true. But merely to assert a theory, however true, in not enough. We must also adopt it as a matter of belief. Only then does it become a plan of life. Until theory takes on the form of belief, it "lacks that confidence

---

[1] *Loc. cit.*, p. 160.   [2] *Ibid.*

[3] All quotations in this section, unless otherwise stated, are taken from R. B. Perry's *Present Philosophical Tendencies*, chs. i. and ii. A first draft of ch. i. appeared in the *Harvard Theological Review*, vol. iii. (1910).

and steadiness without which no consecutive endeavour is possible". Indeed, the difference between theory and belief cuts much deeper still. It is a moral difference. A different motive is involved, a different human good. In the attitude of theory, we care only about the attainment of truth. In the attitude of belief, we assume truth and look to efficiency of action. So again these attitudes differ in their social effects. "To belief, society owes its cohesiveness and stability; to theory, it owes its chance of betterment". But even this is not the last word. Theory, just because its end is truth, is in principle divorced from action. "The theoretical mood, even when a conclusion is reached, is a state of practical doubt." The conclusion need not be, like a belief, assimilated into the agent's life as, so to speak, its inspiration. Indeed, so Perry seems to hold, this divorce from action is a positive advantage for theory, because it secures "that immunity from direct social responsibility which is most conducive to clear seeing and straight thinking". Ultimately this estimate of the place and function of theory in life rests on the view that essentially "to theorise is to doubt". And even though doubting here seems to mean enquiring, investigating, researching as much as disbelieving, still it means playing among hypothetical alternatives, weighing inconclusive evidences, and therefore refusing to commit oneself. And, again, in the pursuit of truth, the theorist is entitled to concern himself with matters minute and remote from all practical interests. "The theoretical mind is not held to those standards of proportionateness which obtain in life".

Even if we have followed Perry's previous argument without a murmur of dissent, this last statement must surely give us pause. True, Perry speaks of this neglect of proportions as an "incident of theoretical analysis", and mentions scientists, not philosophers, as practising it. Still, he fails to make clear that the one kind of theorist who, whatever details he may study incidentally, cannot afford to ignore the standards of proportionateness is the philosopher, especially when his aim is to formulate an adequate "philosophy of life". In fact, the trouble is not that the philosopher is held to these standards, but that they are so hard to discover. Actual life so perplexingly and even cruelly confuses the standards, that it requires trained insight to discern them in the welter of first appearances. Again,

though doubting, investigating, and the trying-out of hypotheses are instrumental to theorising, yet essentially it consists,
not in doubting but in contemplating. This is true not only
because, after all, we do reach conclusions. It is true chiefly
because in philosophy, as we may say in direct challenge to
Perry's dictum, to theorise is to apply to the interpretation of
life the insight gained from one's best, if rarest, experiences.
In the dust of the daily road we need the hill-top views. The
philosopher, above every other kind of theorist, requires the
eye for the fundamental realities which only his deeper
experiences adequately reveal. This is, after all, the spirit in
which Perry himself philosophises when he urges upon our
acceptance his view of man as striving to transform the world
by the realisation of his ethical ideals. There he does not
"doubt". He communicates his insight into life—or, to use
William James's terms, his "vision", his "mode of feeling the
whole push of life".[1] This is, so we suggest, an example of the
kind of thinking on which we ought to model our theory of
what "theory" is and does. A philosopher owes it to his own
enterprise to describe theory where he finds it at its best. And
that is not where it operates amidst the necessary abstractions
of science, but where, as in philosophy, it seeks "to see life
steadily and see it whole".

It is but another way of putting this same point to say that
such a thing as Perry's "philosophy of life" carries us at once
beyond his own antithesis of "belief" and "theory". That it
does so is all to the good. For, if we may judge from the great
thinkers, a Plato, a Spinoza, a Kant, or a Hegel, the divorce of
theory and belief is not characteristic of philosophy at its best.
Such philosophy is too deeply rooted in the realities of
experience to cease "believing" (in Perry's sense) merely
because it reflects and investigates. The experiences which
illuminate life and teach one to read its values aright carry,
so to speak, their own guarantee. There is nothing hypothetical about them. Whatever stability and steadfastness we
need in life we must draw from them. It is precisely the function
of the kind of theory which we call philosophical, to seize upon
these insights and make them available for the interpretation
of our world. But thus understood, philosophy takes us once for

[1] *A Pluralistic Universe*, pp. 20-1.

all beyond the stage where man needs to "convert theoretical probabilities into subjective certainties and to believe more than he knows".

Our concept of philosophy supplies us with a point of view from which to weigh what Perry has to say about the difference between religion and science, and the relation of philosophy to both. "Religion", we read, "has to do with the general character of nature as a whole, or with whatever may lie beyond nature and still belong to the environment of life". It is essentially "a plan of action", "man's hope or despair of salvation". It springs from the need for "a final adaptation", for coming to terms, as it were, once and for all with God, this being "the name for the over-ruling powers as sources of fortune". Whether this description of religion in biological terms of environment and adaptation is adequate, we need not now stop to consider. For the moment we are interested only in its relation to science and philosophy. Science, we are told, is the pure embodiment of the theoretical motive, that is, of disinterested curiosity. Religion similarly is the pure embodiment of the practical motive, that is, the highly interested desire for a plan of action which shall secure the maximum of good fortune from the environment as a whole. But obviously "an enlightened and therefore effective religion" requires itself to be based on a thorough theoretical understanding of this environment, not in its proximate details but in its general and ultimate features. Not science but only philosophy can meet this requirement, for only philosophy deals theoretically with ultimates. Whence it follows that "as popular or applied science is related to pure science, so religion is related to pure philosophy". And again, "it is as important for religion to promote the development of a rigorously theoretical philosophy, as it is for engineering to promote the development of theoretical physics". The qualification "rigorously theoretical" covers the demand that during the course of the enquiry the passions be repressed and the application of results to life ignored, lest hopes and fears beget illusions and dreams. "Religion is no exception to the rule that man conquers his environment and moulds it into good through forgetting his fears and renouncing his hopes, until he shall have disciplined himself to see coolly and steadily". Now religion, as Perry says elsewhere, is the embodiment of man's "optimistic bias".[1] Being "belief", it is the spirit of hope and confidence which sustains him in energetic living, that hope of "salvation" which, for Perry, seems to coincide with "moulding the environment into good". From all this we may conjecture for philosophy, as the theoretical basis of religion, a threefold task. On the one hand it must, in the critical and unprejudiced manner of science, examine the ultimate nature of the environment of human life as a mere matter of fact. On the other it must, with like disinterestedness, study what things are good or have value in virtue of the fact that human beings desire them. Presumably it must also rationalise these desires and their goods, i.e., organise them into a harmonious system, securing the maximum fulfilment of desire and the maximum realisation of what is good. Lastly, philosophy will have to decide whether, the facts being what they are, the maximum fulfilment of interests, or at least a progress towards increasingly complete fulfilment, is possible. If so, we shall be justified in "believing", that is, in labouring with zest and confidence for making the world an ever better and more satisfactory place for human beings to live in. This is what Perry calls "the Baconian idea", the "axiom of modern civilisation". "The good is to be won by the race and for the race; it lies in the future, and can result only from prolonged and collective endeavour; and the power to achieve it lies in the progressive knowledge and control of nature."[2] Science, so we may sum up his view in our own words, supplies the detailed knowledge of causes and effects, without which action would be impossible for lack of means. Philosophy investigates whether as a whole nature is favourable to the realisation of human desires, that is, plastic to human action. Religion turns philosophy's verdict into belief and thus supplies the dynamic element. Its watchword, one feels, ought to be, Full steam ahead for efficiency and reform. Such is, as a matter of fact, the account of the theoretical content of religion, or "religious truth", which Perry offers in his *Moral Economy*.[3] Religious truth consists of ethical judgments concerning human interests ("what the believer has at stake"), and cosmological judgments concerning the en-

[1] *The Moral Economy*, chap. vi., p. 231.
[2] *Present Philosophical Tendencies*, pp. 4, 5.
[3] Chap. vi., on "The Moral Justification of Religion", originally printed in the *Harvard Theological Review*, vol. ii., April 1909.

vironment at large, which in its bearing on the worshipper's interests is called "God".

On the whole theory a single comment will suffice at this stage of our argument. Perry's account of religion entirely ignores the *mystical* element in it. The biological language in which he has cast his description, only serves to throw this neglect into bolder relief. Hence his treatment cannot but strike as inadequate all who regard mystical experience as the intensest and purest form of religion. For such an utterance of religious experience as St. Paul's "Not I, but God that worketh in me", there is no room within Perry's formula. In discussing religion, it is inevitable that every thinker should reveal himself, that he should lay bare, as the basis of his argument, the type of experience through which he "feels his continuity with reality". For Perry this is clearly moral enthusiasm, the reformer's zeal for the bettering of his world through the realisation of his ideals. This he offers as the essence of religion—what religion ought to be, what at its best it is. Though one feels tempted to say that he sacrifices religion to morality, yet such a zeal for progress in human welfare, for rendering service to the cause of reform, for fighting against evil in all its guises, is clearly something without which religion would be poor and ineffective. The question is whether, as it stands, this is equivalent to religion. The answer, it is hardly possible to doubt, must be No. Religion after all is an historical fact in the lives of men and, dogma apart, has found expression in utterance and conduct in so many forms that a comparative study not only reveals the main "varieties of religious experience", but enables us also to discriminate higher and lower forms—experiences, or lives, in which the distinctive and unique character of religion is more completely and adequately exhibited than in others. One might instance Christ or St. Paul or St. Francis. No combination of cosmology and ethics, welded together from a biological point of view, such as Perry offers, seizes the distinctive quality of religion as these "men of God" exhibit it. A philosophical theory of religion which fails to include, not merely one variety of religious experience among others but the most characteristic and revealing variety of all, namely, mysticism, offends against the canon of philosophical interpretation of experience which we laid down above.

III.

But the real trial of strength between these two ways of using experiences as material for philosophical theory, and thus extracting from them that wisdom which both is true as insight and imparts the right temper to conduct, is still to come. The issue so far has been whether religion, as a matter of experience, is identical with "moral enthusiasm", especially when this enthusiasm wears the biological air of an effort so to control and modify the environment that it becomes a better place for men to live in. As the alternative to this we have taken the view that religion, while involving morality as an element within itself, yet is as a whole a distinctive type of experience, of which the keynote is mysticism. The real touchstone of the adequacy of these two views, as we are now about to see, is the problem presented by the fact of evil.

To clear the ground for fruitful debate, let us put aside irrelevant topics and set down explicitly what is common ground for both sides. As irrelevant we shall regard the familiar dialectical puzzle how a perfect whole can consist of imperfect parts, or, to put the puzzle in theological language, how the existence of sin, error, and evil is consistent with the creation of the Universe by God defined as all-wise, all-good, all-powerful. Let it be agreed that evil is neither an illusion nor yet something willed and planned as adding zest and spice to the perfection of the cosmic spectacle for a divine spectator. We will have no God enjoying from the stalls the tragedy of human sin and suffering enacted on the stage. Nor does experience support the suggestion that evil is as unsubstantial as a dream. Such interpretations pervert the judgment of perfection, the roots of which in our experience it will be our task to search out.

Again, let it be agreed that our world and our lives show a pattern of mingled good and ill, and that under these conditions there is as much need for the steadfastness of mind which endures suffering patiently and is not debauched by good fortune, as there is for the moral struggle to defeat evil and realise good. Doing one's best, the "full deliverance of one's self to the cause of goodness", as Perry finely puts it,[1] is essential to happiness, by which we mean the sense that life is worth while. We

[1] *The Moral Economy*, p. 254.

shall make no attempt to call the universe "perfect" in any sense which makes morality meaningless.

Yet again, let it be agreed that we are not to make out a case for or against a surplus of pleasure over pain, nor to show every item of pain and wrong to be overbalanced or cancelled by some compensating joy or good. Least of all shall we pretend that evil is somehow good in disguise, or borrow the convenient philosophy of Pangloss in Voltaire's *Candide*: "Les malheurs particuliers font le bien général, de sort que plus il y a de malheurs particuliers, plus tout est bien".

All these issues being set aside, what issue remains? Where do we differ? The point of deep difference may be put in a nutshell by placing side by side two sentences from Perry's *Moral Economy*: "If life is a real tragedy, it can be endured, and to enter into it will bring the deep satisfaction which every form of heroism affords".[1] And, "The moment evil is conceived as the necessary but diminishing complement to partial success, the sting of it is gone. Evil as a temporary and accidental necessity is tolerable; but not so an evil which is absolutely necessary, and which must be construed with some hypothetical divine satisfaction".[2] We have agreed above to put aside as irrelevant the appeal to a hypothetical divine satisfaction. We are to argue on the basis of human experience, taking it where it is at its best. Thus approached the question is whether the arduous and heroic life with the conditions, that is, the pain and the evil which evoke heroism, is worth while, enduringly and for its own sake, or whether morality is worth while only on the prospect of the final eradication of evil and therefore the abolition of morality itself. The issue is put misleadingly as a choice between "the practical optimism or meliorism which stakes its hope on the chance that the world *may be made* better", and "the contemplative or quietistic optimism, which consists in the faith that the world *is* best".[3] The alternatives are not moral endeavour versus moral holiday, doing one's best versus doing nothing, fighting evil versus resignedly acquiescing in it. The only question worth asking and answering in this matter is, What kind of life, and under what conditions, is fundamentally most worth while as enabling us to make the most of ourselves—life

[1] *Loc. cit.*, p. 251.   [2] *Loc. cit.*, p. 249.
[3] *Present Philosophical Tendencies*, p. 248.

in this actual world of ours with its suffering and evil, or life, as the meliorist's fancy paints it, in a world without either? If the decision is, as we hold it must be, in favour of the former alternative, then the meliorist is deluding us with his promise of a world which, in James's phrase, has been made to "forget the very place and name of evil".[1] He is falsifying the very spirit of morality by his suggestion that only as a means to the realisation of such a world is morality really worth while.

More abstractly the problem might be put in the form of the question, Is the value of evil purely negative, as of something to be once and for all eliminated, or is it so closely interwoven with the whole tissue of this double-edged life of ours that it is not only ineradicable as a matter of fact but positively valuable as the condition without which other values cannot be had? It should be clearly noted that in asking this question, we have left behind the level where desire and aversion, the things towards which and the things against which we are moved, are polar opposites. We are asked to survey life *as a whole*, with its values and their conditions. And "as a whole" means that we are not now to pick and choose, saying we would like to retain this and rather do without that. It means that once we understand the sources of all that is valuable, we shall find evil among these; and we shall find further that if evil were to be eliminated, utterly and in principle, the things which are good would not survive it. It is this reflection which underlies the "judgment of perfection" and leads in a sense to an acceptance of evil, and to a preference for the actual world with evil over an imaginary world without evil. Only let it be noted that this acceptance is not resignation nor a betrayal of morality. It rather begets loyalty to morality by dispelling the illusion that an evil-less, painless world is both possible and, from the profoundest point of view, desirable. Thus the "judgment of perfection" does not contradict or cancel morality, for it is made from a point of view which may be described in all seriousness as "beyond good and evil".

It is not merely as an *argumentum ad hominem*, but as an illustration of the way in which the logic of experience will override the prejudices of inadequate theory, that we shall quote a professed and eager meliorist in support of our contention. The

[1] *Pragmatism*, p. 297.

meliorism of William James is part of the friendly philosophical polemic which he carried on against Royce's defence of the perfection of the universe. That defence James labelled "tender-minded", apparently under the impression that somehow a denial of the reality of evil was involved. But it would appear to require a "tougher" courage to accept both evil and the fight against it as among the *permanent* "hazards and hardships" of finite life than to console oneself with the hope of a world in which there shall be neither. At any rate, James himself, on occasions, when he happily forgot his meliorism, showed himself possessed of this very courage, and made his choice of lives accordingly. There is the famous and oft-quoted passage describing his visit to the Assembly Grounds on Chautauqua Lake.[1] He sets out eloquently the absence of disease, poverty, drunkenness, crime, and the realisation of the meliorist's dream. "You have culture, you have kindness, you have cheapness, you have equality, you have the best of what mankind has fought and bled and striven for under the name of civilisation for centuries. You have, in short, a foretaste of what society might be, were it all in the light, with no suffering and no dark corners". Yet after seven days of this "middle-class paradise, without a sin, without a victim, without a blot, without a tear", he bursts out, on emerging again into the dark and wicked world, with "Ouf! what a relief! Now for something primordial and savage, even though it were as bad as an Armenian massacre, to set the balance straight again. . . . Let me take my chances again in the big outside worldly wilderness with all its sins and sufferings . . . all its moral style, expressiveness and picturesqueness—the element of precipitousness, of strength and strenuousness, intensity and danger".

In this utterance and in the experience which it records we have the very logic of the "judgment of perfection", the acknowledgment that this actual world of ours *is the best* world, in the sense that it is the kind of world in which it is most worth while to live. Beside it melioristic dreams fade into nothingness.

Those for whom the "judgment of perfection" expresses the deepest insight into these matters, accept evil and the struggle against evil as permanent features of the Universe, and they

[1] *Talks to Teachers on Psychology and Life's Ideals*, pp. 268 ff.—quoted and discussed by B. Bosanquet, *The Value and Destiny of the Individual*, pp. 332 ff.

accept life in this Universe on these terms as supremely worth while. They accept it, not with a gesture of despair or condemnation but, like James, confidently and even joyously, content to play a man's part and fulfil a man's destiny under the conditions of finite existence. They accept life, as the marriage-service has it, "for better, for worse". Is this optimism? Is this pessimism? Our classificatory pigeon-holes will not contain such an attitude. It is a recognition of value which carries us, as we said, "beyond good and evil". As the spirit of daily living it is religion. As reflective theory it is philosophy, and, paradoxically enough, though usually called "idealism", it is really the only philosophy which is realistic to the bitter end.

Plato's " Forms " and Plato's " God "

WHAT is the relation of the Forms to God in Plato's philosophy?
More especially, what is the relation of the Form of Good to
God? Above all, how are this Form of Good and God to be
understood in relation to the evil in the universe, the gravity
of which Plato acknowledges even to the point of speaking of
an "immortal conflict" between Good and Evil?[1]

These problems are central, yet it is notorious that Plato's
own text offers but a few scattered passages to guide us, and that
these are to no small extent mutually inconsistent. This being
so, I agree with Professor Boodin that, in the end, there is only
one method to follow, viz., the method of bringing to bear on
the interpretation of the text whatever insight into the nature
of the problem one may have gained from one's own firsthand
study of it.[2] When comparative study of the text, in the light
which philological research can throw on the meaning of the
term "Idea" in the language of Greek philosophy and science
in the 5th and 4th centuries B.C., has done all it can for us,
there still remains the final task of entering into Plato's thought
with as much philosophical insight as one can muster. It is only
by one's own power of philosophising that one can hope to
understand another philosopher.

---

[1] Throughout this paper, I shall use the word "Form" in preference to the
word "Idea" which following current usage I still retain in the passages dealing
with Plato in my book, *Idealism as a Philosophy* (ch. 2). True, "Idea" is Plato's own
word, but in coming down to us through the ages it has acquired, in the language
both of philosophy and of everyday life, meanings so utterly different from Plato's
meaning that the use of it is far more misleading than helpful. If Plato's own
alternative word, "Eidos", were familiar to any but Greek scholars, this would
be the best to use. "Form" has been introduced by Professor Burnet and others,
and I shall follow them rather than employ "Idea" in a meaning which runs
counter to all the familiar associations of this word in current speech. Further,
when I speak of "Plato's Forms" I mean the theory of Forms which we find in
the Platonic dialogues, without prejudice to the question, much debated by some
scholars at the present day, whether Plato or Socrates was the first to formulate it
as we find it in the dialogues, or whether it is perhaps even part of a Pythagorean
tradition common to both Plato and Socrates.
[2] See J. E. Boodin, "Plato's Cosmology". *Mind*, N.S., Nos. 152, 153.

THE GENERAL THEORY OF FORMS

Whatever conundrums the theory of Forms may raise, two points are now generally agreed upon.

The first is that the theory of Forms is for Plato a theory of the objects of knowledge. "Knowledge" is here to be understood in a strict technical sense as opposed to imagination or guess-work or opinion. It is identical with what we nowadays call science and philosophy—the apprehension of the real nature of anything.

Our simplest illustrations of what is meant are, in fact, drawn from the sciences. If an engineer writes a book on "The Steam Engine", or a physiologist on "The Heart", we understand that they are telling us not merely about the limited number of steam-engines or hearts which they have actually studied, analysed, experimented upon in writing their books, but that they are expounding the essential nature, or general principle, of steam-engines or hearts *as such*. In other words, what as scientists they are seeking to discover and explain is the real nature of steam-engines or hearts. The principles they lay down, the truths which they formulate, are meant to apply to, and hold for, all steam-engines and all hearts. If they were using Platonic language, they would entitle their books, "The Form of the Steam-Engine" or "The Form of the Heart".

Let us generalise this. Whenever we ask concerning any particular object, "What is this?" meaning "what kind of thing is this?" we are asking for what Plato would have called its "Idea" or "Form", i.e., for its real nature. We may have to compare a great many particular objects of the same kind, observing them in different circumstances, analysing them, experimenting upon them, before we can say that we know what their real nature is. But that there is a real nature to be discovered in all the particular specimens or instances is the conviction on which the scientist proceeds.

A scientist is not interested in the particular case as such. He studies the particular only for the sake of what he can learn from it, not only about itself, but about all others of the same kind. This is a truth which has been reaffirmed again and again since Plato's time. *Non est singularium scientia*, said the mediaeval

U

logicians. "No science, as science, can deal with the individual
as such," says the modern logician.[1] And scientists themselves
confirm it: "The individual, as such, is not the proper object
of science . . . science aims at determining and characterising
the general and constant (universal), and is concerned with the
individual only in so far as it is reducible to, or exemplifies, the
general, i.e., the typical.[2] This then is the first point to grasp
concerning the meaning of Plato's theory of Forms. "Form" is
Plato's name for the real natures or general principles which
scientific thought seeks to discover in the particular cases which
it studies, and the discovery of which constitutes "knowledge"
of all cases of that sort. We nowadays use a great variety of
words in different contexts for what Plato called "Ideas"
or "Forms". We speak of universals, essences, kinds, types,
laws, principles, etc., but the point is always the same, viz., that
knowledge consists in grasping by thought the universal "Form"
which is embodied or exemplified in the particular instance and
which makes the instance the kind of thing it is.

The second point about Plato's Forms is that they are also
ideal standards by which the individual object can be judged
to be good or bad of its kind. In other words, by knowing the
Form of an object we not merely know what sort of thing it
really is, but we can also determine whether it illustrates or
exhibits its real nature well or badly. If objects of the same kind
did not exhibit their common nature with varying degrees of
completeness or adequacy, we could not grade them as better
or worse. Thus a thing's real nature, or Form, supplies also a
standard or Norm. In a class of students, e.g., some are better
students, others are worse. They differ in the degree of perfection with which they realise in themselves what it is to be a
student—the Form of student. This principle runs through the
whole of nature, though we may not be interested in applying
it throughout. We may proverbially say "as like as two peas",
but if peas of the same kind did not differ as better and worse
of their kind, how could we give a first prize to one lot and an
inferior prize, or no prize at all, to another lot? Forms, then,
in Plato's theory function both as the real natures of particular

[1] See B. Bosanquet, *Science and Philosophy*, p. 175.
[2] See R. S. Lillie, "Science and Life", in the *Journal of Philosophy*, vol. xxvii.,
No. 16, pp. 422-3.

things and as norms, or standards of perfection, by which particular things can be graded.

The use which Plato makes of his theory in its application to Art, and to the distinction between the good and the bad artist according to the power of each to grasp the Form and to express it in his work of art, we must here pass by.

But, with a view to the argument which is to follow, we must notice that Forms do not stand each by itself in splendid isolation. On the contrary, they are related among themselves in various ways. There is, e.g., the relation which makes classification possible. The Forms of red, green, blue, etc., are subordinate to, or, in Plato's language, "participate" in, the Form of colour, which in its turn is subordinated to the Form of quality. Again, the Form of animal is present in the Forms of mammal, bird, fish, insect, etc., and so down through all the subordinate levels of zoological classification until we reach the individual specimens. In its turn, animal is subordinate to organism. Further, Forms are compatible or incompatible with each other according as they can, or cannot, co-exist in the same particular object. A lump of sugar, e.g., exhibits the Forms of whiteness, sweetness, crystallinity, etc., but the realisation in it of the Form of whiteness excludes the simultaneous realisation of the Form of any other colour.

Thus, there are systematic interrelations of co-ordination, subordination, compatibility, incompatibility, etc., possible among Forms, and the discovery and study of these yields what we may perhaps call knowledge of the logical structure of the universe.

This brings us to the Form of Good.

THE FORM OF GOOD

According to a famous passage in the *Republic*,[1] the Form of Good is at once the highest and the most universal of all Forms. It is at once the apex of the whole system of Forms and the pervasive principle which runs through all Forms and their interrelations. To put it in this way is to use modern words. Plato, perhaps for lack of a technical language no less than because of the difficulty of the thought to be expressed, puts his doctrine

[1] See *Republic*, 506-509.

in the form of a simile. He likens the Form of Good to the sun. Just as the sun in its relation to the natural world at the same time causes all things to exist and also makes them visible, so the Form of Good causes the universe to be what it is and also to become intelligible. The Form of Good, says Plato, "imparts truth to the known and the power of knowing to the knower". In apprehending the Form of Good, we grasp the ultimate nature of the universe and thereby know it as it really is. In the technical language of mediaeval logicians we might describe it as at once the *causa essendi* and the *causa cognoscendi* of all that is. It is offered as the principle through which the universe can be fully understood just because the whole universe is the realisation or embodiment of this principle. In this sense, therefore, the whole system of Forms may be said to culminate in the Form of Good, which in its turn includes all subordinate Forms within itself, and thus through their realisation in particular things is itself realised in all that the Universe contains. Malebranche and Spinoza taught that the highest knowledge is "to see all things in God". Of Plato we may justly say in the light of this passage, that, for him, the completion of knowledge is to see all things in the light of the Form of Good.

But how is this possible in the face of all the evil and imperfection which the universe so manifestly contains? And what is the relation of the Form of Good to God?

THE FORM OF GOOD AS PRINCIPLE OF THE UNIVERSE

Does Plato give us any help towards answering these questions? We must try out whether some of the contexts in which the words "good" and "goodness" occur, can be made to yield some light on our problem.

1. At the end of Book I of the *Republic*,[1] we are told that everything has a function which it may perform either well or ill. The function of a knife is to cut. Now, the quality which enables a thing to perform its function well is its characteristic "virtue", its goodness or efficiency. A good knife is a knife which cuts well, just as a blunt knife is a bad knife because it performs its function badly. The principle here illustrated may be generalised to cover the human virtues. Indeed, Plato does

---

[1] See *Republic*, 352d-353c.

so himself. The function of the soul is to guide and direct human conduct. A good soul directs and controls the individual according to the work which falls to him to do in the world. If he be a statesman, he will rule wisely; if he be a soldier, he will fight bravely; as a private citizen, he will obey law and authority and keep a firm hand on his desires. Thus, wisdom, courage, self-control are the Forms of goodness (the "virtues") which the citizens of his ideal state have to practise according to their functions in the social order. These virtues are specialised forms of the general principle, or Form, of human goodness which Plato calls "justice", and which may be defined as doing the work one is best fitted to do and doing it as well as one knows how.

Thus we have a principle here which covers the whole range of what we call "good"—from a good tool to a good dinner, a good dog, a good player, a good worker, a good citizen, and so on. For everything there is the demand to be effective according to the law of its own nature. It realises, we might say, the Form of Good in doing what it is meant to do as well as possible, in being what it is meant to be as well as possible.

In thus connecting the Platonic argument from function and virtue with his Form of Good, we are going beyond Plato's text, yet it is a development which may fairly be said to be in harmony with his thought. But it does not carry us very far towards explaining how the evil, badness, imperfection in the world can be reconciled with the Form of Good as supreme principle. For, even if we argue that everything in the world does its work as well as is individually possible for it, and that the poor performance of one thing is due either to its being inferior of its kind, or to adverse circumstances preventing it from doing better, we only raise the ulterior question, why under the rule of the Form of Good there should be things inferior of their kind, or why there should be circumstances such as to hamper and lower the efficiency of a thing.

2. Another line of thought is suggested by the Platonic argument which grades and evaluates different human activities. The inborn inequality of men was axiomatic with Plato and Aristotle. Both rest their political theories upon it, both try to make provision in the order of their ideal commonwealths for these inherent differences in physical and mental endowment,

so as to make the most of each individual according to the gifts and powers which fit him for one kind of activity and unfit him for others. Both, and especially Plato, are convinced that the ruling of a state for the common good requires the highest qualities of intellect and character. Both know, too, that the interests of men differ. There are the lovers of money, the lovers of honour and power, the lovers of knowledge and wisdom. Each of these groups, so far as successful in its quest, enjoys the pleasure of getting what it wants, but it does not follow that the pleasure of the lover of money ranks equal to the pleasure of the lover of wisdom. And still less does it follow that the activities of the one rank equal to the activities of the other, or that in their intrinsic nature these activities are equally worth while. Thus, we find both Plato and Aristotle evaluating, be it human lives, be it human activities, and thereby laying the foundation of what has come down to us as the doctrine of the *summum bonum*, the highest good. And just as Plato ranks the life of the lover of wisdom above all other human lives, so Aristotle ranks the exercise of the pure intellect above all other human activities, because, as he quaintly puts it, "though small in bulk", the intellect is the divinest element in our nature, and to employ it in thought on the things which are eternal is to come as near to being God as our human nature permits. For Plato, clearly, the highest good will be to see the whole universe in the light of the Form of Good : and if the Form of Good be identical with God, then "to see all things in God". For such a view, all human shortcomings, failures, misdeeds and crimes, no less than all sufferings, pains and unhappiness, will somehow have to appear not only compatible with, but positively justified by, the Form of Good. But how? Instead of getting nearer to an answer to this question, the argument so far only seems to make the problem more insoluble.

3. In one single passage,[1] there is implicit mention of a Form of Bad or Evil. The problem raised by such a Form, especially in a universe which as a whole is dominated by the Form of Good, is nowhere discussed by Plato, not even in the dialogue called the *Parmenides*, in which the logical problems of the theory of Forms are subjected to the most searching examination, and in which even such questions are raised as whether it

[1] See *Republic*, 476a.

is conceivable that there are Forms of mud or hair. Yet, if good things are good by participation in the Form of Good, it would seem by parity of reasoning that bad things must be bad by participation in a corresponding Form of Bad. Certainly, nowhere in Plato's argument do we get any hint of the device by which a later generation of Platonists tried to escape from the difficulties of this supposition, viz., by saying that evil is nothing positive, but mere privation, mere lack of excellence. If we take the Form of Bad seriously, then the Bad must be for Plato as positive as any other character in the universe which is a distinctive Form. And this suggests a mixed world, a world in which things good and things bad exist side by side, and the corresponding Forms divide the realm of being between them or perhaps compete for its exclusive possession. Good and bad seem contradictory and mutually exclusive. What subordinate place, then, can the Form of Bad occupy in a system dominated by the Form of Good? Once more our problem has only become more opaque.

4. Indeed, we can push the problem of evil into the very heart of the realm of Forms, by considering not merely imperfect realisations of Forms, nor merely the presence of a Form of Bad among the other Forms, but by asking whether some Forms may not be inherently bad in their very nature. We may ask, in other words, whether in a universe dominated by the Form of Good it can be good that certain Forms should occur in the system of Forms and have their realisations in the empirical world at all. To illustrate: Given the Form of monarchy, there will be good kings and bad kings, or to put it differently, kings who are all that a king ought to be and kings who fail miserably. But the point now is not whether individual kings are good or bad, but whether monarchical rule *as such* is good or bad. Can it be approved in principle as an eternal constituent, so to speak, of the realm of the Forms which are realised in the details of nature and of history? So, again, the philosophical anarchist objects to government and law *in principle*, though he might readily admit that some governments, as governments, are better than others. Or, again, what of criminal professions? If there is a Form for every classifiable kind of thing, the existence, e.g., of burglars implies a Form of Burglary. It seems obvious that, so long as there are good

burglars ("first-class cracksmen", experts at their job), being a
good burglar rather than an inefficient one is an aggravation,
because in a perfect world there ought to be no burglars nor
any possibility of burglary at all. And so here, again, we are
back at the question how there can be evil in principle in a
world which is to be conceived as good in principle. Moreover,
it should be noted that, although our illustrations, above, have
been taken from human affairs, the problem is not restricted to
the human sphere. All through the world we find life main-
taining itself by destroying other life—"Nature red in tooth
and claw". Granted that, if organisms can live only by destroying life in other organisms, it is better in their own
interests that they be good at destroying, still the question remains whether this spectacle of life flourishing by the destruction of life—with all the incidental results of death, pain,
suffering, development prematurely cut short, capacities left
unrealised—can be interpreted consistently with making the
Form of Good the supreme determining principle in the universe as a whole.

Against this cumulative indictment, what if anything can
be set on the positive side?

The most promising line of defence would seem to be that
of saying that every Form has an intrinsic value which can be
appreciated, if we will but contemplate and enjoy it and all its
manifestations with the detachment of a spectator who, after
the manner of Spinoza, should lay aside all attempts to judge
and content himself with accepting and appreciating all things
sub specie aeternitatis. The practice of such detachment from
approval and disapproval, from the moralising tendency which
is ever sorting out in the universe what ought to be from what
ought not to be, and the possibilities of a deeper insight into
the nature of things as the reward of such detachment, should
not be rashly denied. Experience shows that it has value and
reveals value. Obvious examples are to be found in both the
scientific and the aesthetic attitudes towards the universe. For,
though each of these has its own scheme of value distinctions,
viz., true and false in science, beautiful and ugly in art, yet the
emancipation of both from utilitarian, economic, moral valuations does enable them to face the world with a catholicity of
appreciation, a disinterested curiosity and delight, that have a

legitimate contribution to make to our fuller understanding of it. The modern "camera hunter" who does not go out to kill for food or sport, but risks his life in the effort to observe and record the intimate details of the lives of wild and dangerous animals, may serve to illustrate what is meant. Or, again, consider our modern attitude towards species threatened with extinction. They may have been destroyed by us for the sake of the economic value of their skins or their flesh or some product of theirs, or they may have been exterminated to make room for human herds and fields and towns, but before the process comes to an end a counter effort sets in to save and preserve the remnants. This effort bears witness to a sense of a value threatened with extinction. It acknowledges that the world without the threatened species would be a poorer world. We seek to preserve it both for science and for art, and both these study it and delight in it for its own sake. The game reserves in which the African fauna is now saved from the hunter are at once historical records of a world which elsewhere has vanished, an opportunity for scientific study of forms of animal life, and an inexhaustible source of delight and inspiration to the artist who responds to the beauty of all unspoiled natural things. Are not the bison of North America preserved for the same reason? And if we could still find alive some prehistoric monster like the *Diplodocus Carnegii*, would not our first endeavour be to preserve it alive in the name of science?

Indeed, this objective delight of scientist and artist extends from large-scale appearance and behaviour to the minutiae of structure and adaptation, and here passes into that sense of the marvels of nature which is the empirical basis for the old argument from design for the existence of God. There is always a possible strand of religious experience at the heart of science, provided intellectual curiosity is not simply the bond slave of a desire for results capable of practical application, and provided also it goes together with a disinterested delight in the spectacle of nature—the sort of delight which the Divine Artist experienced when he reviewed his work and saw that it was good. Here, too, we strike the empirical basis of the mood which leads through Spinoza's acceptance of the "necessity" of all things to the "intellectual love of God". Or, again, if we grant the intrinsic value of every Form, but recall that Forms compete, so to speak, with each other in the realm of particular objects where all seek their realisation, we may be tempted to identify the Form of Good with the value of maximum compossibility of values, and thus be led to defend it on Leibnizian lines as the principle of "the best of all possible worlds".

It must, however, be admitted that there is no clear evidence in Plato's dialogues for any of the lines of argument into which we have been following up the possible interpretations and defences of the Platonic Form of Good. The plain fact of the matter is that in the few passages in the dialogues in which the contrast between Good and Evil in the universe comes up for explicit discussion, Plato takes up an attitude so dualistic, that the interpretation of the Form of Good as the ultimate principle of reality and knowledge becomes quite impossible. For, always Evil stands over against Good in a way which makes its occurrence and its opposition to Good unintelligible in terms of the Good itself.

THE FORM OF GOOD AND GOD

This comes out quite clearly when one tries to answer the following two questions:

First, what is the relation of the Form of Evil to the Form of Good?

Second, is the Form of Good identical with God, and, if so, what is the relation of God to the Form of Evil?

As regards the first question, the actual phrase, "Form of Evil", does not occur in Plato's text, not even in the passage from the *Republic* referred to above. But it is implied there, for the passage forms part of Plato's argument distinguishing the singleness of each Form from the multiplicity of its particular embodiments: ". . . and of the just and unjust, good and evil, and of every other class, the same remark holds: taken singly, each of them is one; but from the various combinations of them with actions and things and with one another, they are seen in all sorts of lights and appear many".[1]

The mention, here, of a Form of Unjust, of course, is additional evidence for the application of the doctrine of Forms to evil qualities. So, again, in a passage in the *Laws*, we find the

---

[1] See *Republic*, 476a.

enumeration, "good and evil, base and honourable, just and unjust". And in the *Theaetetus* there is mention of "two patterns set before" men, viz., the one blessed and divine, the other godless and wretched; and the punishment of evildoers is said to be that they do not observe how in their evil deeds they practise the evil pattern and grow like unto it in their very souls.[1]

Lastly, the fundamental opposition of Evil and Good is emphasised in all the passages which repeat that God is the author of good only, and that the evil in the world must be ascribed to some cause other than God, except in the cases in which it can reasonably be interpreted as punishment inflicted by him for the sufferer's good. Thus the *Republic* has it:

> It follows therefore that the good is not the cause of all things, but of the good only?—Assuredly.—Then God, if he be good, is not the author of all things, . . . but he is the cause of a few things only, and not of most things that occur to men. For few are the goods of human life, and many are the evils, and the good is to be attributed to God alone; of the evils the causes are to be sought elsewhere, and not in him.[2]

The *Theaetetus* supports this: "The Truth is that God is never in any way unrighteous—he is perfect righteousness".[3] Finally, in the *Laws*, Plato, after reasserting the goodness of God,[4] speaks of the "immortal conflict" between Good and Evil, and says that God "contrived so to place each of the parts that their position might in the easiest and best manner procure the victory of good and the defeat of evil in the whole".[5] But the whole context of the passage makes it clear that God's arrangements merely favour the victory of Good, secure the possibility of its victory, not that they make that victory inevitable and necessary, still less that the victory consists in an elimination of the very principle of Evil from the universe. No, the thought of Plato, with its emphasis on the immortal conflict of Good and Evil and on the eternal patterns of these two antagonists, remains thoroughly dualistic.

Now, as long as it so remains, it is impossible to see how the Form of Good can be the ultimate principle of explanation of the universe. How can it, how does it, account for the presence of Evil either in fact or in principle in the universe? How does

[1] See *Theaetetus*, 176e-177a.   [2] See *Republic*, 379c.   [3] *Theaetetus*, 176c.
[4] *Laws*, 901d.   [5] *Laws*, 904b.

it make its own opposite and its conflict with that opposite intelligible? How is its supremacy to be understood when Plato repeatedly affirms that human life exhibits more evil than good? Professor R. C. Lodge interprets the Form of the Good as metaphysical principle by describing it as

> the conception of an ideal existence consisting of the fullest and richest development of the potentialities of the universe in a single, self-supporting system, with a complete absence of conflict, waste, privation, and negation.[1]

Even granted that the one passage in the *Republic* about the Form of Good might permit such an interpretation as this, it is quite impossible to uphold it in the face of the repeated affirmations of the fundamental opposition of, and conflict between, Good and Evil in the universe.

Turning now to our second question, concerning the relation of the Form of Good to God, it must at once be confessed that there is no unambiguous statement to be found in Plato's text. No wonder, then, that the chief commentators differ widely from one another, each taking the view which seems to him the most probable in the light of his personal philosophical predilections. Raeder, for example, identifies the God of the creation story in the *Timaeus* with the Form of Good in the *Republic*: God for him is the Form of Good conceived in its true nature as a creative causal agent, a creative world-soul. Natorp, on the other hand, holds that the personification of the Form of Good as God is a pure metaphor appropriate to the "myth" character of the account of creation in the *Timaeus*. J. A. Stewart tries to make the best of both worlds by saying that there is identification, but with a difference corresponding to the scientific and religious interpretations of the world, respectively. Both approaches are equally legitimate and necessary, and the identification affirms them not to be mutually exclusive and destructive.

When eminent students of Plato thus disagree, it is clear evidence that Plato's own words give no unambiguous lead. Indeed, in the *Timaeus*, he warns us himself not to press his statements too hard:

> If then, Socrates, amid the many opinions about the gods and the generation of the universe, we are not able to give notions which

[1] See Plato's *Theory of Ethics*, 141.

are altogether and in every respect exact and consistent with one another, do not be surprised.[1]

And, truly, it is difficult to fit the various statements of the creation story into a consistent pattern. We are told that God made this world of change and becoming, because

> he was good, and the good can never have any jealousy of anything. And being free from jealousy, he desired that all things should be as like himself as they could be. . . . God desired that all things should be good and nothing bad, so far as this was attainable.[2]

This agrees with another statement a little earlier in the same dialogue: "the world is the fairest of creations and he (God) the best of causes".[3] But there is that tantalising hint concerning some obstacle to the realisation of the highest perfection—"so far as this was attainable". What is the cause or source of this imperfection? Perhaps we are meant to find an explanation in the sentence which follows immediately upon the first of the above quotations:

> Wherefore also finding the whole visible sphere not at rest, but moving in an irregular and disorderly fashion, out of disorder he brought order, considering that this was in every way better than the other.[4]

Taken at its face value—and is there any good reason for taking it otherwise?—this can mean only that creation for Plato is not an absolute bringing of the universe into existence *ex nihilo*, but merely an effort to introduce order into a previously existing disorder. And if we connect this in turn with the passages from the *Laws*, quoted above, concerning the "immortal conflict" of Good and Evil, we are back at the severely dualistic position which had been the outcome of our consideration of the relation of the Form of Good and the Form of Evil.

But, prior to all these passages, there occurs in the *Timaeus* the famous argument about the two kinds of "patterns" between which God has the choice in creating the universe:

> The work of the creator, whenever he looks to the unchangeable and fashions the form and nature of his work after an unchangeable pattern, must necessarily be made fair and perfect; but when he looks to the created only, and uses a created pattern, it is not fair and perfect.[5]

[1] See *Timaeus*, 29c.   [2] See *Timaeus*, 29e-30a.   [3] *Ibid.*, 29a.
[4] *Timaeus*, 30c.   [5] See *Timaeus*, 28a.

And then the argument goes on to conclude:

> If the world be indeed fair and the artificer good, it is manifest that he must have looked to that which is eternal. . . . Every one will see that he must have looked to the eternal; for the world is the fairest of creations and he is the best of causes.[1]

This praise of the creation is very difficult to reconcile with all the passages in which Plato appears to estimate that the evil in the world outweighs the good: indeed, I do not know how a reconciliation is intelligibly to be effected. But, leaving this point aside, we have here the passages which have been usually, and plausibly, interpreted by identifying the "eternal patterns" of the *Timaeus* with the "eternal Forms" of the *Republic*; and, further, which have been held to imply that the Forms are not identical with God, nor in any sense created by him, but are independently existing patterns which he follows. No other interpretation seems really consistent with Plato's explicit language. Yet, when we bring into the argument the "created patterns" which God might have followed and which are imperfect, the difficulties become well-nigh insuperable. Who has created these patterns? The language of the text does not suggest that it was God who created them; and if he had been their creator, it is unintelligible why he should not have made them perfect.

And, finally, when we recall that there had been mention of a Form of Evil, we get no answer to the question which we can hardly avoid asking, whether this Form is one of the "eternal patterns", and, if it is, whether God ignores it in his creation: or, if he follows it, how creation can be "the fairest" and yet contain within itself an "immortal conflict" of Good and Evil.

The view that God is the creator of the Forms is generally supported by reference to the argument in the Tenth Book of the *Republic*, where God as the maker of the Form of Bed is contrasted with the carpenter who makes physical beds, and with the painter who "imitates" the carpenter's bed and is thus "twice removed from reality". There, God as the "natural author and maker of the bed" (i.e., of the Form of Bed) is further said to be "by the natural process of creation the author of this and of all other things" (scil. of their Forms).[2] This

[1] *Ibid.*, 29a.   [2] *Republic*, 597d.

statement is explicit enough, but how it is to be reconciled with
the relation of God to the eternal patterns of the *Theaetetus*, or
with the existence of a Form of Evil, there is no means of telling.

So, again, the assertion in the *Philebus* that the universe is not
left to the guidance of unreason and chance, but is "ordered
and governed by a marvellous intelligence and wisdom",[1] conflicts with the existence of Evil in detail and in principle.

One small illustration of the difficulties of eliciting coherent
theory from Plato's scattered references to all these inter-related
topics may be given in conclusion. In the section of the *Republic*
which deals with the Form of Good, there occurs this passage:

> You would say, would you not, that the sun is not only the author
> of visibility in all visible things, but of generation and nourishment
> and growth though he himself is not generation?—Certainly.—In
> like manner the good may be said to be not only the author of
> knowledge to all things known, but of their being and essence, and
> yet the good is not essence, but far exceeds essence in dignity and
> power.[2]

Professor Boodin thinks that the Good which is here said to
exceed essence, whilst being the author of essence, cannot be
the Form of Good. "When Plato makes the good the creator of
essence, he cannot have in mind the idea of good".[3] In other
words, Professor Boodin seeks to distinguish between the Form
of Good as constituting the essence of all particular good things,
and the Good as ultimate creative agent. Now, truly, the passage
quoted is difficult to interpret. Yet one thing seems clear, viz.,
that it belongs to a context in which, according to common
consent, Plato talks throughout of nothing other than the Form
of Good; and there is no trace in his language of any such distinction as Professor Boodin would read into it. The only thing
that seems clear is that Plato means to distinguish cause from
effect both for the sun and for the Good, and to assign to the
cause a more eminent reality. But beyond this it hardly seems
safe to go.

Professor Boodin's interpretation of Plato's cosmology has
the merit of recognising more fully than do most commentators
on Plato the ineradicable dualism in Plato's universe between
Good and Evil. He prefers the cosmology of the *Timaeus* to the

---

[1] *Philebus*, 28d.   [2] *Republic*, 509b, c.
[3] Boodin, "Plato's Cosmology", *Mind*, N.S., No. 152, p. 503. Cf. also No. 153,
p. 70.

cosmology of the *Laws*, on the ground that, whilst in the latter the source of Evil is ascribed to evil souls, in the former the failure of the world to realise the full perfection which God strives to impress upon it, "lies in an inherent indifference or laziness on the part of the world in which God works to create order and beauty".[1]

But even he hardly brings out the full force of the difficulties in which we get unavoidably entangled when we try to think together the main things which Plato says at different times about God, and the Form of Good, and Evil. Let us sum up the main positions which conflict in this way: (1) So long as there is evil in the world, whether it be due to the laziness of a purely materialistic universe or to the recalcitrance of evil souls, there must, it would seem, be a Form of Evil. (2) This Form of Evil must have a place in the system of Forms through which, according to the *Republic*, the Form of Good realises itself in all that exists; yet how Evil can have such a place is unintelligible. (3) If God is, as the creator of the universe, the embodiment of the Form of Good (if he is the utmost perfection become fact), all other Forms, and therefore the Form of Evil along with the rest, must be an expression of his nature, but this supposition repeats the preceding difficulty, and runs flatly counter to all Plato's own statements about the perfect righteousness of God and his eternal opposition to Evil.

What would we not give for the chance of eliciting from Plato another immortal dialogue giving us his definite solution to our difficulties!

[1] *Mind*, N.S., No. 153, p. 77.

Kant's Theory of Freedom[1]

I.

LET me begin by recalling briefly the general setting of Kant's discussion of freedom in this treatise.

The moral worth of an act depends, for Kant, solely on the agent's motive. The act may be objectively right: it may be the act which "duty requires"; but, unless the agent does it "because duty requires" (p. 16), and *from no other motive whatever*, the doing of it has no moral worth: the agent's will is not "good". Kant's "good will" is, as it were, a transposition into philosophical language of the Christian ideal of "purity of heart". Man's nature is composite; more, it is divided against itself. Reason is in principle different from the inclinations and generally at war with them. It speaks through the voice of duty, and "an action done from duty must wholly exclude the influence of inclination" (p. 20). Reason must "overpower" inclination; "or at least in case of choice exclude it from its calculation" (p. 19). The will of man, as a rational being, "takes no account of" and "disregards" all desires and inclinations (p. 93). Kant's language implies that we never get rid of our inclinations: they are always with us. What morality demands of us is that we should emancipate ourselves from them and exclude them from all share in the motivation of our actions, so that our inclinations, though still there, are ineffective and powerless as motives to action. Ideally, "it must be the universal wish of every rational being to be wholly free from them" (viz., the inclinations, p. 55). Actually, inward emancipation is all we can hope to achieve.

Early in the second section of his treatise, Kant talks of this

---

[1] This article deals only with the *Fundamental Principles*, partly for reasons of space, but mainly because Kant's Theory of Freedom in this treatise is the best known and most frequently expounded. The references in the text are to the pages of the separate issue of T. K. Abbott's translation of the *Fundamental Principles* (published by Longmans, Green & Co.).

mastery of reason over the inclinations as if it were easy to achieve and psychologically quite intelligible:

> For the pure conception of duty . . . exercises on the human heart, by way of reason alone . . . an influence so much more powerful than all other springs . . . that in the consciousness of its worth, it despises the latter, and can by degrees become their master (pp. 32-3).

But, this is, I think, an exceptional passage. Ordinarily, Kant regards the attainment of purity of motive as so difficult that he even doubts whether it ever occurs as a genuine fact (pp. 27 ff.). But, his fundamental difficulty goes deeper still: even if this purity of motive were an everyday occurrence; even if we could confidently say concerning the "exclusion" of the inclinations, "it is done and it can be done", there would still remain the *theoretical* problem of *making intelligible how it is, and can be, done.* Given man's composite nature, how does reason actually effect the exclusion of the inclinations from the motivation of our actions?

This is the point of Kant's reiterated question: "How is the categorical imperative possible?" Many Kant students read Kant as intending to argue that the thought of duty, or of the moral law, *can* function as the only motive, even if it remains doubtful whether, in fact, it ever does. I suggest that, even if actions done "because duty requires" were as frequent as they are in fact rare, there would still remain for Kant the problem of making their occurrence intelligible. To talk of reason "over-mastering" and "excluding" the inclinations is easy. To demand that reason should do so is almost as easy. But *to understand how reason can do so*—the theoretical possibility—*that* is the difficulty. And for the solution of this difficulty Kant offers his theory of freedom.

II.

The conceptual apparatus by means of which Kant attempts to construct a solution is introduced in the opening paragraph of section 3 of his treatise (p. 78). We are told that there are two kinds of causality, viz.,

  (1) will, i.e., the causality of living beings "in so far as they are rational"; and

(2) the causality proper to all "irrational beings".
Concerning will, we are told that it is efficient "independently
of foreign causes determining it", and in this sense is *free*. The
activity of irrational beings, on the other hand, is characterised
by *physical necessity*, as being "determined by the influence of
foreign causes" (*ibid.*).

In other words, there is determination in either case, but a
rational being, if purely rational, is self-determined and in that
sense free; whereas an irrational being can never be self-
determined, but is always subject to determination by something other than itself ("foreign").

And, in both cases, too, determination is always subject to
"law", viz., "the moral law", or law of reason, in the former
case; "physical laws", in the latter.

Fundamental, thus, is the sharp contrast between rational
and irrational beings. A purely rational being will always perform that act which is in accord with, and therefore categori-
cally commanded by, the law of its own reason. An irrational
being, if it can be said to "act" at all, will always do that act
which "foreign causes" determine it to do. For a purely rational
being, the principle holds that "a free will and a will subject to
moral laws are one and the same" (p. 79).

Now, when we apply this conceptual apparatus to human
agents, we find that, owing to their composite nature, they are
at once both rational and irrational. We humans have physical
bodies and through them belong to the physical world of matter
in motion, in which all happenings, including human actions
as movements of human bodies, are characterised by physical
necessity. The physical world is, as such, a world of "irrational
beings", and our bodies are but a special class of irrational
beings, at any rate when considered in abstraction from our
rational minds. Moreover, worse still, our minds are irrational,
too, viz., in respect of our inclinations. Our feelings, desires, etc.,
are the effects of causes beyond ourselves—"foreign causes";
more, the inclinations are "foreign" to reason which is the true
self of each of us. Hence, for reason to be influenced by them,
would be to sink to the level of physical necessity and irration-
ality; and, omitting reason, man is clearly to be classed with
plants and animals, living but irrational.

But man has reason; his rational self is his real self; and if he

would be true to himself, his every action must be determined
solely by the law of his own reason which is also the law of
reason for every other rational being. Morality, in short, for
such a composite creature as man consists precisely in behaving
as if he were not composite at all; in achieving, by emancipation from the influence of his inclinations, the same purity of
motive which is the normal condition of rational beings that
have no inclinations at all. How is this "possible"? How can
we conceive this emancipation of the rational in man from the
irrational taking place?

Kant's problem is clear now. It is *not* the problem, What is
the nature of freedom? The answer to *that* problem is settled by
definition, based upon the analysis of the concept of "rational
being" : to be free is to be subject to the law of one's own reason.
Kant's problem concerns the *realisation of freedom, so defined in
composite human nature.* We know what must happen if freedom
is to be realised : the inclinations, always there, must be excluded from determining in any way our choice of action. But,
to *understand* how this is "possible", how reason can effect the
required mastery over the irrational side of human nature—
that is the problem to be solved.

III.

It seems to me that the answer required (though not necessarily an answer that can be established) is a theory of the
power of reason to exclude all irrational motives from the determination of our actions. This power, if we keep within the orbit
of Kant's thought, requires, on the one hand, that reason
should itself remain immune against all influences from our
inclinations; and, on the other side, that reason should somehow itself so influence our inclinations that they cease to be
effective as motives.

Actually, Kant throws out suggestions on both these aspects
of the power of reason, but he does so in passages widely apart
from each other; and nowhere does he state a theory of the
power of reason as a connected whole.

Thus, on the negative side (reason as immune against the
irrational) we read:

we cannot possibly conceive a reason consciously receiving a bias
from any other quarter with respect to its judgments, for then

the subject would ascribe the determination of its judgment not to its own reason, but to an impulse. It must regard itself as the author of its principles independent on foreign influences (p. 81).

And on the positive side (reason itself influencing the irrational) we read:

it is no doubt requisite that reason should have a power to infuse a feeling of pleasure or satisfaction in the fulfilment of duty, that is to say, that it should have a causality by which it determines the sensibility according to its own principles (p. 97).

But, this suggestion, scarcely made, is at once met with the crushing reflection:

But it is quite impossible to discern, i.e., to make intelligible *a priori*, how a mere thought . . . can itself produce a sensation of pleasure or pain . . .

Here, it will be remembered, we reach the point where Kant bids us be content with "comprehending the incomprehensibility" of the realisation of freedom in human life, whether or no such freedom is ever realised in actual fact.

Kant's own clearest formulation of the problem, as I have analysed it, is to be found in the famous "I ought, therefore I can" passage, which Abbott, more accurately, if less epigrammatically, renders: "this 'I ought' is properly an 'I would', valid for every rational being" (p. 82). There we are explicitly told that the problem is to "discern how this comes to pass", when we are dealing with human beings in whom, so far from reason determining their actions "without any hindrance", there are "in addition springs of a different kind, namely sensibility", as a result of which we often fail to do, and fail to want to do, what we ought to do.

But, having thus boldly marched up to the very ramparts of the problem, Kant turns aside into argument "about it and about", though always trying to "see" how it is possible to achieve in men the condition of mind in which "I ought" and "I would" automatically coincide. In the end, he gives up the problem as insoluble: we can only see why we cannot see the solution.

IV.

If I am right in claiming that this is the genuine logical track of Kant's argument, then two famous theories which also occur in these pages of his treatise, must be definitely put aside as leading him and us astray.

There is, first, the theory (pp. 80-1) that freedom must be "presupposed" as the property of the will of *all* rational beings (not merely as a special endowment of rational beings who are also human). This I regard as the first formulation of what subsequently, in the *Critique of Practical Reason*, appears as the "postulate" of freedom:

> Now I say every being that cannot act except *under the idea of freedom* is just for that reason in a practical point of view really free (p. 80).

But, this does not help us forward with the solution of the problem of understanding how freedom can be realised in the rational-irrational nature of man. Kant here merely tells us that freedom (as defined, i.e., as consisting in obedience to the law of reason) is inherent in rational beings, as such. Quite simply: a rational being can only act rationally, i.e., in accordance with the law of his reason, i.e., freely. Such is the nature of every rational being, and such must every rational being conceive his nature to be. But, this does not touch the real problem, viz., how it is possible for a rational being to behave rationally and freely under the "hindrances" of having also an irrational side to his nature, which must somehow be eliminated from the motivation of his actions.

Secondly, there is the famous distinction of two points of view (pp. 84-93), viz., that of *phenomena* and that of *noumena*—that of man as a natural object, an object of sense-perception, even to himself, and that of man as a "thing-in-himself", as a rational being, capable of self-consciousness, and in this aspect of his nature not an object of sense-perception or phenomenon.

This doctrine is, of course, full of philosophical interest and has many merits. Only—helping to solve our problem of understanding how it is possible for a rational-irrational creature to behave as if he were purely rational, is not one of these merits. In fact, considered in *this* context, the doctrine is not only an irrelevance, but it is actually in contradiction with the assumptions underlying the problem to be solved.

These assumptions are that, whilst it is doubtful whether any truly moral action (i.e., any action of which the thought of duty is the only motive) ever occurs, there is no doubt at all

that the motives of most human actions are either pure inclinations, or inclinations and duty mixed. This examination of
motives is possible only on the plane of self-conscious reflection :
the distinction between phenomena and noumena is here
utterly irrelevant and inapplicable. On the other hand, *whatever* the motives and their moral worth, the actions resulting
from them will be movements of the agent's body and their
effects in the physical world. But, the agent's body and its movements and their physical effects are all of them objects of sense-
perception, i.e., phenomena. Thus, *every* action, whether its
motive was pure duty to the exclusion of all inclination or pure
inclination without thought of duty, will on its bodily side be
phenomenon. So considered, it belongs, in terms of Kant's
original conceptual apparatus, to the world of "irrational
beings", and has to be treated as explicable by "physical
necessity", even if its motive was, *ex hypothesi*, pure duty! The
plea that "philosophy must assume that no real contradiction
will be found between freedom and physical necessity of the
same human action" (p. 91) fails. It might have succeeded, if
Kant had merely held that all actions, as phenomena, are irrational, but rational when considered from the noumenal
plane. This would have been equivalent to saying that natural
science, dealing with human actions only as objects of perception, seeks to explain them by natural causes ("physical
necessity"), and leaves completely out of account the question
of their moral value. Correspondingly, moral philosophy considers the moral values of actions and is not interested in their
causes as natural events. This distinction, if carefully maintained, might avoid a "real contradiction". But, actually,
Kant, if he intends this distinction at all, does not maintain it
consistently. The point at which it breaks down is the treatment of *motives*. An inclination, as a motive, is a natural cause,
a phenomenal cause, an irrational cause. The thought of duty,
as a motive, is also a cause, but not a natural cause ; rather it is
a noumenal cause, it is reason exercising its own appropriate
causality. Thus, we have actions of which the motive is an
inclination, when both cause and effect are phenomenal. And
we have actions, themselves still phenomenal, of which the
cause is not phenomenal at all, but noumenal. So far, then,
from a distinction of two points of view being consistently

maintained towards *all* actions, we have a cross-division in that, whilst all actions, as physical events, are phenomenal and nothing but phenomenal, their causes are either purely phenomenal, or purely noumenal, or mixed! And, how a purely rational thought on the noumenal plane can come into conflict with, or exert any resistance against, an inclination which, by definition, belongs to the phenomenal plane, Kant himself has confessed to be unintelligible.

V.

That Kant himself realised the position, taken up by him in this treatise, to be untenable, may be inferred, I think even in the absence of any explicit withdrawal of this theory, from the attempts which he made in his later writings to give a more satisfactory solution of the problem of freedom. Actually, these later attempts are no more successful, but the fact that Kant should have experimented with them may fairly be interpreted as an implicit admission of the failure of the theory put forward in the *Fundamental Principles*.

Kant's Concept of the "Intrinsic Worth" of Every "Rational Being"

SOME time ago, I contributed an article on "Kant's Theory of Freedom" to the pages of *The Personalist*. I welcome this opportunity of pursuing my study of Kant's Moral Theory from another, but closely related, angle, the more so as my present topic might also have been called "Kant's Concept of Man's Moral Personality", and is thus eminently relevant as a contribution to the special issue of *The Personalist* in honour of Ralph Tyler Flewelling.

I propose to divide my discussion into four sections. The first will analyse the concept, or complex of concepts, for which the words "intrinsic worth" stand. The second will offer certain comments of my own, which furnish the basis of my interpretation, and criticism, of Kant's statements concerning what is "a priori synthetic" in his Moral Theory. The discussions of the "a priori" and the "a priori synthetic" will form the third and fourth sections.

As in the previous article, I restrict myself to the little treatise, entitled "Fundamental Principles of the Metaphysic of Morals", because it is—deservedly, I think—the only ethical text of Kant's which is ordinarily read by students of Ethics in English and American Universities. My references are to Thomas Kingswill Abbott's translation, entitled *Kant's Theory of Ethics*.

I.

The material for an analysis and interpretation of Kant's concept of "intrinsic worth" will be found in the following passages, which are listed in the order in which they occur in the text. The list does not claim to be exhaustive, but it does include every passage which adds relevant material. The few passages omitted merely repeat points to be found in the passages included. The key-words for the subsequent analysis are italicised in each passage.

1. "Nothing can possibly be conceived in the world, or even out of it, which can be called *good without qualification*, except a *Good Will*" (9).

2. "Moderation in the affections . . . seems to constitute part of the *intrinsic worth of the person, but* . . ." (9).

3. "There is something so strange in this idea of *the absolute value of the mere will*, in which no account is taken of its utility . . ." (10).

4. "The often anxious care which most men take for it (scil. maintenance of life) has *no intrinsic worth* . . ." (13, 14).

5. "It is just in this that the *moral worth* of the character is brought out which is incomparably the highest of all, namely, that he is beneficent, not from inclination, but from duty" (15).

6. "The purposes which we may have in view in our actions, or their effects regarded as ends and springs of the will, cannot give to *actions* any *unconditional or moral worth*" (16).[1]

7. "The *pre-eminent good* which we call moral can therefore consist in nothing else than *the conception of law* in itself, *which certainly is only possible in a rational being*, in so far as this conception, and not the expected effect, determines the will. This is a good which is always present in the person who acts accordingly, and we have not to wait for it to appear first in the result" (17).[2]

8. "The necessity of acting from *pure respect* for the practical law is what constitutes duty, to which every other motive must give place, because it is the condition of a will being good *in itself*, and the *worth of such a will is above everything*" (20).[3]

9. "Beings whose existence depends not on our will but on nature's, have nevertheless, if they are irrational beings, only a relative value as means, and are therefore called *things*; rational beings, on the contrary, are called *persons*, because their very nature points them out as ends in themselves, that is as something which must not be used merely as means, and *so far therefore restricts freedom of action* (and is an object of respect). These, therefore, are not merely subjective ends whose existence has a worth for us as an effect of our action, but *objective ends, that is things whose existence is an end in itself*: an end moreover for which no other can be substituted, which they should subserve merely as means, for otherwise nothing whatever would possess absolute worth; but if all worth were conditioned and therefore contingent, then there would be no supreme practical principle of reason whatever" (46).[4]

[1] The whole context from which this passage is quoted is relevant.
[2] The italics, here, are Kant's, but coincide with mine, except that I also italicise the words "pre-eminent good".
[3] The first two italicisings are Kant's, the last is mine.
[4] Kant's italics, coinciding with mine.

10. "In the kingdom of ends everything has either Value or Dignity. Whatever has a value can be replaced by something else which is *equivalent*; whatever, on the other hand, is above all value, and therefore admits of no equivalent, has a dignity. Whatever has reference to the general inclinations and wants of mankind has a *market value*; whatever, without presupposing a want, corresponds to a certain taste, that is to a satisfaction in the mere purposeless play of our faculties, has a *fancy value*; but that which constitutes the condition under which alone anything can be an end in itself, this has not merely a relative worth, i.e., value, but an intrinsic worth, that is, *dignity*" (53).[1]

Before proceeding to a systematic statement of the concepts involved in these passages, a word on the translation, which is not always precise. The translator uses for Kant's single word, *Wert*, sometimes "value" (e.g. in quotation 3), but most commonly "worth", especially in the combinations "intrinsic worth", "unconditional worth". But, he also uses "value" for what Kant calls *Preis* in the passages where he distinguishes *Preis* from *Wuerde* ("dignity"). There was no need for the translator to have used "value" for rendering two quite different words, *Preis* and *Wert*. Some inkling of this confusion probably led him to render *Wert* most commonly by "worth". Another inaccuracy is the rendering of Kant's *inner Wert* by "intrinsic worth". Certainly, what has "inner" value has also "intrinsic" value (=absolute value, value for its own sake, or in itself). But, the emphasis of "inner" is on the *motives* for action, as distinct from the actions and their effects. And the use of the word "inner" is essential to Kant's argument that moral judgment should not consider the action and its effects, but only its motive.

Taking for granted, now, these verbal revisions, the system of concepts employed by Kant may be summed up in the following propositions:

1. Every "rational being" (="person") is an "end in himself", and possesses absolute, intrinsic value (="dignity").

2. The "actions" of such a person also possess absolute, intrinsic value, as expressions of "good will".

3. A good will wills only such actions as "are in conformity with the moral law", and it wills them only "because they are in conformity with the moral law". In short, a good will acts

---

[1] Kant's italics. I would italicise only the words *value* and *dignity*.

from "respect for the moral law", i.e., does its "duty" for duty's sake.

These three propositions seem to me to sum up the doctrine of the above quotations. They may be condensed into: Every rational being, acting solely from respect for the moral law, has absolute value (=is an end in himself).

To these three propositions a fourth may be added, to link up with the theory of freedom:

4. The moral law is the law of reason itself, so that every rational being, obeying the law of reason, is autonomous (=free).

When these propositions are applied to human beings, we are met by the difficulty that human beings are composite in nature. They are rational, but they are also non-rational. Reason in them has to realise itself in the midst of, and in conflict with, non-rational impulses. Humans are also creatures of flesh and blood; animals reacting to stimuli from their natural environment; experiencing desires and aversions, feelings and emotions (=Kant's "inclinations"). As rational beings, humans are committed to the task of making every other motive give way to the thought of duty, to "pure respect for the moral law". As having also a non-rational side to their natures, they are divided against themselves, torn by the conflict between their inclinations and their reason—a conflict in which reason is all too often defeated, or in which the "purity" of the rational motive is all too often tainted by the fact that what the moral law commands happens to coincide with what inclination urges. It is in this context of inner conflict that the moral law takes on the stern character of duty ("ought"), whereas in a purely rational being, unhampered by non-rational inclinations, disobedience to the moral law would be impossible. For, in acting in conformity with the law of reason, a rational being is simply true to itself: it does what it wants to do—it could not want or do anything else.

And just as "duty" carries with it a connotation derived from this inward division in human nature, so does "good will". A purely rational creature, e.g., God, has, according to Kant, a "holy will": such a will is not troubled by inclinations which it has to resist, or from the influence of which it has to emancipate itself, lest they become motives of action.

Qua rational, every human being is an end in himself, and for men to treat each other as rational beings, forming together a community of rational beings (="kingdom of ends"), is precisely the command of the moral law, however much the realisation of this ideal may be hampered, and even defeated, by man's non-rational nature.

This is the basis of the distinction drawn by Kant, in the Preface to our treatise, between a "rational" and an "empirical" part of Ethics. The rational part is the "metaphysic of morals", properly so called. The empirical part "might have the name of *practical anthropology*" (2). The former consists of *a priori* propositions; the latter of propositions concerning human nature as an object of (sense-) experience. In the language of Section III of our treatise, the former deals with men as *noumena*, the latter with men as *phenomena*.

The conclusion from all this, which seems to me inescapable, is that the doctrine of the rational person as an end in himself, and as having absolute value (or "worth"), consists of *a priori* propositions, which are true of all rational beings whatsoever, whether human or superhuman. From this point of view we can appreciate, not only why Kant is bound to reject all attempts to derive moral principles from "experience", but also why it is so frequently important for him to insist that the propositions in which he expounds the nature of moral character (the "good will") and moral action (fulfilling the moral law because it is the moral law) are true of all rational beings whatsoever, and are not restricted to reason in its "human" form.

The remaining sections of this paper will be devoted to examining some of the curious consequences of this theory.

II.

I begin by attempting to clear up an ambiguity in Kant's distinction between the "pure" or "rational" and the "empirical" part of Ethics.

Consider the analogy between Physics and Ethics, as pointed out by Kant in the Preface (1, 2).

Both Physics and Ethics belong, in Kant's scheme of classification, to "Material" Philosophy, as distinct from Logic which is "Formal" Philosophy. The latter is said to "be concerned with the universal laws of thought in general without distinction of its objects" (1), i.e., irrespective of what the object of thought may be. "Material" philosophy "has to do with determinate objects and the laws to which they are subject" (*ibid.*). Material Philosophy consists of Physics and Ethics. The pure, or rational, or *a priori*, part of the former consists, if I understand Kant aright, of the concepts and propositions which are true of *any* system of "Nature" (hence ="metaphysic of nature"), and must be taken to be represented by the categories and principles set out in the section of the *Critique of Pure Reason* which is entitled "Transcendental Logic". The "empirical" part of Physics is said to "determine the laws of nature as an object of experience" (2). The only interpretation which I can put on this latter phrase is that this part consists of the propositions which Physicists, observing and experimenting (="experience"), affirm as true of "Nature", sc. Nature as object of sense-perception. But, the body of these propositions will be Physics itself; Physics as a Natural Science. It will not be "part" of Physics, distinguishable from another part, in such wise that the two parts together make up Physics as a whole.

In other words, I believe—and I regard this as the central doctrine of the *Transcendental Logic*—that Physics, as a Natural or Empirical Science, contains both *a priori* and *a posteriori* (="empirical") elements or factors, and that every scientific statement of fact about natural phenomena can be analysed into these two kinds of factors (categories and sense-data). If we abstract the *a priori* elements and formulate them in isolation, we certainly get propositions which may be called the "pure" or "rational" part of Physics. But, there remains no counterpart consisting of empirical propositions without any *a priori* element. For, the point of Kant's *Transcendental Logic* is precisely this, that every empirical proposition ("empirical" by reference to actual or possible sense-data) contains an *a priori* element. It is neither purely *a priori*, nor purely empirical: it is a synthesis of empirical data by *a priori* concepts and principles.

Turn now to Ethics: we know from Section I what its "rational" part is. What is its "empirical" part? Kant assigns to it "the laws of the human will, so far as it is affected by nature" (2), but adds that it "must also consider the conditions under which what ought to happen frequently does not" (*ibid.*). The latter topic presents no special problem. But what can be meant by "laws of the human will, so far as it is affected by nature"? If "affected by nature" refers to the inclinations, the resulting "laws" can certainly not be "laws according to which everything ought to happen". They could at best be "anthropological" or "psychological" generalisations, not "categorical imperatives". According to Kant himself, the only moral laws are the laws which reason *a priori* prescribes to man's will. If, then, we try to interpret the "empirical" part of Ethics as consisting of propositions about human nature as a "phenomenon", i.e., propositions treating human beings *as if they had no rational side to their natures*, the obvious objection is that such propositions have no place in Ethics. The only other possibility is to say that the "empirical" part of Ethics consists of propositions about the way in which the rational nature of man, as defined by the concepts of "rational being", "moral law", "duty", "free will", is realised, or struggles to realise itself, in the hostile medium of his non-rational nature. But, such propositions, of which there are plenty of examples in our treatise, cannot usefully be compared to the propositions of Physics: they exhibit no synthesis of empirical data by *a priori* concepts.

This point is worth insisting on. There is, there can be, according to Kant, no synthesis of *a priori* and empirical elements in man's moral behaviour, comparable to the synthesis of these elements in his scientific judgments. "Inclinations", unlike sense-data, do not function as "matter" for the *a priori* "forms" of reason. On the contrary, the principle of purity of motive ("good will"), i.e., the demand that an action, in order to have "moral" or "absolute" value, must have no motive other than "pure respect for the moral law", entails negatively the elimination of every motive derived from the inclinations. There is here, there can be, no "synthesis" of rational and non-rational.

We must, however, remind ourselves of a point which Kant overlooked, viz., that this very stocktaking of the elements of human nature, which enables us to distinguish what is rational from what is non-rational, requires our rising to a plane of reflection from which we can, as it were, look down on the elements distinguished in the object of our analysis—our own human nature. What name, what characterising label, are we to give to this plane, this highest point of view? If we call it "reason" then we shall have to say that reason, in distinguishing itself from the non-rational, takes stock (or: makes an object) both of itself and the non-rational.

This suggestion, however, undermines Kant's facile distinction between "rational" and "empirical" knowledge. This distinction works smoothly enough, so long as we are content merely to classify propositions into those which are *a priori*, and therefore not verifiable by sense-experience, and those which are "empirical", i.e., refer to matters of fact verifiable by sense-experience. But, the classifying proposition itself, which asserts the distinction between these two types of propositions, certainly is not "empirical" in the sense required, and yet, on the other hand, as referring to what is "empirical", it cannot be called *a priori*, when *a priori* excludes everything empirical.

This leads, finally, to yet a further reflection. If we call "rational" this very plane, and act, of reflection by which "rational" is distinguished from "non-rational", and, in terms of this way of speaking and thinking, attribute to "reason" the power to take stock of (affirm propositions about) itself as well as its "other", we must also set down that for this actually to happen, requires actual reflectings by actual thinkers. More simply: all this argument about reason implies the existence of reasoners, of rational beings. The existential reference cannot be eliminated: Descartes' *Cogito ergo sum* returns upon us at this point.

A theory of reason, in distinction from and in relation to the non-rational, consists of propositions affirmed by thinkers who attribute reason to themselves; who, in this theory, take stock of themselves, of their own natures, as at once both rational and non-rational. Once more, is this sort of self-knowledge "rational" or "empirical", *a priori* or *a posteriori*? Or, does it move on a plane which transcends the mutual exclusiveness of these terms?

This question is fundamental for the remaining two sections.

III.

Consider the famous opening sentence of our treatise, already quoted. "Nothing can possibly be conceived in the world . . . which can be called good without qualification, except a Good Will". This is said by a human thinker to other human thinkers, inviting their assent. It introduces a discussion of the nature of reason, and of the part it should play, in the behaviour of humans as "rational beings" afflicted by non-rational "inclinations". Thus, the whole context of the argument, as addressed by one thinker to others, and having for its topic that human nature of which each of them is an illustration, implies the existence of rational human beings, or of reason as embodied in actual humans.

Yet, it is precisely this implication that reason is exemplified in actual rational beings, and, therefore, that the theory of rational conduct is true of (applies to) actual agents, which troubles Kant in virtue of his sharp distinction between "*a priori*" and "empirical" knowledge. For all that, as has been mentioned above, he classifies Ethics with Physics under the head of "Material Philosophy", as having "to do with determinate objects", the question whether such objects actually exist continues to haunt him.

The reason for the difficulty is that he had inherited the tradition of treating *a priori* propositions as devoid of existential reference. Now, that opening proposition about the absolute value of a will determined to action by no other motive than pure respect for the moral law, is an *a priori* proposition, if ever there was one. It is one of the set of *a priori* propositions which together make up the "rational part", or the "metaphysic", of morals. To this set of propositions, considered on this abstract *a priori* plane, the question whether they apply to, or are true of, any actually existent beings is irrelevant. In the realm of pure thought, the question of the existence of its objects does not arise. In order to affirm the existence of any object of thought—this had been Kant's own teaching in the *Critique of Pure Reason*—empirical data are required.

But empirical evidence for moral action in the sense defined is, from the nature of the case, not to be had. In the opening pages of the Second Section of our treatise Kant heaps argu-

Y

ment on argument, in order to show that no empirical case of the "Good Will" can be exhibited. And the difficulty becomes even more devastating when we remember that all propositions about human beings as existents must, as resting on the evidence of sense-perception, treat them as "phenomena", and, therefore, cannot justify the attribution to them (or their attribution to themselves) of the "reason" which is the topic of the *a priori* propositions of the "metaphysic of morals".

It is as if Kant were saying: "If we human beings are rational, then such-and-such propositions are true of us. But we have no empirical evidence that we are rational beings".

If Kant had merely said: We human beings are composite creatures, and the elements of our human nature are so deeply at war with each other that we can never be sure of achieving that purity of motive of all our actions, which we recognise to be demanded by the rational side of our natures, there would have been no difficulty. And this is what he—rightly—is taken to say by all who ignore the technicalities which he has chosen to introduce. But, for Kant as a philosopher, these technicalities are essential. Hence, as soon as the above statement is broken up into what is *a priori* in it and what is empirical, and the general theory of this distinction is then applied, the inevitable result is that reached by Kant in the last sentences of the Second Section of our treatise, where, addressing himself to those who, with him, "hold morality to be anything real, and not a chimerical idea without any truth", he puts the problem how "to prove that morality is no creation of the brain" (64). The problem is to "prove" that, and how, the *a priori* propositions of the "metaphysics of morals" apply to, or are true of, actual human beings.

IV.

There remains, however, another complication. The metaphysic of morals contains not only *a priori* propositions—which, as such, are "analytic", but it contains also, so Kant insists, at least one *a priori* "synthetic" proposition.

This is, in my judgment, the most difficult—indeed, to me, unintelligible—part of his doctrine. Yet, according to Kant himself, the affirmation of the freedom of the will is necessary in order to prove this *a priori* synthetic proposition—in his own words, "the possibility of the categorical imperative".

This *a priori* synthetic proposition in the body of the metaphysic or morals has nothing to do with the synthesis of the rational and non-rational sides of man's nature, or, better, with making reason, i.e., the moral law, effective in his conduct as sole operative motive to the "exclusion" of all inclination. With freedom of the will as this *power* (or "efficiency") of reason, I dealt in my previous article.

But, now, the problem is the quite different one of the relation of freedom to the *a priori* synthetic proposition that the will of every rational being possesses autonomy, i.e., the "property by which it is a law to itself (independently of any property of the objects of volition)" (59).[1] The terms of this law, or "the principle of autonomy", viz., "always to choose that the same volition shall comprehend the maxims of our choice as a universal law" (59),[2] so Kant claims, are derivable "by mere analysis of the conceptions of morality". What is not so derivable is "that the will of every rational being is necessarily bound to it (scil., the law) as a condition" (59).[3]

To me, the need for introducing a synthetical proposition at this point, in order to "prove" that "the categorical imperative and with it the autonomy of the will is true" (64), remains unintelligible, except on the supposition—which I see no reason to make—that the concept of "rational being" does not contain, analytically, the concept of rational-being-acting-according-to-a-law-of-reason. It is like saying: there is nothing in the concept of reason which implies action; but, if we synthetically form the concept of reason-acting, then there will now be involved "analytically" the concept of reason acting in accordance with a certain principle, viz., the moral law. If *this* is what Kant means to say, I can see, I repeat, no need for it. If he excludes action from his concept of reason, he might—in

---

[1] From the opening of the paragraph entitled: "The Autonomy of the Will as the Supreme Principle of Morality".

[2] The words quoted are another version of the First Formula of the Moral Law (or Categorical Imperative), viz., "Act only on that maxim whereby thou canst at the same time will that it should become universal".

[3] The full sentence reads: "We cannot prove that this practical rule is an imperative, i.e., that the will of every rational being is necessarily bound to it as a condition, by a mere analysis of the conceptions which occur in it, since it is a synthetical proposition".

fact, should—equally have excluded knowledge. And what then remains of "reason"—what content to be analysed—I fail to see. Why not start with the concept of reason knowing and acting,[1] and draw out "by mere analysis" the *a priori* propositions contained in this concept?

For better or for worse, Kant did not choose to take this line. Hence, "proving" that "morality is no creation of the brain" and that "the categorical imperative and with it the autonomy of the will is true", is for him equivalent to establishing the *a priori* synthetic proposition that it is part of rationality to be necessarily bound to act according to the moral law. In order to establish this, Kant claims to be obliged to establish the freedom of the will, for "the concept of freedom is the key that explains the autonomy of the will" (65).[2]

What does Kant actually offer us in fulfilment of his self-imposed task? I do not propose to go through the whole of the Third Section of our treatise, in order to answer this question, the more so as the ultimate outcome, by Kant's own confession, is negative (84). Suffice it to illustrate his method from the first paragraph, which offers us the following propositions, one of which (viz., (e) below) is put by Kant in the form of a rhetorical question:

(*a*) "The will is a kind of causality, belonging to living beings in so far as they are rational";

(*b*) "freedom would be this property of such causality that it can be efficient, independent on foreign causes *determining* it";

(*c*) "the conception of causality involves that of laws" (according to which cause produces effect);

(*d*) "freedom . . . must be a causality acting according to immutable laws, but of a peculiar kind" (i.e., not "physical laws");

(*e*) "What else then can freedom of the will be but autonomy, that is the property of the will to be a law to itself?"

(*f*) "But the proposition: the will is in every action a law to itself, only expresses the principle to act on no other maxim

---

[1] And also remembering the *Critique of Judgment*—reason disinterestedly enjoying beauty.
[2] Title of the Third Section of our treatise. "Explaining the autonomy of the will" must be equivalent to establishing the *a priori* synthetic proposition in the question.

than that which can also have as an object itself as a universal law" (=the formula of the categorical imperative).

(*g*) "A free will and a will subject to moral law are one and the same" (65-6).[1]

Now, so far as I can see, all these propositions would be classified by Kant as *a priori analytic*. Or, if any one of them is *a priori synthetic*, he does not say so; and, if it were, it would only aggravate the problem to be solved. What have we then been given? Nothing but this proposition into which the relevant substance of the above propositions can be condensed, viz., that the will of a rational being (for short, a rational will) acts according to the moral law (=it is autonomous=it is free). But, either this is a purely analytic statement of what is meant by rational will or rational action, or, else, the statement is as synthetic as the statement which it is intended to "prove" and "explain".

V.

The upshot of my examination of Kant's argument may now be briefly summarised.

The abiding interest of Kant's theory of morality is quite unaffected by the technicalities with which he has clogged his exposition of it. It lies in the affirmation of the principle that reason, as embodied in rational beings ("persons"), has absolute value; that each rational being is an end in himself; and that rational beings, living together as members of a rational community ("kingdom of ends"), ought to treat, each himself and each every other, as an end in himself and not as a means. Whether we read this as a secularised version of the Christian doctrine that in God's eyes every human soul is a thing of absolute value, or as a challenging and inspiring formulation of the Humanitarian spirit—its value as a contribution to human culture remains. For, it assigns to that culture the aim of the coöperative realisation of the fullness of rational personality in every one of its members.

But, the exposition of this moral ideal has been complicated by a maze of technicalities, out of which Kant himself has failed to find a way. Trying to apply the apparatus of technical

[1] Kant's italics.

distinctions, like that between the *a priori* ("rational") and the *a posteriori* ("empirical"), between the analytic and the synthetic, and, above all, trying to find a place for his own invention of the "*a priori* synthetic", he ends in entangling himself in insuperable difficulties.

The root of the trouble is that the technical apparatus of concepts which Kant applies in his *theoretical* analysis of human nature has no relevance to the solution of the *practical* problem of realising the ideal (of the Good Will and the Kingdom of Ends), to which men, in the name of "reasons, are committed, in the recalcitrant material of desires and feelings"—a problem of self-discipline or self-mastery which no talk of "*a priori*"and "synthetic" brings nearer to solution.[1]

[1] For Kant's own confession of this, see p. 81.

Index

330

INDEX

signs, 240-1 ; as a system of universals, 41 ; and Universe, 54
Nature of Existence, The (McTaggart), 177
Nazi rise to power in Germany, 56
Necessities, factual, and logical, 41-2
Necessity, and contingence, 40
Negative propositions, 18
Neo-Realism, and Idealism, 206, 210, 265, 267-8 ; and Materialism, 210, 265-7 ; and Mind or consciousness, 205-29 ; and Old Realism, 208-9 ; and Religion, 265-85. See also Realism
Neutral objects, 209
New Realism, The, 205*n*, 212, 223*n*
Nisus, towards harmony, 262-3
Norm, human nature as a, 195 ; Plato's " form " as a, 288-9 ; two senses of, and universals, 190-1
Noumena, and *Phenomena,* 308-10 ; men as, 315
Numerical difference, 182
Numerical limits, in classes and organised groups, 199-200

Object(s), act and relation, 256-7 ; coöperation of, 167, 169, 170, 174 ; independence of, in Neo-Realism, 209-210 ; and mind, 6 ; perception and idea of, 171 ; physical, and perceived, identity of, 31-2 ; real and unreal, mental and non-mental, 161-163 ; 214-17, and value, 53-4
Objective Idealism, 265
Objectivity, 209
One-in-Many, 253-4
Organic Wholes, Moore's Principle of, and values, 53
Organisation, and differences of degree and mode, 199 ; numerical limits in, 199-200
Othello (Shakespeare), 80, 128
Over-statement of case, 85
Oxford University, x, xi

Pain, and pleasure, 51
Parmenides (Plato), 292
Particulars, as real, 164 ; as realisations of universals, 183 ; and science, 287-8 ; and sense-data, 105-7
Particulars and universals, as two classes, 178 ; and Image and meaning, 146-7 ; and language, 134 ; and organized groups, 200
Passivity, of individual in Universe, 39-40
Peirce, Charles S., and signs, 234-5, 238-9
Perception, and apperception, 149 ; and Berkeley, 137 ; deceptiveness of, 91-2 ; intellectual, 81-2 ; and interpretation, 49, 93-4 ; and judgment, 43, 95-6 ; and Kant, 48 ; limits of, and thoughts, 83 ; and mind, 45 ; physico-physiological theory of, 45, 46 ; and Reality, 60 ; and Russell, 121 ; and sense, and idea, 171-2 ; and theory of knowledge,

44 ; and theories of truth, 88-97 ; and thought, 127, 237 ; and truth, 46 ; truths and judgments of, in Russell's theory of Error, 109 ; as a two term relation, 127 ; and value, 49-50
Perfection, and Christianity, 59 ; judgment of, 283, 284 ; striving for, and Nature, 193
Perry, Prof. R. B., xii, 51, 205*n*, 273 ; and consciousness, 223 ; and egocentric theory of mind, 225 ; and four senses of truth, 75 ; and Idealism, 48 ; his Moral Realism, 275-80 ; and Neo-Realism, 269, 270, 271, 272 ; and Realism, 212 ; and science and religion, 266-276
Phenomena and *noumena,* 308-10 ; men as, 315
Phenomenology of meaning, 230-45
Philebus (Plato), 301
Philosophers, and language, 131 ; mutual misunderstanding of, 99-100 ; and practical experience, xii; and the public, 100
Philosophical Essays (Russell), 90, 98, 205
Philosophy, and Biology, 272-3 ; as a continuous debate, xvii ; effectiveness of its teachers, xv ; importance of discussion of theories of, 98-9, 119 ; and Language, 131-40 ; Material and Formal, in Kant, 315-16 ; and physics, 265 ; and science and religion, 278-80 ; and theory and belief, 276-8 ; tidiness in, 75
Physical necessity, in Kant, 305
Physicists, mental character of world of, 217
Physics, 44 ; and Kant, 315-16 ; and Philosophy, 265
Plant-signatures, 240-1
Plato, 49 ; and conflicting data, 94 ; his " forms " and " God ", 286-302 ; and practical experience, xii ; his *Republic,* 198
Pleasure, and pain, 51
Pluralism, 254 ; and Absolutism, 258-64
Possibility, and imaginary objects, 162
Practical experience, and philosophers, xii
Pragmatism, 205, 206 ; and theory of truth, 70
Pragmatism (James), 283
Prediction, and experience, 79-80, 83-4
Premisses, true and false, 34
Present Philosophical Tendencies (Perry), 75*n*, 205*n*, 212, 223*n*, 266-7, 269, 270, 272-3, 275-80, 282
Present reality, and idea, 164-6
Prichard, H. A., 205*n*, 208, 212, 213, 271
Primitive experience, 94
Principles of Human Knowledge (Berkeley), 3*n*, 137
Principles of Psychology (James), 138, 148*n*, 149, 152-3, 155
Problems of Philosophy (Russell), 80, 94, 98, 126, 127, 270
Propositions, *a priori* and *a posteriori,* in Kant, 316-20 ; categorical, and uni-

versals and particulars, 178 ; classification of, 66, 68 ; and facts, 71-2, 100-1 ; and fact, and Correspondence, 125-30 ; negative, 18 ; self-evident, 16 ; stability of, 74 ; true and false, 12-18 ; Universe of, 98-9

Psychic fringe, of James, 155-8

Psychic whole, of sign and meaning, 151, 159-60

Psychological Principles (Ward), 138

Psychological theory of mind, 225

Psychologische Untersuchungen zur Bedeutungslehre (Martinak), 241*n*

Psychology, and Image, Idea and Meaning, 144, 149 ; introspective, and Behaviourism, 136, 139 ; and misuse and limits of introspection, 152-3 ; and language, 138 ; and Metaphysics, 255-256 ; and mind, 136 ; and Russell's theory of Error, 105 ; and self-consistency of knowledge, 87 ; and sign and meaning, 160 ; and theory of knowledge, 20 ; and two modes of experience, 169 ; and word-meaning, 150

Qualities, and classes, 179, 183-4, 188 ; primary and secondary, 47 ; secondary, 216

Questions, and pre-determined answers, 44

Race problem, in South Africa, xiii, xvi

Race and Reason (Hoernlé), xiii*n*

Raeder, and Plato's " form " of Good, 298

Rational, and irrational, in Kant, 304-10, 312-15 ; and non-rational conviction, 55-6 ; and empirical propositions, in Kant, 316-20

Rationalisation, 65

Rationalists, and immediate experience, 25

Rationality, and differences of degree and mode, 184-7

Real, and mental, ambiguity of terms, 216-18

Realisation, of idea, and volition, 173-5 ; and meaning, 134-5

Realisierung (Kulpe), 206*n*

Realism, its analysis of cognitive experience, 256-7 ; Critical, 176 ; and ego-centric theory of mind, 226 ; and Idealism, 123, 136, 206*n*, 210, 211-212, 215*n*, 255 ; and knowledge, 3 ; and mind, 208 ; Old and New, 208-9 ; and perception, 48, 137 ; proper sphere of, 117-18; and propositions, 72; and subsisting propositions, 98-9 ; and values, 51, 53. See also Neo-Realism

Realitas phenomenon, 48 ; and *noumena*, 31

Realitäts-character, 170

Reality, and ego-centric theory of mind, 226 ; and idea, 160-73 ; and immediate experience, 26, 28 ; and mind in Idealism, 211-12 ; Kant's transcendental, 19 ; and logic, 28-9 ; as it is

perceived and thought, 32 ; and perception, 31, 48-9, 60 ; and religion, 59-61 ; and the senses, 81 ; and this-such, 204 ; and unreality, 161-3 ; and values, 50, 53

Reason, as having absolute value, 323 ; and inclination, in Kant, 303-10, 314 ; and revelation, 55

Reasoning, 33-4

Redintegration, and idea, 169, 173

Reflection, forward and backward, 44 ; two planes of, 20

Relating Relation, 116, 117 ; thinking as, 128-9

Relation, act, and object, 256-7

Relational theory of consciousness, 219, 223

Relations, External, 228*n* ; and Realism and Idealism, 215*n* ; and Russell's theory of Error, 103, 107

Relationship, of proposition and fact, 17-18

Relative and Absolute contexts of truth, 68-9

Religion, and faith, 56 ; and moral enthusiasm, 280-1 ; natural and revealed, 57 ; and Neo-Realism, 265-85 ; primitive, and value judgments, 59 ; and science and philosophy, 278-80 ; and values, 61 ; as wishful thinking, 59

Religious experience, types of, 57-8

Republic (Plato), 198, 289-90, 292, 296-8, 300

Retentiveness, 168, 169. See also Memory

Revealed religion, and natural, 57

Revelation, and reason, 55

Revived sensation, and actual, 166-73

Romanticism, 266, 275

Rose, smell of, and consciousness of meaning, 82

Royce, Prof. Josiah, 205, 212*n*, 234*n*; Hoernlé's tribute to, xiv-xv; and James, 246*n*, 284 ; and meaning, 236

Russell, Bertrand, 202 ; and conflict of data, 94-5; and " hard " data, 92 ; and knowing, 270 ; his logical construct, 71 ; and meaning, 232-4, 238, 242 ; and Neo-Realism, 205*n*, 206*n*, 209 ; and religion, 271-2 ; his theory of Error, 98-124 ; and theories of truth, 77, 80, 90, 126-30 ; and universals, 176

Santayana, George, 185 ; and essences, 176

Scepticism and Animal Faith (Santayana), 176

Sceptics, and immediate experience, 25 ; and truth, 36

Schiller, xi

Schiller, Dr. F. C. S., 205 ; and meaning, 231-2, 242, 243

Science, aim of, 54 ; and causality, 30 ; and classes, 180-4 ; and deceptiveness of perception, 92 ; and disinterested delight, 294-5 ; and intelligent perceptions, 96-7 ; as system of judg-

332 INDEX

ments, 86 ; and Kant, 48 ; and knowledge, 6 ; and language, 131 ; mental character of Universe of, 217 ; and Metaphysics, 256 ; and two modes of experience, 168 ; and Neo-Realism, 265-6, 267 ; and perception, 43, 45, 46 ; and Plato's " forms ", 287-8 ; and religion and philosophy, 278-80 ; and self-consistency of knowledge, 87 ; and theory of knowledge, 44 ; and thinking, 63-4 ; and truth, 37 ; and types of proposition, 66
Science and Philosophy (Bosanquet), 288
Scientia, 104
Scientific knowledge, and religion, 56-7
Scientific research, and facts, 40-1
Secondary qualities, 216
Seeing, intelligent, 93 ; as Judgment, 120
Self, as mind, 226
Self-consciousness, 194 ; and desires, 197 ; logic of, 227
Self-consistency, of knowledge, 87, 88
Self-evidence, 16, 250 ; and Russell, 111-112
Self-revealing, Universe as, 252-3, 254-5
Sensation, as immediate experience, 24-25, 27 ; and meaning, 152-3 ; " pure ", 148n ; revived and actual, 166-73 ; and thought, in experience, 172-3
Sense-data, acquaintance with, 101-5 ; aggregate of, 109 ; and facts, 81-2 ; as " hard ", 92 ; and judgment, 119-20 ; and Kant, 48 ; and meaning, 43, 134 ; and sensing, relation between, 103 ; and truths, in Russell's theory of Error, 111 ; and universals, 105-7
Sense-experience, actual and possible, 83 ; complexity of, 173
Sense-perception, and idea, 171-2
Senses, fallibility of, 91-2, 121 ; and science, 44-5
Shakespeare, 77-8, 80
Sign-facts, 73
Signs, indicative and expressive, 241, 243-5 ; and meaning, 144, 147, 150-1, 152-3, 155-60, 230-1, 234-45 ; and Nature, 240-1 ; and significates, 236 ; and symbols, 234-5
Sigwart, 31, 38
Sin, in assent or dissent, 64
Smell, and consciousness of meaning, 82
Smuts, General, xi
Social nature of thinking, 67-8
Society, and differences of degree and mode, 198-9 ; and individual, ix
Sociological Review, 189n
Socrates, and meaning, 132
Socratic irony, caricature of, 4
Sounds, interpretation of, 78-9
South Africa, x-xi, xiii ; formation of Union of, xii ; race problem in, xiii, xvi
Southern California, University of, v, xiii
Space and time, and universals and particulars, 178
Spectator, and agent, and meaning, 242-3
Spinoza, 54, 193n, 228, 263, 290, 294,

295 ; and emotions, 52 ; his parallelism of *ideae* and *res*, 47 ; and terminology, 138
Spirit, The (Streeter), 245
Square circle, 148
Stability, of judgments, 86-7 ; logical, struggle towards, 227-8 ; of propositions, 74
St. Andrews University, xi
State, idealistic theory of, xii
Stewart, Dugald, 152
Stewart, J. A., and Plato's " form " of Good, 298
Stoic ideal, ix
Story of My Life (Keller), 150-1
Stout, Dr. G. F., 232n ; and acquirement of meaning, 155, 157-8 ; and cognition, 153-4 ; and James, 156n ; and revived sensation, 167 ; and signs, 234-5 ; and universals, 176 ; and words and meaning, 147-8, 152
Stream of consciousness, 225
Studies in Contemporary Metaphysics (Hoernlé), xiii, 176, 201, 237, 260
Studies of Realism (Laird), 140
Subject and object, unity of, 19
Subjective nature of values, 50-1
Subjectivity of truths and falsehoods, 115-16
Sullivan, Miss, 150-1
Summum Bonum, 292
Symbol, index and icon, 239 ; and sign, 234-5
Synoptic Philosophy, On the Way to a (Hoernlé), xiii
Synthesis, of Kant, 71
Systematic ambiguity, 12, 20, 31, 55, 56

Table, shape of, and conflict of data, 95
Talks to Teachers on Psychology and Life's Ideals (James), 284
Technicality of philosophy, 131, 134, 137
Terminology, confusion of, 143, 230, 235 ; individual thinkers', 137-9. See also Language
Thaetetus (Plato), 297
Theology, and science, 57
Theories, importance of discussion of, 98-9
Theory, and belief, and Perry, 275-9 ; and data, 96 ; and perception, 88-9 ; and realisation, 135
Things, and Russell's theory of Error, 101 ; and thoughts, 214n
Things that exist, 90-1
Thinking, and the individual, 67-8 ; nature of, 249-50 ; as relating relation, 128-9 ; in right context, 73 ; to satisfy cognitive interest, 63, 67
This-such, 106, 134, 201-4
Thought, and fact, agreement of, 76-7, 81-2, 83-4 ; and limits of perception, 83 ; and perception, 127, 237 ; and sensation, in experience, 172-3 ; and thing, 214n
Tidiness, in philosophy, 75
Timaeus (Plato), 298-301
Time and idea, 164-6 ; and space, 178

GEORGE ALLEN & UNWIN LTD
LONDON: 40 MUSEUM STREET, W.C.1
CAPE TOWN: 58–60 LONG STREET
SYDNEY, N.S.W.: 55 YORK STREET
TORONTO: 91 WELLINGTON STREET WEST
CALCUTTA: 17 CENTRAL AVE., P.O. DHARAMTALA
BOMBAY: 15 GRAHAM ROAD, BALLARD ESTATE
WELLINGTON, N.Z.: 8 KINGS CRESCENT, LOWER HUTT